Sunset

Western Garden Annual

1996 EDITION

By the Editors of *Sunset Magazine* and Sunset Books

NORMAN A. PLATE

Sunflowers for cutting (page 178)

Sunset Publishing Corporation ■ **Menlo Park, California**

NORMAN A. PLATE

GLORIOUS 'GRAHAM THOMAS', *one of the new "English roses" gaining favor in the West (see page 88).*

SUNSET BOOKS

President and Publisher
Susan J. Maruyama
Director, Sales & Marketing
Richard A. Smeby
Director, New Business
Kenneth Winchester
Editorial Director
Bob Doyle
**Marketing & Creative
Services Manager**
Guy C. Joy
Production Director
Lory Day
Coordinating Editor
Suzanne Normand Eyre
Contributing Editor
Philip Edinger
Production Coordinator
Patricia S. Williams

**SUNSET PUBLISHING
CORPORATION**

Chairman
Jim Nelson
**President/Chief Executive
Officer**
Stephen J. Seabolt
Chief Financial Officer
James E. Mitchell
Publisher, Sunset Magazine
Anthony P. Glaves
Director of Finance
Larry Diamond
Circulation Director
Robert I. Gursha
**Vice President,
Manufacturing**
Lorinda B. Reichert
Editor, Sunset Magazine
William R. Marken
Managing Editor
Carol Hoffman
Executive Editor
Melissa Houtte

A Year of Gardening

Now in its third yearly edition, our *Western Garden Annual* is an indispensable companion for the West's home gardeners. Offering a full year's worth of inspiration, this volume gathers all the gardening and outdoor living articles from *Sunset Magazine*'s 1995 regional editions into a single handy reference book.

Each chapter covers one month—and each month begins with the Garden Guide, filled with news and ideas timely for that month around the West. Regional checklists follow, highlighting the month's important gardening activities.

Major articles cover all aspects of Western gardening. You'll meet worthy new plants and get reacquainted with old favorites; you'll learn about helpful new books, labor-saving tools, and outstanding public gardens. Other features this year let you explore the West's diverse climates and offer ideas on garden design, from landscapes designed for water conservation and fire safety to schemes using aquatic plants.

We hope this *Western Garden Annual*, like its predecessors, gives you many months of enjoyment and inspiration.

Cover: 'China Dragon' bearded iris with pink painted daisies (see page 152). Design by Susan Bryant Caron. Photography by Michael S. Thompson

Back cover: Godetia *(Clarkia amoena).* See page 285. Photography by Norman A. Plate.

All material in this book originally appeared in the 1995 issues of *Sunset Magazine.*

Sunset Western Garden Annual was produced by Sunset Books. If you have comments or suggestions, please let us hear from you. Write us at:
Sunset Books
Garden Book Editorial
80 Willow Road
Menlo Park, CA 94025

If you would like to order additional copies of any of our books, call us at 1-800-634-3095 or check with your local bookstore. For special sales, bulk orders, and premium sales information, call Sunset Custom Publishing Services at (415) 324-5577.

First printing March 1996
Copyright © 1996 Sunset Publishing Corporation, Menlo Park, CA 94025. First edition. All rights reserved, including the right of reproduction in whole or in part in any form.

ISSN 1073-5089
Hardcover edition: ISBN 0-376-03859-4
Softcover edition: ISBN 0-376-03858-6

Printed in the United States.

Contents

The Western Gardener's Companion

The West is a world in itself. The landscape encompasses mountains, seashores, deserts, and fertile valleys, and the climate and scenery are just as varied. The same striking diversity characterizes Western gardening—yet for over 60 years, gardeners in every part of the West have been able to find the advice and information they need in a single publication: *Sunset Magazine*. Through our pages, readers keep up to date on new plants and the latest gardening products and methods; they learn about noteworthy books and newsletters, sources for unusual seeds, and places to visit for gardening inspiration.

This third edition of our *Western Garden Annual* follows the format of its predecessors. There are 12 chapters, one for each month of the year. Each month leads off with the Garden Guide, a potpourri of items timely for that month throughout the West. These short features cover such topics as new and award-winning plants; events and public gardens worthy of notice; environmental concerns; and gardening techniques and design.

Following the Garden Guide are our Garden Checklists, focusing on concerns specific to each of the magazine's regions. Starting in July, each checklist is accompanied by a Garden Notebook: our editors' musings on favorite plants, their advice for the month's chores, and their answers to readers' questions. And in August, you'll notice a change in the way our geographic regions are presented. As before, the first four checklists cover the Pacific Northwest, Northern California, the Central Valley, and Southern California. But the fifth checklist, formerly devoted to the Southwest deserts and/or the Intermountain West (the territory between the Sierra-Cascades and the Rockies), now offers advice for the inland West: the eight landlocked Western states.

Following each chapter's Garden Guide and checklists are that month's feature articles, drawn from all regional issues of *Sunset*. This past year offers the usual variety of themes. For example, you'll discover the best trees for growing as houseplants and the best birches to plant for attention-getting bark; you'll learn about the increasing number of different magnolias in Western nurseries. If color is your interest, check out coral bells with dramatic foliage, sunflowers for cutting, and beautiful blue perennials. And those who garden for taste can visually munch on hot peppers, fragrant French melons, and the newest apple varieties.

Reports on plants often refer to climate zones in which a plant will thrive. For maps and detailed descriptions of all Western climate zones, refer to the *Sunset Western Garden Book*, sixth edition, 1995.

NEW DWARF TOMATOES *provide backyard bonanza in close quarters (see page 96).*

COLORFUL BLOOMERS
brighten the dark days
of winter. For more on
these flowering plants,
see page 8.

JANUARY

NORMAN A. PLATE

Instant winter color, rose-planting tips, All-America flowers

During the dark days of winter, color-hungry gardeners in mild parts of the West can use quite a few flowering plants to brighten up the windowsill or the garden. Some colorful options available this month at nurseries and florists are pictured on page 6. Clockwise from top left: red and pink cyclamen, yellow and rose *Primula polyantha,* pink *P. obconica,* and Johnny-jump-up. If you transplant from six-packs and 4-inch pots into decorative containers, these plants can keep on producing their colorful flowers for weeks.

If you grow them indoors, put plants in a spot that gets plenty of light to encourage continued bloom. If you try them outdoors, be prepared to bring them in when frost is predicted. Wear gloves when you plant *P. obconica,* whose hairy stems irritate some people's skin.

All-America Selections for 1995

Each new year ushers in a fresh crop of garden catalogs that trumpet flower introductions, including new plants judged as All-America Selections by the seed industry. The flowers look great on catalog pages, but how do they perform in the garden? To find out, we grew the three 1995 AAS winners—two petunias and a black-eyed Susan—in *Sunset*'s gardens in Menlo Park, California, last summer.

'*Purple Wave*' is a new class of petunia that hugs the ground. This plant grows only 4 to 6 inches tall and spreads to 4 feet wide, making it suitable as a seasonal ground cover or in hanging baskets. But the most outstanding thing about this petunia is the intensely iridescent deep purple of its flowers. The blooms are about 2 inches across, like those of a multiflora. Space plants 3 feet apart.

'*Celebrity Chiffon Morn*', an improved multiflora petunia called a floribunda, was chosen for its beautiful pastel pink flowers that are produced in great profusion on plants growing to 18 inches tall. This petunia tolerates a wide range of garden conditions, including heat and some drought. Space plants 6 to 12 inches apart.

Rudbeckia hirta '*Indian Summer*', a new black-eyed Susan, is a standout in the summer garden. Plants produce huge 6- to 9-inch-wide single or double golden yellow blooms all season long. The 3- to 4-foot-tall plants branch freely at the base, so they don't require staking. Plant 1 to 2 feet apart.

Look for these plants at nurseries this spring. All of them grow best in full sun and well-amended soil.

Space-age shrub for mild climates

So exotic and otherworldly are blooms of the protea family that they were often used as props in the "Star Trek" series. Prices for protea blooms are also out of this world: at $2.50 to $8.50 each, depending on size and variety, cut proteas are among the most expensive flowers on the market.

Which is why many earthlings try to grow their own. Yet home gardeners find the

than 1 gallon per week. Water less frequently along the coast, where soils tend to retain water and temperatures are cooler.

• Don't hoe around roots during the growing season, December through May. Proteas have shallow feeder root systems, so pull weeds by hand.

Very forgiving kinds, easier to grow than most, include duchess protea (*Protea eximia*), king protea (*P. cynaroides*), nodding pincushion (*Leucospermum cordifolium*), and 'Pink Ice' (a protea hybrid). Species of *Leucodendron* and *Banksia*— two other genera in the protea family— are not common in most retail nurseries.

Plants cost about $10 for a 1-gallon container, $30 for a 5-gallon. In Southern California, try Turk Hessellund Nursery in Santa Barbara, Burkard Nurseries in Pasadena, Green Thumb nurseries throughout Southern California, Green Valley Nursery in Escondido, and Walter Andersen Nursery in San Diego.

'PINK ICE' *is a protea hybrid that's more forgiving and easier to grow than most members of this exotic family.*

plants frustrating. As a group, proteas (several genera of the Proteaceae family) are difficult to get started—they have the annoying habit of dying, seemingly for no reason.

The key to getting them going is to provide site, soil, and irrigation similar to what are found in the plants' native Australia and South Africa. So says Ben Gill, owner of California Protea Management and manager of Silvermink Protea Ranch in Pauma Valley. The 93-acre farm, 45 miles northeast of San Diego, grows more than 100 kinds of proteas for the floral market. The fast-draining decomposed granite soil there is, apparently, perfect for the plants. Here's what Gill has learned about these exotic-looking plants.

• Plant during cool weather, now through May.

• Don't amend the soil, and don't fertilize the plants.

• Provide air circulation, but shelter them from high winds.

• Consider an orchard layout. Proteas get large and tend to sprawl, so be sure to give them enough room.

• Good drainage is crucial. Plant on a slope, if possible, and instead of forming a basin to hold water, place a drip emitter 12 inches above the trunk on the uphill side.

• Established proteas growing in decomposed granite (common to inland areas in Southern California) need 1 to 3 gallons of water per week during the dry season. New plants can't take much more

Sweet cherry trees for small gardens

Sweet cherries normally grow on large trees, and that's often bad news on several counts: it makes the fruit hard to protect from birds and hard to harvest, and the tree hard to squeeze into a small city garden. That's why a new dwarfing rootstock for cherries is good news.

The rootstock is called 'Gisela' (or sometimes 'Geissen', for its German city of origin), and it comes in several similar forms. Starting this winter, you should be able to find more than a dozen major varieties of cherries, from 'Bing' to 'Van', grafted onto this dwarfing rootstock. All bear fruit a year or two after planting. Most kinds of sweet cherry trees will remain at less than half the size of those on standard rootstocks, such as 'Mazzard'. At Washington State University's Prosser Research Center, trees have been growing for about 6 years, and they're all under 15 feet tall.

Availability of these dwarf trees will be spotty this first year and prices will be high—$2 to $4 more per tree than cherries on standard rootstocks. Not all cherries labeled "dwarf" are on 'Gisela' roots, so be sure to ask before you buy. Cherries aren't recommended for the desert.

Cherry trees on 'Gisela' roots are also available mail-order from Raintree Nursery, 391 Butts Rd., Morton, Wash. 98356; write for free catalog.

Now or soon, feed citrus trees nitrogen

Six to eight weeks before citrus trees bloom is the most important time to feed them nitrogen fertilizer, and in the Central Valley feeding should be done later this month.

The University of California advises fertilizing according to the age of the tree. Recommendations are given in pounds of actual nitrogen per year. To calculate pounds of actual nitrogen in a fertilizer, multiply the weight of the bag or box by the percentage of nitrogen it contains (the first of the three numbers in the fertilizer's guaranteed analysis, listed beneath the product name). For example, a 20-pound bag of ammonium sulfate (21-0-0) would include 4.2 pounds (20×.21) of actual nitrogen.

UC recommends that a newly planted citrus tree be given 1 tablespoon of a nitrogen fertilizer in May and July. After the tree's first season, fertilizer should be applied in January or early February and again in May, at these rates: a total of ¼ pound of actual nitrogen in the second year, ½ pound in the third year, ¾ pound in the fourth year, and 1 pound in the fifth year.

Trees more than 5 years old should receive 1 to 1½ pounds of nitrogen each year; you can feed them once in January or early February, or in two feedings: half in January, half in May.

Seedless grapes for the Central Valley

Growing clusters of juicy seedless grapes like the ones you see in the supermarket isn't all that easy. Commercial growers use a combination of techniques including fruit thinning and precision pruning to achieve those large, full-fruited clusters.

The most popular seedless varieties for inland California are white-fruited 'Thompson Seedless' and 'Perlette', black-fruited 'Black Monukka', and red-fruited 'Flame Seedless'. With the exception of 'Black Monukka', these varieties unfortunately tend to form small, broken clusters in most home gardens, although the grapes taste good.

Two excellent new varieties developed by the U.S. Department of Agriculture are 'Crimson Seedless' and black-fruited 'Fantasy Seedless'; both kinds produce large clusters with less work, but they still need to be pruned properly.

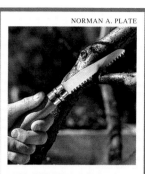

NORMAN A. PLATE

Tool of the Month

Sometimes when you're literally up a tree, it's better to have a serviceable tool at hand than the perfect one back in the garden shed. With this in mind, the French invented the Opinel pruning saw, a folding tool you can tuck in your pocket. The saw's 4¾-inch carbon steel blade will handle branches as thin as a straw or as thick as the grip on a tennis racket. A twisting lock secures the sharp blade in the open position. Price is $24.95. You can buy it at some cutlery stores and at garden shops such as Smith & Hawken, or order it by mail (ask for OP 165) from Boker USA by calling (800) 992-6537.

Bare-root grapes appear this month in most nurseries. For useful tips, order a copy of the 66-page booklet *Growing Quality Table Grapes in the Home Garden*, published by Fresno County UC Cooperative Extension, 1720 S. Maple Ave., Fresno, Calif. 93702. The booklet costs $5 plus $1 for shipping.

Get roses off to a good start

One of the most satisfying and colorful plants to grow in the garden is the rose. To get the best performance from roses, it's important to provide them with optimum growing conditions.

Plant in full sun. For best results, roses need at least 6 hours of sun per day.

Plant in well-drained soil. If your soil is clayey, add compost, well-composted manure, or peat moss to the soil. If your soil doesn't drain well, plant in raised beds about 12 inches high.

Add soil sulfur, if necessary. Roses prefer a soil pH of 6.5. If your soil's pH is 7.5 or higher, apply soil sulfur according to package directions.

Plant bare-root roses right away. If you can't plant for a few days, open the package immediately and moisten the packing material around the roots or place roots in a container of moistened peat moss or sawdust. Keep plants in a cool, dry, shaded place.

Dig a hole to accommodate the roots. A standard hole is usually about 2 feet wide and a foot deep. Build a cone of soil in the bottom of the hole and spread the roots over the top. If the rose is budded onto a rootstock, keep the bud slightly above the soil level. Fill in the hole, making sure to work soil into the gaps. Soak the soil thoroughly to settle it. Add more soil if necessary.

A multimedia garden catalog

Books, videos, and computer software each do different things well, so it's nice to be able to pick and choose when you're looking for gardening information. A new mail-order catalog from A. C. Burke & Co. lets you choose among all three.

The catalog specializes in products that will help you with garden planning, design, and problem-solving. Computer software is mostly geared to IBM-compatible machines, but some Macintosh software is available.

For a free catalog, write to A.C. Burke & Co., 2554 Lincoln Blvd., Suite 1058, Marina del Rey, Calif. 90291.

By Debra Lee Baldwin, Owen Dell, Steven R. Lorton, Jim McCausland, Lynn Ocone, Lauren Bonar Swezey, Lance Walheim

January Checklist

■

PACIFIC NORTHWEST

☐ **BAIT FOR SLUGS.** These relentless nibblers hide under rocks and decks, among ground covers, next to house foundations. Bait liberally on a warm, dry day to reduce damage in spring. Take care to keep bait away from pets.

☐ **BUY BARE-ROOT PLANTS.** West of the Cascades, bare-root fruit trees are the bargains of the month. Roses will be offered, too. East of the Cascades, bare-root stock shows up in early spring. For shopping and planting tips, see page 16.

☐ **CARE FOR HOUSE PLANTS.** Remove dead or damaged foliage, and water plants well. Fertilize only winter-blooming plants. Put dusty plants in the bathtub or shower stall and give them a warm, gentle rinse. If the top layer of soil in the pot is crusty, use a large serving spoon to carefully remove the soil down to the uppermost roots, then add fresh soil. This is also a good time to repot rootbound plants.

☐ **CHECK STORED BULBS.** Examine summer-flowering bulbs, corms, and tubers. Separate and discard those that show any sign of rot, except dahlias. Cut the bad spots out of dahlia tubers, dust the cuts with sulfur, and store separately.

☐ **ORDER SEED NOW.** Seed catalogs start arriving after Christmas. Order now while suppliers are fully stocked.

☐ **PRUNE FRUIT TREES.** Where winters are mild, you can prune fruit trees any day that the temperature is above freezing. In cold inland climates, wait until danger of prolonged hard freeze has passed. First cut out dead, diseased, closely parallel, or crossing branches. Then prune for shape.

☐ **PRUNE ROSES.** Prune hybrid teas to a vase shape, preserving three to five of the strongest upright canes. Cut growth back by about a third. East of the Cascades, hold off on this job until early spring or you'll be encouraging dieback.

Sunset Western Garden Book climate zones

(1–3) (4–7)

☐ **SHOP FOR WINTER-FLOWERING SHRUBS.** In the coastal Northwest, the selection includes cornelian cherry (*Cornus mas*), leatherleaf mahonia (*M. bealei*), Sasanqua camellias, wintersweet (*Chimonanthus praecox*), witch hazel (*Hamamelis*), and *Sycopsis sinensis*.

☐ **SOW PERENNIALS.** Hardy perennials such as delphiniums, hellebores, Oriental poppies, Shasta daisies, veronicas, and violas can be sown in greenhouses and coldframes now. A month after the last hard frost and when plants have developed two or three sets of true leaves, you can set them out.

☐ **SPRAY FOR PEACH LEAF CURL.** On both sides of the Cascades, choose a dry, mild day to spray peach and nectarine trees with fixed copper, lime sulfur, or bordeaux mixture. Use a spreader-sticker to improve coverage. Spray again as buds swell but before they open.

January Checklist

NORTHERN CALIFORNIA

WHERE DO YOU GARDEN?
The following recommendations refer to the elevation at which you garden.

L = Low (zones 14–17)
H = High (zones 1–3)
Climate zones are from *Sunset Western Garden Book*.

CARE FOR GIFT PLANTS. L: After bloom, snip off spent blossoms and move hardier plants such as azaleas, cinerarias, cyclamen, and cymbidiums to a protected spot outdoors. Keep tender plants such as amaryllis and kalanchoe indoors in a well-lighted spot. Water regularly. Repot if plants are rootbound and dry out quickly. Fertilize amaryllis and azaleas after bloom finishes. Fertilize cymbidiums lightly every week, others every three to four weeks. **H:** Keep all gift plants indoors until after the last frost.

CARE FOR LIVING CHRISTMAS TREES. L, H: If you haven't done so already, move living Christmas trees outdoors. Give them part sun to begin with, then move into full sun after a week or two. Rinse off the foliage and thoroughly soak the soil.

ORDER SEEDS. This is a good time to thumb through catalogs and order varieties you can't find on seed racks. **L:** Sow seed of warm-season vegetables and flowers as soon as they arrive, so you can plant them out in March and April; eggplants, peppers, and tomatoes take six to eight weeks to reach transplant size. **H:** Sow seed of cool-season crops such as broccoli and cauliflower indoors in flats six to eight weeks before soil can be worked.

PLANT ANNUALS. L: For midwinter bloom, buy plants in 4-inch pots for instant color. Stuff plants into containers or set them out in flower beds. Try calendula, candytuft, cineraria, dianthus, English daisy, English and fairy primroses, Iceland poppy, pansy, snapdragons, stock, and viola.

PLANT BARE-ROOT. L: This is the best month to buy and plant dormant roses, shrubs, fruit and shade trees, and vines. For more information, see the story on page 16.

PROTECT PLANTS FROM FROST. L: Watch for dry, still nights when it's clear; monitor weather forecasts. If frost is predicted, move tender container plants such as citrus, cymbidiums, hibiscus, and mandevilla beneath overhangs or into the garage. Protect other frost-tender plants in the ground or in containers too large to move with burlap, cloth, or plastic covering; do not let the cover touch the leaves. Remove the cover during the day.

PRUNE. L: This is prime time for pruning dormant deciduous plants such as flowering vines, fruit and shade trees, grapes, and roses. Wait to prune spring-flowering plants such as lilacs and Japanese snowball until after they bloom.

SPRAY FOR PEACH LEAF CURL. L: To prevent this fungus from causing distorted growth in peach leaves and destroying the fruit, spray now with fixed copper or lime sulfur, then again as buds swell but before they open. Use a spreader-sticker to improve coverage; spray on a calm, dry day.

WATER. L: If rains have been light or nonexistent, water plants periodically, especially those planted last fall whose new roots are developing. Drought-stressed plants are susceptible to freeze damage.

January Checklist

CENTRAL VALLEY

APPLY DORMANT SPRAY. To control fungus diseases and overwintering insects, spray deciduous plants, especially fruit trees, with a dormant spray such as horticultural oil or lime sulfur. Hold off spraying if rain is expected.

CARE FOR GIFT PLANTS. After bloom finishes, trim spent blossoms from hardier plants such as azaleas, cinerarias, cyclamen, and cymbidiums, and move them to a protected spot outdoors. Keep tender plants such as amaryllis and kalanchoe indoors in a well-lighted spot. Water regularly. If plants dry out quickly,

repot with fresh soil into the next-larger container. Fertilize amaryllis and azaleas after bloom finishes. Fertilize cymbidiums lightly every week, others lightly every three to four weeks.

CARE FOR LIVING CHRISTMAS TREES. If you haven't done so already, move trees outdoors. Put them in partial shade to acclimatize them, then move into full sun after a week or two. Rinse off foliage and thoroughly soak soil.

CONTROL SLUGS AND SNAILS. Reduce their numbers by reducing hiding places: clean up leaf litter and garden debris. Handpick them, trap by allowing them to collect on the underside of a raised board, or use commercial bait.

ORDER SEEDS. Browse through catalogs and order varieties you can't find on seed racks. Sow vegetable and flower seeds in flats as soon as they arrive, so you can plant them out in February, March, and April.

PLANT BERRIES AND VEGETABLES. Artichokes, asparagus, blackberries, grapes, raspberries, and strawberries are available bare-root. You can also plant onion sets and seed potatoes. Wait until next month to plant seedlings of most other cool-season vegetables.

PLANT BARE-ROOT. This is a prime month to buy and plant dormant roses, fruit and shade trees, shrubs, and vines. Plant as soon as you bring them home or receive them in the mail. If you can't plant right away, temporarily lay them on their sides in a shallow trench and cover with moist sawdust or soil.

PRUNE. Give dormant deciduous plants—cane berries, flowering shrubs and vines, shade trees, and roses—their annual pruning. Wait to prune plants that bloom only in early spring until after bloom.

*Sunset
Western Garden Book
climate zones*

Valley and foothills (7–9, 14)

PROTECT PLANTS. If frost is predicted, move tender container plants beneath overhangs or into the garage. Protect other tender plants with burlap, cloth, or plastic covering. Don't let covering touch the leaves; remove during the day.

January Checklist

FEED CITRUS. In frost-free coastal areas, fertilize citrus during January; inland, wait until next month. Where frost can linger, wait until March so new growth will not be damaged. Water first; a day later, sprinkle slow-release ammonium sulfate fertilizer over entire root area, then water to wash into soil. Wait two months, then apply a second feeding. See item on page 10 for more information.

GROOM CAMELLIAS. If camellia petal blight is a problem, keep the ground clean by removing all fallen flowers promptly. Pick infected flowers from plants.

IRRIGATE BASED ON RAINFALL. Remember to turn off automatic irrigation systems during rainstorms. Empty water from trays under potted plants so roots will not rot. Inland areas may receive more rainfall than the coast. On the coast, move indoor potted plants outdoors to let rain flush salts from soil.

ORDER SEEDS. Place orders for warm-season flowers and vegetables. Mail-order catalogs offer a much wider choice than seed displays in most nurseries, including colors and hybrids you're unlikely to find elsewhere.

PLANT BEDS. Along the coast and in mild inland areas, you can still put out cool-season plants that will provide color through early summer: calendulas, cinerarias (very frost sensitive), dianthus, English daisies, Iceland poppies, pansies, primroses, snapdragons, stock, sweet alyssum, sweet peas, and viola. Watch for seedling flowers that will sprout after rains; dig and replant where you want them.

PLANT BULBS. January is one of the year's most important months for planting bulbs, corms, rhizomes, and tubers. Now in nurseries are calla, canna, crinum, dahlia, gladiolus, nerine, tigridia, tuberous begonia, and watsonia. For a longer bloom season, plant at two- to three-week intervals. Plant tulips after they've chilled in the refrigerator crisper for six weeks.

PLANT DAYLILIES. Red-flowered varieties develop best color in hot areas; for a dependable dwarf yellow, choose 'Stella de Oro'. Evergreen hybrids, sold in gallon containers, like afternoon shade or filtered sun. Use dwarf varieties in rock gardens, as edgings, or as ground covers.

PLANT HYBRID AMARYLLIS BULBS. Amaryllis are often forced into bloom during the holidays and sold as gift plants. You can replant spent bulbs in your garden if you live in a frost-free area, but don't expect repeat bloom until next spring. Plant in a sunny or semishaded area, in loose, fast-draining soil, with the tip of the bulb just showing.

PLANT VEGETABLES. In coastal and inland areas, set out seedlings of the cabbage family, chard, chives, endive, lettuce, onions, and parsley. Plant roots of perennial vegetables such as artichoke, asparagus, and rhubarb. Sow seeds of beets, carrots, greens, and radishes.

PROTECT PLANTS FROM FROST. In frost-prone inland areas, move tender potted plants beneath overhangs or into the garage. On nights when frost is predicted, protect young citrus and other subtropicals by draping with burlap, cloth, or plastic covering. Don't let the cover touch the leaves; remove during the day.

PRUNE DORMANT PLANTS. Begin pruning dormant fruit and shade trees and vines. Cut blackberry canes that bore this year to the ground; remove any suckers that have sprouted. Delay pruning trees, shrubs, and vines that flower only in spring until flower show is over. To avoid winter injury, in coldest areas, delay pruning until late in the dormant season.

PRUNE ROSES. Remove dead or diseased canes; prune healthy canes to 18 to 36 inches depending on the variety's vigor. Clear crossed canes or twiggy growth in the center of the bush. Then remove debris, reshape the soil basin, and apply dormant spray.

SPRAY DORMANT FRUIT TREES. To control many pests that overwinter on deciduous plants, spray roses and dormant fruit trees with horticultural oil, oil and lime sulfur, or oil and fixed copper.

START SEEDS OF ANNUALS. For bedding plants to set in the garden during April and May, start seeds indoors late this month. Encourage germination by using a heat cable; promote healthy growth with a fluorescent lamp.

Bishop ●

● San Luis Obispo

● Tehachapi

● Santa Barbara

● Lancaster

Sunset Western Garden Book climate zones

☐ Mountain (1–3)
☐ High desert (11)
☐ Low desert (13)
☐ Coastal and inland (14–24)

● Los Angeles

Palm Springs

● San Diego

ANYWHERE IN THE WEST, TACKLE THESE CHORES:

☐ **CARE FOR CHRISTMAS TREES.** Move your living Christmas tree outside as soon as possible, putting it on a patio or under a tree where there's filtered sunlight for most of the day. Water well. After two weeks, you can move the tree into full sun or plant it out if it's a kind that does well where you live. If it isn't, you can keep it in a container for years by pruning its roots and repotting occasionally when the soil needs to be renewed.

☐ **CHECK STORED BULBS, FRUIT, PRODUCE.** If you keep apples, squash, and tender bulbs in cool storage, check them every couple of weeks. Shriveling can usually be corrected by sprinkling with water. Throw out anything that has rotten spots except dahlia tubers. You can often save these by cutting out the bad spots, dusting with sulfur, and storing apart from the rest.

☐ **FERTILIZE ASPARAGUS.** To get the best crop this spring, apply a top dressing of rotted manure or some complete fertilizer.

☐ **MAINTAIN GIFT PLANTS.** After the holidays, rinse plants off with a warm shower (cover the soil first with plastic wrap) and put them in a draft-free place that gets plenty of light. To keep flowering plants going, pinch off faded blooms and feed with half-strength fertilizer every two weeks.

☐ **ORDER SEEDS, PLANTS.** Order early to avoid substitutions or out-of-stock notices. Start seeds indoors about six weeks before you intend to plant them outside.

☐ **PRUNE TREES, SHRUBS.** First cut out dead, diseased, and injured branches, then remove crossing or closely parallel branches. Step back, size up the plant, and prune for shape. Make pruning cuts on the main stem, ¼ inch beyond side branches or growth buds.

☐ **SOW PERENNIALS.** Start seeds of delphinium, hellebore, veronica, and viola in a coldframe or greenhouse for planting when at least two sets of true leaves appear (and, in coldest areas, when ground can be worked). To prevent damping-off disease, plant in a sterile potting mix.

☐ **WATER HOUSE PLANTS.** Low humidity and dry house heat can take a toll on indoor plants. Check the soil in potted plants frequently, watering when the top ½ inch has dried out. Don't fertilize most plants until spring growth starts; the exceptions are any plants that are flowering or fruiting now.

IN THE SOUTHWEST'S LOW AND INTERMEDIATE DESERTS:

☐ **BUY AND PLANT BARE-ROOT STOCK.** A host of bare-root plants, from roses to fruit trees, appears in nurseries this month. For shopping tips, see page 16. Ask the nursery staff to wrap roots to keep them moist until you get plants home and into the ground.

☐ **CONTROL APHIDS.** You can control small, localized populations by just blasting them off with a jet of water. For more widespread infestations, blast them off, then spray plants with insecticidal soap.

☐ **FEED CITRUS TREES.** Fertilize trees to prepare them for coming bloom. Water trees first, then apply ammonium sulfate a day later: 2½ pounds per mature grapefruit tree; 4 pounds for orange and tangerine; and 5 pounds for lemon. Water again after application, and fertilize again in May. See item on page 10 for more information.

☐ **MULCH.** A layer of organic mulch can keep down winter weeds and retain water from winter rains. It also protects tender surface roots from frost.

☐ **PLANT CHILLED BULBS.** If you bought crocus, tulips, or hyacinths and chilled them in the refrigerator for at least six weeks, now is the time to plant them.

☐ **PLANT WINTER COLOR.** Shop for bachelor's button, calendula, cineraria, cyclamen, English daisy, pansy, primrose, sweet alyssum, and winter-flowering bedding plants.

☐ **PROTECT CITRUS.** When temperatures below 28° are predicted, cover citrus trees with burlap, cloth, or plastic for the night. Prop the cover over plants so it doesn't hang on leaves. Most fruit is ruined when temperatures remain at 25° for more than 2 hours. (If fruit does freeze, pick it and extract juice right away.)

☐ **PRUNE ROSES.** Prune shrub roses for shape only. Cut back hybrid tea roses by about a third, leaving the strongest three to five canes to produce this year's flowers.

☐ **START VEGETABLES.** In the low desert, start seeds of warm-season vegetables such as cucumber, eggplant, melon, pepper, squash, and tomato indoors for transplanting out into the garden after all danger of frost is past.

☐ **WATER PLANTS.** During dry spells, you'll need to deep-water most trees and shrubs occasionally: irrigate whenever the soil is dry to a depth of 1 inch. Don't irrigate cactus and acacia when it's chilly, since their roots won't take up water in cold weather.

The beauty of bare-root

It's the best way to go—from fruits to flowers, even some vegetables. Here's what you need to know before you shop

A T FIRST GLANCE, there's nothing terribly inspiring about a nursery full of lifeless-looking bare-root plants. But don't let their scraggly appearance fool you. Harbored in the dormant stock is a bounty of fruits, flowers, and vegetables. It can all be yours this month, the height of bare-root season.

Labels and signs at the nursery are your first clue. Looking for figs? A sign at one Southern California nursery promises 'Black Jack', 'Black Mission', 'Brown Turkey', 'Conadria', 'Osborn Prolific', 'White Genoa', and 'White Kadota'. Roses? There are literally hundreds of varieties to choose from. And though you usually don't associate the dead of winter with prime vegetable-planting season, now is the time to plant bare-root perennials such as artichokes, horseradish, and rhubarb. There are even a few surprises, such as ferns, jujube, and a tasty cross between an apricot and plum called a pluot.

CHRISTOPHER GARDNER

IF YOU'VE NEVER BOUGHT *bare-root before, you may be in for a surprise. Plant roots are heeled into sand or wood chips.*

KATHRYN KLEINMAN

WHY BARE-ROOT?

Bare-root plants have numerous advantages over plants in containers.

Price. Bare-root plants typically cost 10 to 40 percent less than comparable container plants, although we've saved 70 percent in a few cases. The savings can add up if you are buying a lot of the same plants (if you're putting in a hedge, for example).

Variety. Unsurpassed selection is another good reason to buy bare-root. Since the plants take up less space than those in containers, nurseries that specialize in bare-root often have extensive seasonal inventories. And if you can't find what you're looking for, you can always order it.

Viability. Bare-root plants often establish themselves more quickly than container plants for several reasons. First, roots in a container can be potbound. Second, though less common, roots in a container can be underdeveloped. Last, bare-roots don't get "spoiled" by container soil. As a result, bare-roots don't have to adapt to any differences between container soil and your garden's.

BEFORE YOU SHOP

Know your source. Your favorite nursery for a splash of annual color or container

plants may not have the best selection of bare-root. Since bare-root plants require special storage, many nurseries don't offer them at all. Twenty minutes spent checking the ads in your local newspaper and making a few phone calls will save you hours of running around to find out who has what.

Know the season. Plants are freshest and most abundant this month. Shop early because a plant's dormant period does not last long. Don't be enticed by deep discounts on bare-root in early spring; if plants start to leaf out, they won't do as well as dormant ones purchased during the peak of bare-root season.

Do you know your roots?

1. 'French Lace' rose
2. 'Olallie' blackberry
3. 'Quinault' strawberry
4. 'Cherry' rhubarb
5. Artichoke
6. Red-hot poker
7. 'U.C. 72' asparagus
8. Bleeding heart
9. Horseradish
10. Astilbe

Know your climate. Some nurseries and chain stores may not offer varieties ideally suited to the climate they are sold in. To ensure that you get the best varieties for your area, shop at nurseries that specialize in regional plants. In mild-winter Southern California, for example, it's important to plant varieties of apples, peaches, and pears that require very little chilling for fruit production.

Know what you want. It's best to plant bare-root immediately after purchase, so you should have a planting plan in mind—and the planting holes dug—before you bring anything home. If you don't know exactly what you want, or where you want to plant it, assess your site's space, light, and soil considerations, then take a scouting trip to the nursery to see what's available. Before you buy, you should return home to dig those holes. If, however, you're an impulse shopper and have not planned ahead, lay the new plants on their sides and cover roots with moist soil until you've prepared planting holes.

SHOPPING SMARTS

At the nursery, you'll notice that some bare-root plants such as berries, grapes, and roses are sold in packages, while others will be truly "bare," with loose roots heeled into bins of moist sand or wood shavings. For the nursery, the advantage of packaged plants is that they require little or no care, but for the consumer, packaged plants are not always best. The roots of packaged plants are trimmed or forced to fit into the package; the package usually hides the roots, so you won't be able to judge their health. And some packaged plants actually cost more than their truly bare-root brethren. Still, fresh packaged plants, purchased early in the season before they dry out on the shelves, should do well once they're planted.

CHRISTOPHER GARDNER

ROOTS WILL STAY MOIST *if they are packed loosely in soil.*

A good nursery will give you plenty of information on the varieties it sells, as well as instructions on how to plant and care for your purchase. To ensure that a particular variety is right for your needs and climate, check the hours of chilling required for fruit production, the season of fruit maturity (early, mid, or late), whether or not a plant is self-fruitful (doesn't need other varieties to be pollinated), and its ultimate size.

Once you've selected your tree, the nursery staff will often prune its top. Horticulturists differ on how much should be pruned; some question whether the practice is beneficial at all. But Bob Ludekens, president of L. E. Cooke Company, one of the largest growers of bare-root stock for home gardens, recommends removing the top third of most trees. He recommends removing 50 percent on pomegranates and almonds, but he doesn't prune birch at all because it ruins the tree's shape.

Finally, make sure the nursery staff wraps the roots in a plastic bag to keep them moist in transit, and plant as soon as you get home.

MANY BARE-ROOT ROSES, *a Southern California specialty, are sold prepackaged. Buy early in the season before the roots dry out.*

BARE-ROOT BUYING GUIDE

The prices given for the plants listed here are only approximate—the price you pay will depend on where you live, how the plant is packaged, the nursery's volume, and the particular variety you choose. When you buy can also be a factor, although it generally doesn't pay to wait until the end of bare-root season for a so-called bargain.

Perennial Vegetables. Buy plants with the largest, plumpest roots you can find. The best root crowns have plenty of fleshy, fibrous, unbroken roots.

Artichoke. 'Improved Green Globe' is most widely available. Artichokes are traditionally sold by root division, but seedlings that are true to the parent plant are also available. Seedlings are less prone to rot than divisions. Both will produce artichokes the first year. Cost: $1.50 to $2.50.

Asparagus. Roots are typically 1-year-old seedlings whose tops have been cut back. Common varieties are 'Mary Washington', 'U.C. 157', and 'U.C. 72'. Plants take two to three years to reach full production. Cost: around $3 for 12 roots.

Horseradish. Crowns from root divisions produce roots for harvest the first year. Cost: $2.50 to $3 for two.

Jerusalem artichoke (also called sunchokes). Edible tubers are gaining in popularity but are still hard to find. Plant the tubers, which multiply underground. Cost: about 60 cents each.

Rhubarb. Several varieties are available, including 'Cherry' (also called 'Crimson Cherry'), 'Strawberry', and 'Victoria'. Sold by division and seedlings. Divisions tend to rot more easily but produce red leaf stalks. Plants from seedlings may include green stalks at maturity. Cost: $1.20 to $2.50 each.

Cane Berries. Several varieties of raspberries and blackberries (including thornless types) are offered, as well as currants and gooseberries suitable for cold climates. Check the *Sunset Western Garden Book* to find the best varieties for your region. Root systems should appear full and balanced. The diameter of the cane should be pencil-size or larger. Some types, such as red raspberries, produce fruit the first year; all should bear well by the second year. Cost: $2 to $4 each.

Blueberries. Choose the varieties appropriate for your climate: southern highbush and rabbiteye types are suited to Southern California; northern highbush varieties grow well in the Northwest. Some rabbiteye types require pollinators, while the northern highbush types are self-fruitful; production for all blueberries increases with pollinators. For a sustained harvest, plant a mixture of early-, mid-, and late-season varieties. Select plants with full, stocky tops and a substantial mat of fine roots. Plants bear some fruit the first year; production increases with age and size. Cost: $7 to $8.50 each.

Strawberries. Essentially, there are three types of strawberries available bare-root. One produces a single, major crop in the spring. Another produces two or three crops during the growing season. The third produces on and off throughout the season, but never a lot all at once. Mix varieties for a prolonged and abundant harvest. Plants are available packaged and bundled. Make sure the roots are moist and plump. Cost: around $3 for a package of 12, less for bundled roots.

Grapes. A better selection of juice, raisin, table, and wine varieties is available loose than in packages. Varieties vary widely in hardiness and heat requirements, so choose ones that are best for your climate. Plants are usually grown from cuttings. Grade No. 1 plants sold loose are larger than packaged grade No. 2 plants. Select plants with roots growing all the way around the basal node, the joint at the very bottom of the plant. Vines bear a partial crop in the third year and a full crop in the fourth. Cost: $2 to $3.50 each.

Fruit Trees. Apples, apricots, Asian pears, cherries, crabapples, figs, jujube, mulberries, nectarines, peaches, pears, persimmons, plums, pluots, pomegranate, and quince are available in increasing numbers. You'll also find fruit trees with multiple-variety grafts. Some trees

THE 'FRENCH LACE' ROSE *in the 2-gallon container (left) was purchased in May for about $17. The same rose bare-root (in terra-cotta planter) was purchased in January for about $4.*

ROSE ROOTS *from packaged plant (left) aren't as extensive as true bare-root version of the same plant.*

need pollinators, notably Japanese plums and older varieties of sweet cherries such as 'Bing'.

Tree trunk diameters usually range from ⅜ inch to 1 inch, with corresponding heights from 4 to 8 feet. Smaller trees are easier to shape and may cost less than larger ones, but larger trees may give you a harvest sooner.

Look for a tree that is relatively straight where the trunk joins the rootstock. The top should be balanced, with branches growing off a single leader. Buds along the

branches should be plump yet closed. The major roots should radiate fairly evenly from the trunk's base—free of kinks or knots but with smaller, fibrous roots attached. Roots should appear plump, not shriveled. Skip trees with diseased or injured bark.

Prices vary by tree type, but the average runs between $12 and $20 for a standard, semidwarf, or genetic dwarf. Specialty trees such as combination grafts, jujube, and persimmons cost more.

Ornamental Trees and Shrubs. A good selection of flowering trees, such as apricot, cherry, crabapple, peach, pear, and plum, is available. Shade trees such as ash, birch, hawthorn, and maple are less available, especially in warm regions of California. Select ornamental trees as you would fruit trees (see criteria under Fruit Trees). Cost: $14 to $20.

The selection of shrubs is limited, although varieties of flowering quince, lilacs, rose of Sharon, and wisteria are increasing. Look for tree forms of shrubs, such as flowering

pomegranate, lilacs, and wisteria. Shrubs are usually sold by height; a 2- to 3-foot plant runs from $8 to $15.

Some nurseries will special order unusual varieties of ornamental trees and shrubs. For example, 12 varieties of birch can be ordered bare-root; there are even more types of ash available.

Nut Trees. Varieties vary by region. 'All-in-One' genetic semidwarf almond is the most available nut tree in California. Occasionally, you'll find additional almond varieties as well as walnuts and, less frequently, pecans. In the Willamette Valley, you'll find filberts, 'Hall's Hardy' almond, and walnuts. Use the same criteria to select a healthy nut tree as you would a fruit tree. Cost: $12 to $30.

Roses. In colder parts of the West, nurseries sell mostly potted roses. Some California nurseries, on the other hand, offer hundreds of rose varieties bare-root. In order to provide the best possible selection, most nurseries sell both packaged and bin-stored bare-root plants.

For largest plants, select grade No. 1 roses from a bin. The roots should be unknotted, unbroken, and developed. On all roses, look for three or more strong, well-spaced canes. Healthy canes are green and hard. Roses sold in packages can be grade No. 1, but they are usually smaller in size. Some packaged roses are of a lesser grade—read the label carefully. Grade No. 1 roses range from $4 to $15. Nonpatented varieties cost less than patented ones.

Ferns and Perennials. Unless you discover a variety that is unusual or hard to find, there is generally no advantage to buying ferns or perennials bare-root. However, you may find root divisions of perennials such as coreopsis and baby's breath. Less common are ferns such as cinnamon, leatherwood, and royal. Roots are sold packaged. Cost: about $3 each. ∎

By Lynn Ocone

Fishtail palm

Ficus maclellandii 'Alii'

Ming aralia

Trees that make the best houseguests

These 12 trees will thrive indoors as long as you take good care of them

L USH-LOOKING HOUSE TREES add natural grace to interior design. Gardeners have been growing trees indoors for the last century or so, and during that time, two classes of trees—palms and ornamental figs—have become favorites, along with a few trees from other plant groups.

We list 12 of the best choices. Average costs are for 5- to 6-foot specimens, but if you're willing to buy a smaller plant and nurse it to maturity, you'll pay a much smaller price. Shop at nurseries that sell indoor plants.

PALMS BRING TROPICAL
ELEGANCE INDOORS

Select a variety that fits your space, since indoor palms can't be top-pruned or they will stop growing and die.

Fishtail palm (*Caryota*). Though this is a feather palm, its fishtail-shaped fronds put it in a class by itself. Give it plenty of light, a high ceiling, and even moisture; fertilize regularly to prevent yellowing. The single-trunked fishtail wine palm (*C. urens*) grows fast; clustered fishtail palm (*C. mitis*) is slower, developing multiple trunks. Cost is around $80.

Kentia palm (*Howea*); the favorite variety is called paradise palm (*H. forsterana*). Kentia's 9-foot feathery leaves emerge from a single, slow-growing trunk. This tree takes relatively low light if you don't overwater. About $150.

Lady palm (*Rhapis excelsa*). One of the finest clumping-fan palms, this one grows slowly and almost never gets too big for indoor display. It likes even moisture, so you can put it in a self-

watering container. About $100.

Triangle palm (*Neodypsis decaryi*). This single-trunked feather palm, which takes its name from the triangular cross section of trunk and frond stems, looks best when planted in groups. Costing about $60, it's a less expensive alternative to the similar kentia palm.

THE FICUS FAMILY

Ornamental fig trees are beautiful and fast-growing, and they do well in relatively low light.

Ficus maclellandii **'Alii'.** You won't think "Ficus" when you see this tree's dark, long, eucalyptus-like leaves, though its size and habit are similar to those of weeping fig. One of the very best figs, 'Alii' doesn't drop

Weeping fig
'Wintergreen'

Lady palm

Kentia palm

Norfolk Island pine

its leaves when moved, and it takes low light if you let it dry out between waterings. About $40.

Indian laurel fig (*Ficus microcarpa nitida*). It looks much like weeping fig, but its leaves are thicker, slightly larger, and less wavy edged. 'Green Gem' is the best choice. About $60.

Nuda fig (*Ficus benjamina* 'Nuda'). Its leaves are much larger, waxier, and less likely to drop than those of standard weeping fig, and this tree's form is more upright. About $100.

Weeping fig (*Ficus benjamina*). This tree is graceful and easy to shape, and it takes an amazing amount of abuse. If you move it from a sunny porch to a darker living room, it will horrify you by dropping all its old leaves, then hearten you by growing a new set. Both 'Wintergreen' and variegated weeping fig are less prone to

shedding and can tolerate lower light. About $40.

OTHER CHOICE TREES

African fern pine (*Podocarpus gracilior*). Thin, dark green leaves cloak this tree, whose upright form tends to be columnar. It likes plenty of light but can tolerate low light; water it well. About $125.

Bottle palm (*Beaucarnea recurvata*). Given good light and little water, bottle palm grows slowly, developing a swollen, bulbous base. Put it where you won't brush against its sharp leaves. About $125.

Ming aralia (*Polyscias fruticosa*). This handsome, slow-growing tree tops out at just under standard ceiling height. It demands bright light, and if you don't let it dry out between water-

ings, especially in winter, it will die. About $150.

Norfolk Island pine (*Araucaria heterophylla*). This symmetrical conifer is a standard tabletop Christmas tree. It grows well indoors if given plenty of light. Don't top it or you'll destroy its form. About $60.

NESTING CONTAINERS

Nesting your house tree's nursery pot in a larger ceramic or plastic container makes it easy to move the tree for root pruning and repotting. If the outer container is waterproof, the inner pot should rest on 2 to 3 inches of river rock to keep the lowest roots out of standing water. If the outer container has a drainage hole, use both a saucer and a trivet below it. ■

By Jim McCausland

LUSH GREEN FOLIAGE *and dozens of colorful blooms are sure signs of healthy plants. Landscape designer Michelle Comeau enjoys 'Sun Flare'.*

Rugged roses for coastal gardens

A list of top performers if you live in a cool, foggy area

Y OU DON'T HAVE TO FORGO growing roses just because you live in a cool, coastal climate. Those shown here, in Elizabeth Kirby's garden in Pebble Beach, California, are visible proof that roses can perform well in less-than-perfect climates—if you choose the right varieties.

To come up with a selection of top performers for Kirby's garden, landscape designer Michelle Comeau consulted with rosarians, avid gardeners, and rose societies.

The garden has been growing for four years. "The summer of '94 was a real test because it was so cool and foggy," explains Comeau. Some roses that she had thought were disease resistant are now on the marginal list.

ROSES THAT LIKE THE COAST

The best performers have been 'Color Magic' and 'Festival Fanfare' (pink blends), 'French Lace' (white), 'Ingrid Bergman' (dark red), 'Paul Shirville' (orange pink), 'Stretch Johnson' (a red blend, also called 'Rock 'n' Roll'), and 'Sun Flare' (yellow).

Roses only minimally affected by disease, such as powdery mildew, include 'All That Jazz' (orange pink), 'Brandy' (an apricot blend), 'Fisherman's Friend' (dark red), 'Graceland' (yellow), 'Honor' (white), 'Lancôme' (deep pink), 'Lavender Dream' (mauve with yellow), 'Medallion' (an apricot blend), 'Olé' (orange red), 'Paradise' (mauve), 'Pascali' (white), 'Pink Meidiland' (a pink blend), 'Playboy' (an orange-yellow blend), 'Pleasure' (medium pink), 'Sexy Rexy' (pink), and 'Voodoo' (an orange blend).

START PLANTS OFF RIGHT

Where you plant roses and how you maintain them are as important as choosing the right varieties. Good air circulation minimizes the chance of disease. Comeau recommends planting roses 5 to 7 feet apart (trunk to trunk) where they get at least 6 hours of full midday sun.

She has developed a maintenance routine to keep the roses healthy. In February, all roses are pruned. Shrubby roses like 'French Lace' need minimal pruning to maintain shape; hybrid teas need more drastic pruning. Then a dormant spray of sulfur mixed with a sticker-spreader or dormant oil is applied to kill overwintering diseases and pests.

In March, the roses get a dose of controlled-release fertilizer. From April through November, plants are drip-watered at least weekly, beds are kept free of debris, and old blooms are pruned off regularly (always prune down to a leaf with five leaflets).

Although these roses are suitable for cool climates, some may become minimally infected with a disease such as mildew. Plants are monitored during the growing season, and any infected leaves are picked off. Roses also may be spot-sprayed with a fungicide; a good organic spray for mildew is 2 teaspoons each baking soda and summer oil per gallon water.

In November, rose hips are allowed to form, so plants begin dormancy. ∎

By Lauren Bonar Swezey

'Pleasure'   'Fisherman's Friend'   'Playboy'   'Voodoo'

A **SHADY GROVE** of three European white birches has shrubs beneath, where the trees' roots grow too thickly for a lawn to succeed.

Birches with striking bark, graceful form

PAPERY LAYERS of bark peel from Betula jacquemontii.

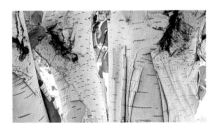

RIVER BIRCH BARK turns to cinnamon brown and flakes as the tree ages.

GROVES OF BIRCHES HAVE A graceful character all their own. In summer, even delicate breezes rustle the small leaves easily; in winter, the bright-barked trunks and barren limbs look like etchings in the landscape.

You can plant any kind of birch in winter, from bare-root stock or from containers. Plant in groups, since birches look most natural in groves.

Don't plant trees where they'll eventually hang over parking areas or patios, since birch leaves attract aphids that drip honeydew. All birches need regular water.

For white bark. No birch can match the chalk white bark of a good *Betula jacquemontii;* grafted trees are usually whitest. This tree won't grow in the coldest parts of the West or in the desert, but it does nicely everywhere west of the Pacific crest and in mild places east of the mountains. It reaches 60 feet.

Japanese white birch (*B. platyphylla japonica*) is a beautiful white-barked tree that grows everywhere but the desert. *B. p. j.* 'Whitespire' is a seed-grown strain with some variability of bark color; 'Whitespire Senior' has a

trunk whose white color is guaranteed by tissue-culture propagation. All Japanese white birches resist borers, have good fall color (yellow), and grow to about 50 feet.

For peeling bark. Paper birch (*Betula papyrifera*), with bark that peels off in white sheets, grows well throughout the Northwest, the Rockies, and California's mountains. Its beauty is almost unsurpassed, but it grows too large for many gardens, topping 100 feet in ideal conditions.

River birch (*B. nigra*) starts out with gray white or cinnamon-colored bark that peels and flakes, darkening with age; *B. n.* 'Heritage' has the lightest bark of the species. *B. nigra* resists bronze birch borers. It grows to 50 to 90 feet.

For weeping form. The European white birch clan (*B. pendula;* also sold as *B. verrucosa*) varies in form from upright to weeping; most top out at 30 to 40 feet. These grow everywhere but the low desert, though in warmer climates they tend to be shorter-lived. The following varieties all do best in cool-summer climates.

For a weeping form, try Young's weeping birch (*B. p.* 'Youngii'), which will grow as high as the stake to which you tie it, or *B. p.* 'Dalecarlica' (also sold as *B. p.* 'Laciniata'), an open-limbed tree whose branches are hung with deeply cut leaves.

For purple leaves and twigs that stand out against white trunks, look for *B. p. purpurea* 'Dark Prince' or *B. p. p.* 'Purple Rain'. *B. p. purpurea* tends to have extremely limber branches; a variety called 'Crimson Frost' is stronger than most.

For cold-winter gardens. Try paper birch, Japanese white birch, or *B.* 'Rocky Mountain Splendor' ('Rocki-mon'), a white-bark hybrid with extra-large leaves that reaches 45 feet.

For desert gardens. For success, abundant water is assumed. It is possible to grow river birch throughout the desert; in high and intermediate deserts, try straight European white birch; in the high desert only, plant Japanese white birch.

SOURCE

If you can't find the tree you want at a local nursery, try Forest Farm, 990 Tetherow Rd., Williams, Ore. 97544; (503) 846-7269. Catalog costs $3. This grower offers a remarkably broad collection of birches. ∎

By Jim McCausland

FEBRUARY IS A GREAT MONTH *to set out bare-root plants, including shade trees such as the 'Purple Robe' locust shown here. For more on this fast-growing deciduous tree, see page 28.*

FEBRUARY

A fine month for shopping, from nursery plants and bulbs to seed catalog offerings

'BLUE STAR' JUNIPER *(foreground) gets sun at the edge of this planting, while moss and sword fern enjoy the shade.*

W inter color choices and combinations may not be so obvious as those for summer, yet the possibilities are limitless. February is a great month to prowl nurseries looking for plants. You can put most landscape plants in the ground this month, as long as the soil is workable. The 'Blue Star' juniper and the native sword fern shown at right growing around a mossy rock provide a refreshing color combination. The rich green of the fern stands out against the sparkling blue of the juniper. But there's another trick to this planting: it combines a sun lover (the juniper) with shade lovers (the fern and moss).

Terry Welch of Woodinville, Washington, carefully studies sunlight boundaries and shade toleration levels in his garden. In the shade of a big conifer, there's just enough sunlight at the edge of the planting to keep the juniper blue and healthy, and enough shade toward the rear to keep the rock mossy and the ferns rich green and a bit rangy. For more about Welch's winter garden, see page 69.

For tomatoes next summer, start now

Every February, Mary Ellen Paulson of Edmonds, Washington, starts 'Early Girl' tomatoes from seed on her kitchen windowsill. She gives some away but saves four of the sturdiest to plant along the south wall of her house. Asked how her plants did last summer, she says, "Those plants went crazy! We ate tomatoes constantly from August into October."

A lot of the bumper crop can be credited to last year's hot, dry summer. But there's more to the story. Just as Mary Ellen started her seeds, her husband, Morvin, began building an 18-inch-high brick retaining wall 2½ feet out from the foundation of the house, forming a raised bed.

Late in May, he filled the bed with compost and mixed in a 20-pound bag of well-rotted steer manure along with 5 cups of 10-15-10 granular fertilizer. Then the Paulsons planted the tomatoes, surrounding each plant with a cylindrical wire cage. Side shoots were not removed, so the plants got bushy. Blossoms and fruits formed until the plants sagged with tomatoes. "It was the combination of the hot, dry summer, the raised bed that kept the soil warm, and the soil itself, I guess," says Morvin.

This month, Mary Ellen will be starting tomato seeds

regularly when the plants are growing.

Tiger flower naturalizes nicely, forming thick clumps in just a few years. If plants become overcrowded or produce fewer blooms, divide the bulbs after foliage dies back in fall.

Drought tolerance in Laguna Niguel

For about 10 years, Friends of the Niguel Botanical Preserve has been quietly working to develop a drought-tolerant botanical garden. Southern California's climate is similar to those of central Chile, the Mediterranean, South Africa, and southwest Australia. Plants native to any of those regions tend to do well in all the others with little or no extra irrigation. With water becoming scarcer, drought or not, Mediterranean-climate plants will play a bigger part in all our gardens.

As the preserve grows (it now sprawls over 20 acres in Crown Valley Community Park), more volunteers are needed to help with planting, propagation, and the myriad daily tasks that go into running a garden. For example, volunteers are needed now to plant trees in areas that won't see development until the year 2000. Gardeners working then will have well-established trees in place.

Friends of the Niguel Botanical Preserve gets its income from plant sales and $20 annual dues. Members receive a quarterly newsletter to keep them current. If you'd like to join or want more information, call the city's main number at (714) 362-4300.

again. And Morvin will replace the old soil mix with more of his private blend.

Plant bulbs of tiger flower for summer color

Tiger flower (*Tigridia pavonia*) is a beautiful summer-blooming bulb that many gardeners overlook. Planted now or soon (when nighttime temperatures are in the 50s or 60s), tiger flower will bloom for several weeks in July and August. The blooms are triangular, 3 to 6 inches across, with three flared petals coming together at the center to form a cup. The flared parts are shaded white, pink, red, orange, or yellow. The center cup has darker spots. Each bloom lasts only a day but is quickly followed by another.

The flowers appear on slender 1½- to 2½-foot stalks over grasslike leaves.

These bulbs are best planted in groups behind lower-growing plants that will cover up the bases of their leaves. Set the bulbs 2 to 4 inches deep and 4 to 8 inches apart. In all but coastal regions, they grow best with partial shade from the afternoon sun. Water and fertilize

Add "pluot" to your fruit vocabulary

What's a pluot, you ask? It's a new type of fruit called an interspecific hybrid (a hybrid between species)—in this case between apricots and plums. In tastings held at Dave Wilson Nursery in

Hickman, California, 'Flavor Supreme' pluot scored highest for flavor and texture when compared with 30 other varieties of fruit, including plums, peaches, and nectarines. Two other top-rated pluots are 'Flavor King' and 'Flavor Queen'.

Pluots have a taste all their own, but they're closest in flavor to plums. Craig Minor of Dave Wilson Nursery (wholesale only) says that you can't taste the apricot parentage, but it influences the flavor of the parent plum. The flavor is described as fruity and sweet.

'Flavor Supreme' has mottled green and maroon skin similar to that of its parent 'Mariposa' plum. The flesh is deep red like a 'Satsuma'. 'Flavor Supreme' is an early ripener, producing in June long before other plums and pluots, which ripen mid-July through August, and it's a most consistent producer, Minor says.

To produce a good crop of fruit, pluots need a pollinizer. 'Flavor Supreme' is pollinated by 'Flavor King' and 'Flavor Queen', or a Japanese plum like 'Santa Rosa'. You can also get a "2N1" tree— 'Flavor Queen' and 'Flavor Supreme' on the same tree. Many nurseries will carry bare-root trees: single trees cost $16 to $25, 2N1s cost $20 to $30.

A new golden crabapple

After years of trials at the Northwest Washington Research and Extension Unit, Washington State University–Mount Vernon has recommended some excellent new crabapples.

One especially attractive small-fruited variety is 'Golden Raindrops' (pictured above). It flowers well in spring and produces scads of pea-size golden fruits in fall.

'Golden Raindrops' is a vigorous plant, growing 12 to 15 feet tall, with an upright habit and oak-shaped leaves.

PHIL SCHOFIELD

'GOLDEN RAINDROPS' *crabapple bears small bright fruit.*

It also resists scab.

Look for bare-root plants at retail nurseries this winter. Crabapples grow in *Sunset Western Garden Book* zones 1 through 21.

A showy shade tree

As winter loosens its grip, gardeners can begin the processes that lead to first-rate summer gardens. Depending on where you live, this is the month to plant spring flower color outdoors or start it indoors, to order or plant summer-blooming bulbs, and to sow cool-season vegetables. And it's a great time to set out bare-root plants, including shade trees like the beauty shown on page 24. It's a variety of flowering locust called *Robinia ambigua* 'Purple Robe' (also sold as *R. pseudoacacia* 'Purple Robe'). This deciduous tree is fast-growing, with a shapely crown; it reaches about 35 feet at maturity.

'Purple Robe' puts on a three-season color show: New reddish bronze foliage appears early in spring. Then from mid-May to early summer, 'Purple Robe' earns its name, bearing fragrant rosy purple blossoms in big clusters that hang delicately among dark green leaves. In fall, the leaves turn bright yellow before dropping.

'Purple Robe' is an excellent shade tree, especially in hot, dry summer climates, where it does well on little water after it's established. Locust trees can be grown in all climate zones. Although branches of 'Purple Robe' are less brittle than those of other locust, it should not be planted in windy locations.

Seed sources for the inland West

When you shop for flower and vegetable seeds to plant this season, you might start by considering regional sources. Here are 10 that specialize in seeds that perform well in the inland West.

Burrell Seeds (Box 150, Rocky Ford, Colo. 81067;

719/254-3318); flowers, vegetables, herbs; catalog is free.

Garden City Seeds (1324 Red Crow Rd., Victor, Mont. 59875; 406/961-4837); heirloom and open-pollinated annuals, herbs, vegetables; catalog is free.

Native Seeds/SEARCH (2509 N. Campbell Ave., Box 325, Tucson, Ariz. 85719; 602/327-9123); Southwestern natives, wild food plants; catalog $1.

Northplan/Mountain Seed (Box 9107, Moscow, Idaho 83843; 208/882-8040); native wildflowers, shrubs, trees; seed list $1.

Plants of the Southwest (Route 6, Box 11A, Santa Fe, N.M. 87501; 505/471-2212); native flowers, vegetables; catalog $3.50.

Roswell Seed Co. (Box 725, Roswell, N.M. 88202; 505/622-7701); flowers, grains, vegetables; catalog is free.

Seeds Blüm (Idaho City Stage, Boise, Idaho 83706); annuals, vegetables, herbs; catalog $3.

Seeds of Change (Box 15700, Santa Fe, N.M. 87506; 800/957-3337); catalog is free.

Seeds Trust, High-Altitude Gardens (Box 1048, Hailey, Idaho 83333; 208/788-4363); open-pollinated herbs, vegetables, wildflowers; catalog $3.

Seeds West (Box 27057, Albuquerque, N.M. 87125; 505/242-7474); short-season and heirloom vegetables, herbs, wildflowers; catalog is free.

Heeding the call of the wild

A home demonstration garden devoted to native plants is now open at Soka University of America on Mulholland Highway just east of Las Virgenes Road in Los Angeles County's Santa Monica Mountains. What separates this garden from other native gardens is that its approximately 100 kinds of plants were collected and propagated on-site.

The garden, designed by landscape architect Rick Fisher of Toyon Design in Altadena, was planted in the fall of 1993. Since then, the drought-tolerant garden has flourished, mostly without irrigation.

A key to growing California native plants seems to be recognizing and developing microclimates within a landscape. For some plants, such as ceanothus, lupines, and white sage (*Salvia apiana*), good drainage is critical. Drainage was encouraged by mounding and contouring the soil. Moisture-loving plants such as deer grass (*Muhlenbergia rigens*), stream monkey flower (*Mimulus guttatus*), and California rose (*Rosa californica*) were planted where water gravitates.

Sunlight was another defining factor. Chaparral currant (*Ribes malvaceum*), hummingbird sage (*Salvia spathacea*), wild Johnny-jump-up (*Viola pedunculata*), and wild peony (*Paeonia californica*) were planted in the cool shade of an immense sycamore tree. Silvery chalk dudleya (*D. pulverulenta*) and the rare Verity's dudleya (*D. verityi*) were planted among stones in full sun.

The garden is open 9 to 5 daily. Tours are offered at 10 on the first Tuesday of every month. For more information, call (818) 878-3763.

Eucalyptus borers found in Fresno

It was only a matter of time before the eucalyptus longhorn borer, the beetle that has wreaked havoc on eucalyptus trees in Southern California, reached the Central Valley. The borer was recently discovered in trees growing on a Fresno golf course, and University of California entomologists fear that the insect may be established in other areas of the valley as well.

The adult longhorn beetle is shiny blackish brown with long antennae and a yellow zigzag pattern on its back. The females lay as many as 300 eggs on a tree or in eucalyptus firewood. The resulting larvae bore into the bark and feed on the cambium of the tree, girdling the trunk. An infested tree begins to turn yellow and may produce a lot of resinous sap. Eventually individual branches, the top of the canopy, or the entire tree dies.

Currently, no effective chemical control exists for the eucalyptus borer. UC entomologists are introducing natural insect enemies from Australia, but they will take time to become established.

However, you can do some things this month to help prevent the spread of the eucalyptus borer. Prune all dead branches. Use a chipper to turn prunings into mulch, or, where permitted, burn them.

If you have eucalyptus firewood that may be infested with larvae (you can sometimes actually hear them chewing under the bark; pull it off to check), use it up before spring. After that, seal the pile with plastic sheeting to prevent the adult insects from escaping.

Petite peas, big flavor

In France, tiny peas called *petits pois* are considered a delicacy because of their tenderness and sweet, succulent flavor. These aren't just immature versions of shelling peas. They're genetically smaller—about half the size of peas typically grown in our country. At maturity, the pods measure 2 to 3 inches long and are filled with six to nine small, round peas.

You can plant these peas in your garden this month if you live in *Sunset Western Garden Book* zone 7, 8, 9, or 14. In the coldest parts of zone 7 (foothills), wait until late this month to plant. Here are two kinds to try: 'Precovelle' (pictured above), a 2- to 2½-foot-tall bush variety that's productive and disease resistant, and 'Waverex', which produces abundant yields on 2½-foot-tall plants.

Sow seeds in well-drained soil about ½ inch deep and 2 inches apart. Train plants on a 3-foot trellis for good air circulation and easy harvest, or allow them to sprawl on the ground. Harvest when peas have just filled the pods but before they turn tough.

You can order seeds from these sources: ***The Cook's Garden,*** Box 535, Londonderry, Vt. 05148, (802) 824-3400; sells 'Waverex'; free catalog. ***Shepherd's Garden***

PETITS POIS *'Precovelle' are about half the size of standard shelling peas.*

Seeds, 6116 Highway 9, Felton, Calif. 95018, (408) 335-6910; sells 'Precovelle'; free catalog.

A rhody for early spring bloom in the Northwest

The clear pink flowers of the deciduous *Rhododendron mucronulatum* 'Cornell Pink' will open in abundance this month. It's one of those sights that remind us how early and long spring is in the coastal Northwest. Hardy to –25°, this rhododendron will herald spring in the same way in the inland Northwest, but about a month to six weeks later.

Native to the mountains of Korea and northern Japan, *R. mucronulatum* and its cultivated varieties are quite at home in the Northwest's climates and deciduous woodlands. This plant has a loose, open form that grows to about 5 feet or taller, with an almost equal spread. Out of leaf it isn't particularly handsome, but it makes a good background plant.

New salvia colors

Salvia coccinea is an extremely long-blooming summer annual. Until this past year, the only readily available variety was 'Lady in Red'. Two new kinds expand this

GIANT WILD RYE, *purple and white sage, deergrass, and rush thrive beneath sycamores at Soka University.*

PETER CHRISTIANSEN

Tip of the Month

After a weekend away, you return home to find that the cat used your potted palm as a rest room, or a squirrel buried nuts in the Japanese maple's container. The humane and handsome way to stop these intrusions: put rocks atop the soil in your big pots. Smooth river rocks (the kind used in ikebana) are sold at flower shops and import marts, or use stones you collect at the beach. You can pour water and liquid plant food through the rocks, and they're easy to move if they crowd the trunk or you want to change soil.

salvia's color spectrum: 'Coral Nymph' and 'White Nymph'.

'Coral Nymph' produces spikes of salmon coral and white orchidlike flowers on bushy 2- to 3-foot-tall plants. 'White Nymph' is similar in form but bears white flowers.

Start seeds indoors and transplant out after the last frost. Here are two seed sources: **Park Seed Co.,** Cokesbury Rd., Greenwood, S.C. 29647, (800) 845-3369; sells 'Coral Nymph' and 'White Nymph'; free catalog. **Shepherd's Garden Seeds,** 6116 Highway 9, Felton, Calif. 95018, (408) 335-6910; sells 'Coral Nymph'; free catalog.

Tough love for ferns

San Diego Fern Society member Robin Halley has a way with ferns. With a few snips of his pruning shears, he gives maidenhair ferns (*Adiantum*) what he calls a "butch haircut," removing all lacy top growth and leaving spiky brown stubs. For leather-leaf ferns (*Rumohra*) and ones less dense than the maidenhair, Halley uses blunt-tipped scissors to sever scraggly fronds at the crown.

But it's the way Halley divides Boston, holly, mother, and sword ferns that causes fellow society members to gasp. After knocking a plant out of its pot, he grabs a pruning saw or knife and unceremoniously slices the root mass in half or thirds. "Ferns aren't the tender things people think they are," he says with a grin.

Yet ferns do require special care to stay healthy. (The quickest way to kill one is to overwater—the roots rot easily.) Halley babies the divisions, planting them in a mix of equal parts redwood compost, perlite, and peat moss. He applies a controlled-release fertilizer only after the new growth has started.

Seed exchanges preserve heirloom flowers, herbs, and vegetables

Many gardeners are familiar with Seed Savers Exchange, an organization that has worked 15 years to preserve heirloom vegetable varieties. Now, an offshoot of Seed Savers, the Flower and Herb Exchange (FHE), has sprung up to preserve flowers and herbs that were part of our grandparents' gardens. FHE publishes an annual seeds yearbook, which its members can order from; this season's edition lists more than 2,500 different types. Among the plants are kiss-me-over-the-garden-gate (*Polygonum orientale*), a 6- to 7-foot-tall pink or purplish flowering annual, and balloon flower (*Platycodon grandiflorus*), a 2- to 3-foot-tall perennial with blue or sometimes pink or white flowers. To become a member and receive a copy of the yearbook, send $7 to FHE, 3076 N. Winn Rd., Decorah, Iowa 52101.

Seed Savers Exchange (SSE) also publishes a yearbook, which lists thousands of kinds of heirloom vegetables available to members. Membership costs $25. Write to SSE at the above address.

Elegant single-flowered roses

When you think of roses, you probably think of the beautiful, full-flowered hybrid teas, which can have more than 60 petals per bloom. Their beauty is undeniable. However, if you're shopping for bare-root roses in nurseries or mail-order catalogs this month, don't overlook varieties with single flowers. Single roses, with five to seven petals, have an elegance and character all their own.

A single rose usually opens wide with flattened petals, looking more like a dogwood than a hybrid tea. Bright yellow stamens add color to the center of the flower.

Single-flowering roses that perform well in the Central Valley and surrounding foothills include the deep red climber 'Altissimo', the lovely pink floribunda 'Betty Prior', the pink hybrid tea 'Dainty Bess', the red-and-white floribunda 'Eye Paint', the yellow shrub 'Golden Wings', the white shrub 'Sally Holmes', and the white miniature 'Simplex'.

Put out the fire on evergreen pears

Evergreen pear (*Pyrus kawakamii*) is usually covered with white flowers in the dead of winter. Lately, though, it's gained a reputation for something else as well—branches scorched by fireblight.

Symptoms are individual twigs or branches that die back suddenly, as though scorched by fire. The leaves appear blackened but usually remain on the stem. Left unchecked, the bacteria can kill the tree and spread to any member of the pome tribe of the rose family, including pyracantha, apple, cotoneaster, crabapple, hawthorn, quince, and even toyon.

Treat the tree by cutting out small diseased branches 4 to 6 inches below the dieback; prune out larger branches 12 inches below dieback. Disinfect shears between cuts. Remove cankered branches, too. Burn prunings or send them out with the trash.

Fireblight spreads during flowering. Protect healthy evergreen pears by applying a fixed-copper spray every four to five days during bloom.

Get ready: the hummers are coming

Lori Newman, a gardener in Perris, California, has made a science out of feeding hummingbirds, and she offers some solid, time-tested advice. Hummingbirds start moving north this month, so you can put these principles into practice as hummers show up in your area.

Basic feeding formula. Mix ¼ cup sugar with 1 cup water and microwave it for 4 to 5 minutes (the sugar must dissolve completely). This small a quantity cools quickly and is easy to handle.

Feeder placement. Hang it in a shady spot where it's easy to see—you'll get the most pleasure from watching the birds that way. Remember to refill and clean the feeder as needed.

Cleaning. Using a small bottle brush and pipe cleaners, scrub the feeder with detergent and a few drops of bleach added to warm water. Rinse the feeder well in hot water, then again in cold.

Insect protection. Buy a feeder with mesh guards to keep wasps away, and put commercial sticky ant barrier around the hanger to keep ants away.

By Debra Lee Baldwin, Melanie Baer-Keeley, Peter Jensen, Jim McCausland, Lauren Bonar Swezey, Lance Walheim

BAIT FOR SLUGS. Control slugs early in the season before they reproduce and multiply your problem. Set out bait: scatter it around the bases of pots, along foundations, and through ground covers. Be careful to keep bait away from pets and children.

BUY CYCLAMEN. You'll find them in bloom, ready for valentine giving, at florist shops, nurseries, and supermarkets. Set them in a sunny location. Keep the soil moist, but don't let pots stand in water. Pinch off faded blooms and foliage. West of the Cascades (zones 4–7), gardeners have had some luck with florists' cyclamen (*C. persicum*) outdoors. When the danger of hard frost is over, put plants outside in bright, indirect light. Keep them well watered and fed. They'll produce good foliage and a few blooms for many years unless they get snuffed out by a killer freeze.

CARE FOR HYDRAN-GEAS. West of the Cascades, prune plants lightly to shape them into a sculptural bush form. Cut back branches to an outward-pointing bud. Remember, hydrangeas bloom on old wood, so don't remove too much or you'll lose this year's flowers. Feed plants with a complete granular plant food. In this month's cool, moist weather, hydrangeas can take a heavy feeding: a fertilizer with a 15-15-15 formula isn't too strong if used according to manufacturer's directions. East of the Cascades (zones 1, 2, and 3), do this in late March or early April.

FEED HOUSE PLANTS. If house plants are showing new growth, flowering, or fruiting, feed them now. Otherwise, wait until April to begin feeding (when days are longer and sunlight stronger). It is safest at this time of year to use a half-strength plant food, unless you have an unusually robust producer of foliage or flowers.

PLANT BARE-ROOT STOCK. West of the Cascades, plant bare-root cane berries, trees, shrubs, and vines. Buy early. Plant them as soon as you get them. In the inland Northwest, bare-root planting opportunities will come in the spring.

Sunset Western Garden Book climate zones

(1–3) (4–7)

PRESPROUT PEAS. West of the Cascades, gardeners can sow peas this month. To hasten germination, place the peas between several layers of wet paper towel on a cookie sheet set in a warm place. When they sprout in a few days, plant them outdoors and they'll start growing.

PRUNE ROSES. Toward the end of the month, gardeners west of the Cascades can prune roses. Cut hybrid teas back by about a third. Remove injured or dead canes. Cut out parallel or crossing branches. Prune with an eye for a handsomely shaped plant. East of the Cascades, hold off on pruning roses until early April, when temperatures will be safely above 25°.

February Checklist

NORTHERN CALIFORNIA

Where do you garden?

The following recommendations refer to the elevation at which you garden.

L=Low (zones 14–17)
H=High (zones 1–3)

Climate zones are from *Sunset Western Garden Book.*

CONTROL SLUGS AND SNAILS. L: As night temperatures rise, snails and slugs become more active and can quickly consume plants such as crocus, daffodils, pansies, primroses, and vegetables. Go on a search-and-destroy mission at night, when they're active, or use beer traps or commercial bait.

CUT BACK FUCHSIAS. L: To stimulate lush new growth, cut back woody growth to main branches, then remove interior twiggy growth. Container fuchsias can be pruned back to the pot rim.

FERTILIZE. Feed fall-planted annuals and perennials, and established trees and shrubs, if plants need it—if they lack vigor or leaves look pale. Wait to feed azaleas, camellias, and rhododendrons until after bloom, then use an acid-type fertilizer. Later this month, fertilize lawns.

PLANT FLOWERING CHERRIES. Plant several kinds for staggered bloom. **Early blooming:** single pink 'Akebono'; double dark pink 'Royal Burgundy', with purplish foliage; single rosy pink 'Taiwan'. **Midseason:** bright pink 'Beni Hoshi'; double rose pink 'Kwanzan'. **Late:** semidouble light pink 'Mt. Fuji-Shogetsu'.

PLANT FOR SPRING BLOOM. L: Choices include calendula, candytuft, cineraria, dianthus, English daisy, English and fairy primroses, forget-me-not, Iceland poppy, pansy, *Primula obconica*, snapdragon, stock, sweet William, and viola.

PLANT PERENNIALS. L: Among the spring-blooming perennials, try alstroemeria, bergenia, bleeding heart, campanula, candytuft, columbine, coral bells, delphinium, dianthus, foxglove, marguerite, Oriental poppy, and violet.

PLANT SUMMER-BLOOMING BULBS. L: Set out calla lilies, cannas, crocosmias, dahlias, gladiolus, tiger flowers (*Tigridia*), tuberoses, and tuberous begonias.

PLANT VEGETABLES. L: Set out artichokes and asparagus, and seedlings of broccoli, cabbage, cauliflower, celery (only in zones 15, 16, and 17), green onion, kohlrabi, and lettuce. Sow beets, carrots, chard, lettuce, peas, and spinach. Sow seeds of eggplant, pepper, and tomato indoors; allow six to eight weeks to reach transplant size. **H:** To get a jump on the season, start seeds of broccoli, cabbage, and cauliflower indoors or in a greenhouse at the end of the month. When seedlings are ready to plant (in six to eight weeks), set them out in the garden and drape floating row covers over plants for weather protection.

SET OUT EVERGREEN VINES. Good choices for zones 14 through 17 are Carolina jessamine (*Gelsemium sempervirens*), with fragrant yellow flowers; *Hardenbergia violacea* 'Happy Wanderer', with pinkish purple flowers; *Jasminum polyanthum*, with fragrant pinkish white flowers; and violet trumpet vine (*Clytostoma callistegioides*), with violet flowers. All these vines are vigorous, growing 15 to 20 feet or more.

SPRAY FOR PEACH LEAF CURL. L: Around the second or third week in February, just when the tips of flower buds show color, is the best time to apply a second dormant spray to prevent peach leaf curl—a fungus that distorts peach leaves and destroys the fruit. Even if you didn't spray earlier, you haven't missed your chance: doing it at pink bud stage is most effective in controlling the disease. Use lime sulfur with a spreader-sticker to improve coverage; spray on a calm, dry day.

WATER. L: If winter rains are light or sporadic, water plants deeply when the soil is dry.

February Checklist

CENTRAL VALLEY

APPLY DORMANT SPRAY. If you haven't already done so, control fungus diseases and overwintering insects on deciduous plants (especially fruit trees) by spraying with a dormant spray such as horticultural oil or lime sulfur. Hold off spraying if rain is expected.

BUY FLOWERING PLANTS. Nurseries carry a good selection of early spring–blooming shrubs and vines, such as azalea, camellia, Carolina jessamine, daphne, and hardenbergia.

CONTROL SLUGS AND SNAILS. As night temperatures rise above 40°, slugs and snails become more active. They can quickly consume flowers as well as vegetables. To reduce these pests, handpick and destroy them at night (carry a flashlight), when they are most active. Or use beer traps, copper barriers, or commercial baits.

FERTILIZE PLANTS. Fall-planted annuals and perennials benefit from feeding now. Also feed established trees and shrubs if they lack vigor or their leaves look pale as new growth appears. If you haven't fed citrus trees, do so now. Later this month, feed lawns. Wait to feed azaleas, camellias, and rhododendrons until after bloom, then use an acid fertilizer.

PLANT FOR SPRING BLOOM. Consider bleeding heart, calendula, campanula, candytuft, cineraria, coral bells, dianthus, English daisy, English and fairy primroses, forget-me-not, Iceland poppy, marguerite, pansy, *Primula obconica*, snapdragon, stock, sweet William, and viola.

PLANT SUMMER BULBS. Set out tuberous begonias, calla lilies, cannas, crocosmias, dahlias, gladiolus, tiger flowers *(Tigridia)*, and tuberoses.

PLANT VEGETABLES. Set out plants of asparagus and artichokes as well as seedlings of broccoli, cabbage, cauliflower, kohlrabi, green onion, and lettuce. Sow seeds of beets, carrots, chard, lettuce, peas, and spinach in the garden. Start eggplant, pepper, and tomato seedlings indoors.

PRUNE. If you haven't pruned deciduous trees and shrubs, do so by midmonth. Wait until after they flower to prune deciduous shrubs that bloom only in spring.

WATER. If rains are light or sporadic, water plants deeply when the soil is dry.

Redding

Lake Tahoe

Sacramento

Fresno

Bakersfield

Sunset
Western Garden Book
climate zones

Valley and foothills (7–9, 14)

WEED. Hand-pull or hoe them, or spray with a nontoxic weed killer (one made from fatty acids) or glyphosate; spray on a calm, dry day so the herbicide doesn't drift onto desirable plants.

February Checklist

SOUTHERN CALIFORNIA

BUY SUMMER BULBS. If you live along the coast (zone 24), plant tuberous begonia, caladium, and gloxinia. Inland (zones 14–23), plant heat-tolerant babiana, canna, and gladiolus. If you get glads in the ground now, they'll bloom before thrips attack in summer. Also in nurseries now are calla, dahlia, nerine, and tigridia.

COLD-WEATHER TIPS. In mountain zones (1–3), keep snow from accumulating on trees and shrubs. Don't fertilize if below-freezing nights are expected. Delay pruning frost-damaged limbs until toward the end of the dormant season, just before growth starts.

CONTROL PESTS. The reproductive season is just beginning for gophers, so trapping now means fewer to deal with in summer. Handpick snails at night; eliminate their hiding places, such as leaf litter, old pots, and debris.

CUT BACK TROPICALS. Along the coast (zone 24), cut back begonia, canna, and ginger to promote fresh spring growth. Delay this in inland areas (zones 22 and 23), where late frosts may damage new growth.

DESERT BED PREP. Work compost or other organic matter into alkaline desert soils. Add 2 pounds of ammonium phosphate and 3 pounds of soil sulfur per 100 square feet.

FEED DECIDUOUS FRUIT TREES. In coastal and mild inland areas (wait until next month in colder areas), apply a complete fertilizer two to three weeks before trees begin to bloom.

FERTILIZE ROSES. As the coast and low-elevation inland areas warm, roses pruned last month will begin to show new growth. Wait until leaves turn from red to green, then give the first feeding of the year. Water thoroughly unless rains are sufficient.

PLANT PERENNIAL WILDFLOWERS. In the low desert (zone 13), plant coreopsis, desert marigold, evening primrose, penstemon, and salvia.

PLANT WINTER COLOR. For colorful bloom now through spring in frost-free areas, plant calendula, cineraria, dianthus, English daisy, Iceland poppy, larkspur, lobelia, pansy, primrose, snapdragon, stock, sweet alyssum, sweet pea, and viola.

Sunset
Western Garden Book
climate zones

Mountain (1–3)
High desert (11)
Low desert (13)
Coastal and inland (14–24)

Map locations: Bishop, San Luis Obispo, Tehachapi, Santa Barbara, Lancaster, Los Angeles, Palm Springs, San Diego

PRUNE DORMANT PLANTS. If you didn't get to it last month, prune deciduous trees, fruit trees, grapes, roses, shrubs, and vines before weather warms and growth begins.

PRUNE HYDRANGEAS. Remove old, brittle hydrangea canes clear to the ground; shorten others halfway, cutting just above a bud. Leave canes that have large, fat flower buds at tips.

PURCHASE AZALEAS. Visit nurseries now to view azaleas in bloom and to select plants. Enjoy potted plants indoors until blooms fade, then plant in the garden. Azaleas do best in fast-draining acidic soil; they are a garden staple along the coast but must be protected from harsh sun and intense summer heat inland.

SEND FOR FLOWER SEEDS. Order warm-season bloomers now. Start seeds indoors as soon as they arrive, then plant out after six to eight weeks.

SPRAY DORMANT PLANTS. To reduce aphids, scale, and diseases such as black spot and peach leaf curl, spray leafless and dormant fruit trees and roses. Use horticultural oil alone, or combine it with either lime sulfur or fixed copper.

START VEGETABLES. In coastal and inland zones (14–24) and the high desert (zone 11), set out seedlings of broccoli, cabbage, cauliflower, celery, chard, chives, endive, lettuce, onions, and parsley. Many warm-season vegetables, including tomatoes and peppers, can go into the ground after midmonth.

TEND LAWNS. Fertilize cool-season lawns every six weeks, and water if rains are inadequate; mow with blades set at 1½ to 2 inches. Warm-season lawns will begin to grow midmonth along the coast and early next month inland; they should be dethatched, fertilized, and watered thoroughly. Before midmonth, apply a preemergence herbicide to control crabgrass..

ANYWHERE IN THE WEST, TACKLE THESE CHORES:

☐ **CLEAN UP HOUSE PLANTS.** Most kinds will start growing again next month. Get them ready by gently showering both sides of leaves with lukewarm water, then trimming off dead and yellowing leaves. If you have to spray for insects, cover plants with a plastic garment bag (the kind you get from the dry cleaners), then apply the spray inside the bag and seal it temporarily to confine the chemical.

☐ **FEED WINTER RYE LAWNS.** Give them a boost with 2½ pounds ammonium sulfate per 1,000 square feet of turf. Water well afterward.

☐ **PLANT COLE CROPS.** In warm-winter areas, direct-sow cole crops (broccoli, brussels sprouts, cabbage, cauliflower, kale, kohlrabi, and many Chinese vegetables) this month. In cold-winter areas, start seed indoors.

☐ **PREPARE SOIL.** Get garden beds ready for planting by digging in generous amounts of compost, well-rotted manure, and peat moss. After beds are dug, water, let them settle for a week or two, and pull out weed seedlings before you plant.

☐ **WATER INDOOR CACTUS.** If you held off watering spring-flowering cactus in December and January, now's the time to start watering and feeding again.

IN THE SOUTHWEST'S LOW AND INTERMEDIATE DESERTS:

☐ **CONTROL APHIDS.** Check tender new growth daily. When aphids show up, wash them off with a spray of water, then follow up by spraying plants with an insecticidal soap if needed .

☐ **FEED BEARDED IRISES.** Late in the month, work a complete fertilizer into the soil around irises and water it in well.

☐ **FEED CITRUS.** If you haven't done so already this year, feed all kinds of citrus by sprinkling a complete fertilizer over each tree's root zone (essentially the area covered by the drip line of the tree). Water the fertilizer in well.

☐ **FEED ROSES.** On a day when night temperatures are expected to remain above freezing, water roses, then apply a complete fertilizer and water it in thoroughly.

☐ **MAINTAIN DRIP SYSTEMS.** Test drip-irrigation systems now, before new plant growth covers them; check filters, emitters, and flow (especially at the ends of the lines). Unclog emitters, and replace each one that can't be unclogged by plugging a new emitter in beside it.

☐ **PLANT GROUND COVERS, VINES.** Set out Hall's honeysuckle, perennial verbena, star jasmine, trailing indigo bush, and *Vinca major* or *V. minor*.

☐ **PLANT PERENNIAL WILDFLOWERS.** If you set out plants of desert marigold, evening primrose, paperflower (*Psilostrophe cooperi*), penstemon, and salvia, they'll bloom this spring.

☐ **PROTECT TENDER CROPS.** Eggplant, pepper, and tomato plants started indoors in January can go into the garden this month, but give them protection from late frost.

What's your garden climate?

Sunset's exclusive climate zones, newly revised and updated, can help you choose the right plants to grow in every region of the West

West, revising the climate zone maps to make them even more useful.

Since climate determines what you can and cannot grow, here is a look at the all-new *Sunset Western Garden Book* climate maps and climate zone descriptions. Scan the maps in the following pages to find where you live, then read about the zone that defines your gardening.

What defines a climate zone?

Six important factors determine each of the zones.

Latitude. Generally, the farther a spot is from the equator, the longer and colder its winters, and the more daylight in its summers.

Elevation. High gardens get long, cold winters and low night temperatures all year.

Ocean influence. Weather that blows in off the Pacific Ocean tends to be humid and mild, and laden with precipitation in winter.

Continental influence. Our continent originates its own weather, which is colder in winter than in areas of ocean influence, hotter in summer, and more likely to get precipitation any time of year. The farther inland you live, the stronger the effect.

Mountains and hills. The Coast Ranges take some ocean influence out of the air as it passes eastward over them. The Sierra further weaken ocean influence. East of the Rocky Mountains, continental and Arctic air dominate. In the opposite order, first the Rockies, then the Sierra, and finally the Coast Ranges reduce the westward influence of continental air.

Local terrain. South-facing slopes get more solar heat than flatland; north-facing slopes get less. Slope also affects airflow: warm air rises, cold air sinks. Because hillsides are never quite as cold in winter as the lower ground beneath them, they're called thermal belts. Above thermal belts, elevation makes the air cold. Lowlands are cold-air basins.

A "classic California landscape of Mediterranean heritage" describes the garden shown at left in the Napa Valley—in climate zone 14. Below, thyme softens rock edges at Ohme Gardens in Wenatchee, Washington—in zone 2.

THERE ARE NO GREEN THUMBS, ONLY PEOPLE who give plants what they need to thrive. Most plant needs—good soil, water, fertilizer—are easy to satisfy. You can't, however, change the climate to suit the plant. So it makes sense to choose the plant to suit the climate.

To supply that crucial information, the present incarnation of *Sunset Western Garden Book* was first published in 1967 (previous versions go back to the 1930s). It identifies 24 different climate zones and provides an encyclopedia of plants that tells which zones each grows in. We've just completed the book's most extensive revision ever, expanding the encyclopedia to cover some 6,000 garden plants and, with the help of about 70 weather observers around the

By Jim McCausland

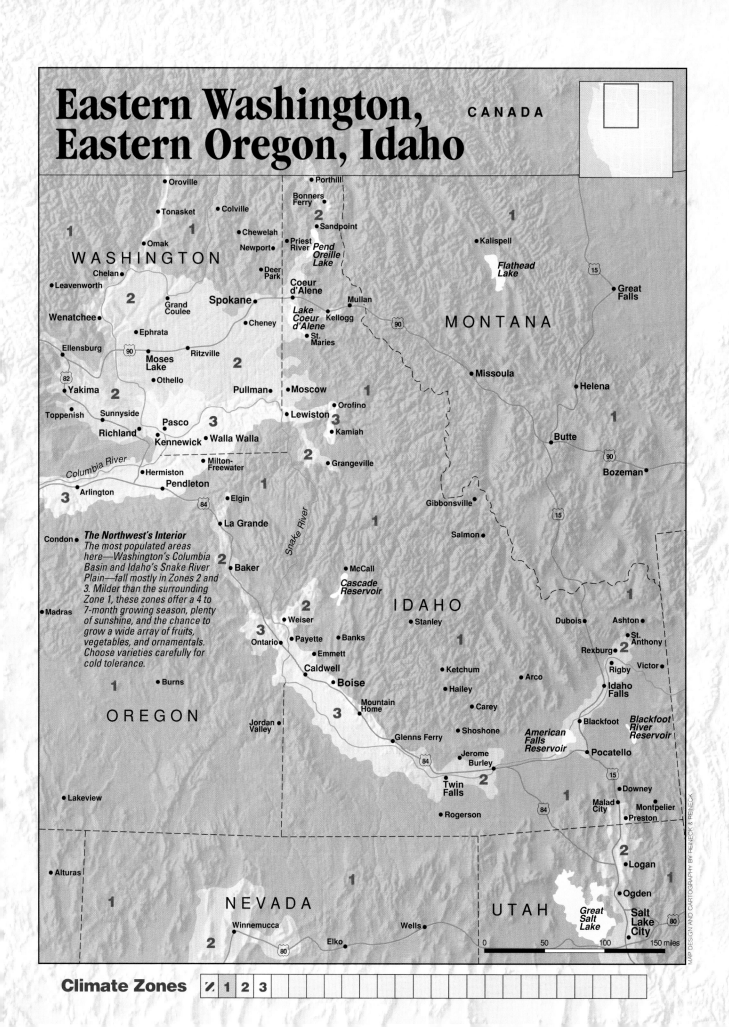

Eastern Washington, Eastern Oregon, Idaho

CANADA

WASHINGTON

Oroville
Tonasket • Colville
1   1
Chewelah
Omak
Newport
Chelan
Leavenworth
2   Grand   Spokane
         Coulee   Cheney
Wenatchee
Ephrata
Ellensburg
         Moses
         Lake
Yakima   Othello   2   Pullman
2
Toppenish Sunnyside
Richland   Pasco   3
         Kennewick Walla Walla
                              2
                    Milton-
         Hermiston Freewater
3 Arlington Pendleton

Porthill
Bonners
Ferry
2   Sandpoint
Priest   Pend
River   Oreille
          Lake
Deer
Park
         Coeur
         d'Alene
Lake   Mullan
Coeur   Kellogg
d'Alene
         • St.
         Maries
Moscow
         1
Lewiston Orofino
         3   Kamiah

MONTANA

Kalispell
                    1
         Flathead
         Lake
                         Great
                         Falls
                    15

Missoula
              Helena
                         1
         Butte
                    90
              Bozeman
                    15

Elgin
La Grande
84

Condon •

The Northwest's Interior
*The most populated areas
here—Washington's Columbia
Basin and Idaho's Snake River
Plain—fall mostly in Zones 2 and
3. Milder than the surrounding
Zone 1, these zones offer a 4 to
7-month growing season, plenty
of sunshine, and the chance to
grow a wide array of fruits,
vegetables, and ornamentals.
Choose varieties carefully for
cold tolerance.*

Madras •

Baker
2

Weiser
2
Ontario
3
Payette
Emmett
Caldwell
Boise

Grangeville
2

1

1

McCall
Cascade
Reservoir

IDAHO

Stanley

Gibbonsville

Salmon

1

Dubois   Ashton
                    1
                         St.
Rexburg   2   Anthony
                    Rigby   Victor
Ketchum
Hailey   Arco
         Carey
                    Idaho
                    Falls
Shoshone   Blackfoot   Blackfoot
         American   River
         Falls   Reservoir
Burns •   1   Reservoir
                    Pocatello
Jordan   Mountain
Valley   Home 3   Jerome
         Glenns Ferry Burley 2
OREGON   Twin
              Falls   1   Downey
         Rogerson   84   Malad   Montpelier
Lakeview •   City   Preston

Alturas •   1
                                        2
                                   Logan
         1   1
                                   Ogden
NEVADA   **UTAH**   Great   Salt
                         Salt   Lake
Winnemucca   Lake   City
         80   80
2   Elko   Wells
80
         0   50   100   150 miles

Climate Zones ⬚ 1 2 3

Get to know your zone

Sunset Western Garden Book climate zones are listed in numerical order, from harsh zone 1 to mild zone 24. Temperatures are given in degrees Fahrenheit. Here we describe the characteristics of each zone, accompanying these profiles with regional maps of the West showing where the zones occur.

Why don't we use the U.S. Department of Agriculture's 11-zone climate map? Its zones are based on minimum winter temperatures alone; that's useful for determining plant hardiness, but just not sufficient for predicting how plants will perform from region to region. For example, the USDA map puts the Olympic rain forest into a zone with parts of the Sonoran Desert. Try growing grapefruit in Port Angeles.

Sunset Western Garden Book's zone scheme considers winter minimums, too, but it also factors in summer highs, length of growing season, humidity, and rainfall patterns to give a more accurate picture of what will grow where.

As you scan the information that describes your zone, you may find that your garden has different characteristics. If, for example, winter lows in your garden are different from what your zone would lead you to expect, chances are you're gardening in a microclimate that pushes you into another zone. Local terrain is almost always the cause of such microclimates. Read descriptions of the nearest climate zones, and you'll probably find one that fits your situation better.

High elevation, predictable snow, and a short growing season characterize zone 1—the West's coldest climate.

Z O N E 1

Coldest-winter West

Zones 1, 2, and 3 are regions where snow falls and stays on the ground (for a week or all winter) every year. Zone 1 is coldest, its extreme winters caused by latitude, influence of the continental air mass, elevation (the higher you go, the colder it gets), or some combination of the three. In this zone, gardeners plant with a 75- to 150-day growing season in mind, though frosts can occur any night of the year.

Z O N E 2

Second-coldest Western climate

Gardens in zone 2 get snow in winter, but because they're usually lower in elevation or modified by a large body of water (Lake Coeur d'Alene, for example), they don't get quite as much cold as zone 1. The difference is crucial: 'McIntosh' and 'Sierra Beauty' apples, for example, grow well in zone 2 but not in zone 1.

In zone 2, windbreaks, trees planted for shelter, and heavy mulches can make it possible to grow plants that would otherwise perish from the effects of wind, cold, and the low winter sun, which can burn the trunks of young thin-barked trees.

During a 20-year period in zone 2, annual low temperatures ranged from –3° to –34°.

Z O N E 3

Cold country's "banana belt"

This is the mildest of the snowy-winter climates, thus a "banana belt." Gardeners grow such plants as

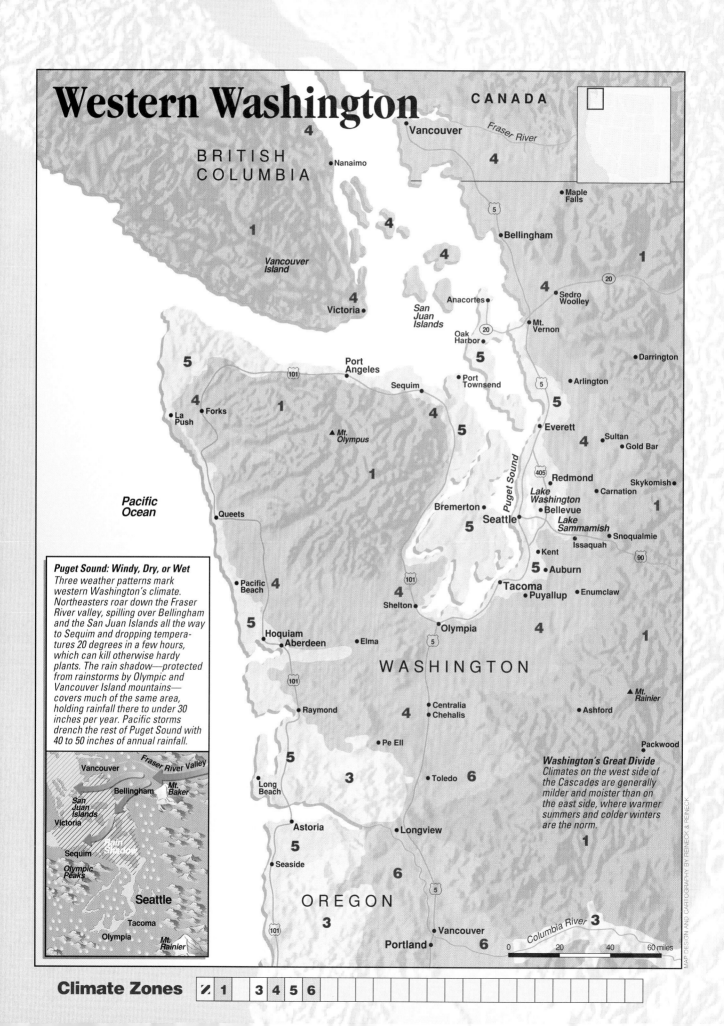

Western Washington

CANADA

BRITISH COLUMBIA

Pacific Ocean

WASHINGTON

OREGON

Fraser River

Vancouver
4
Nanaimo

4

Vancouver Island

1

Victoria
4

Maple Falls
4

Bellingham

1

Sedro Woolley
4
20

Anacortes
San Juan Islands
Mt. Vernon
20
Oak Harbor

Darrington

5
Port Angeles
Sequim
Port Townsend
5
Arlington

5

5
4

5
Everett
4
Sultan
Gold Bar

Forks
4
La Push

1

Mt. Olympus

Skykomish
Carnation
1

405
Redmond
Lake Washington
Bellevue
Lake Sammamish
Snoqualmie
Issaquah
90

Queets

1

Bremerton
Seattle
5

Kent

5
Auburn

Pacific Beach
4

5

Hoquiam
Aberdeen
Elma

101
Shelton
4
Olympia
5

Tacoma
Puyallup
Enumclaw

4
Mt. Rainier

101

Raymond
4
Centralia
Chehalis

Ashford

Packwood

Pe Ell

5

Long Beach
3
Toledo
6

Washington's Great Divide
Climates on the west side of the Cascades are generally milder and moister than on the east side, where warmer summers and colder winters are the norm.

Astoria
5
Longview

1

Seaside

6

Portland
6
Vancouver

3

Columbia River
3

0   20   40   60 miles

Puget Sound: Windy, Dry, or Wet
Three weather patterns mark western Washington's climate. Northeasters roar down the Fraser River valley, spilling over Bellingham and the San Juan Islands all the way to Sequim and dropping temperatures 20 degrees in a few hours, which can kill otherwise hardy plants. The rain shadow—protected from rainstorms by Olympic and Vancouver Island mountains— covers much of the same area, holding rainfall there to under 30 inches per year. Pacific storms drench the rest of Puget Sound with 40 to 50 inches of annual rainfall.

Fraser River Valley
Vancouver
Bellingham
Mt. Baker
San Juan Islands
Victoria
Rain Shadow
Sequim
Olympic Peaks
Seattle
Tacoma
Olympia
Mt. Rainier

MAP DESIGN AND CARTOGRAPHY BY REINECK & REINECK

Climate Zones   1   3 4 5 6

Sheltered from Columbia Gorge winds by rows of poplars, peach orchards thrive in zone 3.

English boxwood and winter jasmine here (but not bananas). From Hood River to Walla Walla, zone 3 is slightly lower and warmer than sur-

Columbines are tough enough to take the coldest Northwest winters.

rounding zone 2. These conditions and the Pacific air that pushes through the Columbia Gorge moderate most winters.

Much planting is based on winter lows of 10° to 15°, though in an occasional winter Arctic air forces temperatures low enough to limit the selection of broad-leafed evergreens.

Absolute cold is not so much the enemy here as drying winds that dehydrate plants growing in frozen soil. Wind protection, mulching, shade planting, and careful late-autumn watering will help you grow many borderline evergreens.

During a 20-year period, minimum temperatures in zone 3 ranged from 13° to −24°. While growing seasons can be shorter in zone 3 than in zone 2, winter minimum temperatures are always higher in zone 3. In Walla Walla, the growing season lasts longer—almost 220 days—than in much of zone 3, where it averages 160 days.

ZONE 4

Cold-winter areas west of the Cascades

This zone gets considerable influence from the Pacific Ocean and Puget Sound, but also from the continental air mass, higher elevation, or both. Zone 4 touches salt water only from Mount Vernon, Washington, into British Columbia.

Zone 4 has much lower winter temperatures than zone 5, a shorter growing season, and, in most locations, considerably more rainfall. No zone grows better perennials and bulbs; people who like woodland plants and rock-garden plants love zone 4.

Zones 4 and 5 can often be found in the same neighborhood, a fact that explains much of the familiar Northwestern talk about warm or cold gardens. During a 20-year period, the average winter lows in zone 4 ranged from 19° to −7°.

ZONE 5

Mild Northwest coast

Ocean air brings relatively mild winters to this zone, which is on the same latitude as Duluth, Minnesota, and Bangor, Maine. The region is one of the world's great centers of rhododendron culture and rock gardens. Native woodland plants like trillium, piggy-back plant, and a host of ferns thrive here, as do shade-tolerant

Tons of tulips bloom in rows at a commercial field in Washington's Skagit Valley—in zone 4.

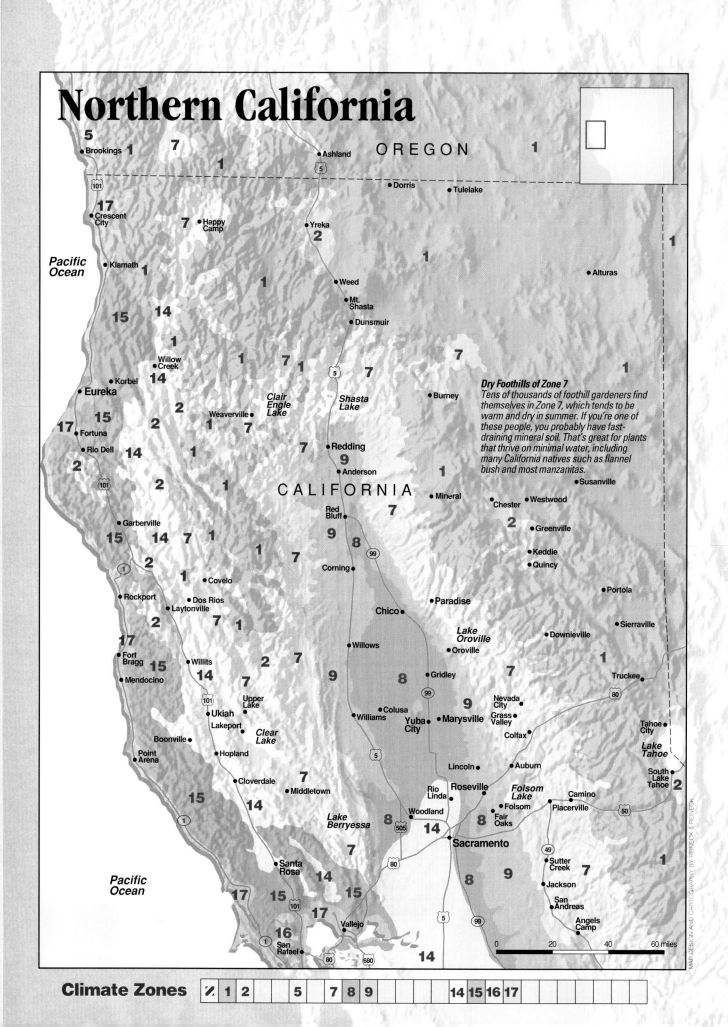

Northern California

OREGON

Pacific Ocean

5 Brookings 1   7   1   Ashland   1

17 Crescent City   7 Happy Camp   Dorris   Tulelake   1

Klamath 1   Yreka 2   1   Alturas

15   14   Weed   Mt. Shasta   Dunsmuir

1   Willow Creek   1   7   1   7   Burney

14   Korbel   Clair Engle Lake   Shasta Lake   7

Eureka   2   Weaverville   7

17 Fortuna   15   2   1   7   Redding   9   *Dry Foothills of Zone 7*
Tens of thousands of foothill gardeners find themselves in Zone 7, which tends to be warm and dry in summer. If you're one of these people, you probably have fast-draining mineral soil. That's great for plants that thrive on minimal water, including many California natives such as flannel bush and most manzanitas.

Rio Dell 14   2   1   Anderson

2   2   1   **C A L I F O R N I A**   Mineral   Susanville

Garberville   Red Bluff   7   Chester   Westwood

15   14   7   1   9   8   Greenville   2

2   1   Corning   99   Keddie   Quincy

Covelo   7   Paradise   Portola

Rockport   Dos Rios   Lake Oroville   Sierraville

2   Laytonville   7   1   Chico   8   Oroville   Downieville

17 Fort Bragg   15   Willits   Willows   9   Gridley   7   Truckee   80

Mendocino   14   Upper Lake   9   8   99   Nevada City   Grass Valley   Tahoe City

Ukiah   Colusa   Marysville   Colfax   Lake Tahoe

Lakeport   Clear Lake   Williams   Yuba City   9

Boonville   Hopland   Lincoln   Auburn   South Lake Tahoe   2

Point Arena   Roseville   Folsom Lake   Camino   50

Cloverdale   7   Rio Linda   Folsom   Placerville

15   Middletown   505   Woodland   Fair Oaks   8   49

14   8   14   Sacramento   Sutter Creek   7

Lake Berryessa   7   80   9   Jackson

Santa Rosa   14   San Andreas

Pacific Ocean   15   15   Angels Camp   1

17   101   5   99

17   Vallejo

16   San Rafael   80   680   14

0   20   40   60 miles

Climate Zones   ⧄   1   2   5   7   8   9   14   15   16   17

Apple trees like these in an orchard near Winters grow best in the valleys of zone 8.

ZONE 1

Coldest-winter West

Zones 1 and 2, as well as 3 (described on page 39), are regions where snow falls and stays on the ground (for a week or all winter) every year. Zone 1 is coldest, its extreme winters caused by latitude, influence of the continental air mass, elevation (the higher you go, the colder it gets), or some combination of the three. In this zone, gardeners plant with a 75- to 150-day growing season in mind, though frosts can occur any night of the year.

ZONE 2

Second-coldest Western climate

Gardens in zone 2 get some snow in winter, but because they're usually lower in elevation or modified by a large body of water (Lake Tahoe, for example), they don't get quite as much cold as zone 1. The difference is crucial: 'Sierra Beauty' and 'McIntosh' apples, for example, grow well in zone 2 but not in zone 1.

In zone 2, windbreaks, trees planted for shelter, and heavy mulches can make it possible to grow plants that would otherwise perish from the effects of wind, cold, and low winter sun, which can burn the trunks of young, thin-barked trees.

During a 20-year period in zone 2, lows ranged from –3° to –34°.

ZONE 7

California's foothill pine belt

This zone covers several thousand square miles west of the Sierra Nevada, mostly at middle elevations in country whose signature tree is the foothill, gray, or digger pine (*Pinus sabiniana*). A few gardens in the hills near San Francisco Bay are mapped in zone 7, even though there isn't a foothill pine in sight. These are hilltop areas that are too high and cold in winter to be included in milder zones.

Hot summers and mild but pronounced winters please plants that require a marked seasonal pattern to do well—peony, iris, and lilac, for example, and pears, apples, peaches, and cherries.

At weather stations in zone 7, typical winter low temperatures range from 23° to 9°, and record lows vary from 15° to –1°.

ZONE 8

Central Valley's cold-air basins

Only a shade of difference exists between zone 8 and zone 9, but it can be crucial. Zone 9 (see page 49) is a thermal belt, meaning that cold air can flow from it to lower ground—which is zone 8. Lemons, oranges, and grapefruit flourish in zone 9 but suffer in zone 8's cold nights. The same winter cold can damage many garden plants.

Zone 8 differs from zone 14, which it joins near Sacramento and Modesto, in that zone 14 occasionally gets some marine influence. During a 20-year period, low temperatures in zone 8 ranged from 29° to 13°.

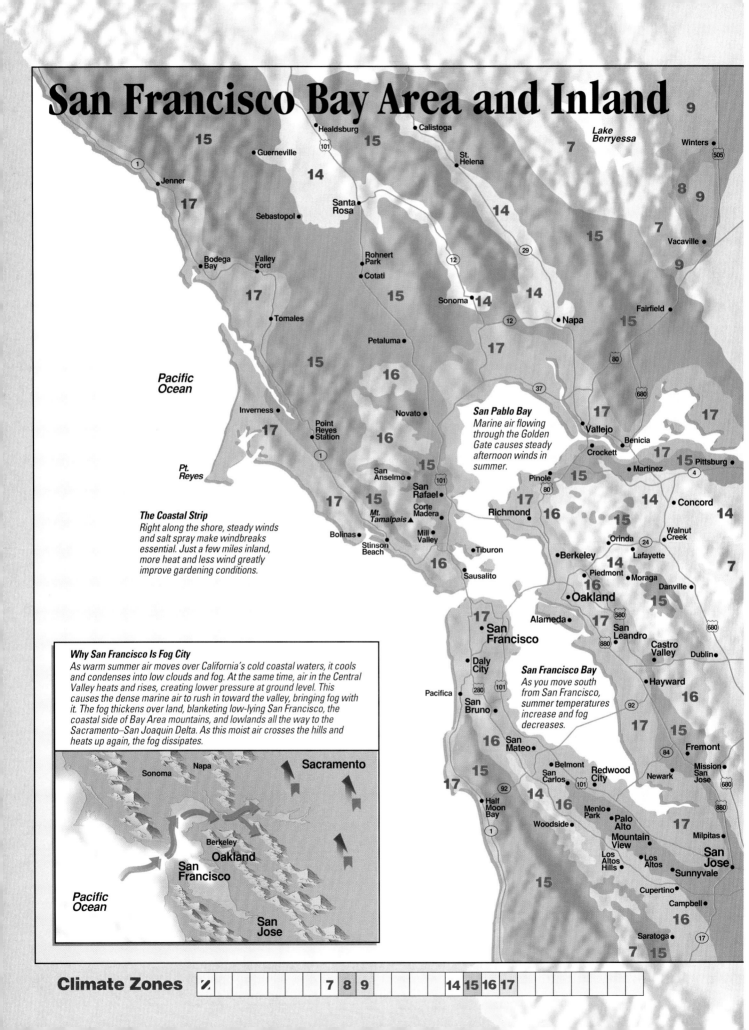

San Francisco Bay Area and Inland

The Coastal Strip
Right along the shore, steady winds and salt spray make windbreaks essential. Just a few miles inland, more heat and less wind greatly improve gardening conditions.

San Pablo Bay
Marine air flowing through the Golden Gate causes steady afternoon winds in summer.

San Francisco Bay
As you move south from San Francisco, summer temperatures increase and fog decreases.

Why San Francisco Is Fog City
As warm summer air moves over California's cold coastal waters, it cools and condenses into low clouds and fog. At the same time, air in the Central Valley heats and rises, creating lower pressure at ground level. This causes the dense marine air to rush in toward the valley, bringing fog with it. The fog thickens over land, blanketing low-lying San Francisco, the coastal side of Bay Area mountains, and lowlands all the way to the Sacramento–San Joaquin Delta. As this moist air crosses the hills and heats up again, the fog dissipates.

Climate Zones 7 8 9 14 15 16 17

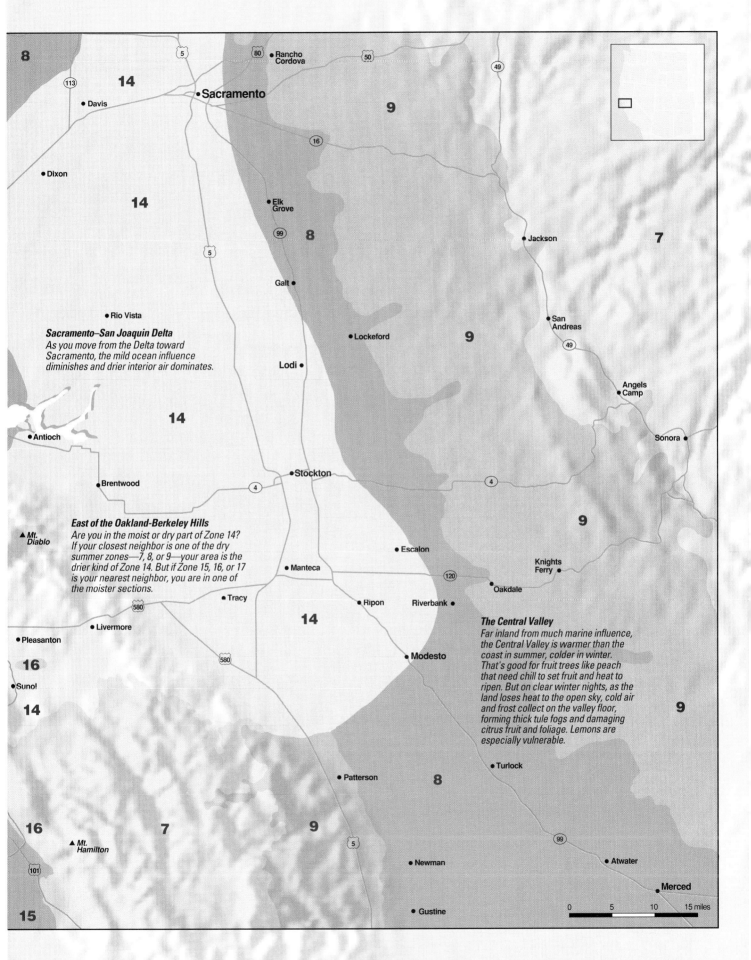

8

14

● Davis

113

5

80 ● Rancho
Cordova

50

49

9

● Dixon

16

14

● Elk
Grove

7

99

8

● Jackson

5

Galt ●

San
Andreas ●

● Rio Vista

● Lockeford

9

49

Sacramento–San Joaquin Delta
As you move from the Delta toward
Sacramento, the mild ocean influence
diminishes and drier interior air dominates.

Lodi ●

Angels
Camp

Sonora ●

14

● Antioch

● Stockton

4

● Brentwood

4

9

▲ Mt.
Diablo

East of the Oakland-Berkeley Hills
Are you in the moist or dry part of Zone 14?
If your closest neighbor is one of the dry
summer zones—7, 8, or 9—your area is the
drier kind of Zone 14. But if Zone 15, 16, or 17
is your nearest neighbor, you are in one of
the moister sections.

● Escalon

Knights
Ferry ●

● Manteca

120

● Oakdale

● Tracy

580

14

● Ripon

Riverbank ●

The Central Valley
Far inland from much marine influence,
the Central Valley is warmer than the
coast in summer, colder in winter.
That's good for fruit trees like peach
that need chill to set fruit and heat to
ripen. But on clear winter nights, as the
land loses heat to the open sky, cold air
and frost collect on the valley floor,
forming thick tule fogs and damaging
citrus fruit and foliage. Lemons are
especially vulnerable.

● Livermore

● Pleasanton

580

16

● Modesto

● Sunol

14

9

● Turlock

16

7

● Patterson

8

▲ Mt.
Hamilton

9

5

101

● Newman

99

● Atwater

Merced

15

● Gustine

0   5   10   15 miles

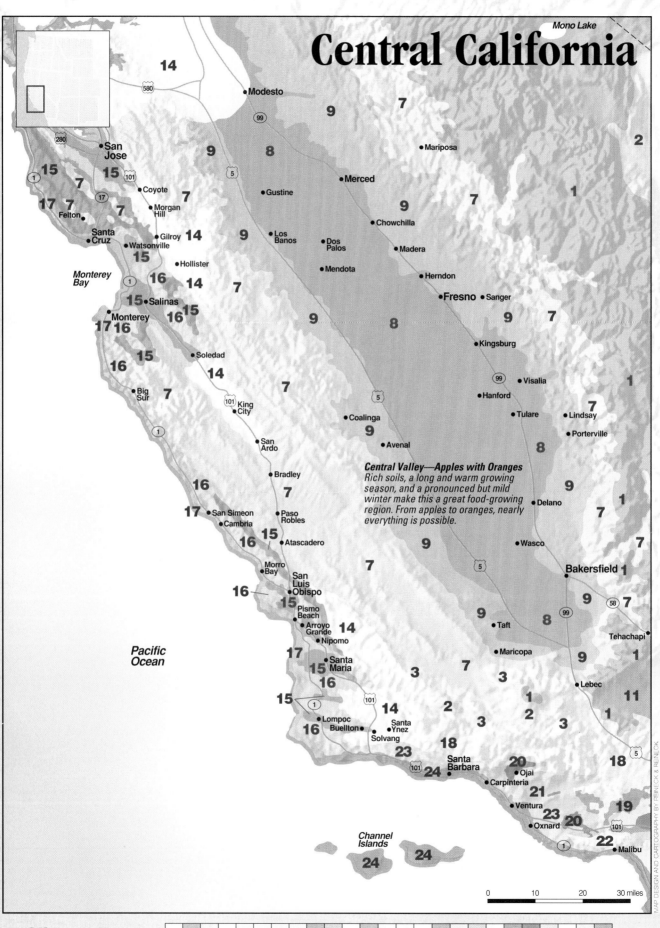

Central California

Mono Lake

580

14

Modesto

99

9

7

San Jose

280

2

Mariposa

15

7

15

101

Coyote

9

8

Merced

7

1

17

7

Morgan Hill

7

Gustine

9

Chowchilla

17

7

Felton

Santa Cruz

Watsonville

15

Gilroy

14

9

Los Banos

Dos Palos

Madera

9

Monterey Bay

16

Hollister

14

Mendota

Herndon

7

Fresno

Sanger

1

15

Salinas

14

9

8

9

7

17

16

Monterey

16

15

Soledad

Kingsburg

15

16

99

Visalia

1

Big Sur

7

14

Hanford

7

1

101

King City

7

8

Tulare

Lindsay

Porterville

San Ardo

Coalinga

9

Avenal

8

9

Delano

1

16

Bradley

7

Central Valley—Apples with Oranges
Rich soils, a long and warm growing
season, and a pronounced but mild
winter make this a great food-growing
region. From apples to oranges, nearly
everything is possible.

7

7

17

San Simeon

Cambria

Paso Robles

9

Wasco

7

16

15

Atascadero

9

Bakersfield

1

Morro Bay

San Luis Obispo

7

5

9

58

7

16

15

Pismo Beach

9

Taft

8

99

Tehachapi

Pacific Ocean

Arroyo Grande

14

Nipomo

9

Maricopa

1

17

Santa Maria

3

7

1

Lebec

11

15

16

2

1

2

1

15

1

101

14

Santa Ynez

3

3

5

16

Lompoc

Buellton

Solvang

18

23

20

18

101

24

Santa Barbara

Ojai

Carpinteria

21

Ventura

23

19

20

Oxnard

101

Channel Islands

22

Malibu

24

24

0   10   20   30 miles

MAP DESIGN AND CARTOGRAPHY BY: REINECK & REINECK

Climate Zones

| ⁄ | 1 | 2 | 3 | | | | 7 | 8 | 9 | | 11 | | | 14 | 15 | 16 | 17 | 18 | 19 | 20 | 21 | 22 | 23 | 24 |

ZONE 9

Central Valley's thermal belts

Zone 9, a thermal belt, is safer for citrus, hibiscus, melaleuca, and pittosporum than zone 8, which is a cold-air basin.

In both zones, summer temperatures are high, summer sunshine is abundant, and growing seasons are long. Plants that like summer heat—oleander and crape myrtle, for example—excel in both zones. Most vegetables and deciduous fruits also thrive here, and winter cold satisfies dormancy requirements of fruit trees. Fiercely cold, piercing north winds blow for several days at a time in winter, but they are harder on gardeners than on plants.

Tule fogs (dense fogs that rise from the ground on cold nights) appear and stay for hours or days during winter. These fogs usually hug the ground at night and rise to 800 to 1,000 feet by afternoon.

In zone 9, winter lows ranged from 28° to 18° during a 20-year period.

ZONE 14

Inland areas with some marine influence

This zone is moderated by marine air pushing through the Coast Ranges at San Pablo and San Francisco bays, and up the Salinas Valley. Zone 14 also includes the cold-winter valley floors, canyons, and land troughs in the Coast Ranges from Mendocino to Santa Barbara.

The milder-winter, marine-influenced areas and the cold-winter inland valleys within zone 14 differ in humidity. For example, lowland parts of Contra Costa County are more humid than Sacramento.

Fruits that need winter chilling do well here, as do shrubs needing summer heat (oleander, gardenia). During a 20-year period, this area had lows ranging from 26° to 16°.

ZONE 15

Cold-winter coastal areas

Zone 15 is influenced by marine air approximately 85 percent of the time and by inland air 15 percent of the time. Note that although zone 16

Coast redwoods, like these 80-foot trees at *Sunset*'s headquarters in Menlo Park, thrive in zone 15.

is within the Northern California coastal climate area, its winters are milder because this zone is in a thermal belt. The cold-winter areas that make up zone 15 lie in cold-air basins, on hilltops above the thermal belts, or far enough north that plant performance dictates a zone 15 designation.

Many plants recommended for zone 15 are not suggested for zone 14 because they must have moister air, cooler summers, milder winters, or all three. On the other hand, zone 15 still receives enough winter chilling to favor cold-winter specialties such as herbaceous peonies.

Most of zone 15 gets a nagging afternoon wind in summer. Trees and dense shrubs planted on the windward side of a garden can disperse it, and a neighborhood full of trees can keep it above the rooftops. Low temperatures ranged from 28° to 21° during a 20-year period, and record lows ranged from 26° to 16°.

ZONE 16

Coastal thermal belts

This benign Coast Range climate exists in patches and strips from northern Marin County to western Santa Barbara County. It's one of Northern California's finest horticultural climates, consisting of thermal belts in an area that's dominated by

ocean weather about 85 percent of the time and by inland weather about 15 percent.

Typical lows in zone 16 ranged from 32° to 19° during a 20-year period. The lowest recorded temperatures range from 25° to 18°. This zone gets more heat in summer than zone 17, which is dominated by maritime air, and has warmer winters than zone 15. That's a happy combination for gardening.

A summer afternoon wind is an integral part of this climate. To help disperse the wind, plant trees and shrubs on the windward side of your garden.

ZONE 17

Temperate coastal strip

Dominated by ocean weather about 98 percent of the time, this zone features cool, wet, almost frostless winters and cool summers with frequent fog or wind. The fog tends to come in high and fast, creating a cooling and humidifying blanket between the sun and the earth, reducing the intensity of the light and sunshine. Some heat-loving plants (citrus, gardenia, hibiscus) don't get enough heat to fruit or flower reliably. The climate favors fuchsias, hydrangeas, azaleas, and rhododendrons.

During a 20-year period, the lowest winter temperatures in zone 17 ranged from 36° to 23°, with all-time record lows from 30° to 20°. In the summer, highs are normally in the 60° to 75° range, with the average highest temperature in the 90s. ∎

Mounding aloes and spiky agaves bloom by the ocean in this garden at Pacific Grove—in temperate zone 17.

Los Angeles and Inland

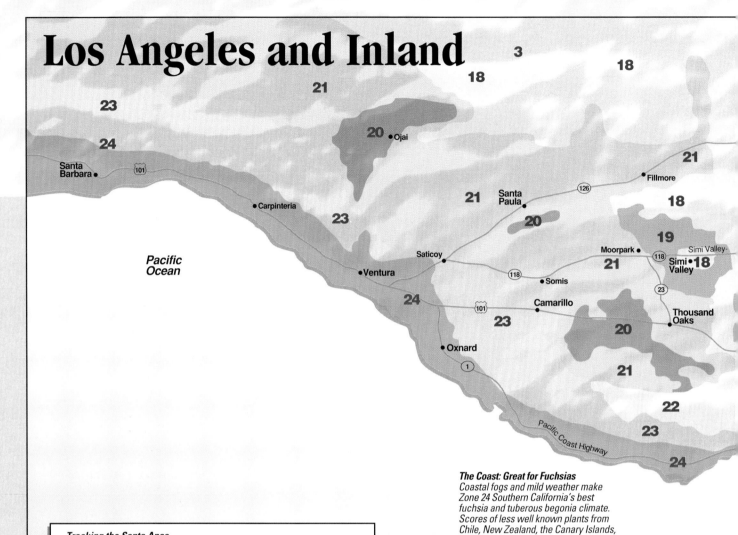

3

18

18

21

23

24

20 •Ojai

21

21 Santa Paula•

18

Santa Barbara •

19

(101)

Moorpark• Simi Valley-

• Carpinteria

20

21 Simi •18 Valley

(118)

23

Saticoy•

(126)

Fillmore•

Pacific Ocean

21

(118)

• Somis

Camarillo•

Thousand Oaks

(23)

•Ventura

24

(101)

23

20

•Oxnard

21

(1)

22

23

Pacific Coast Highway

24

The Coast: Great for Fuchsias
Coastal fogs and mild weather make Zone 24 Southern California's best fuchsia and tuberous begonia climate. Scores of less well known plants from Chile, New Zealand, the Canary Islands, and the moister parts of South Africa do well here for the same reason.

Tracking the Santa Anas
Every fall and winter, the Santa Ana wind revs up as the interior's cold, heavy air flows downhill toward the Southern California coast. As this air loses elevation, it compresses, heats up, dries out, and roars fero-ciously through the passes behind Los Angeles and San Bernardino. Cajon Pass and Soledad Canyon are two main routes, although the wind is named for Santa Ana Canyon. When the Santa Ana wind hits the Los Angeles basin, it's so hot and dry that it desiccates plants. Sprinklers, windbreaks, and row covers help protect them. Santa Anas usually play out near the coast, though sometimes they blow clear to Santa Catalina Island. They reach as far north as Oxnard and as far south as San Diego.

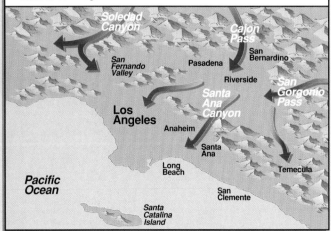

Climate Zones | 🔲 | 2 | 3 | | | | | | | | 11 | | | | | | | 18 | 19 | 20 | 21 | 22 | 23 | 24

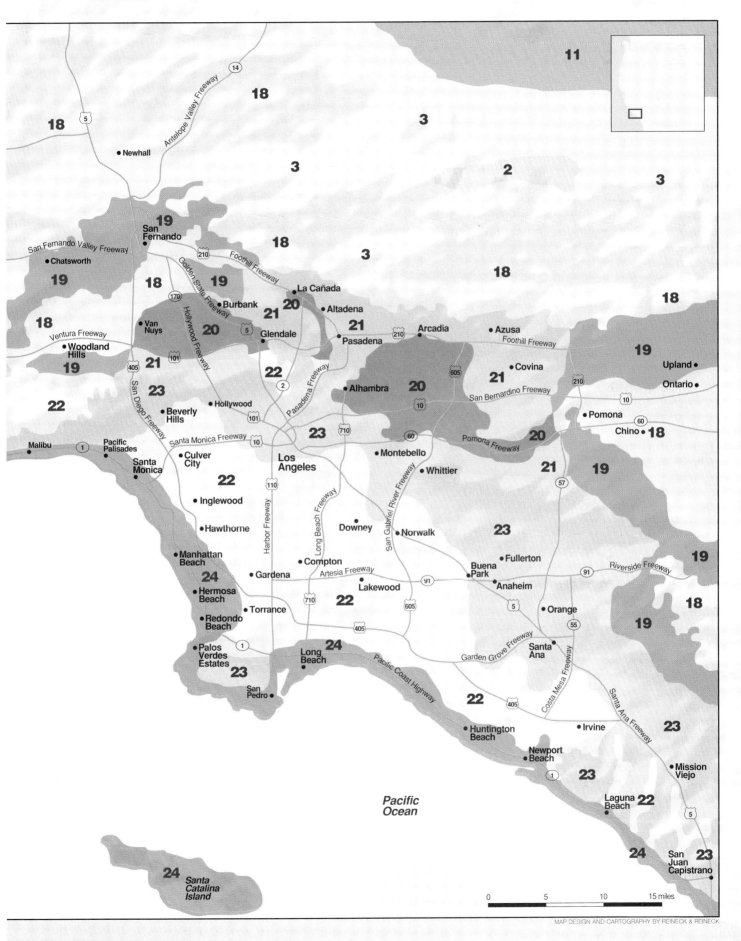

11

18

18 ⑤

● Newhall

3

18

2

3

3

19 San Fernando

San Fernando Valley Freeway

● Chatsworth

19

18

18 ⑰⓪

Golden State Freeway

19

Foothill Freeway

Burbank ●

18

3

18

21

20

La Cañada ●

● Altadena

21

Arcadia ②⑩

18

Ventura Freeway

● Woodland Hills

19

Van Nuys ●

20 ⑤

Hollywood Freeway

Glendale ●

Pasadena

Foothill Freeway

● Azusa

19

Upland ●

18

21

⑩①

22

②

⑥⓪⑤

21

● Covina

San Bernardino Freeway

②⑩

Ontario ●

23

San Diego Freeway

21

⑩①

Pasadena Freeway

● Alhambra

20

⑩

20

● Pomona

⑥⓪

● Hollywood

22

Malibu ● ①

Pacific Palisades ●

Santa Monica ●

● Beverly Hills

Santa Monica Freeway ⑩

23 ⑦①⓪

⑥⓪

● Montebello

Pomona Freeway

Chino ●

18

● Culver City

⑩①

22

● Inglewood

Harbor Freeway

Long Beach Freeway

San Gabriel River Freeway

● Whittier

21

19

● Hawthorne

● Downey

23

● Manhattan Beach

24

● Gardena

⑦①⓪

Artesia Freeway

● Norwalk

⑨①

● Fullerton

Buena Park ●

Riverside Freeway ⑨①

19

● Hermosa Beach

22

● Lakewood

⑥⓪⑤

● Anaheim

⑤⑦

18

● Torrance

● Compton

● Redondo Beach

● Palos Verdes Estates

23

④⓪⑤

22

● Orange

⑤⑤

19

● San Pedro

24

Long Beach ●

①

Pacific Coast Highway

Garden Grove Freeway

Santa Ana ●

Costa Mesa Freeway

Santa Ana Freeway

23

22 ④⓪⑤

● Huntington Beach

● Irvine

● Mission Viejo

Newport Beach ●

①

23

Pacific Ocean

Laguna Beach ●

22

⑤

24

24 Santa Catalina Island

0   5   10   15 miles

San Juan Capistrano ●

23

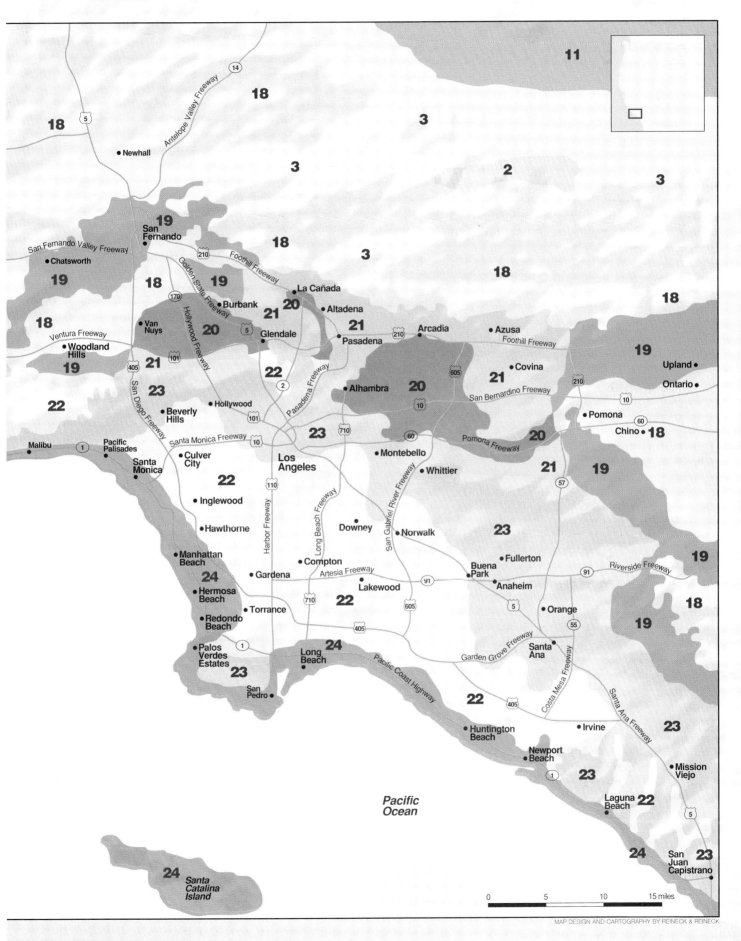

MAP DESIGN AND CARTOGRAPHY BY REINECK & REINECK

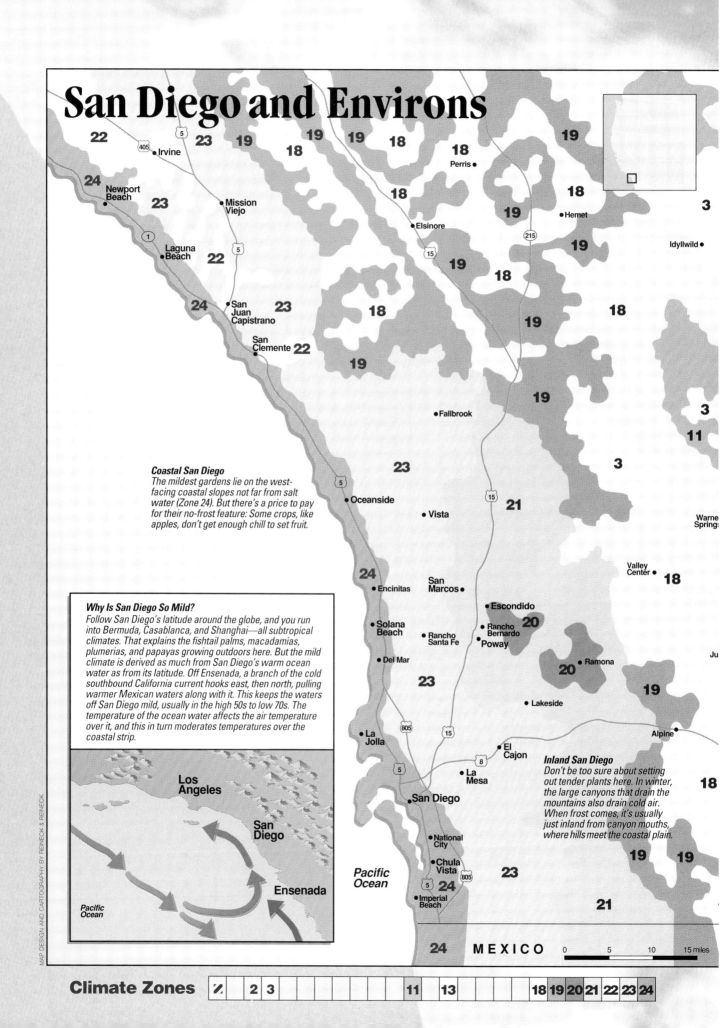

San Diego and Environs

22 23 19 18 19 19 18 18 19

• Irvine

24

Newport Beach   23   • Mission Viejo

Coastal San Diego
The mildest gardens lie on the west-facing coastal slopes not far from salt water (Zone 24). But there's a price to pay for their no-frost feature: Some crops, like apples, don't get enough chill to set fruit.

22   • Laguna Beach

24   • San Juan Capistrano   23

San Clemente   22

19

• Fallbrook

23

• Oceanside

24   • Encinitas

Why Is San Diego So Mild?
Follow San Diego's latitude around the globe, and you run into Bermuda, Casablanca, and Shanghai—all subtropical climates. That explains the fishtail palms, macadamias, plumerias, and papayas growing outdoors here. But the mild climate is derived as much from San Diego's warm ocean water as from its latitude. Off Ensenada, a branch of the cold southbound California current hooks east, then north, pulling warmer Mexican waters along with it. This keeps the waters off San Diego mild, usually in the high 50s to low 70s. The temperature of the ocean water affects the air temperature over it, and this in turn moderates temperatures over the coastal strip.

• Vista

21

San Marcos •

• Escondido

• Solana Beach

• Rancho Santa Fe

• Rancho Bernardo   20

• Del Mar   Poway

23   20   • Ramona

19

• Lakeside

• La Jolla

Los Angeles

San Diego

Ensenada

Pacific Ocean

Pacific Ocean

805   15

• El Cajon   8

• La Mesa

Inland San Diego
Don't be too sure about setting out tender plants here. In winter, the large canyons that drain the mountains also drain cold air. When frost comes, it's usually just inland from canyon mouths, where hills meet the coastal plain.

• San Diego

• National City

• Chula Vista   805

23

5   24

• Imperial Beach

Pacific Ocean

24   **MEXICO**   0   5   10   15 miles

Perris •

18

• Hemet

• Elsinore   215

18   19

15   19

18

19

18   Idyllwild •

18

3

3

11

3

Warner Springs

Valley Center •   18

Ju

19

Alpine •

18

19   19

21

MAP DESIGN AND CARTOGRAPHY BY REINECK & REINECK

Climate Zones   2   3   11   13   18 19 20 21 22 23 24

Z O N E 18

Chilly hilltops and valleys

This zone is influenced by continental air 85 percent of the time. Although the climate supplies enough winter chill for tree peonies and fruits like apple, it is not too cold for many of the hardier subtropicals like cymbidiums. Many avocado varieties do well here, and you can grow citrus if you're willing to put up with occasional minor fruit loss due to frost.

During a 20-year period, winter lows ranged from 28° to 10°.

Z O N E 19

Warm slopes

Zone 19 is little influenced by the ocean, but good air drainage makes it prime country for citrus, macadamias, and most avocados.

Plants that grow here but not in zone 18 include bougainvillea, bouvardia, several kinds of coral tree (*Erythrina*), livistona palms, myoporum, and lady palm (*Rhapis excelsa*).

Winter lows during a 20-year period ranged from 27° to 22°.

Z O N E 20

Cold-air basins

In zones 20 and 21, the same relative pattern prevails as in zones 18 and 19: the even-numbered zones are made up of cold-air basins and hilltops, while the odd-numbered zones are comprised of thermal belts. Influenced by maritime air and interior air, zones 20 and 21 often see climate boundaries move 20 miles in 24 hours.

Maritime influence makes zone 20 favorable for a wide variety of plants. During a 20-year period, winter lows ranged from 28° to 23°.

Z O N E 21

Where oranges meet lilacs

Gardens in zone 21 can be in ocean air or a high fog one day and in a mass of interior air the next.

This is fine citrus-growing country, but it's also the mildest zone that still gets enough winter chilling for most forms of lilacs and certain other plants.

During a 20-year period, winter lows ranged from 36° to 23°.

Z O N E 22

Cold-winter coastal canyons

Big coastal canyons are numerous between Irvine and the Mexico border. Exposed hilltops and canyon floors (where cold air settles in winter) are in zone 22, while the slopes on each side are zone 23 thermal belts.

Temperatures rarely fall below 28° in this zone, but that's enough to damage the tender subtropicals and citrus that thrive on the slopes.

Areas in zone 22 are influenced by the ocean about 85 percent of the time. Annual 20-year winter lows ranged from 24° to 21°.

Z O N E 23

The protea belt

One of the most favored areas in North America for growing subtropical plants, zone 23 has always been Southern California's best zone for avocados and proteas. Frosts don't amount to much here, because 85 percent of the time Pacific Ocean weather dominates.

Zone 23 lacks either the summer heat or the winter chill necessary to grow pears, most apples, and most peaches. But it gets just enough heat to grow gardenias and oleanders. Temperatures are mild, but severe winters descend at times. During a 20-year period, low temperatures ranged from 38° to 23°.

Z O N E 24

The morning fog belt

Stretching along Southern California's beaches, zone 24 is almost completely dominated by the ocean. Where the beach runs below high cliffs or palisades, zone 24 extends only to that barrier. But where hills are low or nonexistent, it runs inland several miles.

Winters are mild, summers are cool, and the air is seldom really dry. On many days, the sun doesn't break through the high overcast until afternoon. Fuchsias like it here, and figs, rubber plants, and scheffleras can grow into jungles.

Zone 24 is coldest at the mouths of canyons that channel chilly air down from the mountains on clear winter nights. During a 20-year period, lows ranged from 44° to 24°. ∎

Cactus and fountain grass get plenty of sun in this Hollywood Hills garden—in zone 23.

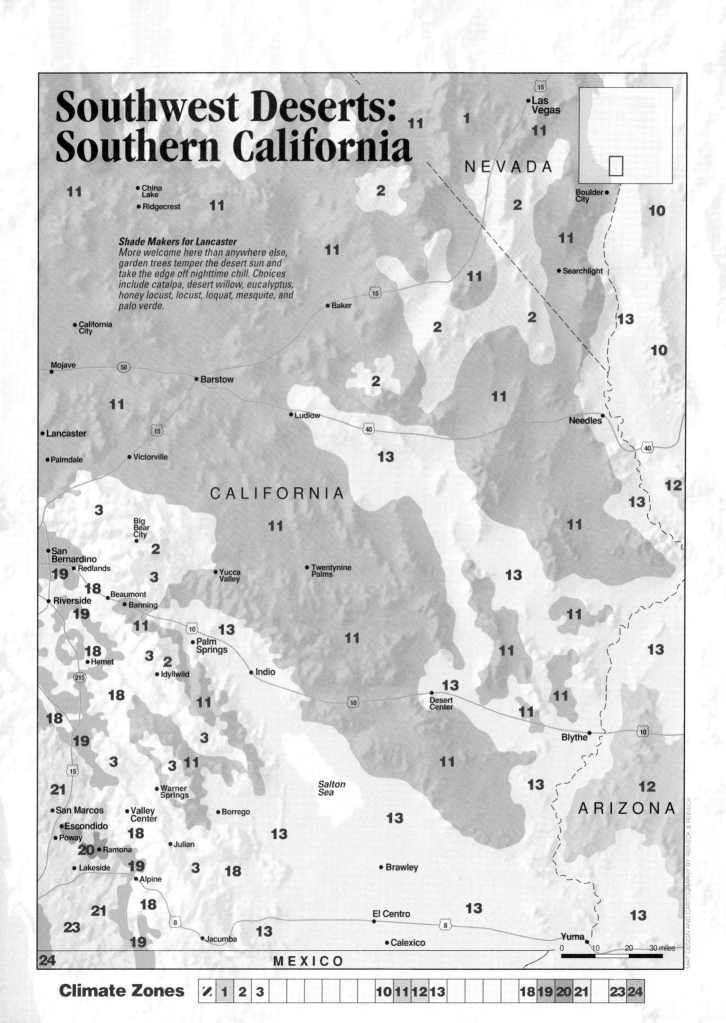

Southwest Deserts: Southern California

Shade Makers for Lancaster
More welcome here than anywhere else, garden trees temper the desert sun and take the edge off nighttime chill. Choices include catalpa, desert willow, eucalyptus, honey locust, locust, loquat, mesquite, and palo verde.

NEVADA

CALIFORNIA

ARIZONA

MEXICO

Las Vegas
Boulder City
Searchlight
Needles
Blythe
Yuma
China Lake
Ridgecrest
California City
Mojave
Barstow
Baker
Ludlow
Lancaster
Palmdale
Victorville
Big Bear City
San Bernardino
Redlands
Beaumont
Banning
Riverside
Hemet
Palm Springs
Yucca Valley
Twentynine Palms
Indio
Idyllwild
Desert Center
Salton Sea
Warner Springs
Borrego
San Marcos
Valley Center
Escondido
Poway
Ramona
Lakeside
Julian
Alpine
Brawley
Jacumba
El Centro
Calexico

Climate Zones

| ⊘ | 1 | 2 | 3 | 10 | 11 | 12 | 13 | 18 | 19 | 20 | 21 | 23 | 24 |

0 10 20 30 miles

Palms are among the many plants that flourish in the Los Angeles Arboretum in Arcadia—in zone 20 (see page 53).

ZONE 2

Second coldest Western climate

Gardens in zone 2 are usually lower, thus milder, than zone 1. The difference is crucial: 'McIntosh' and 'Sierra Beauty' apples, for example, grow well in zone 2 but not in zone 1.

In zone 2, windbreaks, shelter trees, and heavy mulches can make it possible to grow plants that would otherwise perish from the effects of wind, cold, and the low winter sun, which can burn young thin-barked trees.

During a 20-year period in zone 2, annual low temperatures ranged from –3° to –34°.

ZONE 3

Cold country's mildest zone

Milder still, zone 3 allows gardeners to grow such plants as English boxwood and winter jasmine. Winter minimums limit the selection of broad-leafed evergreens, because drying winds dehydrate plants growing in frozen soil.

Much planting is based on winter lows of around 10°, though in an occasional winter, Arctic air forces temperatures much lower. During a 20-year period, minimum temperatures in zone 3 ranged from 13° to –24°.

ZONE 11

Medium to high desert

Zone 11 shares cold winters with neighboring zones 1–3, and hot summers with zone 13. Overall, zone 11 is characterized by hot summer days followed by chilly nights.

On average, 110 summer days go above 90°, with the highest recorded temperatures hovering between 111° and 117°. About 85 nights have temperatures below 32°, with maximum lows between 11° and 0°.

Late-spring frosts and desiccating desert winds pose the biggest risks to plants here. Shelter trees and windbreaks help on both counts.

ZONE 13

Low desert

Ranging from below sea level in the Imperial Valley and Death valley to an elevation of 1,100 feet around Phoenix, Zone 13 is rightly classified as subtropical desert. Summers are hot—from 106° to 108°—and winters are short and mild, with just 15 nights below freezing. Lows of 19° to 13° have been recorded.

The gardening year begins in fall for most vegetables and flowers here, although crops like corn and melons are planted in late winter. Fall-planted crops grow slowly in winter, pick up speed in mid-February, then race as temperatures rise in March and April.

Heat-loving subtropicals like dates, grapefruits, and many cassias do well here. Spring winds and summer storms affect gardening: rains help with watering, and dense clouds shield plants from the hot sun.

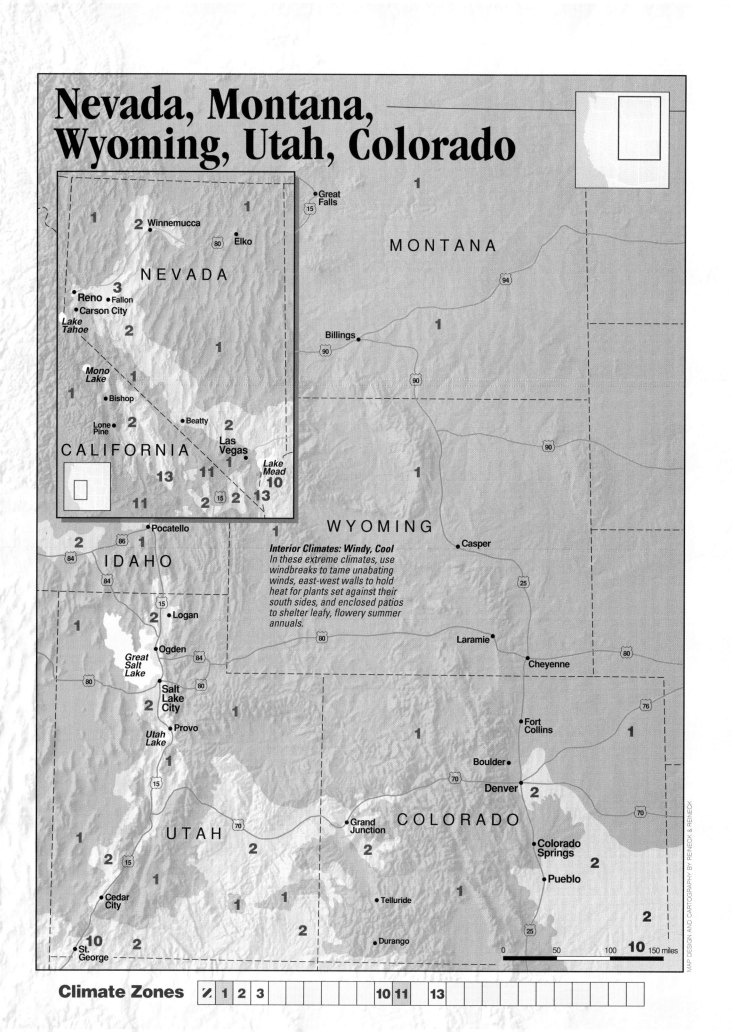

Nevada, Montana, Wyoming, Utah, Colorado

MONTANA

NEVADA

CALIFORNIA

IDAHO

WYOMING

UTAH

COLORADO

Great Falls 1

Winnemucca 2 1

Elko 1

Billings 1

Reno 3 **Fallon**
Carson City 1
Lake Tahoe 2

Mono Lake 1
Bishop 1

Lone Pine 2 **Beatty** 2
Las Vegas 2 1

Lake Mead 13 10
13 11 11
11 2 2 13

Pocatello 1
2 1
Casper 1

Logan 2

Ogden 2
Great Salt Lake 1
Salt Lake City 2
Provo 1
Utah Lake 1

Laramie 1
Cheyenne

Fort Collins 1
Boulder
Denver 2

Grand Junction 1
2 2
Colorado Springs 2
Pueblo

Cedar City 1
2 1
Telluride 1 1

St. George 10 2 2
Durango

Interior Climates: Windy, Cool
In these extreme climates, use windbreaks to tame unabating winds, east-west walls to hold heat for plants set against their south sides, and enclosed patios to shelter leafy, flowery summer annuals.

0 50 100 **10** 150 miles

MAP DESIGN AND CARTOGRAPHY BY REINECK & REINECK

Climate Zones Z 1 2 3   10 11 13

ZONE 1

Coldest-winter West

Zones 1, 2, and 3 are regions where snow falls and stays on the ground (for a week or all winter) every year. Zone 1 is coldest, its extreme winters caused by latitude, influence of the continental air mass, elevation (the higher you go, the colder it gets), or some combination of the three. In this zone, gardeners plant with a 75 to 150-day growing season in mind, though frosts can occur any night of the year.

ZONE 2

Second-coldest Western climate

Gardens in zone 2 get some snow in winter, but because they're usually lower in elevation or modified by a large body of water (Great Salt Lake, for example), they don't get quite as much cold as zone 1. The difference is crucial: 'McIntosh' and 'Sierra Beauty' apples, for example, grow well in zone 2, but not in zone 1.

In zone 2, windbreaks, trees planted for shelter, and heavy mulches can make it possible to grow plants that would otherwise perish from the effects of wind, cold, and the low winter sun, which can burn the trunks of young thin-barked trees.

During a 20-year period in zone 2, annual low temperatures ranged from –3° to –34°.

ZONE 3

Cold country's "banana belts"

This is the mildest of the snowy-winter climates. The zone 3 areas of Idaho and Nevada are the ones that are often called "banana belts." Of course, the only place you can grow the banana satisfactorily outdoors is in tropical climates. But the comparatively mild winter lows of zone 3 allow gardeners to grow such plants as English boxwood and winter jasmine.

Much planting here is based on winter lows of around 10°, though in an occasional winter, Arctic air forces temperatures much lower. Winter minimums limit the choice of broad-leafed evergreens, because drying winds dehydrate plants growing in frozen soil.

DAVID McDONALD

Hardy perennial flowers flourish in Aspen, Colorado, in zone 1—the West's coldest climate.

Wind protection, mulch, shade, and careful late-autumn watering will help with many borderline evergreens.

During a 20-year period, minimum temperatures in zone 3 ranged from 13° to –24°. While growing seasons can be shorter here than in zone 2, winter minimums are always higher in zone 3.

ZONE 10

Southwest's high desert

Zone 10 consists mostly of the 3,300- to 4,500-foot elevations in parts of Arizona and New Mexico. It also includes parts of southern Utah and southern Nevada. It has a definite winter season; from 75 to more than 100 nights each year have temperatures below 32°. In the representative towns of Douglas, Arizona, and Albuquerque, average winter minimums range from 31° to 24°. Lows of 25° to 22° often come in April. The lowest temperature recorded is –17°.

The cold winter season calls for spring planting and a spring-through-summer growing season. (In neighboring zones 12 and 13, most planting is done in fall.)

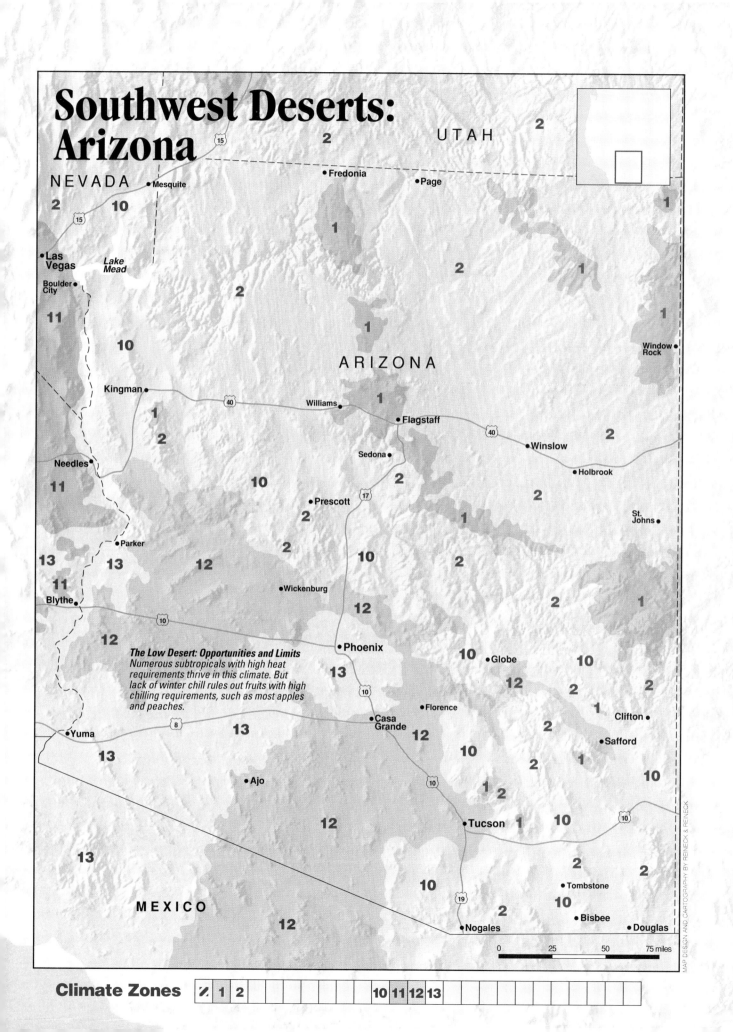

Southwest Deserts:
Arizona

UTAH

NEVADA

The Low Desert: Opportunities and Limits
Numerous subtropicals with high heat
requirements thrive in this climate. But
lack of winter chill rules out fruits with high
chilling requirements, such as most apples
and peaches.

ARIZONA

MEXICO

Las Vegas
Boulder City
Mesquite
Fredonia
Page
Kingman
Williams
Flagstaff
Winslow
Holbrook
Window Rock
Sedona
Needles
Prescott
St. Johns
Parker
Wickenburg
Blythe
Phoenix
Globe
Yuma
Florence
Clifton
Casa Grande
Safford
Ajo
Tucson
Tombstone
Bisbee
Nogales
Douglas

Lake Mead

0   25   50   75 miles

Climate Zones ⧄ 1 2   10 11 12 13

Yellow-flowering verbascum (left, foreground) and other heat-resistant plants ornament an outdoor room in New Mexico's high-desert zone 10.

What distinguishes this climate from zone 11 are more rainfall and less wind. Annual rainfall averages 12 inches, with half that amount falling in July and August. In the eastern parts of zone 10 (Pecos River drainage), the summer provides more precipitation than does the winter.

ZONE 11

Nevada's medium to high desert

This zone shares some similarities with its extremely different neighbors—the cold-winter zones 1, 2, and 3, and the subtropical low-desert zone 13. Like zones 1, 2, and 3, zone 11 has cold winters, and like zone 13, it has hot summers. Overall, zone 11 is characterized by wide swings in temperature. Hot summer days are followed by cool nights; freezing nights are often followed by daytime temperatures of 60°. On average, 110 summer days go above 90°, with the highest recorded temperatures hovering between 111° and 117°. About 85 nights have temperatures below 32°, with maximum lows between 11° and 0°.

Zone 11 includes Las Vegas, where gardeners lose many trees and shrubs every year, blaming the climate when the problem is usually bad soil or inadequate water (dry wind and bright sunlight combine to dry out evergreen plants). If you've been careful about watering and your correctly zoned plants still don't grow well, talk with your county extension agent about plants suited to your native soil.

ZONE 12

Arizona's intermediate desert

The crucial difference between zone 12, the intermediate desert, and zone 13, the low desert, is the amount of winter cold. Even though zone 12 averages only 5 more freezing nights than zone 13 (20 in Tucson compared to 15 in Phoenix), it has harder frosts spread over a longer winter cold season. Put another way, zone 12 averages about eight months between freezes, nine months between killing frosts (28° or lower). Zone 13, on the other hand, averages more than 11 months between killing frosts, if it gets them at all. Extreme low tempera-

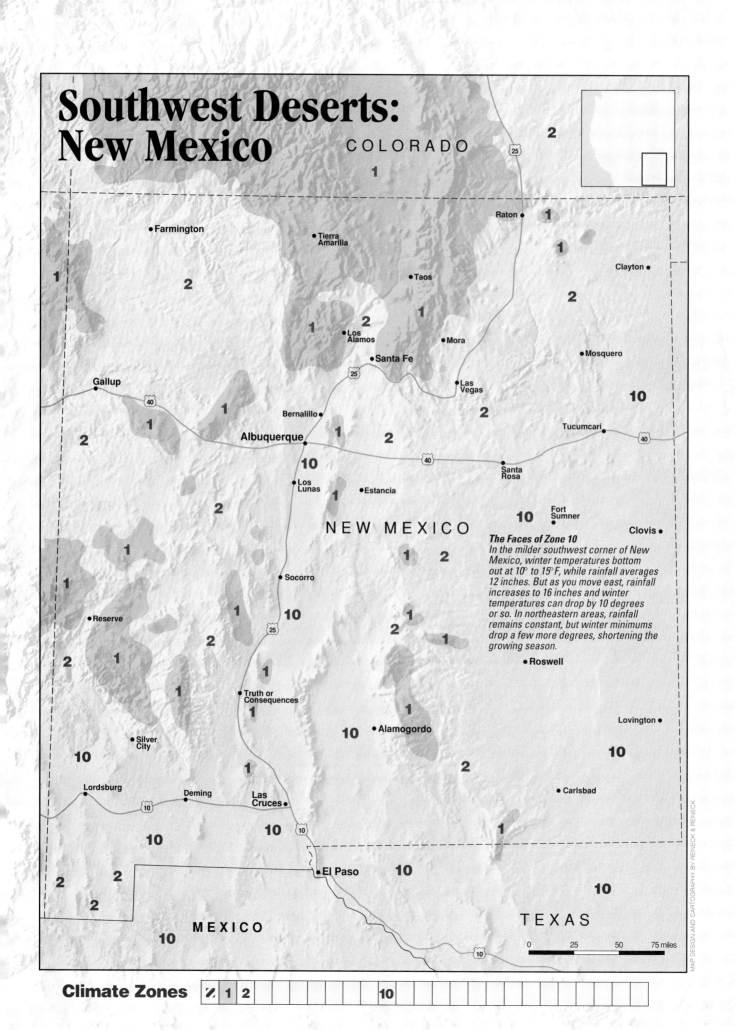

Southwest Deserts: New Mexico

COLORADO

The Faces of Zone 10
In the milder southwest corner of New Mexico, winter temperatures bottom out at 10° to 15° F, while rainfall averages 12 inches. But as you move east, rainfall increases to 16 inches and winter temperatures can drop by 10 degrees or so. In northeastern areas, rainfall remains constant, but winter minimums drop a few more degrees, shortening the growing season.

NEW MEXICO

MEXICO

TEXAS

0   25   50   75 miles

Climate Zones   1   2   10

Cities and towns: Farmington, Tierra Amarilla, Raton, Clayton, Taos, Los Alamos, Mora, Mosquero, Santa Fe, Las Vegas, Gallup, Bernalillo, Tucumcari, Albuquerque, Santa Rosa, Los Lunas, Estancia, Fort Sumner, Clovis, Socorro, Reserve, Roswell, Truth or Consequences, Alamogordo, Lovington, Silver City, Carlsbad, Lordsburg, Deming, Las Cruces, El Paso

Saguaro, cholla, organpipe cactus, and yellow-flowering brittlebush shine in zone 12—Arizona's intermediate desert.

tures of 6° have been recorded in zone 12. The mean maximums in July and August are 5° to 6° cooler than the highs of zone 13.

Many subtropical plants that do well in zone 13 aren't reliably hardy here, but with protection they succeed against the extreme winters.

Although winter temperatures are lower than those in zone 13, the total hours of cold are not enough to provide sufficient winter chilling for some deciduous fruits.

From March to May, winds to 40 miles per hour can damage young, tender growth. Windbreaks can help. Here, as in zone 13 and the eastern parts of zone 10, summer rains are usually more dependable than winter rains. And as in zone 13, the best planting time for cool-season crops (cabbage family members, salad greens, root vegetables) starts in September or October.

ZONE 13

Arizona's low desert

Ranging from below sea level in California's Imperial Valley to 1,100 feet around Phoenix, zone 13 is subtropical low desert. Average summer maximum temperatures range from 106° to 108°. Winters are short and mild. Frosts, anticipated between December 1 and February 15, are brief. Although the average minimum winter temperature is 37°, with just 15 nights below freezing, lows of 19° to 13° have been recorded.

The gardening year begins in September and October for most vegetable crops and annual flowers, although crops like corn and melons are planted in late winter. Fall-planted crops grow slowly in winter, pick up speed in mid-February, then race as temperatures rise in March and April. Spring winds and summer storms are factors in gardening: the rains help with watering, and dense clouds shield plants from the hot sun. ■

Bauhinia is one of the subtropical plants that grow in zone 13—Arizona's low desert.

Getting to know the other magnolias

Beyond the standard saucer magnolia are rich new yellows and huge-flowered hybrids

O N A SPRING DRIVE PAST Western gardens or parks, you can't miss the dramatic white, pink, or purple flowers that blanket magnolia branches like a fancy party dress. That's why deciduous magnolias are often referred to as the aristocrats of the garden.

These magnificent trees produce some of our grandest flowers, which start appearing in late January or February in mild climates and can continue into summer when you mix in late-blooming varieties.

The saucer magnolia (*Magnolia soulangiana*) is a standard in many gardens around the West, but dozens of other outstanding though less well-known magnolias are just as magnificent. A number of these trees also are much more restrained in size, making them suitable for smaller gardens.

Roger Gossler of Gossler Farms Nursery in Springfield, Oregon, has spent years testing new magnolias and introducing them to Western gardens. He attributes the bias toward the saucer magnolia to the fact that it was developed in the 1850s (it is a hybrid, and breeding continued through the 1920s and '30s), so it was the first magnolia to become well known here. Other magnolias weren't bred until the mid-1950s. Since it can take 20 or 30 years to introduce a new tree, availability has been more limited and, up until recently, the trees were primarily collectors' items.

Even now, only a few retail nurseries offer significantly more than the standard saucer and star magnolia (*M. stellata*), although dozens of other

NORMAN A. PLATE

TWELVE-YEAR OLD 'ELIZABETH' *growing in this Menlo Park, California garden is about 17 feet tall.*

species and varieties are available. Gossler says the hottest new magnolias are the rich yellows ('Butterflies' and 'Elizabeth') and the big-flowered hybrids out of New Zealand, such as 'Iolanthe' and 'Vulcan'. "The next colors you'll see are peach and salmon," says Gossler. "Unfortunately, they won't be available for a few years."

If your local nursery doesn't offer a good selection of trees, the best way for home gardeners to get them is

YELLOW FLOWER *of 'Elizabeth' is a magnolia color breakthrough. A bonus: the flowers are fragrant.*

'Galaxy'

M. veitchii

M. loebneri 'Spring Snow'

through sources listed on page 65. Now is the time to order and plant trees, while they're dormant.

MAGNOLIAS THROUGH THE AGES

Although hybrids are relatively recent, species magnolias have a long history. The first written references to magnolias were to their medicinal use in China as far back as 1083 B.C., according to a new reference by Dorothy

Magnolia 'Butterflies'
Sunset Western Garden Book Zones 1–9, 14–24
30 feet tall, 20-foot spread
Rich yellow, 3- to 4-inch-wide flowers. Upright tree with deeper yellow flowers than *M.* 'Elizabeth', below.

M. denudata
Yulan magnolia
Zones 2–9, 14–24
35 feet tall, 30-foot spread
Fragrant, white flowers, 6 to 7 inches wide. Tree has handsome, irregular form; great in Southern California.

M. 'Elizabeth'
Zones 1–9, 14–24
30 to 40 feet tall, 20-foot spread
Fragrant medium yellow flowers (lighter in mild climates) that are 6 to 7 inches wide.

M. 'Galaxy'
Zones 1–9, 14–24
20 to 25 feet tall, 12- to 15-foot spread
Many light purplish pink flowers, 8 to 10 inches wide. Columnar tree good for street or patio.

M. 'Iolanthe'
Zones 4–9, 14–24
Fast-growing to 40 feet tall, 25-foot spread
Large 10- to 12-inch-wide flowers, pink outside, white inside. Blooms at a young age, even on a 2-foot-tall plant.

M. liliiflora 'O'Neil'
Zones 2–9, 14–24
12 feet tall, 15-foot spread
Very dark purple-red flowers that are 8 inches wide. Shrubby tree; blooms over a long period.

M. loebneri 'Spring Snow'
Zones 1–9, 14–24
20 to 30 feet tall, 12- to 15-foot spread
Fragrant pure white many-petaled flowers, 4 to 5 inches wide. Light, airy patio tree that flowers at a young age.

M. macrophylla
Bigleaf magnolia
Zones 2–7, 14–17
Slow-growing, 30 to 60 feet tall, 30-foot spread
Creamy white flowers to 12 inches wide after leaves emerge in June. Huge leaves to 30 inches long, 12 inches wide; protect from wind.

M. salicifolia 'Iufer'
Zones 2–9, 14–24
Slow to 20 feet tall, 12-foot spread
Many 4-inch-wide white, star-shaped flowers with red-tipped stamens. Small, light, airy, columnar tree.

M. sieboldii
Oyama magnolia
Zones 3–9, 14–17
Slow to 15 feet tall, 15-foot spread
Fragrant 4- to 5-inch-wide white flowers with red stamens. Flowers from late spring to mid-August; bright pink pods follow.

M. denudata

M. stellata 'Jane Platt'

'Star Wars'

J. Callaway called *The World of Magnolias* (Timber Press, Portland, 1994; $44.95). Their use as ornamental trees can be dated to at least A.D. 650, when Buddhist monks planted *M. denudata* at their temples. The lilylike flowers were a symbol of purity.

More than 13 centuries later, Gossler identifies this same species as his absolute favorite magnolia. "The reason it has been grown for so long is that nothing compares to it. The pure white 6-inch-wide flower has a grace and form like no other. It's unmistakable, even when you see it depicted on a 500-year-old porcelain. The tree also grows in almost any climate, from Los Angeles to the Northwest."

Of course, that's not to say Gossler doesn't rave about many of the 100-plus other magnolias he sells, all of which he grows for their individual beauty and form. The selection that begins on the facing page includes some of his favorites. He chose them for their outstanding flowers (large or prolific), unusual flower color (yellow), or handsome form, and, in most cases, for their adaptability to a range of climates. All bloom fairly young, at 2 to 6 years of age (others can take 10 to 15 years to bloom).

Many of the trees are small, suiting them to smaller gardens. Gossler also selected a few outstanding larger trees, such as *M. denudata* and 'Elizabeth'. Note that trees grown in California tend to be smaller and bloom earlier than trees grown in the Northwest (our selection lists Northwest heights).

(Although referred to as petals in the listing that begins on page 64, magnolia petals are actually tepals, a flower part that is not separated into sepals and petals as on most plants.)

LOW-MAINTENANCE AND ALMOST PEST-FREE

Their beauty might make one think magnolias are fussy trees. But given the proper growing conditions, they're easy to maintain.

First, choose a location suitable for the size of the tree. The large magnolias need plenty of room. Although the trees are considered woodland plants, they don't bloom well in shade. But some of them do prefer part shade in hotter climates.

In inland areas and in Southern California, plant *M. veitchii* and large-flowered types such as 'Iolanthe' where they will get afternoon shade. From the San Francisco Bay Area to the Northwest, plant trees in full sun. Avoid windy sites in any climate.

Magnolias aren't fussy about soil type, but they need good drainage and thrive in soil amended with lots of hu-

M. 'Star Wars'
Zones 3–9, 14–24
Fast-growing to 30 to 40 feet
Rich pink-purple flowers, 10 inches wide; long bloom. Especially good magnolia for Southern California and inland areas.

M. stellata 'Jane Platt'
Zones 2–9, 14–24
15 to 20 feet tall, 20-foot spread
Star-shaped soft pink flowers that don't fade, 5 inches wide. A slow-growing, shrubby tree.

M. 'Susan'
Kosar-De Vos Hybrid
Zones 2–9, 14–24
12 to 15 feet tall, 15-foot spread
Many red-purple flowers, 5 inches wide and slightly twisted. Shrubby tree; blooms over a long period.

M. veitchii
Zones 4–9, 14–24
40 to 50 feet tall, 30-foot spread
Many soft white flowers, flushed with pink, 8 to 10 inches wide. The best magnolia for Southern California; give afternoon shade inland.

M. 'Vulcan'
Zones 5–9, 14–24
Fast-growing to 40 feet tall, 20-foot spread
Large 10- to 12-inch-wide dark purple-red flowers. The tree blooms at a young age; the trees are in limited supply.

mus. They prefer slightly acid soil but do well in neutral soil, too.

In areas where the soil can be fairly alkaline, such as Southern California, you'll need to apply iron chelate periodically to prevent chlorosis (yellow leaves with green veins). Fertilizing

with ammonium sulfate will also help. If your irrigation water is high in salts, be sure to periodically leach the salts down below the roots with a heavy irrigation.

Dig a planting hole so that the tree sits slightly above its original soil level, and mound soil up to the trunk. Cover the soil area with several inches of mulch. Magnolias need regular water, although *M. veitchii* can take some drought (it survived six years of drought in Santa Barbara). To help maintain soil moisture, renew mulch each season. Don't cultivate around the roots; handpick weeds if necessary. Fertilize trees with nitrogen if leaves look pale.

Pests aren't usually a problem, but trees can get scale, aphids, and spider mites (in warm weather). Summer-weight oils control all of the insects, or you can use insecticidal soap for aphids.

WHERE TO GET TREES

Bay Laurel Nursery, Scotts Valley, Calif. Wholesale only; order through your retail nursery.

Gossler Farms Nursery, 1200 Weaver Rd., Springfield, Ore. 97478; (503) 746-3922. Sells 105 kinds (500 are growing in the nursery's garden), including all mentioned in this story, by mail order or on site.

Greer Gardens, 1280 Goodpasture Island Rd., Eugene, Ore. 97401; (800) 548-0111. Sells 42 kinds, including 12 of the 15 mentioned here, by mail order or on site. ∎

By Lauren Bonar Swezey

CLEAR WHITE FLOWERS of 'Spring Snow' blanket branches of a 20-year-old tree.

MICHAEL THOMPSON

MULTICOLORED SHOW *of 400 early-, mid-, and late-season tulips lasts for three months in this Lafayette, California, garden.*

MARCH

GARDEN GUIDE

Here comes the parade of spring color—and the promise of summer edibles

LYNNE HARRISON

Across much of the far West, the first wave of spring flower color sweeps into gardens. Just look at Brian Coleman's Seattle garden (shown at right), which was designed by Charles Price and Glenn Withey. It's a symphony of early spring blooms: pink-flowered *Bergenia purpurascens,* tall pink tulips, yellow daffodils, purple grape hyacinths, and *Rhododendron* 'Ramapo', *R. pseudochrysanthum,* and *R. yakushimanum.* Don't overlook the subtle mix of evergreen colors—the silvery bluish gray of the rhododendron leaves contrasts with the creamy spring green foliage of *Pieris japonica* 'Variegata' and the dark green background of a boxwood hedge. Off to the left, the strong line of bluish green *Yucca recurvifolia* helps frame the scene. After the spring bulbs have finished blooming, annuals and perennials carry the flower show into summer and fall bloom.

You can find these plants and more in bud or in bloom this month at nurseries. Bring them home and slip them into decorative pots next to a door or outside a window for close-up enjoyment of this year's blooms. When flowers fade, plant them out into the garden.

Flocks of phlox

In the summer, huge, fragrant clusters of phlox blossoms atop sturdy stems grace Elizabeth Lair's garden in Eugene, Oregon. What's her secret? In early March, she thins root clumps so that each crown of roots supports no more than five flower stems. Using a sharp pocket knife, she cuts out all but the most vigorous shoots, sometimes eliminating as many as 90 percent of them. Then, three weeks later, she goes back over the clumps, cutting off all the new shoots that emerge after the first thinning.

She also feeds plants heavily. During March, she gives each plant a generous dose of phosphorus (about 2 cups of bonemeal per established plant) and a top dressing of compost. When the weather warms, she puts about 2 cups of cottonseed meal around each plant.

Big and bold daylilies

Few flowering perennials have as many admirers as the daylily (*Hemerocallis*). Indeed, few plants deliver more reliable bloom and foliage year after year and require so little care. They're tough and persistent plants, too, as the common orange daylily (*H.*

DAINTY GRAPE HYACINTHS *(center foreground) and pink bergenia bloom along a sidewalk. Daffodils and tulips provide splashes of color around the garden.*

'*Isaiah*' grows fast to 3 feet and thrives on steep slopes and in weedy gullies. It bears golden orange blooms on 4½-foot stems.

'Stupice' tomatoes are a smart choice for early crops

The Czechoslovakian 'Stupice' tomato may give the ever-popular 'Early Girl' a run for her money. The fruit is said to be more flavorful, arrive a little earlier, and be more abundant. 'Stupice' tomatoes (pictured below) are, however, a little smaller—about the size of apricots.

Plants are indeterminate—they keep growing until they die—but are not especially vigorous, so you can train them up a 6-foot pole and not bother to prune out leaf suckers. Fruits will keep coming until frost in mild-summer areas, or until they're overwhelmed by heat in the desert.

You can order 'Stupice' seed from High Altitude Gardens, Box 1048, Hailey, Idaho 83333. Catalog is $3.

VERNA VAN DE WATER

SLIGHTLY LARGER *than cherry tomatoes, 'Stupice' tomatoes are abundant and flavorful.*

fulva) demonstrates: it can hold its own along a country road, battling it out with vigorous native grasses (no wonder it's sometimes called tiger lily). Daylilies aren't bothered by most insect pests and plant diseases, and they are adaptable enough to grow in all the West's climate zones. March and April are prime spring months to plant. If you set out plants now, you can expect a few blooms this summer.

Several daylilies form especially big plants. Here are four choices.

'*Sherwood Gladiator*', one of the biggest, forms foliage clumps that often top 4 feet, with an equal or bigger spread. The plant's bright yellow blooms stand atop 5-foot stems.

'*Johnny Reb*' is a strong, tough plant with foliage to 3½ feet and Confederate-flag-red blooms on 4½-foot stems.

'*August Cheer*' bears big pink flowers fading to orange with green throats. Its foliage reaches about 3 feet tall with a 4-foot spread.

Salvaging native plants

It's sad but true: as timber becomes less available on public lands, it is being cut on more private lands around the Northwest. When trees with market value are cut, undergrowth is lost: salal, sword ferns, vine maple, and even rare plants such as the dwarf mountain hemlock (*Tsuga mertensiana*) are casualties.

Jeff McClelland didn't like seeing these plants lost, so he figured out a way to save these and other precious trees and plants. Through his business, Skagit Landscaping, in Mount Vernon, Washington, McClelland contracts with landowners who have sold their timber. He gets a digging permit, and before logging starts, he carefully removes as much vegetation as he can. It's moved to a holding area, then used in landscaping projects or sold to customers who visit McClelland's sales lot.

With good equipment and know-how, the survival rate, even for large trees, is high (only 1 in 10 trees is lost). McClelland will also search

for specific plants (he often takes clients to the site before he digs). Skagit Landscaping, at 1859 State Highway 9 in Mount Vernon, is open by appointment; call (206) 422-8200.

New colors for a Southern California favorite

Even though its botanical name is *Mandevilla,* many people still refer to one of coastal Southern California's most popular flowering plants by its former name, *Dipladenia.* Whatever you call it, though, you'll want to know that Weidners' Gardens in Encinitas is introducing the first new varieties in almost a decade.

'Scarlet Pimpernel' and 'My Fair Lady', both hybridized in Denmark, are natural mutations of 'Red Riding Hood', which has been available in nurseries for about 10 years. 'Scarlet Pimpernel' produces yellow-centered dark red flowers that fade to cherry pink. 'My Fair Lady' has white flowers with a pink blush and yellow centers. 'Red Riding Hood', in contrast, produces dark pink flowers that fade to lighter pink.

Mandevillas can be planted directly in the garden, but the plants seem to do better in containers. Because they have a naturally floppy habit, these plants also do well in hanging baskets.

The plants usually produce their most prolific blooms in March, but all varieties will bloom year-round if cared for. The key is to give them at least half a day of sun, although in hot inland areas you should shade the plants at midday. In all areas, feed with a complete liquid fertilizer about once every two weeks, or a controlled-release fertilizer about once a month. The plants also prefer loose soil that doesn't stay wet.

The new varieties should be widely available by summer; a 10-inch pot will sell

STEPHEN SIMPSON

'SCARLET PIMPERNEL' *is one of two new varieties of mandevilla (dipladenia).*

for around $15. In the meantime, visit Weidners' Gardens at 695 Normandy Road in Encinitas (from Interstate 5, take the Leucadia exit east). Smaller sizes may be available by mail; for information, call (619) 436-2194.

Tulip bonanza

Nothing says spring has sprung like a garden full of blooming tulips. Last year, Bob and Joan Hughey planted 400 tulip bulbs of 15 varieties from around the color wheel, including shades of yellow, red, orange, white, purple, and pink, along with bicolors. To extend the show (featured on page 70), the Hugheys chose early-, mid-, and late-blooming types. The spectacle lasted for almost three months, from late February to early May.

The Hugheys started planting bulbs four years ago. Each year when the bulbs arrive, the Hugheys chill them in the refrigerator for about six weeks. They plant from early November to mid-December, placing the bulbs in groups (6 to 12 of each variety) around existing shrubs and beneath ground covers.

For each bulb, the Hugheys dig a hole 6 inches deep, then add a mixture of 1 teaspoon 5-10-5 bulb food and about ½ cup compost. They cover the bulbs with a mix of soil and compost. The bulbs grow through winter. If spring rains are light, they are given supplemental water.

Snail problem? Maybe you need more

Ten years ago, Mary Borevitz of San Marcos, California, tossed a handful of decollate snails, a predator of the common garden brown snail, into her 7-acre orange grove. "The decollates looked dead when they came in the mail, so I threw them away," she says. "I thought it was a joke."

Evidently, the inch-long, conical-shelled snails were

merely dormant. They multiplied, consuming immature brown snails, snail eggs, and decaying organic matter. Borevitz says she hasn't had a problem with brown snails in years. Now she has so many decollate snails, she sells them by mail order (100 for $19.50, 500 for $80; plan on two snails per square foot).

Decollate snails, *Rumina decollata,* are permitted everywhere in the United States except California north of Santa Barbara County. They don't kill slugs, but slug populations diminish in their presence—an indication that they may consume slug eggs. One drawback: they also eat tender seedlings if preferred foods aren't present.

If you have a severe brown snail infestation, it may be years before the predatory decollates take over. Continue to handpick brown snails at night. And, since brown snails climb but decollates don't, wrap trunks of citrus with snail-deterring copper bands and keep branches from touching the ground. Decollates are susceptible to snail bait, so wait six weeks for bait to dissipate before you release them.

In addition to Mary's Decollate Snails (619/744-9233), sources include most nurseries and garden centers.

California wildflowers bloom in Pasadena

You needn't travel the state to see the profusion of California's spring wildflowers. Blazing stars, spider lupine, tidytips, and other natives are just a few of the flowers flourishing now at Earthside Nature Center in Pasadena.

To see the state's blooms at a glance, join the Wildflower Walkabouts held each year in late March. You can meander through the 2 acres of native plants on your own, or join a guided tour through designed habitats, including a redwood forest and a desert oasis. Plants are labeled for easy identification, and many are

SPIDER LUPINE *is just one of many wildflowers from around the state now in bloom at Earthside Nature Center in Pasadena.*

in *Sunset Western Garden Book* climate zones 1–3 and 10; big-tooth maple grows in zones 1–10 and 14–20. On dry sites and in shallow soil, both these trees grow as shrubs, while in deep soil with ample water they can reach 20 to 30 feet. If you're after height, it also helps to fertilize and train trees to a single trunk (in the wild, they form multiple trunks).

Publish your own plant portfolio

Think of your time. Think of your money. Think of your back. This year, plan before you plant. Jill Dale of North Tustin, California, does, and she makes it sound like fun.

Dale begins by cutting photos of plants she is interested in from catalogs and magazines and saving them in a folder. When she's ready to design a new perennial bed, she pulls out the folder and experiments.

"I play with the pictures almost as if I had the plants there," says Dale. "It helps me see how textures, colors, and shapes work together."

She avoids gardening mistakes in the process. "I was thinking of combining cosmos and coneflowers," she says in illustration, "but once I saw the pictures together I changed my mind. The colors

available for sale.

Earthside is at 3160 E. Del Mar Boulevard. From Interstate 210 in Pasadena, take Madre Street about ¼ mile south, then go west a block on E. Del Mar. A donation of $5 ($3 for students and seniors) is requested. Group tours can be arranged. For more information, call (818) 447-2830.

A pepper you can eat like an apple

Pimiento peppers are some of the best types for eating fresh because of their sweet, juicy flesh and crunchy texture. A newly available heirloom pimiento called 'Figaro' is the tastiest of all. This old-time variety was rediscovered at a produce stand in Yakima Valley, Washington; it had been in the Italian American owner's family for five generations. Unlike the usual pimiento, which is wide on top and tapers to a point, 'Figaro' is 3 to 4 inches wide and shaped like a flattened scallop. It starts out dark green and ripens to a rich crimson red. The thick walls are crunchy,

very juicy, and extremely sweet, especially when the peppers change to red.

'Figaro' is available from Shepherd's Garden Seeds, 6116 Highway 9, Felton, Calif. 95018; (408) 335-6910. Seeds cost $2 (plus shipping).

Two great native maples

Maples are a delight, supplying leafy green shade in summer and beautiful yellow-to-red color in fall. Two native Western maples that fit well into gardens are big-tooth maple (*Acer saccharum grandidentatum*) and Rocky Mountain maple (*A. glabrum*), also sold as dwarf maple.

Big-tooth maple generally has more deeply divided leaves than its Rocky Mountain cousin. In fall, big-tooth maples color Utah's Wasatch Range with shades of yellow, orange, and scarlet. Dick Hildreth, director of education at University of Utah's Red Butte Garden and Arboretum, calls this maple "one of Utah's best-kept secrets."

Rocky Mountain maple has reddish shoots and twigs, and yellow to yellow-orange or golden autumn color. It prefers sun and higher elevations (you'll find it growing with aspen, fir, and spruce).

You can grow these maples throughout the West's mountain and intermountain regions, and in the high deserts of Arizona and New Mexico. Rocky Mountain maple grows

JILL DALE'S *garden planner is full of magazine clippings, drawings, and copious notes. No design that started out in her trusty book has failed yet.*

worked, but the shapes were too much alike."

When Dale is pleased with a particular grouping, she transfers the pictures to a notebook and lets the idea incubate. Over time, she'll usually come up with several refinements. For instance, Dale improved a basic pink, mauve, and silver combination by adding a few purple plants for depth and a dash of yellow for energy.

Once she is completely satisfied with a combination, Dale adds a color pencil sketch to the page illustrating how she would arrange the selected plants. She might also add a vellum overlay to remind her where sun and shade occur. And then, and only then, does she plant.

"The longer I do this, the better my pages look," says Dale. And the better the pages look, the better her garden looks.

Spider flower: a summer beauty with a creepy name

Bearing fluffy clusters of pink, rose, purple, or white blossoms, spider flower (*Cleome hasslerana*) can add an unusual accent to a large border.

This summer- and fall-flowering annual grows 4 to 6 feet tall and about as wide. Flower heads (pictured above) form on tops of upright branches. The blossoms get their airy look from the stamens, which extend a couple of inches beyond the flower. After the blooms drop off, long, narrow seed heads that look like spider legs form, while new flowers continue to open on top.

Grow spider flower as a hedge, against fences, or in large containers.

Direct-sow seeds sparsely in garden soil in a sunny spot after the last frost. Thin to 24 inches apart. Once plants are well established, keep them on the dry side to avoid rank growth. Spider flower can self-sow in the garden.

NORMAN A. PLATE

FLUFFY HEADS *of undemanding spider flower appear from mid- to late summer until frost.*

Seeds are available at many nurseries and from most mail-order seed suppliers that sell flowers. You can get single colors such as 'Cherry Queen' or 'Rose Queen', or buy mixed colors.

Sacramento's most colorful public garden

For more than 20 years, the rock garden in Sacramento's William Land Park languished in obscurity, suffering from the lack of a loving horticultural touch. That changed six years ago, when city employee Daisy Mah, a former art student, and a group of volunteers set out to rejuvenate the garden. They bought seeds from around the world, propagated plants from local gardens, and began to replant the 1-acre site.

Today the public garden ranks among the Central Valley's most beautiful. The first things you notice as you stroll through the garden are the wonderful foliage colors, shapes, and textures. Lacy ornamental grasses are set off by soft gray artemisias and the large, toothy leaves of *Gunnera manicata*. This month there will be plenty in bloom, including flowering fruit trees, hellebores, and irises. Most of the plants are drought tolerant.

The rock garden is adjacent to Fairytale Town (across from the zoo) in William Land Park. From Interstate 5, take Sutterville Road east ½ mile to the park. Most of the plants in the garden aren't labeled, but Mah is working on that. If you visit the garden in the afternoon, chances are she'll be there to answer your questions. The garden is open sunrise to sunset daily.

Gray-water guide promotes resource resourcefulness

We've all heard about gray water, the runoff from household sinks, showers, and washing machines. But until late last year, there wasn't much most Californians could do to take advantage of this potential resource.

Now that gray-water systems are legal throughout California, it's worth checking out a new booklet titled *Create an Oasis With Greywater.* Author Art Ludwig developed Oasis biocompatible cleaning products for use in gray-water systems. After years of experimenting with gray water and researching work done by others, Ludwig has written an exceptionally thorough treatise on the subject.

Even if you're an all-thumbs, nonplumbing type of person, you'll soon be conversant with such arcane matters as eco-chambers, surge capacity, and automatic backwashing sand filters. Some of the systems presented in the book, like the venerable "dishpan dump," are pretty simple ("When the dishpan water gets dirty," writes the sometimes deadpan Ludwig, "carry it outside and dump it in a flower bed"). Others, though, are quite complex (it's unlikely that most readers will put down the book and run out to buy a $3,200 automated system).

To order a copy ($7), call Real Goods Trading Company at (800) 762-7325. For more information, call Oasis Design at (805) 967-3222.

Water-thrifty roses? Here are 22 choices

Although many roses prefer regular watering, a number of heirloom and old species roses can thrive on the coast as well as in inland valleys with little or no water during the summer months.

Alice Flores of Mendocino Heirloom Roses in Mendocino, California, has studied roses in both areas extensively. She explains: "Many roses have naturalized in Mendocino and other coastal areas where it's dry, but not hot. You can also find the same roses in hot inland areas, such as the Napa Valley." Although some of these roses can look ratty with no supplemental water, they thrive if given a minimal amount.

The following list identifies some of the roses that Flores has found to be drought resistant: 'Albertine', 'American Pillar', 'Belle of Portugal', 'Cl. Cécile Brunner', 'Complicata', 'Dorothy Perkins', 'Excelsa', 'François Juranville', 'Gardenia', 'Madame Plantier', 'Navarro Ridge Noisette', 'Paul's Double Musk', 'Paul Ricault', double yellow Lady Banks' rose (*Rosa banksiae* 'Lutea'), *R. corymbifera, R. rubiginosa, R. rugosa* ('Alba' and 'Rubra'), 'Russelliana', 'Silver Moon', 'Veilchenblau', and 'White Dorothy Perkins'.

Most of these roses are available from Mendocino Heirloom Roses, Box 670, Mendocino, Calif. 95460; (707) 877-1888. Catalog $1.

Drought-tolerant plants for the Northwest

Population in the Northwest is growing, but the water supply is not. So it's important that gardeners learn to use plants that will flourish on the water that nature provides and that can withstand dry summer months. The Northwest Perennial Alliance (NPA) has just published an encyclopedic list of plants that, once established, tolerate drought or require minimal water in Northwest gardens. Plants are also categorized by type (annual, perennial, bulb, grass, shrub, tree, vine) and by size.

More than 1,400 plants are on the list. You'll see dozens of roses; two of the toughest are *Rosa rugosa,* prized for its big hips in autumn, and *R. glauca,* admired for its handsome bluish foliage. If you want a maple for a small garden, *Acer campestre* is one good choice; it grows slowly to a height that rarely tops 30 feet. If you want a vine that is equally colorful in summer and autumn, consider *Parthenocissus henryana.* And if you're looking for a broad-leaved evergreen for a dry corner, consider *Co-*

toneaster glaucophyllus with its dusty blue-gray leaves.

The NPA plant list costs $12. To order by mail, send a note of request and a check for $15 (which includes $3 for postage and handling) to NPA, Box 45574, University Station, Seattle 98145.

Buddleia: fragrant blooms attract butterflies

Few shrubs can stand up to California's Central Valley heat and still bloom from early summer through fall. One hardy shrub is butterfly bush (*Buddleia*), and March is the ideal month to plant it. *B. davidii,* the most common species, is a vigorous deciduous to semi-evergreen shrub that can reach 10 feet in height. Long, arching branches are topped with slender 6- to 12-inch clusters of colorful flowers. The blooms are sweetly fragrant and, as the plant's common name suggests, are favored by butterflies. There are many varieties available, including ones with pink, lilac, blue, purple, and white flowers. Some are more compact and lower growing.

Butterfly bush is not a demanding shrub, but it does need room to grow. Plant in full sun and water regularly. To keep the plant in bounds, cut it back to about a foot high in winter.

If local nurseries don't carry butterfly bush, a mail-order source that sells 10 varieties is Mountain Valley Growers, 38325 Pepperweed Rd., Squaw Valley, Calif. 93675; (209) 338-2775. Catalog is free.

New climate maps

When the U.S. Natural Resources Conservation Service decided to produce the most accurate climate maps yet of the United States, they called George Taylor, the Oregon state climatologist, at Oregon State University in Corvallis. He's been on the project ever

since, using computers and huge climatological data bases to create state-by-state pictures of precipitation.

Publication of the maps has just begun. So far, you can get 11- by 17-inch color precipitation maps of the United States, the West, Idaho, Montana, Nevada, Oregon, and Utah; other Western states should be mapped and the results available within a few months.

Maps cost $5 each, including shipping. If you'd like one, specify the region or state and send a check payable to Oregon Climate Service to the service at 316 Strand Hall, Oregon State University, Corvallis, Ore. 97331.

Bottlebrush tree tips

When we asked Lew Whitney of Roger's Gardens in Corona del Mar how he cares for the striking lemon bottlebrush (*Callistemon citrinus*) growing at Casa Pacifica in San Clemente, at first he

sounded a bit puzzled. "We do absolutely nothing to it," he responded. "It thrives in the lawn. We mow the lawn, and we water it."

It's true that lemon bottlebrush demands little and will tolerate a range of conditions from poor soil to heat to smog to wind. To look its best, however, the plant prefers plenty of sun, a moderate amount of moisture (not constantly wet), and good drainage. In alkaline or soggy clay soils, leaves yellow and show signs of chlorosis.

Lemon bottlebrush naturally develops into a large mounding shrub, but with training, it makes a striking small tree that grows to around 20 feet. Nurseries such as Bukhard Nurseries in Pasadena (818/796-4395) sell shrub and tree forms. If it's a tree you want, buy a tree to start with; a 5-gallon standard costs $29 to $35.

Although the plant is somewhat self-shaping, with tight, evenly spaced branches, it's important to maintain the

LEMON BOTTLEBRUSH *demands little care, but early shaping will give it an especially graceful form.*

WOODWIND SECTION *of the garden plays a rustling rhapsody. Keeping a bamboo clump thinned gives stems and leaves more room to move and rub together in the wind. Fatsia (below) music depends on size and number of raindrops that play it.*

Don't talk to your plants— listen to them

They could be giving an open-air concert

LISTEN CAREFULLY. THERE'S music in your garden. The percussion and woodwind instruments are needles, stems, leaves, and branches that patter and tap, whistle and rustle. The musicians that play these instruments are wind and rain, as well as the occasional passing human or pet.

This is a good time to discover plant music, with drippy and blustery weather outside and human noises driven inside, reducing competition with the natural symphony. Winter's cool, moist weather is also conducive to adding sonorous plants to your garden; put dormant plants in the ground now and they'll be ready to grow in spring.

WHISTLES AND RUSTLES

The expression "whistling pines" evolved honestly. With long needles and an open branching pattern, pines make a pleasant whoosh when wind blows through them. In the Northwest, the great native whistlers are white pine (*Pinus monticola*) and ponderosa pine (*P. ponderosa*). These are big trees, though. For garden-scale musical pines, try Tanyosho pine (*P. densiflora* 'Umbraculifera') or Austrian black pine (*P. nigra*). Less melodious because of shorter needles, but still quite tuneful, are shore or beach pine (*P. contorta*) and mugho pine (*P. mugo*).

The best rattlers have leathery leaves set on generous stems. Two eucalyptus (*E. gunnii* and *E. niphophila*) that thrive in the Northwest rattle beautifully, as do members of the genus *Populus*: aspens, cottonwoods, and poplars.

As for rustling, the bamboos are a one-instrument symphony. And big grasses, such as *Miscanthus sinensis,* play well, too. Grasses are especially effective in winter when they are dry and have been left standing. Cut them back in early spring just before new growth emerges at the base.

For maximum resonance, be sure to place plants where they'll be exposed to the wind, unsheltered by your house or other structures. You can play conductor by putting plants of different heights in the wind path.

PATTERS AND PLOPS

"It's a wonderful, restful sound," says Seattle gardener Homer Harris, who used a roofing nail to put a few holes in a rain gutter so that water would drip onto the leaves of his *Fatsia japonica*. Big, firm leaves make the best drums for rain. In addition to fatsia, large-leafed ivies like *Hedera canariensis, H. colchica,* and *H. helix* make excellent water music, as do the large leaves of *Acanthus mollis* and hostas like *H. sieboldiana*. Leaves to be dripped on fare better under low overhangs; if raindrops fall too far, they can riddle the leaves.

TAP, TAP, TAP . . .

A stiff twig on a deciduous tree, judiciously pruned to tap against a window in the wind, will make its presence satisfyingly known all winter. Vine and Japanese maples are excellent tappers. Dogwoods (especially *Cornus kousa* and *C. florida*), as well as the deciduous magnolias, are also good choices. ∎

By Steven R. Lorton

FRAGRANT CLOUDS OF LILAC BLOSSOMS *are a sure sign of spring. Here, 'True Pink' scents the Hulda Klager Lilac Garden in Woodland, Washington. For more on the many species and varieties of lilacs, see page 107.*

APRIL

New plants, new techniques, lovely gardens—check them out in April

Roses are the raison d'être of Diane Johnson's garden in Newport Beach. Everything else is just an accessory. Her French provincial–style house is nothing more than a backdrop for her climbing roses. "You could almost say it was designed for them," Johnson says. Even the annuals and perennials in her bayside cutting garden must share space with roses—in this case, a hybrid tea called 'Royal Highness'.

"I prefer flowers in blues, whites, and pinks because they look best with the French roses I love, both in the garden and in bouquets," she says. Her favorite rose companions include lavender, daisies, and ranunculus.

Finding roses that have the subtle coloring and multipetal shape Johnson adores, as well as long stems and strong fragrance, is challenging enough. But roses in coastal cities such as Newport Beach need to be mildew resistant, too.

Johnson has found no easy answers to the mildew problem. No one family of roses is immune. Among her successes are 'Sombreuil', a climbing tea, 'Cornelia' and 'Danaë', hybrid musks, and 'Belle Story' and 'Heritage', two of David Austin's English roses. Trial and error determines the winners, but patience is necessary, too.

"English and French roses need longer to adjust," she says. "'Jacques Cartier' didn't really take off until the third year. But it was worth waiting for."

Johnson buys roses from nurseries and mail-order catalogs. Her favorite source is the Antique Rose Emporium in Texas. For a catalog ($5), call (800) 441-0002.

Lilac time

Perfuming the air with fragrance, lilacs burst into bloom after the last frosts. They bear single or double flowers in familiar shades of white, blue, pink, and that classic pinkish purple blend we call lilac. You can also find these shrubs with flowers in red, purple, and other colors.

In older plantings, like the one in the Hulda Klager Lilac Garden in Woodland, Washington (pictured on page 104), you'll see mostly big lilac plants. But many newer gardens favor smaller species and varieties. Some are small enough to put in tubs beside your front door, where you can enjoy the perfume every time you pass. You can buy many kinds of lilacs from nurseries.

In the Southwest, look for early lilac flowers now; farther north, bloom comes in May. Colorado gardeners can see a good collection of lilacs at the Denver Botanic Gardens. Wherever you live, you can bet on one thing: when you smell lilacs, you smell spring.

Sweet but seedless watermelons

If you enjoy watermelon but don't like spitting out the seeds, try planting some seedless varieties this month. Two popular varieties are 'Sweet Heart', which has red flesh and weighs 8 to 10 pounds, and 'Redball Seedless', which is a bit larger, weighing as much as 12 pounds. Both are round, icebox-type melons.

Plants that produce seedless watermelons need to be pollinated by regular types to produce a good crop. Put in one plant of a seed-bearing variety for every two to three seedless ones. Choose a seeded melon that looks different from the seedless so

DIANE JOHNSON tends 'Royal Highness' roses, lavender, daisies, and ranunculus in her Newport Beach garden.

you don't confuse fruits at harvest time.

Plant watermelon seed about an inch deep after the soil has warmed (later this month). Keep the soil moist and well fertilized. Fruit of most varieties will be ready to harvest 80 to 85 days after sowing. Look—and listen— for these signs of ripeness: the spot on the bottom turns from white to cream, the two tendrils nearest the fruit dry out, and you hear a dull thump when you tap on the fruit.

Most nurseries and garden centers sell seed of various watermelons. Seed of 'Sweet Heart' can be ordered from Park Seed Co., Cokesbury Road, Greenwood, S.C. 29647; call (800) 845-3369. 'Redball Seedless' can be purchased from W. Atlee Burpee & Co., 300 Park Ave., Warminster, Pa. 18974; call (800) 888-1447. Both mail-order companies offer free catalogs.

A tree that resists Dutch elm disease

During the past 60-plus years, the American elm (*Ulmus americana*) has taken a beating from Dutch elm disease, a devastating fungus that kills trees. Many of the grand old elms across the country have died from the disease, and it has been illegal to plant new elm trees in California— up until now, that is.

The state of California recently approved the sale of American Liberty elm, a disease-resistant strain developed by researchers at the University of Wisconsin through grants from the nonprofit Elm Research Institute (ERI) in Harrisville, New Hampshire.

American Liberty elm is available from ERI when you become a new member. Memberships cost $25 and include a 1- to 2-foot tree and the opportunity to buy six additional trees, ranging from 2 feet ($15 each, plus shipping) to 6 feet ($100 each, plus shipping).

American elms reach as tall as 100 feet, so they need

'TORONTO' TULIPS *bloom around the bases of paper birch trees in a Seattle parking strip.*

plenty of room to grow and spread. They are ideal for large landscapes, parks, and open spaces, and as street trees.

For more information, write to ERI, Elm St., Harrisville, N.H. 03450; call (603) 827-3048.

Rings of tulips around trees

The parking strip planting pictured above employs two simple components: paper birch (*Betula papyrifera*) and 'Toronto' tulips. The planting was designed by Charles Price and Glenn Withey for Brian Coleman of Seattle.

Each 5-foot circle has about 50 bulbs snugly planted in a rich soil mix fortified with a couple of handfuls of 12-12-12 granular fertilizer. When the tulip show fades, the spent blooms are deadheaded. As soon as the foliage begins to yellow, the tulip bulbs are dug and laid out to dry for replanting elsewhere in fall (tulips are notorious for not coming back strongly in consecutive years). In summer, bedding annuals go in the circle.

As the birches grow bigger, their aggressive roots make it difficult to grow plants around them. A deciduous magnolia might be a better choice.

Miniature flax for small spaces

'Jack Spratt' flax is a little hedgehog of a plant, about the size and shape of a clump of blue fescue but with dusky blood red leaves. This miniature mountain flax (*Phormium colensoi*) adds drama to a perennial border, looks handsome spilling over rocks (especially when backed by silver plants), and makes a splendid foil for bright or pastel cut flowers in a colored bowl. Like blue fescue, 'Jack Spratt' makes a good ground cover for a small area. Or you could try combining the two in a checkerboard pattern.

If your nursery doesn't stock 'Jack Spratt', ask it to order the flax from San Marcos Growers in Santa Barbara or Hines Nurseries in Irvine; both are wholesalers.

Flowering maple: a beautiful gamble in the Northwest

Flowering maple (*Abutilon megapotamicum*) is a Brazilian native only marginally hardy in the mild climates of the coastal Northwest. Nevertheless, it's a plant that Portland landscape designer John Nausieda loves to use. "It's filled with those little Chinese lantern blossoms from May right up until frost," says Nausieda. "It survives 8 out of 10 winters. I always have a plant or two in pots to move indoors for winter. And it's a cinch to grow from cuttings."

This flowering shrub is well worth a try in climate zones 4–7. It's a deciduous plant in the Northwest. Some winters, it dies to the ground and springs back later from the roots. It bears dangling bell-shaped red and yellow flowers and maplelike leaves. In the Northwest, this plant can reach 8 to 10 feet.

Plants can be hard to find; you may see them at arboretum and botanical garden plant sales. If a friend has a plant, ask for a few pieces of stem, dip them in rooting hormone, plant the cuttings in potting soil, keep them moist until roots form, then transplant into larger containers. One mail-order source for *A. megapotamicum* is Trans-Pacific Nursery, 16065 Oldsville Rd., McMinnville, Ore. 97128; (503) 472-6215. Plants cost $5 each, including shipping.

Give the plant full sun and loose, rich soil. If you plant it in a protected spot, such as next to the foundation of a house, you'll increase its chances of surviving a cold winter.

Speedy, supersweet white corn

If you like supersweet white corn, try a new one called 'Sweet Magic'. It races from seed to harvest in 74 days, making it the earliest supersweet white on the market. If you live in a short-summer area, plant it after all danger of frost is past. You should have 7-inch ears by summer's end.

'JACK SPRATT' FLAX *is a miniature phormium that's perfect in small borders or as a ground cover.*

'Sweet Magic' is available from Harris Seeds, Box 22960, Rochester, N.Y. 14692. Catalog is free.

Arizona's sweet antique melon

For decades, gardeners in northern Arizona have shared seed of a sweet, early-maturing heirloom cantaloupe with no name. Now it's available commercially, and it holds promise for anybody who wants to grow melons in borderline melon climates. Cataloged as Northern Arizona melon, it has pink-orange flesh and yellow skin with orange and green markings. At maturity, it's about the size of a large cantaloupe.

Seed of this melon is available from Bountiful Gardens, 18001 Shafer Ranch Rd., Willits, Calif. 95490. Seed list is free.

Need a quick vine to cover a fence?

Silver lace vine (*Polygonum aubertii*) is a delicate but dense plant that blooms prolifically and thrives throughout the West. In fact, it's such a rampant vine that many gardeners choose to avoid it. But it has great value, especially in the cold, dry climates of the inland Northwest (*Sunset Western Garden Book* climate zones 1–3), where it will scramble up and spread out 12 to 15 feet in the first year.

Silver lace vine bears sprays of foamy white flowers in midsummer that stay on till fall. Its leaves are heart shaped and 1½ to 2½ inches long. Once established, the vine tolerates drought and poor soil. If you give it a rich growing medium and regular irrigation, it grows faster.

This plant is a great candidate for covering a chain-link fence. As it grows, you can push the new shoots through the links until it reaches the top. Shear the vine in late fall or early spring to keep it from growing out of bounds. If the

K. BRYAN SWEZEY

FLOWER SPIKES *of pink and white foxglove dominate this spring border in Michael Bates's garden in Santa Rosa, California. Beyond, roses cascade over trellises.*

vine gets scraggly, cut it to the ground and it will spring up anew. If you set out plants from nursery cans now, you'll see amazing growth and a great bloom show by August.

Spring-blooming border

If you love flowers, you've got to be crazy about April. Tulips are at their peak early this month, spring-flowering perennials fully awaken from their winter slumber bursting with blooms, and roses are starting to strut their stuff. The garden above, belonging to landscape designer Michael Bates of Santa Rosa, California, epitomizes this April floral bonanza. On 1½ acres of cultivated land, Bates grows perennials and more than 100 different roses.

In spring, the border edging the front of the lawn is full of flowers in shades of pink, white, blue, purple, and yel-

low: pink and white foxglove (*Digitalis purpurea*), tall white *Nicotiana alata,* white peonies, deep blue 'Belladonna' delphiniums, blue Chinese forget-me-nots, purple Siberian irises, low-growing catmint, dwarf lavender, pale yellow daylilies, and gray-leafed verbascum.

The rest of the garden is full of mostly old roses, including hybrid musks such as 'Penelope' and noisettes such as 'Madame Alfred Carrière'. Bates also grows old-fashioned-looking David Austin's English roses; two favorites are 'English Garden' and 'Symphony'.

Seed-spacing tool you can make

Evani Lupinek is a San Luis Obispo artist and gardener who designs basic tools for easy, productive raised-bed gardening. She created these seed-planting templates,

for example, to simplify planting, save seeds, and eliminate the need for thinning. She presses a template into a prepared garden bed, and the protruding dowels make planting holes for seeds. The template also flattens the area around the holes, making them easier to see. Spacing of the dowels varies by template to accommodate the seed spacing requirements of different types of plants.

To make a template, Lupinek starts with a square-foot piece of ¾-inch plywood or particleboard and marks locations for the ½-inch-diameter dowels. She then drills ½-inch-deep holes into the board using a ½-inch bit, and glues and taps the 1½-inch-long dowels in place. When in place, each dowel extends 1 inch beyond the board. On the reverse side of the board, Lupinek attaches a handle or knob, used to press the template into the ground.

EVANI LUPINEK of San Luis Obispo designed these seed-planting templates to save time and eliminate the need for thinning.

The key to the template is the spacing of the dowels. When planting seeds for beets, carrots, onions, and radishes, Lupinek uses a template with 16 dowels spaced 3 inches apart. A template with nine dowels at 4-inch intervals is used for bush beans. She employs a template with four dowels spaced 6 inches apart for chard and leaf lettuce. For larger plants like corn, peppers, broccoli, cabbage, and eggplant, a template with a single centered dowel works best.

Lupinek sells detailed plans for the templates, as well as plans for shade structures and other homemade garden accessories. For a free brochure, send a self-addressed, stamped business-size envelope to Growing Solutions, Box 842, Grover Beach, Calif. 93483.

Buffalo grass without tears

You almost need a full-time sentry to start buffalo grass from seed. That thug, Bermuda grass, is always lurking in the neighborhood, just waiting to invade. Starting a lawn from sod is a lot easier. Now it's cheaper, too.

West Coast Turf, the only supplier of buffalo grass sod in Southern California, recently reduced its price from 40 cents per square foot to 35, delivered. Though still expensive compared with Bermuda sod (about 25 cents), buffalo grass sod costs only pennies more than dwarf fescue.

Two hybrids are '609' and 'Prairie'. '609' is the darker and denser of the two, but both hybrids are more turflike than Texas buffalo grass, and neither forms seed heads.

Since buffalo grass is a warm-season type, April is a good month to install sod. Gardeners in interior Southern California and high-desert areas should wait another month, until the danger of frost has passed.

"Water savings with buffalo grass is considerable," says Jeff Cole of West Coast Turf. He's even more impressed with its energy savings: "You only have to mow it about once a month, even during the summer."

For more information, call (800) 447-1840.

Customized plant markers

During the past few years, new designs of plant markers have been showing up in catalogs and garden stores. Some are made of plastic or metal that you can write on. Others are made of clay or plastic and come with plant names already printed on them.

Now a company called Garden Expressions is going one step further by offering custom-engraved plant markers. The attractive, durable plastic markers come in several sizes and shapes, four lettering styles, and 17 plain colors, five faux-stone designs, and eight metallic colors. You can have any text you want engraved on the marker as long as it fits in the allotted space.

Depending on style, size, and quantity ordered, prices (per marker) range from 75 cents to $5. For more information or a catalog ($2), write to Garden Expressions, Box 1358, Loveland, Colo. 80539; call (303) 663-7989.

A colorful, flavorful winter squash

With its unusual markings and multicolored skin, acorn squash elicits a "wow" and a smile from just about anyone who sees it. But 'Carnival' squash (pictured below) is worth growing for its flavorful golden yellow flesh alone.

Last year, head gardener Rick LaFrentz grew 'Carnival' in *Sunset*'s display garden in Menlo Park, California. It's a vigorous, semibush plant that produces six to eight 4- to 5-inch-diameter squash per plant. LaFrentz finds this squash particularly tasty and says it stores well because of its tough skin. The firm exterior also makes it a bit difficult to cut, so you'll need a large, sharp knife on hand when you're ready to cook it.

Sow seeds in an area that gets full sun and offers plenty of room for plants to spread. Water regularly. Allow squash to mature on the vine; pick when the skin is hard (you can barely dent it with a fingernail).

Seed of 'Carnival' is available from Harris Seeds, 60 Saginaw Dr., Box 22960, Rochester, N.Y. 14692; (800) 514-4441. Catalog is free.

Heirloom vegetable seedlings by mail

Heirloom vegetables are all the rage, as you may have noticed by scanning this year's seed catalogs. If you don't have the space or time to sow seeds, you can now buy more than 200 different types of heirloom vegetable seedlings by mail from Santa Barbara Heirloom Seedling Nursery.

'CARNIVAL' *winter squash has colorful skin, tasty golden flesh.*

Owners JoAnna LaForce and Russ Waldrop are avid organic gardeners who have searched throughout the United States for authentic family or cultural heirloom seed stock. Some of the vegetables they sell come from seed that has been grown in the U.S. since the mid-1800s. 'Tom Thumb', an English-American lettuce dating to 1853, is the oldest continuously grown lettuce in the United States, and 'Brandywine' is an Amish tomato dating back to 1910.

Organically grown seedlings are sold in 3-inch pots in multiples of six (varieties can be mixed) for $2.95 per seedling plus $5.45 for shipping. Seedling choices include 35 tomatoes, 40 culinary herbs, 34 sweet and hot peppers, 12 squash, 10 edible flowers, and six watermelons. They also sell specialty gift seed assortments, such as exotic lettuces and plants for salsa.

For a free list, send a self-addressed, stamped envelope to Santa Barbara Heirloom Seedling Nursery, Box 4153, Santa Barbara, Calif. 93140; call (805) 968-5444. The seedlings are unconditionally guaranteed.

Pampas grass: exotic beauty or invasive pest?

There's a debate going on in the horticultural world about *Cortaderia selloana,* commonly known as pampas grass. This large plant, which can grow 20 feet tall, has sawtoothed, grassy leaves and produces long stalks of white to pink plumes. This isn't the same species of pampas grass known as *C. jubata,* which often grows wild by roadsides and invades native habitats; horticulturists agree that *C. jubata* is an exotic pest.

The current debate concerns whether *C. selloana* also is an invasive weed. Many gardeners and horticulturists have thought this pampas grass to be the benign rel-

ative of its pesky cousin. But recent research in San Luis Obispo County and reports from Northern California have shown that under some circumstances, *C. selloana* can naturalize and spread.

The California Exotic Pest Plant Council lists both types of pampas grass as invasive weeds. Carla M. D'Antonio, assistant professor in the Department of Integrative Biology at UC Berkeley, recommends halting the importation of all *Cortaderia* and discouraging the use of pampas grass in all landscape plantings.

For now, the best advice is to avoid planting *Cortaderia,* remove it from areas that border wildlands, and dig out and destroy volunteer seedlings whenever they appear.

Korean grass grows between patio pavers

To soften the hard lines of a patio in Exeter, California, the owners planted Korean grass (*Zoysia tenuifolia*) between adobe pavers. Korean grass is a slow-growing, warm-season grass that spreads by underground runners. It grows best in full sun or partial shade and should be planted in midspring with the onset of warm weather. Korean grass rarely grows over 4 inches high. It goes dormant and turns brown in winter.

The adobe pavers were spaced about 2½ inches apart on a bed of sand. Quarter-inch-diameter drip irrigation lines were laid in one direction between the pavers. The Korean grass, which is sold in flats, was cut into inch-wide strips, planted between the pavers, and firmed-in with sand. It took several months for the grass to fill in the gaps.

In areas where there is constant foot traffic, the Korean grass stays neat without mowing. In other parts of the patio, it is mowed twice during the growing season to keep it from getting too tall and becoming a hazard. Once established, this grass needs

FUZZY STRIPS *of Korean grass grow in gaps between adobe pavers on a patio.*

SCOTT ANGER

water only once a week in summer. In fall, it is cut back to paver level with a nylon string trimmer.

'Sweet 100' bears thousands of tomatoes

In a poll of *Sunset* readers, 'Early Girl' emerged as one of the best tomatoes for flavor. But Al Hangge of Alameda, California, begs to differ; he says that you can't beat the 'Sweet 100' cherry tomato for flavor and production.

Last year, Hangge planted a 'Sweet 100' seedling in a flower bed next to a 6-foot fence. He tied the plant to the fence. By summer, it had reached 7 feet tall and 18 feet wide. Just for fun, Hangge decided to keep track of his harvest. By the time the plant finally froze in December, it had produced 2,890 ripe tomatoes and 274 green tomatoes.

'Sweet 100' is adapted to any climate. Most nurseries sell seedlings; look for plants sometime this month in mild climates, May and June at higher elevations.

Red as a ... sunflower?

In this year's crop of new seed catalogs, you'll find a pleasing exception to the rule that sunflowers are always yellow: a multiflowered red called 'Prado Red'.

It produces 15 to 20 blooms

per plant, each 5 to 6 inches in diameter. They grow on long stems, so you can easily use them in cut-flower arrangements. Plants grow 5 to 6 feet tall.

Give 'Prado Red' full sun and regular feeding and watering (as you would any other sunflower), and you'll have abundant blooms by summer's end.

You can order seed of 'Prado Red' from Territorial Seed Co., Box 157, Cottage Grove, Ore. 97424. Catalog is free.

New biocontrol nips gnats

Fungus gnats, often mistaken for fruit flies, are tiny (⅛ inch or smaller) flying insects with clear mosquito-like wings. They are common in greenhouses and many homes where house plants are grown. Fungus gnats are usually just a nuisance, occasionally flying into food or drink or showing up dead along windowsills. However, their larvae can sometimes damage plant roots, causing the foliage to wilt and die. Susceptible plants include bulbs, gerbera daisies, gloxinia, and ornamental peppers.

Fungus gnats breed in decaying organic matter such as is found in most potting soils. To check for them, purchase a yellow sticky trap (a yellow card covered with a sticky material) at a nursery or garden center. Place it near your plants this month (gnats are most active in spring), and count the number of flies stuck to it after a few days.

If you catch more than a few gnats, use a new form of the biological control *Bacillus thuringiensis,* sold as Knock-Out Gnat, to control the larvae. Apply it as a soil drench according to label instructions. If you can't find Knock-Out Gnat locally, send for a free catalog from Gardens Alive, 5100 Schenley Place, Lawrenceburg, Ind. 47025. One pint costs $12.95, plus shipping.

NORMAN A. PLATE

Tool of the Month

You mow the lawn. You fertilize the lawn. Maybe the jobs could be combined into one, or so thought one manufacturer. The result is Mow & Feed, the fertilizer hopper attachment shown above. You mount it to any recent 21-inch Lawn Boy or Toro mower, adjust the flow rate, then spread fertilizer, compost, or lime over your lawn as you mow. Mow & Feed is available from Toro dealers for around $50. A separate attachment allows the spreader to be used on its own, apart from a mower.

Reining in a beautiful pest

On the surface, Mexican evening primrose (*Oenothera berlandieri*) is the perfect plant. It's an easy-to-grow spring-summer bloomer with airy, poppylike pink flowers. It's drought tolerant, requires little or no maintenance, and grows well in just about anything.

But in warm and sunny Southern California gardens, especially in amended, fast-draining soils, the plant turns into a tiger, rivaling Bermuda grass with its tenacity.

Weeding won't work; the plant propagates fast with prolific underground runners. An herbicide such as Roundup will slay the lovely monster but may have to be painted on leaf by leaf, since Mexican evening primrose tends to intertwine with prized plants.

If your flower bed is overrun, there is one surefire solution: dig up the entire bed and start over. It's a year-long process that begins in fall, so forget about trying to control the plant this season. Sometime in October, dig up any beloved perennials, wash roots to remove invasive runners, and plant in containers—their homes for the next year. Beginning in spring, spray young Mexican evening primrose sprouts with an herbicide. If you continue to see active growth, spray monthly until sprouting ceases. In fall, replant your perennials.

An almost everblooming strawflower

In mild climates, sunny yellow flowers decorate *Helichrysum bracteatum* 'Dargan Hill Monarch' for most of the year. A perennial form of the annual species, this plant bears 3-inch-wide daisylike strawflowers. The flowers actually dry on the plant and hold their color for several months. Blooms also can be cut fresh and allowed to dry for use as everlasting

NORMAN A. PLATE

EVERLASTING FLOWERS *cover Helichrysum bracteatum 'Dargan Hill Monarch' almost year-round.*

flowers. They are short-stemmed, so you may need wire to extend stems for use in dried arrangements.

The shrubby gray-leafed plant grows 2½ feet tall and 3 to 4 feet wide, making it useful as a specimen plant or a medium-size ground cover when plants are grouped together. It looks particularly handsome when planted with other dry-climate plants, such as the colorful dwarf forms of New Zealand flax (*Phormium tenax*) and ground-hugging 'Homestead Purple' verbena.

Plant 'Dargan Hill Monarch' in full sun and, preferably, well-drained soil

(it's shorter-lived in heavy soil). Water regularly to get the plant established the first season of growth, then cut back to watering once every couple of weeks. Trim off old flowers when they lose their color.

If you can't find 'Dargan Hill Monarch' at your nursery, ask it to order the strawflower from Rosendale Nursery (wholesale only) in Watsonville, California.

By Debra Lee Baldwin, Sharon Cohoon, Steven R. Lorton, Jim McCausland, Lynn Ocone, Feliz E. Satir, Lauren Bonar Swezey, Lance Walheim

April Checklist
■
PACIFIC NORTHWEST

AMEND SOIL. You can amend soil when the ground is dry enough to dig. Spade planting beds, adding generous amounts of peat moss, leaf mold, compost, and well-rotted manure. Rake the amended soil, let it settle for a week, then plant.

BUY BEDDING PLANTS. In zones 4–7 (see map), you can buy tender bedding plants to set out once all danger of hard frost has passed. Celosia, geraniums, impatiens, marigolds, and sweet alyssum are good candidates. If you're itching to plant, buy frost-tolerant plants such as dusty miller and lobelia to set out now. In zones 1–3, wait until May.

CHECK DAHLIAS. Many gardeners in zones 4–7 leave dahlia tubers in the ground during winter. If you dug yours up, take them out of storage this month and plant them. In zones 1–3, leave the tubers in storage for another month. Look for signs of rot or dehydration on stored tubers. If you find rot, cut out bad spots and dust tubers with sulfur. If tubers are withered, sprinkle them lightly with water to plump them up.

COMPOST. Add garden debris to the compost pile. Mixing new material with old compost and high-nitrogen fertilizer helps speed decomposition. Turn the pile; if rains are scant, keep it moist.

CONTROL TENT CATERPILLARS. In the coastal Northwest, tent caterpillars camped out in cherry trees spin webby tents this month. You can blast the tents out of trees with a strong jet of water from the hose, then spray with *Bacillus thuringiensis*.

DEADHEAD FLOWERS. Removing faded flowers improves the look of a plant, arrests the process of seed development (thereby channeling a plant's energy into growth), and encourages more bloom. You can snap most rhododendron blossoms off with your fingers, but be careful not to take the new growth buds that appear just below the old bloom head.

FEED CONIFERS. Conifers wake from dormancy this month. Scratch the soil under the plant and scatter some high-nitrogen fertilizer around it.

FEED SPRING-FLOWERING SHRUBS. As soon as blooms fade, feed plants with a high-nitrogen fertilizer to encourage strong new growth.

FIGHT SLUGS. If a run of dry days is forecast, bait liberally to rid the garden of overwintered and newly hatched slugs. Keep toxic bait away from pets and small children.

Sunset Western Garden Book climate zones

(1–3)　(4–7)

MOVE OUT OVERWINTERED PLANTS. In zones 4–7, cymbidiums can go outdoors early in the month. Begonias, fuchsias, and geraniums should go out mid- to late month; they can take a chill but won't survive a frost.

MOW LAWNS. If the grass is dry enough to cut, mow the lawn.

PLANT BARE-ROOT. In zones 1–3, you can still plant bare-root stock, but do so quickly. Everything from cane berries to ornamental trees will be available in nurseries. Keep roots moist and put plants in the ground as soon as the soil is workable.

PLANT BERRIES. Throughout the Northwest, this is a good month to plant blackberries, blueberries, raspberries, and strawberries.

PLANT SUMMER BULBS. In zones 4–7, nurseries will offer calla, crocosmia, dahlia, gladiolus, ranunculus, tigridia, tritonia, and others.

PLANT VEGETABLES. Throughout the Northwest, plant cabbage, carrots, lettuce, parsnips, peas, potatoes, radishes, spinach, and Swiss chard.

April Checklist

■

NORTHERN CALIFORNIA

Where do you garden?

The following recommendations refer to the elevation at which you garden.

L=Low (zones 14–17)
H=High (zones 1–3)

Climate zones are from the *Sunset Western Garden Book.*

APPLY MULCH. L: To save water, smother weeds, and keep soil cool, spread 1 to 3 inches of bark chips, compost, wood shavings, or other organic material under shrubs and trees, around flowers and vegetables, and in pots. To prevent crown rot, keep mulch away from trunks and stems.

CARE FOR POTATOES. L: Pinch off flower buds before they open so more energy goes into tuber production. Keep soil moist but not soggy, especially while tubers are beginning to set (this happens soon after plants flower, if buds are not pinched off).

CARE FOR SPRING GIFT PLANTS. To keep plants such as cineraria, Easter cactus, Easter lily, gloxinia, kalanchoe, and Rieger begonia blooming longer indoors, set them in a cool place away from drafts that gets bright, indirect light. Or set plants outdoors in filtered sun (in high elevations, wait until last frost has passed). Keep the soil moist but not wet, except for kalanchoe, which grows best if the soil almost dries out between waterings.

CONTROL ANTS. L: Ants feed off honeydew secreted by aphids, scale insects, and other pests. To keep ants off trees and shrubs such as camellias, citrus, and roses, wrap the trunks with a 1- to 2-inch-wide strip of masking tape and coat with a sticky barrier like Tanglefoot. Keep the barriers free of dirt and check them for breaks; reapply barriers when necessary.

FEED ACID LOVERS. L: After azaleas, camellias, and rhododendrons finish blooming, feed them with an acid fertilizer. Also, remove spent blooms on azaleas and rhodies; be careful not to damage emerging growth.

PLANT BARE-ROOT. H: Deciduous plants such as cane berries, flowering shrubs, flowering vines, deciduous fruit and nut trees, grapes, rhubarb, roses, and strawberries are available now. Bare-root

planting is the best and least-expensive way to start many new trees, shrubs, and perennials.

PLANT CITRUS. L: 5- to 7-gallon trees are likely to become established faster than older, larger ones. Plant in full sun. Dig a planting hole at least twice as wide as the rootball, but not much deeper. Water thoroughly—about twice a week until established, then once a week or so (more often in sandy soil).

PLANT SUMMER FLOWERS. L: All warm-season flowers can be planted now. Try ageratum, dwarf dahlias, globe amaranth, impatiens, lobelia, Madagascar periwinkle, marigold, petunia, phlox, portulaca, salvia, sanvitalia, statice, sunflower, sweet alyssum, verbena, and zinnia.

PLANT VEGETABLES, HERBS. L: Sow seeds of beans, corn, cucumbers, greens (chard, lettuce, mustard, spinach), most root crops (beets, carrots, radishes, turnips), and squash. Leave space for another planting—two to three weeks later—of bush beans and root crops. Set out seedlings of eggplant, peppers, and tomatoes. Shop nurseries for herbs, including basil, chives, mint, oregano, parsley, and thyme.

PRUNE. L: After new growth appears, prune freeze-damaged wood on tender plants such as bougainvillea and citrus. Also, prune to shape spring-flowering shrubs (after bloom) and overgrown hedges. **H:** Finish pruning deciduous fruit and ornamental trees before new growth emerges. Prune flowering vines, grapes, and roses. Wait until after bloom to prune forsythia, spiraea, and other spring-flowering shrubs.

SOW HARDY VEGETABLES. H: As soon as soil can be worked, sow seeds of beets, broccoli, cabbage, carrots, cauliflower, endive, kohlrabi, lettuce, onions, parsley, parsnips, peas, potatoes, radishes, spinach, Swiss chard, and turnips.

WATCH FOR INSECTS. Be on the lookout for aphids; hose them off with a strong blast of water or spray with insecticidal soap. If unfamiliar pest problems arise, county extension agents and master gardeners in your area can help identify the cause and suggest solutions (look in the phone book under Cooperative Extension in the county government listings).

April Checklist
CENTRAL VALLEY

COMPOST. Add lawn clippings and garden debris to the compost pile. Keep the pile moist but not wet, and add a handful or two of high-nitrogen fertilizer per 18 to 24 inches of depth. Turn the pile with a pitchfork every week or two.

CONTROL PESTS. Control snails and slugs by handpicking or putting out bait or copper barriers. Hose aphids off foliage. Cover seedlings with netting or floating row covers to protect them from birds. Spray *Bacillus thuringiensis* or pyrethrins to control worms on maturing cole crops.

FERTILIZE. Now is the time to feed lawns, citrus, roses, fall-planted shrubs, and ground covers. Bedding plants benefit from monthly feedings. To keep citrus leaves deep green, spray leaves with liquid fertilizer containing chelated forms of three essential micronutrients: iron, zinc, and manganese.

PLANT ANNUAL FLOWERS. Set out spring bedding plants such as dianthus, nemesia, pansy, and viola; sow or set out summer favorites such as cosmos, marigolds, and zinnia. Also consider heat lovers such as annual salvias, asters, celosia, dwarf dahlias, Madagascar periwinkle, petunias, and portulaca. Fibrous begonias and impatiens do well in shady gardens.

PLANT CITRUS, SUB-TROPICALS. Now that the danger of frost is past, start planting tender plants such as bougainvillea, citrus, and hibiscus.

PLANT PERENNIALS. Easy-care choices now flowering (or about to) in nurseries include bearded iris, coreopsis, dianthus, echinops, gaillardia, penstemon, salvia, and yarrow.

PLANT SUMMER BULBS. For planting beds or containers, try caladium, calla, canna, dahlia, gladiolus, lily, montbretia, tuberose, tuberous begonia, and watsonia.

PLANT VEGETABLES, HERBS. Set out seedlings of eggplant, pepper, and tomato. Sow seed of beans, carrots, corn, cucumbers, and radishes. Herbs to plant this month include basil, oregano, rosemary, tarragon, and thyme.

THIN FRUIT. Pinch off excess pea-size fruit from apples, apricots, peaches, plums, and nectarines. Remove injured or weak-looking fruit first, then all but one or two in each cluster. Thin fruits to at least 4 to 6 inches apart.

TRIM HEDGES. Shear soon after the big flush of spring growth, cutting the top a little narrower than the base to compensate for faster top growth and to let light reach the lower limbs.

WATER AS NEEDED. Watch young seedlings and transplants carefully. If the weather warms, water when the top few inches of soil is dry.

Redding

Lake Tahoe

Sacramento

Fresno

Bakersfield

*Sunset
Western Garden Book*
climate zones

Valley and foothills (7–9, 14)

WEED. Pull or hoe out weeds soon, before they scatter seeds. Spray stubborn types with a chemical herbicide such as glyphosate.

April Checklist

SOUTHERN CALIFORNIA

CARE FOR GRAPES. In high- and low-desert areas (zones 11 and 13), control mildew with sulfur dust or lime sulfur spray when new shoots are 5 to 8 inches long. Repeat as needed. Water deeply while plants are actively growing.

CHECK FOR IRON DEFICIENCY. Along the coast (zones 22–24) and in inland areas (zones 18–21), treat yellowing camellias, citrus, geraniums (*Pelargonium*), hibiscus, roses, and other ornamentals with chelated iron.

CHOOSE SUMMER ANNUALS WISELY. Most summer annuals need lots of water; use them sparingly and cluster for more impact. Less thirsty varieties include celosia, cosmos, portulaca, sanvitalia, and verbena. Choose healthy plants that are not rootbound; smaller plants in cell-packs generally adjust more quickly to the garden than plants in 4-inch containers.

COMPOST. Put grass clippings (except grasses that reproduce by runners, such as Bermuda), kitchen vegetable waste, leaves, and prunings on the compost pile. For fastest breakdown, chop or shred branches. Add a layer of garden soil and a handful of fertilizer every foot or so. Turn and mix pile frequently for quicker results, and keep it moist as a damp sponge.

CONTINUE PLANTING SUMMER BULBS. In coastal, inland, and low-desert areas, cannas and dahlias are available now. Both grow fast and provide a long season of bloom. Tuberoses, which bear deliciously fragrant flowers, are also available this month. In low-desert areas, buy gladiolus corms; store in the refrigerator crisper until planting time in August.

CONTROL WEEDS. Dig out deep-rooted weeds such as dandelions with a hand weeder (water first to loosen soil). Slip weeder into soil and pry against taproot to make sure you get the entire length. Use a sharp hoe to scrape out other kinds of weeds while they're small; cut them just below the soil surface.

DIVIDE CYMBIDIUMS. In coastal and inland areas, it's time to refresh plants in pots packed with bulbs. Knock the root mass out of the pot and separate as many clumps as you can by hand or with pruning shears. Keep at least three healthy bulbs (with foliage) in each division. To discourage rot, dust cuts with sulfur.

Bishop ●

● San Luis Obispo

● Tehachapi

● Santa Barbara

● Lancaster

Sunset Western Garden Book climate zones

● Los Angeles

● Palm Springs

Mountain (1–3)

High desert (11)

Low desert (13)

Coastal and inland (14–24)

● San Diego

FERTILIZE PLANTS. Everything from turf to trees will appreciate a feeding (10-10-10 is a good choice). Apply lightly, though. Overfeeding now will result in softer, thirstier growth in summer.

MANAGE PESTS. April and aphids are practically synonymous. To control pests, blast foliage and flowers with strong streams of water or apply insecticidal soap. Prevent severe caterpillar damage with *Bacillus thuringiensis* (BT), sold in liquid or powder form. Look for Safer and Attack brands or the trade names Dipel and Thuricide.

MULCH TO COOL SOIL. Spread 1 to 3 inches of mulch in flower beds and around trees and shrubs to keep soil cool as temperatures warm. In sandy soil, cultivate mulch into the soil to keep spring winds from blowing the mulch away.

PLANT SUMMER VEGETABLES. Coast gardeners can plant another round of quick-maturing, cool-season crops such as arugula, chard, lettuce, and spinach. Inland, plant warm-season crops such as beans, corn, cucumber, and squash. In late April, add heat-loving eggplant, peppers, and tomatoes. High-desert gardeners should delay planting for two to four weeks, until the danger of frost has passed.

SPRING-CLEAN HOUSE PLANTS. To remove winter dust and soot, treat plants to a spring shower from the garden hose. Now is also a good time to repot crowded plants, leach salts from the soil, and control pests with insecticidal soap.

ANYWHERE IN THE WEST, TACKLE THESE CHORES:

☐ **APPLY MULCH.** Spread a 2- to 3-inch layer of organic mulch to suppress weeds, hold in moisture, and keep roots cool when the weather heats up. Put it around annuals, perennials, trees, and shrubs, espe-cially if summers are hot and dry where you live. Until the weather warms up, keep mulch a few inches back from warm-season vegetables—their roots can use the heat to get started.

☐ **CONTROL WEEDS.** Hoe tiny weeds early in the day, when sun and dryness can help kill tiny roots. Wa-ter areas with larger weeds to loosen roots' grip on the soil, then take weeds out by hand.

☐ **ROTATE VEGETABLE BEDS.** To prevent dis-ease build-up in the soil, ro-tate crops. The best strategy is to keep any given bed from holding the same kinds of plants more than once every few years. A good ro-tation might be solanaceous plants (eggplants, peppers, potatoes, tomatoes) one year; cucurbits (cucumbers, melons, pumpkins, squash) the next; corn the next; legumes (beans, peas) the next; cole crops (broccoli, cabbage, cauliflower) after that; and finally, salad crops (carrots, lettuce).

IN THE INTERMOUNTAIN WEST, DO THESE CHORES:

☐ **APPLY DORMANT SPRAY.** Apply a mix-ture of horticultural spray, oil, and lime sulfur or oil and copper to control insects and disease. If rain washes it off within three days, re-apply. Keep oil and copper off walls, fences, and walks, which might become stained.

☐ **FEED LAWNS.** Apply 1 to 2 pounds high-nitrogen fertilizer per 1,000 square feet of turf. Use 2 pounds if your lawn grows in poor soil or is heavily used. Water in well.

☐ **PLANT BARE-ROOT.** Set out bare-root straw-berries, raspberries, black-berries, blueberries, and fruit and ornamental trees. Don't let roots dry out before you plant, or plants will die.

☐ **PLANT HARDY VEG-ETABLES.** Beet, carrot, endive, kohlrabi, lettuce, onion, parsley, parsnip, pea, radish, spinach, Swiss chard, and turnip can all be sown as soon as soil is pre-pared. Also, set out bare-root asparagus, horserad-ish, and rhubarb, and transplants of broccoli, brussels sprouts, cabbage, cauliflower, and onion; plant seed potatoes.

☐ **PRUNE.** Finish pruning deciduous trees, vines, and roses early in the month before new growth emerges. After bloom, prune for-sythia, spiraea, and other early-flowering shrubs.

IN THE SOUTHWEST'S LOW AND INTERMEDIATE DESERTS:

☐ **FEED LAWNS.** Give Bermuda grass 3 to 4 pounds high-nitrogen fertil-izer per 1,000 square feet about two weeks after the grass greens up. Be sure to water it in well.

☐ **PLANT ANNUALS.** Set out ageratum, calliop-sis (*Coreopsis tinctoria*), celosia, cosmos, four o'clock, globe amaranth, gloriosa daisy (*Rudbeckia*), kochia, lisianthus (*Eustoma grandiflorum*), Madagascar periwinkle (*Catharanthus roseus*), marigold, Mexican sunflower (*Tithonia*), portu-laca, strawflower, and zin-nia.

☐ **PLANT CITRUS.** Plant citrus from 5- to 7-gal-lon containers this month. All kinds like full sun. Plant in a hole that's the same depth as the rootball, but three times as wide. Build a watering basin around the tree. At first, water two or three times per week, then less often as the season pro-gresses. To protect trees from sunburn, wrap trunks in white cloth or newspa-pers, or apply a coat of white latex paint.

☐ **PLANT LAWNS.** When average night tempera-tures top 70°, plant hybrid Bermuda grass.

☐ **PLANT PERENNIALS.** Buy seed or plants of chrysanthemum, columbine, coreopsis, gaillardia, ger-bera, hollyhock, Michael-mas daisy, salvia, and Shasta daisy; gazania and geranium are usually sold only as plants. Water new plants well, and mulch to conserve soil moisture.

☐ **PLANT SUMMER BULBS.** Set out summer bulbs such as caladium, canna, crinum, dahlia, daylily, gladiolus, iris, and montbretia (*Crocosmia* and *Tritonia*). You can also buy agapanthus, society garlic (*Tulbaghia violacea*), and zephyranthes in containers.

☐ **PLANT VEGETABLES.** In the low desert (Phoenix), sow beans and cucumbers by mid-April; set out eggplant, okra, peanut, squash, and sweet potato any time this month. In the intermediate desert (Tucson), sow cucumber, melon, okra, pumpkin, soybean, squash, and wa-termelon, and set out seedlings of eggplant, pep-per, sweet potato, and tomato. Stake tomatoes at planting time.

Wake up in a dream

AT THESE SIX

BED-AND-BREAKFASTS

AROUND THE WEST,

THE GARDENS ARE

AS MUCH A DRAW

AS THE ACCOMMODATIONS.

THE INNKEEPERS

SHARE THEIR TIPS

BY   FOR BEAUTIFUL

JEFF

PHILLIPS   LANDSCAPES

garden

WHAT GARDEN LOVER hasn't dreamed at least once of waking up in a sun-filled room overlooking a garden in which everything is green, blooming ... in a word, perfect? For the price of a night's lodging, you can wake up in that sunny room, stroll outside to smell the flowers, kick off your slippers to feel the cool grass under your feet, even pull up a lounge chair in a quiet corner to read a novel or sip a cup of coffee and listen to the birds sing.

In a *Sunset* survey of hundreds of bed-and-breakfasts and inns with fewer than 25 rooms, we turned up dozens of gorgeous gardens, but the six on the following pages ranked among the best at achieving dramatic, problem-solving landscape design on

SOOKE HARBOUR HOUSE guest relaxes amid splendors of a Vancouver Island gourmet's garden, where every plant but the lawn contributes to the kitchen.

an intimate, residential scale. The innkeepers themselves are knowledgeable gardeners who have used their enthusiasm for plants and gardening to create showcases that are not only appealing to the eye but also loaded with good ideas and answers to the kinds of challenges most homeowners confront in their own yards.

While each garden has a different theme, the bottom line for all six B & Bs is atmosphere. "We are in the business of creating moods and settings, and an atmosphere of total relaxation for our guests," says one innkeeper. "An inviting garden completes the fantasy."

A GOURMET'S GARDEN
Sooke Harbour House, Vancouver Island, British Columbia

*F*ocus on the obvious big picture—the neatly ordered English country garden with benches and chairs strategically positioned to take in the dramatic waterfront views—and Sooke Harbour House on Vancouver Island is a feast for the eyes. Even on gloomy days when clouds ride low in the sky, guests amble among raised beds and along manicured paths overlooking the Strait of Juan de Fuca.

But what makes Fredrica and Sinclair Philip's intensely cultivated acre and a half truly remarkable is that it is also a feast for the palate: 95 percent of what grows here is edible.

"Our goal is to produce a beautiful garden that is totally useful to the kitchen," says Sinclair as he breaks off a sprig of pungent garden sage to smell and taste. "This is more in the tradition of a European curate's garden, where plants were grown primarily for food and medicine."

When the Philips bought the property in 1979, the local standard for fresh produce was iceberg lettuce. For the aspiring restaurateurs, who had developed cooking and gardening skills while living in France, the garden was essential. Today they still grow most of their own edible flowers, herbs, salad greens, and specialty vegetables.

In March and April, when the tulips bloom, guests will find flower petals in their salads. The flowers of tuberous nasturtiums lend a peppery bite and almondy aftertaste to sauces, and in winter, when the flowers have stopped blooming, the tuber will be used as a vegetable. The garden's influence is evident even at breakfast, in ripe berry compotes and in flavorful medallions of freshly picked lavender blossoms embossed on a batch of cornmeal pancakes.

The secret to keeping the garden visually appealing is showcasing beds of seasonal color, such as tulips, against permanent backdrops of herbs or slower-growing vegetables, then filling in with other plants after harvest. Plant selection is the result of years of careful research on what is safe to eat and the most effective uses of those plants in the landscape.

"What makes this all worthwhile is learning to understand how what we grow seasonally translates to the kitchen and makes our menu special," says Sinclair. "We get a lot of satisfaction from the combination."

MICHAEL SKOTT

KITCHEN WORKER at Sooke Harbour House harvests ingredients ranging from grand fir needles and wild berries to daylily buds.

GARDENS IN MINIATURE
Seal Beach Inn and Gardens, Seal Beach, California

*C*rammed onto six dinky lots in the small coastal town of Seal Beach, near Long Beach, the Seal Beach Inn and Gardens has precious little space for parking and a pool, let alone a garden. That hasn't proved a deterrent to owner Marjorie Bettenhausen Schmaehl and landscape consultant Dawn Pope. Using minuscule planting beds, pots, hanging baskets, walls, and arching trellises over walkways, the duo has elevated the challenge of small-space gardening

SMALL IS BEAUTIFUL at Seal Beach Inn, where the gardener's art is revealed in the details. At the entrance (above), guests are greeted with massed pots of seasonal color; passageways (right) are pleasant alcoves with wall-hugging vines, planters, strategically placed furniture, and a fountain. Narrow beds along a path leading to rooms (left) are anchored with azaleas, ferns, lavender, and roses highlighted by changing annuals including hollyhocks, marigolds, and penstemon.

JOHN HUMBLE

into an art that yields a palette of year-round color. "Luckily, we're only a block from the beach and have the perfect climate for it," Schmaehl says.

The planting beds to the left of the main entry are the largest on the property and are put to full use. Pope starts each bed with a basic framework of evergreens for height, depth, and texture, combining azaleas, camellias, ferns, podocarpus, and unstructured hedges with herbs such as lavender, rosemary, and scented geraniums. Every possible space is planted: paved corners are softened with tiers of containers, and climbing roses in big hanging baskets scale walls with closely cropped Boston ivy.

"Variety of heights is an important element a lot of people overlook," says Pope, "but it helps create depth and space to highlight showy annuals."

Pope's secret for continuous color is to "backplant" with seedlings so that something is always coming into bloom as other plants begin to fade. For example, in spring Pope will transplant ready-to-bloom nursery foxgloves into big pots for immediate show. As the blooms wilt, the foxgloves will be transplanted to a nook under a fern or behind another evergreen, where they will rest until they're ready for one more show.

Where planting beds are impossibly narrow between buildings and walkways, walls become extensions of the landscape, with bougainvillea and trumpet vines trained to create niches for artwork, tiles, flowering pots, or small fountains.

Although Schmaehl has owned the inn for 18 years, she still considers the gardens a work in progress. "Dawn and I still aren't happy with the pool area," she says as they wander off, taking the measure of a bare wall and underutilized corners for a place to expand their herb garden.

A NICHE CARVED into an immense wall of eugenia at Simpson House Inn created a cozy bower for a trellis and bench.

A GARDEN OF "OUTDOOR ROOMS"
Simpson House Inn, Santa Barbara

*W*hen Linda and Glyn Davies bought the historic Simpson House in Santa Barbara in 1976 with the idea of turning it into a bed-and-breakfast inn, they acquired a classic Victorian house surrounded by an old, tired garden consisting mostly of a huge lawn. And, like most homeowners, the Davieses spent their initial energy and budget on making the house livable.

But three years ago, after adding several cottages to the back of the property, they wanted to provide more inviting outdoor spaces for the increased number of guests to spread out in. It quickly became clear that the first step was to break up the lawn.

Today the large city lot surrounding Simpson House has been redefined as a series of "outdoor rooms" that are screened with plants for a sense of visual privacy and sprinkled with seven strategically placed fountains. "It's really amazing how guests are drawn to the water," says Linda. "Hearing other noises, from the street or even other guest conversations, is intrusive. Water sounds are soothing while creating a natural sense of intimacy."

Local designer Patrick Omweg first helped the Davieses decide on the placement of patios and walkways to incorporate existing large trees and plants. Then he suggested combinations of rock and wood fencing with espaliered *Ficus benjamina*, *Pittosporum undulatum*, and other shrubs to separate spaces and screen cottages. The lawn isn't totally gone, but what's left is divided into pocket spaces that invite lingering.

On sunny mornings, guests can always be found sitting under a huge pittosporum on a round brick patio set right in the middle of the lawn. You can also usually find someone with a book on the comfortable park bench next to a fountain that transforms a once-unloved corner into a serene nook for reading and watching visiting birds.

A STROLLING GARDEN
Château du Sureau, Oakhurst, California

*W*ith all the luxurious comforts and services of a French country estate at their beck and call, you'd think guests at Château du Sureau in California's Gold Country would spend most of their visit sipping sherry in the ornate Grand Salon or listening to Vivaldi in the privacy

PLAN AHEAD FOR A GARDEN VISIT

The gardens at the small inns and bed-and-breakfasts listed here are reserved for use by guests, who can enjoy the surroundings at their leisure. All prices include a full breakfast, and most include an afternoon tea or sherry service.

Blue Lake Ranch (970/385-4537) is 18 miles southwest of Durango, Colorado, on the way to Mesa Verde. It has four rooms in the main farmhouse plus five separate cottages and cabins suitable for families. Rates range from $85 to $225.

Château du Sureau (209/683-6860) is on the outskirts of Oakhurst, California, a 20-minute drive from the south entrance to Yosemite. Rates for the nine impeccably decorated rooms range from $260 to $360. Erna's Elderberry House Restaurant (683-6800 for reservations) is open for dinner nightly except Tuesdays and offers lunch Wednesdays through Fridays and brunch on Sundays.

Puanani, near Kailua-Kona

of their own richly appointed, firelit rooms. Instead you find them strolling around the 7½-acre property, where native trees and wildflowers are invited into a Sierra foothill country garden.

"The original plans called for a more formal European landscape," says owner Erna Kubin-Clanin of the 3-year-old garden, "but it never felt quite right. The spring before we started construction on the château, I sat on the rock outcropping just near the tower and looked down over the hill. The elderberries were in bloom and the ground was covered in wildflowers, and I decided then that I wanted the grounds to reflect the nature of the place."

The result is a landscape that blends a base of existing mature native pines, oaks, manzanitas, elderberries, and spring wildflowers with more structured plantings of ornamental box hedges, azaleas, roses, and beds of massed annuals. Small meadows of manicured lawn form a civilized corridor between the château and Erna's Elderberry House Restaurant just down the hill.

While only an acre or so of the property is intensively landscaped, showcasing mature natives in these planted areas softens the transition to the surrounding woodlands. Follow a walkway wandering past the clipped-hedge primness of the small swimming pool area and you hardly notice the transition into sparser natural oak- and pine-covered hillsides, where you'll stumble upon quiet retreats for enjoying foothill views or watching deer, birds, and other wildlife.

In dry years, most of the flowering plants have burned out by August, but foothill seasonality doesn't bother Kubin-Clanin. "We want the grounds to look natural, and autumn, when most of the ornamentals are tired, is when our backbone of native plants really shows its worth. Even when the leaves are falling, guests love to explore the grounds."

FOOTPATHS at Château du Sureau lead from a planted environment near the breakfast patio into the Sierra foothill forest.

NORMAN A. PLATE

LAURIE E. DICKSON

FRILLY, FANCIFUL IRIS hybrids of nearly every hue except red fill a June meadow at Blue Lake Ranch.

TWO COLLECTORS' GARDENS
Blue Lake Ranch, Durango, Colorado
Puanani, Kailua-Kona, Hawaii

For two B & Bs that feature plant collections, Blue Lake Ranch in Colorado and Puanani on the Big Island of Hawaii couldn't be more different: One features flowers; the other features palms. One location is challenging; in the other, almost anything grows.

Blue Lake Ranch is an old homestead on a 7,500-foot

on Hawaii's Big Island, has one comfortably furnished suite, with access to a workout room, for a bargain $85; two more suites are expected to open this year. Make reservations through Hawaii's Best Bed & Breakfasts, (800) 262-9912, (808) 885-4550 in Hawaii.

Seal Beach Inn and Gar- dens (310/493-2416) in Seal Beach, California (near Long Beach), has 23 individually decorated rooms ranging from $118 to $255 for a suite with fireplace.

Simpson House Inn (805/ 963-7067) in Santa Barbara has six period-furnished rooms in the main Victorian house, four contemporary suites in a restored barn, and four individual cottages (some suites and cottages have water-jet baths and fireplaces). Rates range from $105 to $245.

Sooke Harbour House (604/642-3421) is an hour's drive southwest of Victoria, British Columbia, and has three individually decorated rooms in the old house and 10 in a separate wing (built in 1986) that overlooks the ocean. Rates range from $150 to $212 and include both full breakfast and lunch. Nonguests are welcome for dinner at the award-winning restaurant by reservation.

mesa near the base of Colorado's rugged La Plata Mountains. "The season's short, the soil isn't very good, there are occasional plagues of grasshoppers, and some summers we only get 15 minutes of real rain," says owner David Alford as he walks through a grove of purple and pink heirloom hollyhocks that take the full measure of his 6-foot-4 frame. "But this is a great place to live, and I have this gardening problem, so I've just had to make do."

Making do for Alford and his wife, Shirley Isgar, has meant 19 years of hard work and "lots of manure" to transform nearly 3 acres of sheep pasture around the comfortably refurbished early-1900s ranch house into a summer garden of annual and perennial blooms that is as productive as it is eclectic. The only real theme is Alford's enthusiasm for whatever plant grabs his interest, tempered with a decidedly Darwinian approach to horticulture that favors survival of the fittest over use of chemical fertilizers and insecticides.

One of the most spectacular times of year at the ranch is the three weeks in June when an acre of hybrid irises ex-

hung in bunches over a porch for the dried-flower market.

"It's amazing how many of our guests really get into the spirit of the garden," says Alford as he pulls a few weeds among the hollyhocks. "They come out and get their fingers in the dirt, or pick flowers, or just sit in the shade. They take home some seeds, then six months later we get a letter telling us what they're doing in their own garden."

A world away, on the Kona Coast of the Big Island, Michael Raymond and his wife, Christina, have built a contemporary single-suite hideaway up-country from the town of Kailua-Kona. They call it Puanani, Hawaiian for *beautiful flower*. While flowers and seasonal sprays of orchids do add subtle touches of color to more than an acre of landscape, what makes the garden so inviting—and so unusual—is Michael's collection of more than 50 kinds of palms. Nearly 300 palms define the boundaries and structure of the landscape. The result is a sunny, tropical oasis that irresistibly draws guests outside to enjoy distant ocean views from the poolside or to pull up a chair in the shade of swaying fronds.

PETER FRENCH

In a climate where almost anything grows, why the focus on palms? Michael, a landscape contractor by trade, isn't bashful about their virtues. "Each variety is unique in color, size, shape, trunk, and frond. They aren't invasive or overbearing, allowing in plenty of light while providing a little shade. Instead of dropping a bunch of little leaves, palms drop a whole frond, and they stand up to big winds, yet have a nice soothing sound when the trades blow through."

They are also fast growers. Planted in February 1994, the gardens already had an established feel just nine months later. Michael's favorites include 18-inch-tall dwarf lady palms (*Rhapis excelsa*) and lacy

PALMS ARE THE BACKBONE trees, shrubs, and understory of gardens at Puanani. Red-leafed ti plant (foreground) and hibiscus and gardenia (not shown) provide bolder spots of color.

plodes in constellations of yellow, blue, orange, white, pink, and purple, mingled with the deep red of Flanders poppies. Last June, Alford estimated that he had at least 250 unique iris hybrids that produced 10,000 blooms.

As the iris bloom winds down and rhizomes are dug and divided, collectors arrive to buy many of the rare hybrids. Later in summer, guests are invited to help pick edible blossoms from small fields of calendula and bachelor's button; these are dried, bottled, and sold by the ounce as a colorful garnish for salads and vegetable dishes.

By mid-July, most guests can't resist wandering among the towering stalks of heirloom hollyhocks, which have grown on the ranch since the early 1900s. The seeds are collected in September for mail-order sale, along with other packaged seeds. Peonies, statice, and delphinium stalks are

fern palms (*Cycas circinalis*); tall, slender MacArthur palms (*Ptychosperma macarthuri*); bottle palms (*Mascarena*—or *Hyophorbe*—*lagenicaulis*), with matted basket-weave trunks; and Mexican fan palms (*Washingtonia robusta*), native to desert canyons near Palm Springs. He even has palms growing inside the dramatic two-story glass atrium that is Puanani's grand entrance.

The biggest challenges have been rocky soil, low rainfall, and finding ground covers compatible with the thick, thatchy palm roots. Michael now favors red-flowered boleria, mondo grass, and white butterfly syngonium.

"I have more palm varieties here than you'll find in many botanical gardens, and I still have more I want to put in," Michael says. "I guess I'm kind of like a chef: you like to show what you can do, and palms are my main dish." ∎

'MAMMOTH' SUNFLOWERS
dwarf Hilary Byk, at far left. Low boxwood hedges encircle beds bursting with zinnias. Sweet alyssum spills onto the granite pathways. Byk's favorites include Queen Anne's lace, below, and love-lies-bleeding, left.

RUSS A. WIDSTRAND

Fanciful formality in Los Angeles

The classic lines of a French garden are a surprising complement to exuberant zinnias and overgrown sunflowers

HILARY BYK'S RIOTOUS Brentwood, California, garden is not the sort you ease yourself into. It cries out for attention, grabs you, pulls you in all at once. "It's not peaceful," says Byk. "It has a lot of energy because of all the yellow and red." Huge, brilliant sunflowers and a mosaic of radiant zinnias are the attention-getters, but it's the garden's design—with its tidy annual beds, intersecting pathways, and permanent plantings—that draws you in.

The garden was not always so arresting. In fact, it started out as an ordinary lawn. Byk had other ideas—a geometrically precise parterre like the ones she'd seen at Château de Villandry in the Loire Valley

of France. To this end, she ripped out the lawn and put in a network of decomposed-granite paths intersecting six 6- by 18-foot planting beds. Each bed is ringed with a neat, clipped boxwood hedge.

Through the years, Byk has let the garden evolve, allowing exuberant flowers to push the boundaries of the boxwood. Twelve-foot-high sunflowers arch over the paths, while sweet alyssum spills from the beds. Easy-to-grow annuals and biennials add volume, texture, and color. Two of Byk's favorites are Eastern Queen Anne's lace, with cushions of tiny white flowers atop long wiry stems, and love-lies-bleeding, with burgundy-pink flowers forming dangling chenillelike ropes.

BEHIND THE SCENES

Of course, it takes a lot of planning and care to create such an enticing and seemingly casual tangle. Take, for example, the big sunflowers. Byk starts 'Mammoth' seeds at the beginning of April outdoors in nursery flats. She prefers this method to sowing in the garden because it's easier to protect the vulnerable seedlings from birds (she covers the flats with netting). The sunflowers are transplanted in early May when they are 3 to 4 inches tall; she spaces them 18 inches apart.

At the same time she also plants purchased seedlings of 'California Giant' zinnias from cell-packs; she spaces them about 6 inches apart. Both sunflowers and zinnias require full sun. All flowers start blooming in June and peak about mid-July.

Byk starts a second batch of smaller-flowered sunflowers in flats around mid-May. As the 'Mammoth' sunflowers fade, she pulls some and replants with a variety such as the 2-foot-tall 'Teddy Bear', with double-flowered golden blooms.

As for routine maintenance, Byk gives the boxwood hedges a trim every six to eight weeks during the growing season. She waters the garden consistently through the summer, and clips spent flowers to keep the garden looking fresh and to encourage more blooms. About the only things she doesn't have to worry about are pests and diseases, because the garden is not especially prone to either.

All of which is not to imply that the garden is all work and no play. Byk likes the structure of the beds and is willing to keep them at their best. But she also uses them as places to experiment, to try out new plants and planting schemes as her interests evolve. "The garden," she says, "is wilder than when it started." ■

By Lynn Ocone

Designing with herbs

Five Western herb gardens show a diversity of sizes, styles, and plants

STEPHEN SIMPSON

W HAT'S AN HERB GARDEN? TO SOME, IT'S any small patch of earth that produces basil, chives, oregano, and other culinary herbs that are snipped and pinched for cooking.

To others, an herb garden means something much grander. It could be a formal layout with geometric brick paths, boxwood borders, and a mixture of culinary and medicinal herbs. Or it could be much more casual, with large beds of loosely arranged plants that include the broadest definition of an herb—a plant or plant part valued for its medicinal, savory, or aromatic qualities.

In keeping with their generally casual lifestyles, Westerners don't seem constrained in their designs or by what goes in them. And rather than being herbal purists, most add dashes of color with annuals and perennials. We found five gardens, from Southern California to the Pacific Northwest, that represent the wide range of sizes, styles, and plants that make up herb gardening in the West.

By Lauren Bonar Swezey

Backdoor kitchen garden

T homas Gaston of Menlo Park, California, created what might be called the ultimate easy-care, easy-to-pick kitchen herb garden, just two steps from his back door.

Gaston learned about herbs from his Swiss mother, an avid herbalist. "All Swiss are herbalists to some degree, " he says. "I guess I'm carrying on the tradition." He started with mints; they're invasive, so he contained them in old chimney pipes left over from remodeling. The rest of the herbs were at ground level. But Gaston liked not having to bend over, so he put many of the others in raised containers, too.

Mainstays for cooking (all in containers) are thyme, tarragon, spearmint, peppermint, rosemary, oregano, and mar-

PETER CHRISTIANSEN

OLD CHIMNEY PIPES *were filled with dirt and gravel for stability, topped by about a foot of soil, and then planted with herbs. Thomas Gaston harvests thyme beneath.*

joram. In the ground beneath, he grows basil, caraway-scented thyme, chives, garlic chives, Greek oregano, lemon and lime thyme, lemon verbena ("I dry it and make sachets for the linen closet"), parsley, and sage.

Maintenance is simple. Gaston installed a drip-irrigation system with hidden emitter lines that climb the backs of the containers. When plants get woody, he cuts them back to initiate new growth. Basil and parsley are replanted every year.

126

A PEDESTAL SUNDIAL *at the center of a spoke design is the focal point of an herb garden in Flinn Springs, California.*

A Shakespearean garden

After researching herb gardening, Sheryl Lozier of Flinn Springs, east of San Diego, realized that an herb garden, like other kinds of gardens, needs a focal point. She chose a favorite sundial (a bench, bird feeder, or topiary also would work), and designed her garden around it. The garden radiates from the center, which Lozier says is a colonial design that she finds appropriate for her country garden. A split-rail fence adds to the rustic look.

Lozier decided she needed a theme for the plants, too, so she chose plants that Shakespeare wrote about. Many of them are culinary—Greek oregano, lavender, rosemary, sage, tarragon, and thyme (she grows five kinds: camphor thyme, caraway-scented thyme, elfin thyme, mother-of-thyme, and woolly thyme).

Among the flowering plants are ones she dries and uses in wreaths. Kinds include armeria, catmint, dianthus, larkspur, Queen Anne's lace, salvias, yarrow, and old-fashioned-looking David Austin's English roses.

Lozier lets her plants grow unchecked through spring. "I love the wild look—everything gets big and beautiful." Around the Fourth of July, before it gets hot, she cuts back plants for potpourri, collects seed of larkspur and Queen Anne's lace, and harvests herbs.

The garden suffers in the summer, but when the heat breaks in fall the plants perk up again. In winter, the garden gets another round of maintenance, and most things get cut back. But the garden isn't entirely bare. Lozier plants pansies for color and often has roses blooming in winter.

"The land around us is our inspiration for herb gardening," explains Lozier, referring to the foothills near San Diego in which she lives. "Gardening is a real pleasure with our healthy soil and great weather."

CIRCULAR THYME GARDEN *grows where a lawn used to be. It is surrounded by flowering plants such as hollyhocks.*

A matter of thyme

When Olive Curtis of Acme, Washington, was a busy home economics teacher, she and her students used dried herbs out of jars. Now that she's retired and has time to grow her own herbs—as well as teach cooking classes—she uses fresh herbs exclusively. One of her favorites is thyme.

Six years ago, Curtis told her husband that she needed more room for her new passion, herb gardening. "He told me, 'You can have the lawn,' so I took him up on it," says Curtis. A friend helped her husband take down huge birch and cedar trees. Then the lawn came out.

"I like circles and meandering paths," she says, "so first I put in a curving brick path. Then I planted a circular thyme garden bordered by rocks and divided into sections with bricks." The garden

now contains 100 thyme plants of eight kinds. At the center is woolly thyme; around the outside is creeping thyme. The sections contain English, French, Dutch tea, lemon, orange balsam, and

variegated lemon thymes.

"I used to have more kinds, but some froze. Now I mulch heavily with bark in winter and, as a security and to fill in the following spring, I take many cuttings, which overwinter indoors."

The rest of her garden expanded to include many more herbs and flowering plants. She now has a semicircle of chives, a sage garden, and a cutting garden of culinary herbs. For convenience, she has pots of herbs on her deck that she harvests at the last minute to sprinkle into soups, breads, and sauces.

EIGHT KINDS *of thyme grow in circular bed divided into sections by bricks and rocks.*

Medicinal garden in Gold Country

For more than 15 years, Candis Packard has been fascinated by herbs. For the last 11 of them, she has been developing her herb garden in the Sierra foothills in Placerville, California.

She bought her three acres not because of the house, which she barely took notice of, but because of the beautiful land and its incredible soil. The topsoil runs 18 to 20 inches deep. Her intent was to cultivate a botanical herb garden.

"All of the herbs I grow are for my family's use, but they're also part of my demonstration garden," explains Packard. "I teach herbalogy and prefer that the students develop a relationship with living plants instead of just dried materials."

The main herb garden was designed to reflect a Native American medicine wheel, with the paths aligned on the cardinal points. The herbs come from around the world. They're not arranged in any particular order, but since it

gets very hot in the Sierra foothills, Packard planted them according to their needs for sun, shade, and moisture.

Most of the herbs are medicinal. But Packard also has planted some flowers strictly for show. At the wheel's center are calendula, garden sage, and pennyroyal. Petunias and sweet alyssum add long-lasting color. In surrounding beds, Packard grows five kinds of echinacea, used for colds and to aid the immune system, and low hedges of chrysanthemum, whose flowers are used to reduce fevers and inflammations.

Beneath large oak trees, Packard planted shade-loving herbs such as angelica, Chinese foxglove *(Rehmannia glutinosa)*, skullcap *(Scutellaria laterifolia)*, and wood betony *(Stachys officinalis)*.

She also grows rare herbs from China and India, including *Astragalus membranaceous*, dong quai *(Angelica sinensis)*, fo-ti *(Polygonum multiflorum)*, which climbs on a tripod, and ashwaghanda

PATHS OF LAWN *circle beds of herbs from around the world. Straight paths radiate in the cardinal directions.*

(Withania somnifera).

An unusual herb in her garden grew in almost every European garden in the 1500s. It's called costmary *(Chrysanthemum balsamita)* or bibleleaf plant because its 4- to 5-inch-long leaves made good bookmarks. It's used to reduce fevers and aid digestion, and has a sweet minty taste.

To keep the beds healthy and to reduce water use in her

hot climate, Packard adds composted manure, compost, and worm casings. Then she fertilizes with fish emulsion and kelp during the growing season. Since Sierra soils are low in phosphorus, she also adds organic phosphate.

The entire garden is on an irrigation system—sprinklers for the lawn and soaker hoses, sprayers, and emitters for the rest of the plants.

A Victorian herb garden with a casual flair

Peter and Carol Ann Irsfeld of Cambria, California, wanted their herb garden to be both useful and decorative, since it would be in front of their Victorian home, a bed-and-breakfast called the Ollalieberry Inn. They chose a formal design to suit the house's era, with paths radiating from a circle accented by an old birdbath. But that's where the formality ends.

"We didn't want anything with too much structure," explains Peter. "The garden has a cottagey feel."

The plants in the free-form beds are a mixture of culinary, fragrant, and flowering herbs. "Ninety percent of the plants are herbs, but we use only 40

FREE-FLOWING *beds of herbs surround birdbath at center of garden. Flowering perennials add color.*

to 50 percent of them," says Peter. Favorites for cooking are chives, French thyme, golden marjoram, oregano, rosemary, savory, and society garlic *(Tulbaghia violacea)*. "We enjoy going out and picking herbs to make meals

for the guests. One of the favorite evening hors d'oeuvres is goat cheese and roasted garlic with fresh herbs."

They planted other old-world herbs such as catmint, comfrey, lamb's ears, and lemon verbena. For fragrance

and color, they added herbs such as feverfew, lavender, and rosemary. Long-blooming perennials such as Santa Barbara daisy and penstemon provide points of interest.

More pungent herbs like rosemary and lavender are used freely inside the inn. "We like to use them around the house instead of traditional flowers," says Peter. "People enter and often ask us what the wonderful smell is."

Maintenance is straightforward. Cooking herbs are constantly being nipped at, which keeps them in bounds. The garden also gets several prunings through the year—one major pruning in winter, when most things get whacked back (the Irsfelds add winter vegetables to fill in bare spots), and two or three less severe trims in late spring and summer to control growth. ■

MARION BRENNER

CHEERFUL *spring flowers of California poppy (Eschscholzia californica) aren't appealing to deer, unlike the shrubbery nibbled above right.*

Can you grow perennials in deer country?

Here are some best bets

BROWSING DEER ARE charming to watch, but they do considerable damage to gardens. There are various ways to discourage deer; another solution is to grow perennials they find unpalatable. However, deer in different areas seem to have somewhat different tastes. Also, young plants may be eaten but older ones left alone; plants untouched in spring may be eaten in fall. As a final frustration, what deer pass by one year they may find irresistible the next. Despite these variables, the perennials listed here—taken from a complete list in the new *Sunset Western Garden Book*—are "best bets" in deer country.

By Lauren Bonar Swezey

Acanthus mollis
BEAR'S BREECH
☼ ◑ ◐ ● ⦚ 4–24

Achillea
YARROW
☼ ○ ◐ ⦚ ALL ZONES

Agave
NEEDS, ZONES VARY

Aloe
☼ ◑◐⦚ 8, 9, 12–24

Aquilegia
COLUMBINE
☼ ◑ ◐ ⦚ ALL ZONES

Armeria
THRIFT
☼ ◑ ◐ ⦚ ALL ZONES

Artemisia
☼ ○ ◐ ⦚ ALL ZONES

Aster
☼ ◐ ⦚ ALL ZONES

Astilbe
FALSE SPIRAEA
☼ ◑ ◐◐ ⦚ 2–7, 14–17

Brachycome
SWAN RIVER DAISY
☼ ◐ ⦚ ZONES VARY

Campanula poscharskyana
SERBIAN BELLFLOWER
☼ ◑ ◐ ⦚ 1–9, 10–12, 14–24

Carex
SEDGE
☼ ◑ ◐◐ ⦚ 4–9, 14–24

Centaurea
⦙ NEEDS, ZONES VARY

Centranthus ruber
JUPITER'S BEARD
☼ ◑◐ ○ ◐ ◐⦚ 7–9, 12–24

Cerastium tomentosum
SNOW-IN-SUMMER
☼ ◑ ◐ ◐ ⦚ ALL ZONES

Chrysanthemum frutescens
MARGUERITE
☼ ◐ ✸ ⦚ 14–24

Coreopsis
☼ ◐ ⦚ ZONES VARY

Dicentra
BLEEDING HEART
● ◐ ⦚ 1–9, 14–24

Dietes vegeta
☼ ◑ ◐ ◐ ⦚ 8, 9, 12–24

Digitalis
FOXGLOVE
☼ ◐ ◐ ⦚ ALL ZONES

Echinacea purpurea
PURPLE CONEFLOWER
☼ ◐ ◐ ◐ ⦚ ALL ZONES

Echium fastuosum
PRIDE OF MADEIRA
☼ ◐ ◐ ◐ ⦚ 14–24

Erigeron
FLEABANE
☼ ◑ ◐ ◐ ⦚ ZONES VARY

Erodium reichardii
CRANESBILL
☼ ◑ ◐ ◐ ⦚ 7–9, 14–24

Erysimum 'Bowles Mauve'
☼ ◑ ◐ ◐ ⦚ 4–6, 14–17, 22, 23

Erysimum cheiri
WALLFLOWER
☼ ◑ ◐ ◐ ⦚ 4–6, 14–17, 22, 23

Eschscholzia californica
CALIFORNIA POPPY
☼ ○ ◐ ⦚ ALL ZONES

Euphorbia
NEEDS, ZONES VARY

Euryops
☼ ◐ ⦚ 8, 9, 12–24

Felicia amelloides
BLUE MARGUERITE
☼ ◐ ⦚ 8, 9, 13–24

Ferns
⦙ NEEDS, ZONES VARY

SYMBOLS:

☼ Grows best with direct sunlight all day long

◑ Needs partial shade—for half the day or for at least 3 hours during the hottest part of the day

● Prefers little or no direct sunlight

○ Needs no supplemental watering once established

◐ Tolerates some aridity

◐ Needs regular irrigation—weekly or more often during extreme heat

◐◐ Needs wet or constantly moist soil

⦙ Plants are eaten in some areas

✸ Plants whose flowers are sometimes eaten

▦ Plants that must be protected when young

⦚ Zone numbers refer to a plant's adaptability in *Sunset Western Garden Book*

NEW ZEALAND FLAX
Phormium hybrid

SWAN RIVER DAISY
Brachycome

MARION BRENNER

YOUNG FOLIAGE *of Euphorbia martinii turns burgundy and yellowish orange in cold weather. Plant grows 2½ feet tall and 3 feet wide.*

LAMB'S EARS
Stachys byzantina

Festuca ovina 'Glauca'
BLUE FESCUE
☼ ◐ ◖ ◖ ✂ ALL ZONES

Gaillardia grandiflora
BLANKET FLOWER
☼ ◖ ✂ ALL ZONES

Geranium
CRANESBILL
NEEDS, ZONES VARY

Helichrysum
☼ ◊ ◖ ✂ ZONES VARY

Helleborus
HELLEBORE
NEEDS, ZONES VARY

Hemerocallis
DAYLILY
☼ ◐● ◖ ✂ ALL ZONES

Herbs (except basil)
NEEDS, ZONES VARY

Iberis
CANDYTUFT
☼ ◖ ✂ ALL ZONES

Kniphofia uvaria
RED-HOT POKER
☼ ◐◊ ◖ ✂ 1–9, 14–24

Lamium maculatum
DEAD NETTLE
● ◖◖ ✂ ALL ZONES

Limonium
SEA LAVENDER
☼ ◖ ✂ ZONES VARY

Liriope and Ophiopogon
LILY TURF
☼ ◐● ◖ ◖◖ ✂ 5–10, 12–24

Lithodora diffusa
☼ ◐◖ ✂ 5–7, 14–17

Lupinus
LUPINE
NEEDS, ZONES VARY

Lychnis coronaria
CROWN-PINK
☼ ◐◖ ✂ ALL ZONES

Mimulus
MONKEY FLOWER
NEEDS, ZONES VARY

Miscanthus sinensis
EULALIA GRASS
☼ ◐● ◖◖ ✂ ALL ZONES

Monarda
BEE BALM
☼ ◐● ◖◖ ✂ ALL ZONES

Myosotis scorpioides
☼ ◖ ✂ ALL ZONES

Nepeta
☼ ◖ ✂ ALL ZONES

Origanum
NEEDS, ZONES VARY

Papaver orientale
ORIENTAL POPPY
☼ ◖ ◖ ✂ 1–17

Pennisetum setaceum
☼ ◊ ✂ 8–24

Penstemon
BEARD TONGUE
◖ NEEDS, ZONES VARY

Phlomis fruticosa
☼ ◐◖ ✂ 4–24

Phlox subulata
MOSS PINK
☼ ◖ ✂ 1–17

Phormium
NEW ZEALAND FLAX
☼ ◐◊ ◖ ◖ ✂ 7–24

Romneya coulteri
MATILIJA POPPY
☼ ◊ ◖ ◖ ▦ ✂ ALL ZONES

Rudbeckia hirta
GLORIOSA DAISY
☼ ◖ ✂ ALL ZONES

Santolina
☼ ◊ ◖ ✂ ALL ZONES

Saxifraga
SAXIFRAGE
NEEDS, ZONES VARY

Scabiosa (some)
PINCUSHION FLOWER
☼ ◖ ◖ ✂ ZONES VARY

Sisyrinchium
☼ ◖ ◖ ✂ 4–24

Stachys byzantina
LAMB'S EARS
☼ ◐◖ ✂ ALL ZONES

Stipa
FEATHER GRASS
NEEDS, ZONES VARY

Tagetes lemmonii
☼ ◖ ▦ ✂ 8–10, 12–24

Thymus
THYME
☼ ◐◖ ✂ ALL ZONES

Tulbaghia violacea
SOCIETY GARLIC
☼ ◖ ✂ 13–24

Verbena
◖ NEEDS, ZONES VARY

Veronica
SPEEDWELL
☼ ◖ ✂ ALL ZONES

Viola odorata
SWEET VIOLET
☼ ◐◖ ✂ ALL ZONES

Zauschneria
CALIFORNIA FUCHSIA
☼ ◊ ◖ ✂ 2–10, 12–24

CLAIRE CURRAN

NORMAN A. PLATE

Decorative grains for fall color indoors

Plant ornamental corn and wheat now for long-lasting color in your home this autumn

MANY GARDENERS plant and harvest everlasting flowers for colorful arrangements in fall. But just as decorative, though usually more subtle, are the ornamental grains—corn and wheat.

Standard Indian corns have long been popular in autumn arrangements, but miniature varieties are more of a novelty. Less well known are the broom corns, with their decorative seed heads, and pod corns, with papery husks covering each kernel.

Ornamental wheat is often used as a filler in everlasting flower arrangements. But when several sheaves are bunched together, wheat makes a dramatic presentation on its own or in combination with ornamental corn, as shown at left.

DECORATIVE CORN IN A RAINBOW OF CHOICES

Although shocks of bundled cornstalks set a festive harvest scene, the primary reason to plant ornamental corn is for its shiny, colorful ears, which offer endless possibilities for long-lasting wall hangings, baskets, and table decorations.

Ornamental corn comes in a range of sizes, shapes, and colors—even textures.

Standard varieties, often called Indian corn, produce one or two 7- to 10-inch-long ears per plant and are usually multicolored. A common variety is 'Calico Indian'.

Multicolored 'Fiesta' matures in about 92 days, 8 to 10 days earlier than 'Calico Indian'. This is advantageous in short-season areas where late-maturing varieties are marginal. 'Fiesta' has variable multicolored ears; stems and husks of about half of the plants are an attractive reddish purple.

'Red Stalker' was bred for its showy reddish purple stalks, which appear on about 65 to 70 percent of the plants; the remaining stalks are green, or green with red streaks. Ears are multicolored.

Miniature varieties produce smaller ears, usually 3 to 6 inches long. Expect two to four ears from the main stalk; often, additional smaller ears appear on side sprouts called tillers. With the exception of a few early varieties, such as multicolored 'Chinook', which matures in 85 to 90 days, most miniature varieties require 100 days or more for maturation.

Attractive companions are 'Cutie Blues', with uniformly blue kernels, and 'Mini Pink', a light pink shaded with blue. You may find similar blue or pink varieties by other names. Miniatures also include petite ornamental popcorns, such as burgundy 'Strawberry' (shaped like a 2-inch strawberry) and multicolored 'Cutie Pops'.

Pod corn has papery mini-husks that range from buff to reddish brown and cover each kernel of the 5½- to 6-inch ears. 'Feather Mixed' gives a variety of colors and reaches maturity in approximately 110 days.

Broom corn is actually a type of sorghum. It has decorative seed-studded tassels that bush from the plant's top. Colors vary from standard buff-khaki to striking red. Plants can be large—as tall as 12 feet—and require a long growing season (120 days).

CORN PLANTING AND CARE

Isolate ornamental corn from sweet corn to prevent cross-pollination, which will adversely affect sweet corn. Or juggle planting dates and use types with different days to maturity so the two types won't cross.

Grow ornamental corn just as you would sweet corn.

'Cutie Blues' miniature corn

'Cutie Pops' popcorn

'Red' broom corn

'Fiesta' Indian corn

'Strawberry' popcorn

'Feather Mixed' pod corn

Plant in rich soil in a location that gets full sun. Amend soil with compost or fertilizer according to package directions. Plant corn when soil is warm, at least 60° to 65°. To ensure pollination, sow seeds in blocks of at least four rows; space rows 2 to 3 feet apart. Plant seeds 1 to 1½ inches deep, 6 inches apart. Use netting or floating row covers to protect young seedlings from birds. Thin young plants to 1 foot apart.

Water consistently to provide about an inch of water a week until the corn silks turn brown and wither and ears are fully formed. When the corn begins tasseling, side-dress with additional fertilizer or compost.

Harvest corn when ears are full and kernels are hard. When cutting ear from plant, include 1½ inches of stalk. Pull husks back and leave them attached to the ear.

Harvest broom corn when the brooms color up and stalks are still green. Hang them to dry broom end down for straight strands, or place stem end down in a bucket to dry in a fan shape.

WHEAT'S WILD RELATIVES

Ornamental wheat is the wild relative of commercial types. The awns, which look like bristles, are longer and more decorative than those of commercial wheat.

Each variety has a slightly different characteristic. 'Blocky' looks like it sounds: the head is short (about 2 inches long), so it's almost square, with long awns. 'Black Eagle' has a dark head and long black awns. 'Black Tip' has a lighter appearance than 'Black Eagle' because the long black awns are attached to a tan (referred to as white) head.

'Gigas' is especially unusual. Unlike the others with uniform rows of seed, 'Gigas' seed rows are distorted, giving the heads a wild look. 'Silver Tip' has the largest head of all the ornamental wheats (about 4½ inches long, excluding awns) because of its wheat-rye heritage. It's completely tan with somewhat shorter awns.

GROWING AND HARVESTING IS EASY

You need only a small plot of soil to grow wheat. In spring, plant seeds in soil that's been amended with compost, tilled or turned, and raked level. Broadcast seeds thinly over soil (the general guideline for wheat is ¼ pound per 100 square feet) and rake in so seeds are buried to about three times their diameter. Sowing seeds a little deeper than normal helps plants get a strong roothold.

Soak the soil thoroughly, then water once a week or so to keep it moist; avoid overhead watering to keep plants from falling over. Weed regularly to prevent invaders from competing with the wheat. In windy areas, or if the wheat starts falling over, tie the plants up by placing heavy stakes at the four corners of the wheat bed and encircling them with twine.

When wheat starts turning brown, stop watering. Heads develop the best color with cool nights and warm days. Harvest wheat when seeds (inside the husks) are at the "soft dough stage"—when you can still barely dent them with your fingernail. You may still see some green streaks in the plants. If you wait too long, heads can shatter (open and spill the seeds).

Cut the long stalks at the base and hang most upside down. Others can be placed upright in a 5-gallon bucket so that heads nod over and dry gracefully. Use these at the edges of an arrangement.

SEED SOURCES

The corn and wheat varieties described here are found in these mail-order sources (catalogs are free).

Liberty Seed Company, Box 806, New Philadelphia, Ohio 44663; (800) 541-6022. All wheat varieties. Ornamental corn: 'Red Stalker', 'Mini Pink', 'Strawberry' popcorn, pod corn ('Feather Mixed'), and broom corn ('Red', 'Standard', and 'Highlights Mix').

Stokes Seeds Inc., Box 548, Buffalo, N.Y. 14240; (716) 695-6980. 'Calico Indian', 'Fiesta', 'Cutie Blues', 'Cutie Pops', ornamental popcorn ('Strawberry'), and pod corn ('Feather Mixed').

Territorial Seed Company, Box 157, Cottage Grove, Ore. 97424; (503) 942-9547. 'Chinook'. ∎

By Lynn Ocone and Lauren Bonar Swezey

'Black Tip'   **'Silver Tip'**   **'Blocky'**   **'Black Eagle'**   **'Gigas'**

'SUM AND SUBSTANCE' *hosta has light green leaves.*

Hostas that make life tough for slugs, snails

Leaves with "substance" resist nibbling pests

I F YOU WERE TO ASK a knowledgeable gardener to make a list of perennials that resist snails and slugs, chances are hostas would not be on the list. After all, crawling pests make many kinds of hosta look like Swiss cheese by season's end.

Yet snails and slugs are a picky lot, devouring some hostas and ignoring others. Choose carefully and you can have attractive plants until late summer, when leaves start looking tattered anyway.

Certain hostas have leaves with "substance." A leaf with good substance feels thick and comparatively stiff between your fingers. That substantial feel comes from a thick cuticle that covers the leaf's surface. Snails and slugs have a hard time chewing through thick cuticles, so they glide on by in search of more tender leaves.

Hostas that have leaves with good substance also tend to hold up better toward the end of the season than the papery-leafed ones.

LET YOUR FINGERS DO THE SHOPPING

When you shop for hostas, gently feel the leaves of one or two kinds from each of the following groups, and you'll get a sense of what we mean by substance.

Slugs usually ignore these plants, whose leaves have good substance: *H. montana*, *H. sieboldiana* (and most other blue-leafed hostas), 'Halcyon', 'Love Pat', and 'Sum and Substance'.

Slugs love these plants with little leaf substance: 'Kabitan', *H. montana aureomarginata*, *H. undulata*, 'Shade Fanfare', the Tiara series ('Golden Tiara', for example), and *H. venusta*.

Some hostas have such beautiful leaves that they're worth fighting for regardless of substance. Start baiting for snails and slugs when hosta leaves emerge from the ground—as early as January or February in mild-winter areas. Remove garden debris, and mulch where slugs hide. Wherever you find slug eggs (light-colored eggs the size of BBs), squash them.

Handpick the pests at night, after you water, or whenever it rains. Carry a pair of pruning shears to cut the offending gastropods in two when you find them, then return later to dispatch the ones feeding on the remains of their recently departed kin. ■

By Jim McCausland

A **THICK CUTICLE** *covers the bluish green leaves of Hosta sieboldiana.*

Pushmowers hit the grass again

They're lighter and quieter than power mowers

THERE'S A THING about the lawn mower I can't even tell you, but to me it's the most beautiful sound in the world, the freshest sound of the season, the sound of summer, and I'd miss it fearfully if it wasn't there." So said Grandpa in Ray Bradbury's *Dandelion Wine*.

The *thwack-thwack-thwack* that was music to Grandpa's ears is being heard again as push-type mowers regain turf. Push mowers make sense for small lawns. You can buy a first-rate, American-made model for $100 to $200, and mow a ¼-acre lawn in about an hour. Reel mowers (which have four to seven blades in a cylinder shape) cut more cleanly and stay sharp longer than rotary power mowers. Most are also considerably lighter than both power mowers and old-time reel mowers and therefore easier to push.

On the downside, compared with rotary mowers, push mowers can't be adjusted to cut as high (a problem in taller grass), don't cut wet grass as well, and have more blades to sharpen. They don't cut grass into as many short pieces as mulching power mowers. But on balance, they're still good choices for small lawns.

When you shop, you'll find great differences among push mowers.

Weight. Most reel mowers weigh considerably less than 40 pounds, so you can hang them up, out of the way, on your garage wall. Some of

them weigh as little as 16 pounds.

Reel width. Standard reels are 14, 16, 18, and 20 inches. The wider the reel, the faster the job gets done, but the harder the mower is to push.

Blades. Low-end push mowers come with four blades, standard models with five, and top-of-the-line mowers with six or seven. Generally, more blades give a more even cut. (If you want to mow bent grass to putting-green perfection, for example, buy a seven-blade mower.) Use fewer blades for rougher, more uneven turf. One manufacturer, American Lawn Mower, sells a sharpening kit with a compound that enables you to use the mower to sharpen itself.

Accessories. If you prefer not to leave grass clippings on your lawn, you can buy a detachable grass catcher for $20 to $50.

SOURCES

Many garden centers and hardware stores stock at least one model of push mower. A wider selection is offered by mail-order suppliers, including these three: Gardener's Supply Co., 128 Intervale Rd., Burlington, Vt. 05401, (800) 955-3370; the Natural Gardening Co., 217 San Anselmo Ave., San Anselmo, Calif. 94960, (707) 766-9303; and Smith & Hawken, 2 Arbor Lane, Box 6900, Florence, Ky. 41022, (800) 776-3336. All offer free catalogs. ■

By Jim McCausland

NORMAN A. PLATE

THE FASTER HE PUSHES *the mower, the faster its blades spin around to trim a regularly mowed lawn.*

A BASIL FOR EVERY TASTE: *In front is 'Lettuce Leaf'; behind (from left) are 'Anise', 'Napoletano', 'Dwarf Bush', and a dark purple selection of 'Dark Opal'. For more on this indispensable herb, see page 143.*

MAY

Sunset's GARDEN GUIDE

Discover new, improved—and overlooked—trees, shrubs, perennials, and vegetables

DRIFTS OF SNOWY BLOSSOMS *fill a 'Mt. Fuji' flowering cherry blooming at Lakewold Gardens, near Tacoma.*

Bearing a blizzard of blossoms, the 'Mt. Fuji' cherry tree, shown at right in Lakewold Gardens, near Tacoma, Washington, will be in full flower this month. See it in person, and you'll understand why this variety is so revered on both sides of the Pacific. Also flowering in May, besides 'Mt. Fuji', will be azaleas, rhododendrons, magnolias, clematis, tulips, and wisteria. You'll see, as well, a large old dove tree (*Davidia involucrata*) covered with enormous white flowers that look like doves perched on its branches.

Lakewold is a perfect place to study the spring-flowering plants and note which kinds you might like to grow. The gardens are open from 10 to 4 Thursdays through Mondays. Admission costs $6, $5 seniors and ages 11 and under. Lakewold is at 12317 Gravelly Lake Drive. From Interstate 5 south of Tacoma, take the Gravelly Lake exit. For more information, call (206) 584-3360.

The great American tulip tree

Not well known and certainly underused in the West, the native American tulip tree (*Liriodendron tulipifera*) has begun to appear in nurseries in 1- and 5-gallon cans. If you have room for a big deciduous shade tree, this one is well worth growing.

Tulip tree grows straight and tall, quickly reaching a height of 60 to 80 feet. (East of the Rockies, old tulip trees have reached 200 feet.) It sends out mighty limbs that spread to 40 feet; the crown is a graceful pyramid. Its deeply lobed, lyre-shaped leaves measure 5 to 6 inches long and across and turn from bright green to bright yellow in autumn. In late spring, mature trees produce masses of 2-inch-wide tulip-shaped flowers that are greenish yellow, with orange at the base (the tree rarely produces blooms until it is at least a decade old).

The tulip tree is hardy enough to grow in the West's coldest climate zones, and it will thrive in any good garden soil. For the first two years while it is becoming established, give it plenty of water; after that, give it regular watering wherever summer is dry. Several cultivated varieties exist. *L. t.* 'Fastigiatum' and *L. t.* 'Arnold' are narrow and columnar. *L. t.* 'Majestic Beauty' ('Aureomarginatum'), has leaves edged in yellow and does not grow as large as the species.

DON NORMARK

Plant a bean of a different color

Beans aren't just green. Snap beans come in purples (they usually turn green when cooked) and yellows. Dried shelling beans come in almost every color imaginable. Many bean plants also have colorful flowers that look great in the garden.

Here are a few especially tasty and colorful bean varieties to plant this month.

Shelling bean: 'Borlotto' is an heirloom Italian variety that produces flecked rose-red and cream pods on bush-type plants.

Snap bean: 'Beurre de Roquencourt Wax' and 'Roc D'Or' both produce delicious yellow beans on low-growing, bushy plants. 'Royalty' is a purple-podded snap bean that develops from red flowers on a bushy plant.

Runner bean: 'Red Knight' produces bright red flowers. The dried seeds are mottled purple and black. This bean's vigorous vines need a trellis for support.

All beans grow best in full sun and require regular watering. Most seed racks carry one or more varieties of yellow- and purple-podded beans, as well as runner beans. 'Beurre de Roquencourt Wax' and 'Royalty' are available from Seeds of Change, Box 15700, Santa Fe, N.M. 87506; (505) 438-8080. Catalog is free. 'Borlotto',

'Roc D'Or', and 'Red Knight' are available from Shepherd's Garden Seeds, 6116 Highway 9, Felton, Calif. 95018; (408) 335-6910. Catalog is free.

If gophers have you fighting mad, switch plants

That's what Robert Semon of Watsonville, California, finally decided to do after battling gophers with baits, traps, and chemicals only to lose many prize plants.

Now he's found a way to coexist with gophers—by landscaping with plants they don't eat. Semon has spent 14 years experimenting. If a gopher eats a plant, Semon eliminates it from his list and doesn't plant another one.

"I am certain that there are no 100 percent guaranteed gopherproof plants that survive everywhere," says Semon. But he has found many that are 90 percent safe and some that are gopherproof, at least in his garden.

"Gophers show no mercy to apples, cherries, and roses. Camellias are unpredictable. We've lost some and have other plants that are 14 years old," he says. The rodents also go after blue fescue, daylily, flax, liquidambar, *Trachelospermum asiaticum,* and Transvaal daisy.

Here are Semon's suggestions for gopher-resistant plants.

Perennials: Agapanthus, armeria (broad-leafed types like *Armeria alliacea*—gophers devour fine-leafed types such as *A. maritima*), bird of paradise, borage, calla, clivia, coral bells, ferns, fibrous begonia, fortnight lily, foxglove (eaten now and then), iris (about 90 percent safe), lantana, lavender, *Nepeta,* penstemon (young plants may be vulnerable), salvia, and Shasta daisy (stems get nibbled now and then).

Woody plants: Apricot, avocado, banana shrub, bottlebrush, breath of heaven, ceanothus, escallonia, eucalyptus (protect the first year or two), fuchsia, grevillea, heavenly bamboo, holly, hydrangea, lemon, natal plum, oleander, photinia, plum, pomegranate, rhaphiolepis, rosemary, strawberry tree, and toyon.

A rosemary that's rugged enough for the cold West

Visit Corsica or Capri and you may see rosemary growing wild, but here in the West, it's strictly an import. You may wonder how rosemary can thrive so far from its mild Mediterranean origins. Its adaptability comes from built-in toughness and from centuries of selection—Europeans in general, and the British in particular, have been cultivating rosemary since Shakespeare's time.

In colder parts of the West, one rosemary is especially worth a try: *Rosmarinus officinalis* 'Arp', which has survived -15° weather in Cleveland, Ohio. As with all marginally hardy plants, it should be grown in a sheltered spot—against a south wall, for example—protected from cold, drying winds. The evergreen shrub, which has slightly gray green leaves, produces light blue flowers in spring. It grows upright to 5 feet, with an equal spread after a time.

In milder winter climates (*Sunset Western Garden Book* zones 7–9 and 12–24), you have many choices, from standard rosemary (to 6 feet tall, blue flowers) to the more upright white form 'Albus' to light pink–flowered 'Majorca Pink'. There's also a prostrate form (*R. o. prostratus*) that can spread to 8 feet fairly quickly.

All rosemaries do best in full sun and fast-draining soil. They respond well to pruning, especially tip pinching. All forms have edible leaves used for tea and seasoning.

You can find a few kinds of rosemary at many nurseries. One mail-order source with a large selection, including 'Arp', is Mountain Valley Growers, 38325 Pepperweed Rd., Squaw Valley, Calif. 93675. Catalog is free.

Wine grape bonsai

You don't need 5 acres or even a backyard to grow your own grapevines. Petite Vines Co., in Healdsburg, California, can supply you with 7- to 18-year-old vines of four varietal grapes—Cabernet Sauvignon, Chardonnay, Sauvignon Blanc, and Zinfandel—in 4-inch pots.

The idea for these handsome bonsai came from St. Émilion, France, where a clever Frenchman, François Brun, has been growing bonsai grapevines for a number of years. Stephen Mandy admired the petite vines and started producing them in California with help from M. Brun.

Jere Michael, general manager of Petite Vines, says bonsai make unusual house plants (they also grow well outdoors on a patio).

Grapevine bonsai need to be watered fairly often, since they grow in small containers. Water every three to four days during the summer (more often in hot weather, less in cool). They'll also need pruning about once a month during the growing season (instructions come with the plant). The grapevine bonsai often produce fruit, although perhaps not every year.

Plants 7 to 12 years old

GOPHER-RESISTANT LANDSCAPE *in Watsonville, California, includes colorful perennials such as (from left) pink penstemon, blue agapanthus, golden callas, and coral bells.*

PROFUSE 'ETOILE VIOLETTE', *a deep purple hybrid of Clematis viticella, is well suited to arid climates that characterize Southern California.*

STEVE SMITH

good start, plant where it will get at least 6 hours of full sun daily, or filtered sun all day. It prefers rich, well-draining soil and plenty of water, especially during the first year, when it's developing a deep root system. Feed monthly with a complete liquid fertilizer such as 5-10-10; apply half-strength feedings once the clematis begins putting out fresh growth. If pruning is necessary, wait until early next spring to avoid losing flowers—this type of clematis blooms on new growth.

If your nursery or garden center does not have any of these clematis varieties in stock, ask it to order from a wholesale grower such as Monrovia Nursery Company or Monterey Bay Nursery; each propagates several varieties. Or you can order from Wayside Gardens in South Carolina (800/845-1124) or Greer Gardens in Oregon (800/548-0111).

A nursery worth a visit—in Yuba City

Imagine the ideal nursery. It would have a huge selection of plants displayed in a spacious, beautiful setting, with garden art and outdoor furniture arranged among the plants. It would have a gift shop where you could purchase the latest books and garden supplies. Best of all, it would be surrounded by display gardens where you could actually see how the plants grew and get ideas about plant combinations.

There is such a place in Yuba City, California— Seedling Nursery. Started more than 20 years ago by owner Ron Eckard, Seedling is part nursery, part arboretum. The sales area, which alone is worth a visit, is surrounded by 2 acres of display gardens, all expertly designed and beautifully manicured. These include a peaceful Oriental garden with a meandering stream, a Shakespearean garden, a rose garden, a water

with ¾-inch (or smaller) trunk diameters start at $60; plants 13 to 18 years old with 1¼- to 1½-inch-diameter trunks cost about $80 (plus packaging and shipping, about $15 to Bay Area cities). To order a plant, write or call Petite Vines Co., 766 Westside Rd., Healdsburg, Calif. 95448; (707) 433-6255.

An ornamental grass for shade

Though most grasses are creatures of field and meadow, Japanese forest grass (*Hakonechloa macra* 'Aureola') is a low, almost weeping grass that thrives in woodland gardens and grows in all Western climate zones. The 'Aureola' part of its name hints at its golden green stripes, which stand out well in shade.

Unlike many sun-loving grasses, this well-mannered variety doesn't spread uncontrollably, though it does have underground runners that increase clump size gradually. Use it with hostas for a nice interplay of textures.

Planted now from a nursery can, Japanese forest grass will grow to 18 inches tall by summer's end.

You can find Japanese forest grass at nurseries that specialize in perennials and grasses.

New clematis for arid climates

Sunny tops and cool bottoms are the usual formula for growing clematis. But that combination can be tricky to pull off in our arid climate. If you would like to grow this traditional rose companion

plant but haven't had much luck with it in the past, try *Clematis viticella.*

This clematis isn't so intolerant of warm roots. It originated in southern Europe and western Asia and is better adapted to our Mediterranean climate than are kinds such as *C. montana,* which originated in cooler, damper regions.

'Etoile Violette', with its deep violet flowers, is one readily available *C. viticella* hybrid. Others to try include 'Alba Luxurians' (solid white), 'Little Nell' (pale mauve with ivory stripes), 'Mme. Julia Correvon' (wine red), and 'Polish Spirit' (deep purple with cerise stripes). These are all small-flowered clematis, but they make up for their diminutive size by blooming practically nonstop from May through September.

To get clematis off to a

garden, and an English cottage garden filled with flowering perennials.

Seedling Nursery is at 1499 Lincoln Road in Yuba City. Hours are 10 to 5 daily except Tuesdays. For directions, call (916) 674-5263.

Putting a fallen tree to work

Losing a mature tree, whether to wind, rain, or disease, can be heart-wrenching. But putting the fallen tree to work again will give you a memento of its presence.

That's what Hortense Miller did when a rare 45-year-old sugar gum (*Eucalyptus cladocalyx*) mysteriously toppled over one night last August. Miller, the creator of the Hortense Miller Garden, a 2½-acre garden in Laguna Beach that she deeded to the city as a public garden in the late 1970s, sorely regretted the loss. So did visitors to her garden: "It was the one [tree] whose white trunk everyone touched," she says.

But Miller is a practical woman. She had the tree's

CHAD SLATTERY

SIX-INCH-THICK PAVERS *cut from a fallen 45-year-old sugar gum now line a path.*

3-foot-diameter trunk sawed into thick slabs that now provide a hard, durable surface on a gravel pathway. Rounds this size—as much as 6 inches thick and 3 feet across—are not readily available, she says.

The fine-grained cross sections are not only highly ornamental, Miller says, but also sturdy enough "to accommodate even the largest feet securely." She predicts the tree rounds will outlast her. In the meantime, they'll provide a continual remembrance of a stately old friend.

Garden preview in San Luis Obispo

It's been a long time since a botanical garden opened in California, but it looks as if the new San Luis Obispo Botanical Garden will be worth the wait. Though still in the planning stages, the 150-acre site holds great promise.

The first project, a ¾-acre demonstration garden, is scheduled to open in late summer or fall. Its collection of California natives and natives from other Mediterranean climates will be a preview of the botanical garden. Look for California buckeye, hummingbird sage, toyon, and other common natives as well as some unusual kinds such as *Eriodictyon capitatum,* a central coast native.

Why we love spiders

If you've ever blundered into a web and felt like apologizing to the spider, you already recognize the importance of arachnids in your garden.

David Faulkner, a research associate for the San Diego Natural History Museum and entomologist with the Wild Animal Park, says that nocturnal orb weavers, those that spin what he calls "bicycle wheel webs," are particularly beneficial in gardens.

"This time of year, many spiders are just emerging from egg cases," says Faulkner. "You don't really notice them

GARY BRAASCH

SPIDER WEBS ARE LOVELY *unless you're an aphid or a whitefly, which is why you want webs in your garden.*

or their webs because they're so tiny, but they're eating small insects, including whiteflies, adult winged aphids, and the fly species of leaf miners." Later in the year, large orb weavers trap moths, flies, mosquitoes, winged termites, and even small grasshoppers.

Spiders spin webs where flying insects gather, which is why they frequently set up shop near outdoor lights. To move an intrusive orb weaver, trap it between its web and the bristles of a broom, then brush the spider off onto a bush. And if you inadvertently destroy the glistening geometry of a fresh web, don't be concerned. A mature spider can spin two or three a night.

Organic controls for two common rose diseases

When it comes to controlling rose diseases, it's important to know all your options. The most widely used fungicides are strong chemicals that are dangerous if used improperly. One of the most popular fungicides, triforine, is one of the few garden chemicals to carry the warning "Danger—Poison."

Two of the most common rose diseases—especially in Southern California—are powdery mildew and rust. If you had problems with these ailments last year, here are some less-toxic control measures to try this spring. If you are thinking about planting new roses, ask your nursery about disease-resistant varieties—you may have more choices than you thought. And always plant roses in full sun.

Powdery mildew. This whitish, powderlike fungus disfigures leaves and flower buds. Mildew builds up when days are warm and nights are cool, and it can spread on dry leaves.

Experienced rose growers have two alternative controls. Spray the plant with an anti-transpirant such as Cloud Cover or Wilt-pruf, which appears to prevent infection. Or spray a mixture of 2 teaspoons summer oil and 2 teaspoons baking soda dissolved in a gallon of water. Either spray needs to be repeated on new foliage. Be careful with oil spray; it may burn leaves. Don't try it if temperatures are expected to top 85°, and don't use it in combination with sulfur-based sprays.

Rust. This fungus is easy to recognize by the orangish pustules that cover the undersides of older leaves. Tops of the leaves are mottled yellow. Since rust spreads on wet foliage, the first step in prevention is to avoid overhead watering, or to irrigate in the morning so leaves dry quickly. Picking off the first infected leaves can also help. Warm, dry weather usually stops the spread of rust. Wettable sulfur is one of the least-toxic fungicidal controls.

Two other simple, nontoxic practices can help control rose diseases. Clean up and discard fallen leaves and prunings, where diseases can overwinter. And prune to increase air circulation around the foliage.

'L. D. BRAITHWAITE' *is a fragrant new addition to the family of David Austin English roses.*

New book sings the praises of natives

"Los Angeles ought to look like Los Angeles, not Managua," writes Sally Wasowski in the newly released hardbound book *Native Gardens for Dry Climates* (Clarkson N. Potter Publishers, New York; $35). Instead of trying to reshape our arid environment into a tropical paradise, she suggests, we ought to appreciate its unique beauty and emulate it in our gardens through the use of indigenous plants.

Wasowski's book, which she coauthored with her husband, Andy, is illustrated with examples shot in Southern California neighborhoods, including the Home Demonstration Garden at the Santa Barbara Botanic Garden and Roy and Ysabel Fetterman's dry-wash garden in Pasadena.

The book begins by defining three chaparral and four desert regions in Southern California and the Southwest. It describes landmark plants in each area, then applies those plants in various gardening schemes. Cleveland sage, woolly blue curls, and California bay are suggested as the backbone of a fragrance garden, for instance.

Next comes an extensive

plant portfolio, organized by landscape-use category (border, ground cover), followed by charts indicating where each plant grows naturally.

Native Gardens for Dry Climates should give you plenty of ideas. It's available in most bookstores, or from the publisher at (800) 733-3000.

Grow your own basil

If you love to cook with your own fresh produce, basil is indispensable in the summer garden. What would homemade spaghetti sauce be without it? Large-leaf types like 'Lettuce Leaf' and 'Napoletano' are great for pesto. Scented basils such as 'Anise', 'Cinnamon', and 'Lemon' are perfect for flavoring fruit salads as well as chicken and fish dishes. A new introduction this year called 'Red Rubin' falls in the purple basil category. It's a descendant of 'Dark Opal', one of the first purple basils, with beautiful dark plum foliage considered to have the best flavor. But seed-grown plants vary tremendously, so you get everything from green to purple, with variegated

plants in between. 'Red Rubin' has a more consistent purple color and more uniform size than 'Dark Opal'. It is best used in salads and pasta dishes, rather than for pesto. (For tips on freezing basil, see page 120.)

Here are two mail-order seed sources that sell a wide variety of basils. Their catalogs are free.

Park Seed Co., Cokesbury Road, Greenwood, S.C. 29647, (800) 845-3369; sells 12 kinds.

Shepherd's Garden Seeds, 6116 Highway 9, Felton, Calif. 95018, (408) 335-6910; sells 11 kinds including 'Red Rubin'.

More new English roses from David Austin

Big shrubby bushes of David Austin English roses will be in bloom this month all over the West. These roses are cherished for their vigorous growth, resistance to disease, repeat flowering habit, and large, fragrant blooms. One of the favorites is 'Mary Rose', a rose pink variety that Austin introduced in 1983. Now 'Mary Rose' has two offspring that are living up to

their parent's reputation: 'L. D. Braithwaite' and 'Winchester Cathedral'.

'L. D. Braithwaite' (shown at left) is a hybrid of 'Mary Rose' and 'The Squire'. It bears brilliant crimson blooms with a pleasing scent and has handsome, dark green foliage. The plant reaches 4 feet tall with an equal spread.

'Winchester Cathedral' is a white sport of 'Mary Rose'. Occasionally the blossoms show a pink blush or a bit of rose speckling, but in general this rose looks like its mother made over in white. Let it grow to its full height and breadth of 4 to 5 feet for a summer-long cloud of fragrance.

You can order both these roses in 3-inch pots now for immediate planting. One good source is Heirloom Old Garden Roses, 24062 N.E. Riverside Dr., St. Paul, Ore. 97137; (503) 538-1576. Catalog costs $5.

Limas that work where summers are short

Like sweet corn, garden-fresh lima beans are markedly tastier than their grocery store counterparts. But because most limas take a long time to mature, gardeners who live where the growing season is short don't even consider planting them. A new lima, however, may succeed where others fail.

'Betty', an early pole-type lima, races from sowing to harvest in around 10 weeks. It has the ability to germinate in relatively cool (for limas) soil, so you can plant anytime after daytime temperatures get into the 70s. It also tolerates relatively cool nights. (For optimum performance, most other limas need warm nights.)

Give this lima a 6- to 8-foot pole to climb, but expect the heaviest production near the bottom of the vine. After harvest, you can eat the beans fresh or dried.

You can buy 'Betty' from

Peters Seed and Research, 407 Maranatha Lane, Myrtle Creek, Ore. 97457. Catalog costs $2.

Sage advice: plant Salvia greggii

One of the sage clan's shining stars is *Salvia greggii,* a perennial in *Sunset Western Garden Book* climate zones 8–24. This waist-high plant blooms for months, attracting hummingbirds all the while.

Salvia greggii has become easier to find recently, and is available in more colors than before. All have a remarkably long season of bloom, but not all are equally strong growers.

The red-flowered *S. greggii* is the bushiest and strongest grower, with the pink-flowered one a close second, and salmon-flowered versions just behind pink. Purple and rare white forms are weaker and not quite as floriferous. You can buy most kinds in 1-gallon containers for around $5 each, or 5-gallon containers for about $17.

Plant *S. greggii* in well-drained soil in a place that gets full sun. Go easy on the water; plants are quite drought tolerant once established.

Flannel bush, an uncommonly showy California native

The common flannel bush (*Fremontodendron californicum*) is one of the showiest and most distinctive California native plants. An evergreen shrub reaching 10 to 20 feet high, flannel bush bears big lemon yellow flowers in May and June.

Native to the Sierra foothills, flannel bush can be grown in *Sunset Western Garden Book* climate zones 7–24. However, plants must have excellent drainage or they'll quickly succumb to root rot. They do best planted with other drought-tolerant natives such as ceanothus.

NORMAN A. PLATE

BRANCHES GLOW *with lemon yellow flowers when Fremontodendron 'California Glory' blooms.*

Nurseries also carry hybrids of *F. californicum* and *F. mexicanum,* the Southern flannel bush. These hybrid plants generally resemble common flannel bush but have larger flowers and bloom over a longer period. 'California Glory' (pictured above) bears cup-shaped yellow flowers as wide as 3 inches on an upright plant.

Nurseries sell plants in 5-gallon cans for $22 to $30.

Mildew-resistant bee balm

Bee balm (*Monarda*) is to bees and hummingbirds what a magnet is to iron. The pleasant fragrance of the leaves leads many gardeners to put bee balm into the herb garden, where they can brush against this 2- to 3-foot plant frequently. Bee balm grows in all Western climate zones, and does best in moist soil with plenty of organic matter. However, it has one weakness: it is susceptible to mildew.

But breeders have developed several forms that resist mildew. (Remember, resistance is not immunity, so put plants in a place with good air circulation.)

Monarda didyma 'Gardenview Scarlet', with its extra-large red flower bracts, is probably the most attractive red. For raspberry-colored flowers, try *M. d.* 'Raspberry Wine'. *M. d.* 'Marshall's Delight' produces pink flowers during a season that can run through September. It's one of the longest-flowering bee balms, and probably the most mildew resistant. For intensely violet-purple flowers, try *M. fistulosa* 'Violet Queen'.

You can get most of these plants from perennial specialists or from mail-order suppliers. Two good sources are White Flower Farm, Box 50, Litchfield, Conn. 06759, (203) 496-9600; and Wayside Gardens, Hodges, S.C. 29695, (800) 845-1124. Catalogs are free.

Tips for seed-starting success

Starting plants from seed can be a very satisfying—or discouraging—experience, depending on how you go about it. Here are 10 tips to help you get the best germination and growth.

• First thoroughly soak seed flats or pots in a solution of 1 part bleach to 10 parts soapy

water. Then rinse them off well.

• Use a commercial seed-starting medium, or combine equal parts potting soil, perlite, and vermiculite.

• Moisten the growing medium before sowing seed.

• Sow seed according to package directions. When in doubt, sow thinly.

• Keep the growing medium evenly moist. Don't let it fluctuate between wet and dry, or stay soggy.

• Most warm-season plants germinate best when the soil temperature is between 75° and 95°. If soil is cooler, seeds take longer to germinate. To speed germination, use either a soil-heating cable or a heat mat.

• To avoid leggy plants, move containers into bright light, but not direct sun, immediately after sprouts poke through the soil.

• Thin crowded seedlings by clipping them with scissors at soil level until remaining seedlings have at least an inch between them.

• Start fertilizing when seedlings have two sets of true leaves (but don't fertilize right after transplanting). Every fourth watering, use a half-strength liquid fertilizer or a fertilizer sold for starting seeds.

• Transplant seedlings started in flats to larger containers when they have two to four sets of leaves.

Bromeliads in Balboa Park

For garden enthusiasts, any day in May is a good one to enjoy the verdant gardens of the San Diego Zoo and Balboa Park. But if you are a bromeliad fancier, or are simply curious about these exotic plants, Memorial Day weekend is best. That's when the zoo's bromeliad garden is in its spring glory, flaunting flamboyant blooms and fantastic forms. That weekend, the park also hosts its yearly bromeliad show and sale.

Leonard Kent Bromeliad

Garden, maintained by volunteers from the Bromeliad Study Group of Balboa Park, is on the eastern side of the zoo, between the children's zoo and the hummingbird aviary. Follow the pathway running about 150 feet through the garden, and you'll see outstanding specimens chosen from more than 2,000 bromeliad species and thousands of hybrids and varieties. A garden display case will feature a dozen or so labeled plants in their prime.

The bromeliad show and sale are held at Casa del Prado, on El Prado just a few blocks south of the zoo. There, you can admire artfully arranged bromeliad displays and chat with knowledgeable study group members who sponsor the event, grow plants for the sale, and give a portion of the proceeds back to the bromeliad garden. Most plants, in 3- to 6-inch pots, cost $3 to $5. The event is held on Saturday and Sunday, in the Majorca Room. Admission is free. For more information, call (619) 484-5948.

Also worth a visit is the 80-year-old Botanical Building, adjacent to Casa del Prado. It houses some 1,200 permanent plants, as well as seasonal color displays. Admission is free.

To reach the zoo from Interstate 5, take the Pershing Drive exit. Hours are 9 to 4 daily. Zoo admission ($13, $6 ages 3 through 11) is required for entrance to the garden. For zoo information, call 234-3153.

Flower bulbs that made our forebears swoon

Early flower bulbs won the hearts of plant fanciers from Thomas Jefferson to Gertrude Jekyll. But as breeders and growers focused on newer varieties, many of the old ones disappeared. Scott Kunst, a landscape historian, became interested enough in these old gems to bring them back onto the market.

Now in its third year, Kunst's mail-order bulb business, Old House Gardens, lists about six dozen kinds of antique bulbs in its catalog. Most are crocuses, daffodils, hyacinths, and tulips, though there are also listings for crown imperial, grape hyacinth, hardy gladiolus, Siberian squill, snowdrop, and winter aconite.

The catalog is fascinating, giving dates when various bulbs were popular (some in the 1600s), historical background, and information about where these heirloom bulbs are currently grown.

To receive a catalog, send $1 to Old House Gardens, 536 S. Third St., Ann Arbor, Mich. 48103.

Where have all the honeybees gone?

If you live in the San Francisco Bay Area, the Napa Valley, or the Monterey Bay area, your garden is one of the fortunate ones: it's probably still being visited by plenty of honeybees pollinating your crops and fruit trees. But it may not be for long.

STEPHEN SIMPSON

FLAMBOYANT CHERRY BROMELIADS *(Guzmania) are in their prime during May at the San Diego Zoo. A show and sale occurs there at Casa del Prado on Memorial Day weekend.*

Up and down California, honeybees are being killed by the varroa mite. This ⅟₂₅-inch-long pest, which looks like a tiny crab, feeds primarily on developing honeybee larvae called brood, thus depleting a colony's work force. Honey production declines and the colony dies. When healthy honeybees raid weakened nests for honey, they pick up the mites and spread them to stronger colonies.

The honeybee population in the San Francisco Bay Area and nearby counties is mostly feral, or wild. The mites have reduced colonies of these feral bees by only about 16 percent, according to a survey by UC Davis entomologist Robert Page. But in counties where beekeeping is substantial, around Sacramento, Los Angeles, and Riverside, feral colonies have almost disappeared.

Page says the decline in Northern California will only get worse. One way gardeners can help maintain the feral honeybee population is by not spraying pesticides on bee-pollinated plants, such as melons, squash, and fruit trees, when there is a danger of killing bees. If you have to use insecticides like carbaryl

BILL ARON

TOMATOES UNCAGED: *A good way to support your tomatoes is to tie them to wire strung between pine stakes.*

(Sevin) that kill honeybees, spray in the evening when the bees aren't active.

If you're a hobbyist bee-keeper, you can treat colonies with a miticide containing fluvalinate (called Apistan), available from beekeeping supply companies.

Tying tomatoes? Plan ahead

If you're like most home vegetable gardeners, you've probably used the standard conical tomato cages commonly sold at nurseries to control your tomato plants. A cage works well enough while a plant is small, but just when the plant is laden with fruit, forget it. At that point, there's little you can do to keep the plant from sprawling about and flopping over, often taking the entire cage with it.

A good alternative is a trellis system that can support a whole row of vigorous plants. Once the structure is in place, you can reuse it every year.

Prepare your soil and install the trellis before planting your tomatoes. A good choice for vertical supports is 8-foot lodgepole pine stakes, pounded 2 feet into the ground at 6-foot intervals. Strands of wire should be strung between the poles at 10-inch intervals from the ground up. Most any heavy-gauge wire will do, but plastic-coated wire is best because it won't rust or heat up in the summer sun.

A simple way to string the trellis is to work one rung at a time. Start a strand of wire at an end pole, and wrap it twice around each stake as you move down the row. For additional support, tack or staple the wire in place.

Space tomatoes 4 feet apart in a row along the wire. Plants are easy to handle and less apt to break if you tie them to the wire as they grow. Any type of garden tie works if you wrap stems loosely to prevent girdling as they grow. Strips of old nylon stockings work particularly well.

NORMAN A. PLATE

Tip of the Month

Few vegetables can turn a food garden into a jungle faster than the cucurbits—squash and melon family members. At planting time, you stick a tag in the ground next to each seedling, and within weeks a riot of leaves covers everything. In Sunset's test garden, we keep track of tag-eating cucurbits by starting with extra-tall plastic tags. As plants reach the tags, we staple them to 30-inch lengths of 1-by-1 cedar stakes. At harvesttime, the extended tags stick out like battle flags.

A new history of California landscape design

Anyone interested in landscape design and California history will want a copy of *California Gardens: Creating a New Eden,* by David C. Streatfield (Abbeville Press, New York, 1994; $55). This 271-page book is much more than a coffee-table conversation piece. Although it has plenty of color photographs, it holds your attention with fascinating facts and historical information about gardens in California.

The book begins by describing Spanish-influenced gardens in the early to late 1800s. "The transformations of the California landscape during the Spanish and Mexican occupation of Alta California have become part of the romantic mythology of a proud, aristocratic society that

lived on the land with elegant grace," states Streatfield.

After the Hispanic period came the Victorian era. "American garden design in the 19th century was dominated by European ideas," writes Streatfield. From there, he takes the reader through the Arts and Crafts movement of the early 20th century to the imported styles of Northern and Southern California, where wealthy entrepreneurs funded designs based on "Japanese and Mediterranean design traditions, the French Baroque, and English gardens, both formal and naturalistic."

Streatfield continues through the 20th century, ending with designs by contemporary artists such as Topher Delaney and Isabelle Greene.

An okra for Yankee gardens

Gumbo is another name for okra, and no self-respecting pot of gumbo soup is complete without its namesake. But Yankee gardeners who try to grow this Southern vegetable up North are often frustrated. Away from the long, hot summers of Dixie, okra plants just sulk and refuse to set fruit.

Now W. Atlee Burpee & Co. has introduced a new okra called 'North & South' that tolerates cool weather and matures in 48 to 50 days. The pods can grow to 6 inches and still be tender, and they're also good for freezing.

If you order seeds now and start plants to set out in July, you should be harvesting pods by September. Set out okra plants in rich, well-drained garden soil where they'll get sun all day long. Provide plenty of water. A packet of 30 'North & South' okra seeds costs $1.75 from W. Atlee Burpee & Co., 300 Park Ave., Warminster, Pa. 18991; (800) 888-1447.

By Debra Lee Baldwin, Sharon Cohoon, Owen Dell, Steven R. Lorton, Jim McCausland, Lynn Ocone, Lauren Bonar Swezey, Lance Walheim

May Checklist

▪ PACIFIC NORTHWEST

BAIT FOR SLUGS. Put bait around newly set out seedlings, broadcast it over ground covers, and put it near rocks, the bottoms of big pots, and other places slugs like to hide. But be careful to keep bait away from pets and small children.

CONTROL WEEDS. Handpick, hoe, or spot-spray them with a chemical herbicide. If you pull weeds, lay them on the compost pile and allow the roots to dry out and die before turning them into the pile.

DIVIDE PERENNIALS. Throughout the North-west, you can divide peren-nials that have just finished blooming. If you act fast, you can divide late summer- and fall-blooming plants and not lose a year of flow-ers. Gingerly dig a circle around clumps with a spade or shovel and pop them out of the ground. Cut a clump the size of a dinner plate into three or four pieces. Replant and water well.

FEED FLOWERING SHRUBS. Apply a high-nitrogen fertilizer this month to bloomed-out flowering shrubs to encourage produc-tion of leaves and branches and to help set a strong crop of flower buds for next year.

FEED LAWNS. Through-out the Northwest, mid-May is the perfect time to give lawns a strong feeding. Apply ½ to 1 pound actual nitrogen per 1,000 square feet of turf to keep grass green and vigorous.

FEED SUMMER-FLOWERING PLANTS. As soon as you've set out summer-flowering plants, give them their first feeding (early in the month in zones 4–7, later in the month in zones 1–3). Liquid applica-tions of a balanced fertilizer work well. Feed plants at three-week to monthly inter-vals with a full-strength solution, more often with a weaker mixture.

GROOM BULBS. Dead-head flowers, fertilize, and continue to water any bulbs that have bloomed, until leaves die down in summer. Don't cut leaves off now—you'll damage the bulbs' ability to store energy for next year's bloom.

MOW LAWNS. All through the Northwest, lawns explode with growth now. You may have to mow more than once a week. On the rainy west side of the Cascades, don't miss a chance to mow when the sun is shining.

PLANT ANNUALS. Throughout the North-west, direct-sow seeds of bachelor's buttons, calen-dula, clarkia, cosmos, impa-tiens, marigolds, nastur-tiums, nicotiana, pansies, salvia, and sunflowers.

PLANT BEGONIAS, FUCHSIAS, GERANI-UMS. In zones 4–7, put these summer flower factories into the ground or set them out in pots early this month. In zones 1–3, wait until the end

Sunset Western Garden Book climate zones

☐ (1–3) ▨ (4–7)

of the month, after the threat of frost has passed.

PLANT PERENNIALS. Buy plants now and put them in the ground immediately.

PLANT VEGETABLES. Get warm-season crops—beans, corn, cucum-bers, eggplant, melons, pep-pers, and tomatoes—into the ground soon.

PRUNE LILACS, RHODIES. For cut flow-ers indoors, judiciously take off branches in bloom. Other-wise do any needed pruning as soon as blooms fade. Af-ter pruning, water well and scatter a complete granular fertilizer (12-12-12 is a good choice) around the base of each plant.

REMOVE FADED BLOOMS. Deadheading improves a plant's looks and stops it from developing seeds, thereby channeling energy into production of foliage and roots. Remove spent blooms from peren-nials, rhododendrons and other flowering shrubs, and newly set out annuals.

SET OUT HERBS. Throughout the North-west, set out herbs. Most like full sun and coarse, well-drained soil.

'CHINA DRAGON', *introduced in 1979, has brilliant red-orange beards. The irises are backed here by pink painted daisies in a Salem, Oregon, garden.*

Bearded and beautiful, irises stand tall in the West

I N THE MYTHOLOGY of ancient Greece, the goddess Iris had an ostentatious way to travel: she would ride on rainbows from Mount Olympus to her destination. With that in mind, the Greek botanist Theophrastus bestowed her name on an extremely colorful group of flowers. We grow their descendants—mostly tall bearded irises—in our gardens today. You'll see them in flower around the West this month; they bloom reliably in all Western climate zones. In fact, the world's two biggest iris growers are in the West.

Like most flowering plants, bearded irises are best chosen at bloom time so you know what to buy for planting season—starting in July, just four to six weeks after the last flowers fade. Indeed, bearded irises are one of the few spring-flowering "bulbs" that you plant in midsummer.

RAINBOW COLORS, FLAMBOYANT FORMS

Looking through the catalogs of three major iris growers (Aitken's Salmon Creek Garden, Cooley's Gardens, and Schreiner's Iris Gardens), we counted nearly 1,000 varieties of tall bearded iris, ranging in price from $3 to $40 per rhizome (a thickened underground stem).

In recent years, breeders have been working to produce varieties with bigger flowers, more flowers per stem, purer colors, laced and ruffled blossoms, and more striking or subtle patterns. And they've made a lot of progress: for example, the 1940 Cooley's catalog crowed about one iris with "huge" 3¼-inch flowers; today, the same catalog

bulges with flowers almost twice that size.

Irises come in every color of the rainbow except true red and green, and breeders are working on that. The wide range of colors as well as varying patterns and sizes allow you to achieve almost any effect you want. Mass irises for impact or salt them into mixed borders. You can grow them for cut flowers, or raise them for show.

It usually makes the most sense to decide where and how you'll use irises, then choose the varieties that suit your purposes.

For massed display, there's much to be said for solid colors. Seen from across the garden, masses of irises stand out as whole color blocks, while individual ruffles and subtle details aren't readily visible at a distance.

Flower form can also play an important part in massed displays. Blooms seen mostly from above, as from a porch or deck, should have flared falls (see the illustration on page 155), which are nearly parallel to the ground, such as 'Sultan's Palace'. Irises seen more often from the side—lining the back of a perennial border, for example—look

A POTPOURRI *of tall bearded iris varieties colors a cottage garden near Durango, Colorado.*

THREE FAVORITES, *from left to right: pink 'Beverly Sills' (1979); velvety maroon-red 'Sultan's Palace' (1977); and delicately edged 'Laced Cotton' (1980).*

best if they have falls that hang down like 'Laced Cotton' or have showy ruffles like those of 'Beverly Sills'.

For cut flowers, check out bicolors, flowers with contrasting beards, ruffles, or any other feature that catches your eye in iris catalogs. All tall bearded irises make fine cut flowers (blooming stems can last a week in water). Some irises are delightfully fragrant: purple varieties often smell like grapes.

Bloom time for bearded irises is fairly concentrated, but if you buy early-, mid-, and late-season varieties, you can extend the bloom season to five or six weeks (shorter in hotter climates).

Also look in catalogs for rebloomers (or remontants) and everbloomers. In some areas, including much of California, reblooming irises can flower a week ahead of their tall bearded brethren in spring, then bloom again in fall. Everbloomers flower every three months or so for most of the year in warm climates. Rebloomers and everbloomers are most reliable in California, less so in the Pacific Northwest.

THE IRIS BREEDING GAME

Tall bearded irises bred in the early part of this century have a tailored look: narrow, elegant, smooth-edged falls and standards. Though few of them are sold anymore, you'll occasionally see classics like 'Dauntless', winner of the 1929 Dykes Memorial Medal—the highest award an iris can receive.

To achieve commercial staying power, a variety has to be outstanding, and—happily for gardeners—popularity brings down the price. Good examples of outstanding varieties include 'Full Tide' (blue, 1972), 'Sultan's Palace' (red, 1977), 'Beverly Sills' (pink, 1979), and 'Skating Party' (white, 1983).

Solid colors. Yellows, whites, and purples have always been easy to breed, so you have many to choose from. Blacks (mostly purples so intense they look black) have been in favor recently, and catalogs list many good ones: 'Hello Darkness', 'Night Ruler', and 'Paint It Black'. A host of blues now exists ('Blue Luster', 'Sapphire Hills', and 'Silverado' among them), but breeders are still working on something in a forget-me-not shade.

No clear reds exist (so-called reds tend to be on the brown side), but 'Sultan's Palace' comes close. Orange and rust flowers abound (the orange 'Good Show' grows

AT THE IRIS RANCH *(opposite page) in Cerrillos, New Mexico, shoppers can choose their favorites from thousands of plants. Western growers offer irises in a wide spectrum of colors; from left to right are 'Paint It Black' (1994), 'Competitive Edge' (1991), and 'Magic Show' (1994).*

almost everywhere). Among pinks, 'Beverly Sills' is a brilliant pink classic, and 'Vanity' is extremely hardy. Burgundy is common and appealing: 'Burgundy Bubbles' has fine wine-colored petals; 'Thriller' is intensely colored and very popular.

Patterns. Iris jargon is replete with names describing various color combinations, stippling, and so forth. The bottom line: buy what you like, and if you're especially drawn to a particular pattern, learn its name and look for others like it. Some of our favorites: 'Edith Wolford' (see the illustration at right); 'Abstract Art' (orange falls stippled with burgundy along the edges); 'Spirit World' (orange beard surrounded with a white glow melding into violet, and creamy petal edges).

Shapes. Almost all flowers are ruffled these days. The lace-edged category has been strong for about 25 years, and new ones are still being developed. Good examples include 'Lace Legacy' (medium orange) and 'Michele Taylor' (white). Other choices include "horned" irises, whose beards extend into a small horn; check out 'Mesmerizer' to see whether you like them.

Height. Under good conditions, many varieties reach a height of more than 50 inches (they have to be more than 28 inches to qualify as tall bearded iris). But breeders are trying to reduce the height, since relatively short irises stay more upright in wind and rain. Many new varieties are coming in at around 40 inches, depending on where and how well they're grown.

To link up with other iris fanciers, you can become a member of the American Iris Society. For information, write to Marilyn Harlow, Box 8455, San Jose, Calif. 95155.

PLANTING AND DIVIDING RHIZOMES

Iris rhizomes look something like flattened potatoes. The rhizomes grow just under the soil's surface, sending up a small fan of leaves in late winter. Plants reach their prime in spring. In hotter climates, most tall bearded irises die back somewhat in summer, though rebloomers should be encouraged to stay green with regular watering. In milder climates, iris leaves can live through fall, then die back in winter.

When you buy rhizomes in summer, most come with a trimmed leaf fan remaining from the spring's growth. (You can buy iris rhizomes through New Year's, but summer plantings are more successful.)

Plant rhizomes with leaf fans facing up. New growth proceeds from the fan end of the rhizome, so point that end in the direction you want growth to occur. In multiple plantings, orient all fans the same way. Irises like fertile, well-drained soil and full sun (filtered shade in hottest climates). Plant rhizomes just below the soil surface. Soil should be well amended with compost before planting.

Dig and divide irises every three or four years to maximize the size and quality of flowers. Cut rhizomes apart with a sharp knife, heavy-duty pruning shears, or a very sharp spade. Leave at least one fan on each division.

The standards: the three upper petals. They can be laced, ruffled, or smooth-edged.

The falls: the three lower petals. Falls can flare out or hang down. Each fall has a beard.

The beard: the tuft of fine hairs down the top center of each fall. Sometimes beard hairs grow together into a horn.

CHAD SLATTERY

VIOLET SEASIDE DAISIES *tucked within mounds of deer grass give this meadow its wild feel. Other native plants include Cape Mendocino reed grass, asters, and poppies.*

Turn your lawn into a water-wise meadow

California native grasses, perennials, and bulbs work hard in this playful planting

BACK IN 1989, DEAD lawns were common in many California neighborhoods. The drought was at its height, making it impractical—in some places illegal—to water with abandon.

That was the year Dave Fross, owner of Native Sons Wholesale Nursery in San Luis Obispo County, planted a meadow at his coastal Arroyo Grande home. What began as an experiment in drought-tolerant gardening has evolved into a lush, low-maintenance landscape. Today, with the drought on hiatus, the coastal meadow hardly looks like an austere relic of a drier time.

Fross began his experiment with drought-tolerant native plants, including some that hadn't made their way into home gardens but seemed to hold promise. He chose plants that would accept overhead watering rather than drip irrigation so that existing systems wouldn't have to be converted. And he selected plants that adapted to a broad range of soil types—from sandy loam to clay.

A MEADOW IN MOTION

"I feel like the meadow is teaching me and designing itself," reflects Fross today. Which is not to say that it has evolved without guidance. Fross did start with a plan. "It has a backbone of grasses," he explains. "The flowering plants are used as highlights."

Deer grass (*Muhlenbergia rigens*) is the foundation plant. This robust, clumping warm-season grass grows to 3 feet wide and equally tall. It holds its green color in summer, even with little water. The flowering stalks develop in early summer and turn a buff color later in the season.

Cape Mendocino reed grass (*Calamagrostis foliosa*) is also prominent. This clumping grass has a gray-blue cast and grows 1½ feet tall and 2 feet wide. The flowering stalks emerge in spring a burgundy rose and turn a tawny color by summer.

The grasses carry the meadow and lend continuity from year to year, while a variety of perennials and native bulbs, including brodiaea and alliums, punctuate the garden with color in an ever-changing display. "The color schemes develop naturally with the seasons," says Fross. He likes the way the yellows and blues come on strong early in the year, with the reds and pinks dominating later.

California poppies (*Eschscholzia californica*) are abundant. Two prized varieties are lemon yellow 'Maritima' and pale yellow 'Moonglow'. For a touch of orange, Fross also plants standard California poppies.

Golden asters (*Chrysopsis villosa*), with daisylike yellow flowers, brighten the meadow in summer. These mounding evergreen perennials reach 8 to 12 inches high.

Seaside daisy (*Erigeron glaucus*), a compact perennial with evergreen foliage, graces the meadow with colorful violet flowers with yellow centers. They reach peak bloom in spring and flower sporadically much of the year.

Rose pink and white yarrows (*Achillea millefolium*) lace through the deer grass with their feathery, fernlike leaves. They bloom most abundantly in summer and early fall, with occasional flowers throughout the year.

In late summer and autumn, when little else is blooming, the scarlet tubular flowers of California fuchsias (*Zauschneria californica*, sometimes called *Epilobium californica*) take center stage and provide nectar for hummingbirds.

MEADOW MAINTENANCE

The fast-growing meadow is easy to maintain. Without fertilizer or special soil preparation, plants filled in during the first season.

Before planting, Fross mulched the entire area, then cleared planting spots. The mulch kept the weeds down, conserved soil moisture, and kept flowers from spreading out of bounds.

To help establish plants, he watered regularly through the first year. Now he gives the meadow just 2 inches of water each month from April through October.

Pulling out or cutting back unwanted plants is the primary maintenance task. Every couple of years, in January or February, Fross cuts back the deer grass to freshen it up.

Reflecting on the six-year process, Fross muses, "I've learned not to control the meadow and force things where they don't want to grow. The plants let me know where they want to be." ■

By Lynn Ocone

TWO-LAYER BAGS *slip over young apples in June (above left), protecting fruit. The outer bag comes off 21 days before harvest, leaving colored inner bag (above right). At harvest (below), apples have a polished look.*

The secret to perfect apples is in the bag

PERFECT APPLES DON'T grow on trees. Orchardists thin, spray, sort, wash, and even wax the fruit before it goes to market. Backyard apple growers usually settle for less, consigning the scabby, wormy fruit to the compost pile or the cider press.

But there's a simple way to improve your apple crop: bag it.

This technique was developed in Japan, where orchardists slip a small bag over each fruit in early summer. The bags protect developing fruit from codling moths (the source of worms), apple maggots, sunburn, russeting, and scratching from nearby twigs. They can also help protect fruits against diseases such as scab and mildew.

The process is labor-intensive, but it gives you near-perfect fruit at harvesttime. Apples protected by bags emerge looking as if they'd been waxed and polished. The beauty is more than skin-deep: "Bagged apples can be firmer, providing a nice crunch when bitten into, and, depending on variety, can have slightly more sugar compared with regularly grown apples," says Eric Curry, a researcher for the U.S. Department of Agriculture.

Order apple bags now (see source below) so you'll have them when you need them. Put the bags on after normal June fruit drop and thinning. (Apple trees naturally drop part of their crop at the beginning of summer. Finish the process by removing any misshapen, imperfect, injured, and diseased fruit, along with all but one apple in each cluster.)

Just slip a double paper bag over each remaining fruit, and crimp it closed. Once apples are bagged, leave them alone until about three weeks before harvest (open one bag to check fruit). Then remove all the outer bags, leaving the colored translucent inner bags in place.

About a week after you remove the outer bags, take off the inner bags and let the uncovered fruit finish coloring up. Harvest the crop about two weeks later.

Bags can be difficult to find. One mail-order source is AppleCorps, 700 13th St. N.E., East Wenatchee, Wash. 98802; call (509) 886-9204. Cost is $10.50 per 100 bags, shipping included. ■

By Jim McCausland

'BARBARA KARST' *bougainvillea and 'Peace', a climbing rose, are unlikely companions in this Orange County, California, garden. For details, see page 164*

JUNE

Sunset's GARDEN GUIDE

Spring moves into summer: time to gather ideas from nurseries and successful gardens

In planning any landscape design, don't overlook the style of your house. Stephen Greenholz of Carmichael, California, carried the Mediterranean theme of his Spanish-style house into the garden, with attractive results, shown at right. With the help of landscape architect David Yakish of Garden-makers in Sacramento, he removed the lawn and surrounded the backyard with white stucco privacy walls. Spanish tiles, which cover the floors inside the house, were used for garden paths and patios. A sturdy wooden arbor provides a shady outdoor dining area.

To soften the hard lines of the swimming pool and give it a pondlike look, planting beds were positioned within 16 inches of the edge of the pool (its interior was finished with deep blue plaster). The beds were filled with water-thrifty flowering plants, including garden penstemon, gaura, lavender, rudbeckia, *Salvia greggii*, verbena, and yarrow. A variety of ornamental grasses, including feather reed grass, fountain grass, and maiden grass (*Miscanthus sinensis* 'Gracillimus') contribute to the Mediterranean ambience.

A colorful twist of fate

Bougainvillea and roses aren't a combination Lew Whitney usually recommends to his customers. Roses, after all, are much thirstier than bougainvillea, which are not only drought tolerant but also tend to take over, making them poor companions to just about anything other than another bougainvillea.

But Whitney has a lot of experience with vines, both at Roger's Gardens, the nursery he runs in Corona del Mar, California, and Casa Pacifica, the San Clemente estate whose gardens he

POOLSIDE PLANTS *include maiden grass at far left and scarlet-flowered bee balm (Monarda didyma). Both plants grow in all Western climate zones.*

maintains. "I like combining vines that bloom at different times of the year for more interest," he says. "If the blooms happen to overlap part of the time, so much the better."

In one corner of Casa Pacifica, Whitney wanted something bold that would show off from a distance. He started with 'Barbara Karst', a red-

pink bougainvillea, and paired it with a climbing yellow 'Peace' rose, chosen for its vigor. "I knew it could hold its own," he says.

What Whitney didn't know was how well the dipped-in-pink edges of 'Peace' would echo the deeper-toned bracts of the bougainvillea, or how successfully the large roses

Shrub Pest Table lists [c]
mon problems and their
causes for each plant.

The book is available [f]
$32 (plus $5 shipping) fr
ANR Publications, Unive
of California, 6701 San P.
Ave., Oakland, CA 94608
(800) 994-8849 (inside Ca
fornia), (510) 642-2431
(everywhere).

Freewheeling foxgloves

Few plants self-sow as freely
as common foxglove (*Digitalis purpurea*). If you have
these plants blooming in your
garden, you can allow them to
set seed, then let it scatter naturally or broadcast the seed
by hand. The foxgloves pictured at right in Beverly and
Jerry Gleeson's Seattle garden
send up their flower spikes in
early June. When the flowers
fade, Beverly Gleeson leaves
the stalks standing. Seeds are
ripe if the stalk rattles when
shaken. She either allows the
seeds to spill naturally, or cuts
the stalk and shakes seeds
around the garden. Early the
following spring, plants pop
up around beds, among rocks
in the retaining wall, and from
cracks in paving.

Common foxglove is a biennial plant: it spends its first
year developing clumps of
woolly light green leaves,
then blooms the second year.
Blossoms are typically rosy
pink, but they can range from
purple to shades of pink that
fade to almost white.

This foxglove grows in all
Western climates. Set out
transplants from nursery cans
now, or sow seed early next
spring. Although they flourish
in light shade, plants can also
take full sun and poor soil.
Note that foxglove is the
source of digitalis, a valued
but poisonous medicinal drug.

Zinnias for color in the garden or a vase

Your grandmother probably
had a garden full of zinnias,
and they're still one of the

TALL SPIRES *of ros*
Seattle garden. As
left to form seed po

DON NORMARK

NORMAN A. PLATE

would stand out against the
darker background (see the
photo on page 162). "The
plants relate to each other
very well visually, and
they've proved to be quite
compatible," says Whitney.
"Gardeners understand: sometimes you just get lucky."

Summer rose grooming

Most rose growers know
that you should remove faded
flowers from floribundas,
grandifloras, hybrid teas, and
miniature roses to encourage
a new crop of buds to form.
To promote good flowers on
strong stems, the general recommendation is to snip them
off just above the first leaf
(down from the top) with
five leaflets. The cane at this
point should be about the diameter of a pencil. For a
long-stemmed rose, cut above
the second leaf with five
leaflets.

Follow this method only if
the rose bush is vigorous and
healthy. If the plant is weak,
diseased, or young, it's best to
remove faded flowers down
only to the first set of leaves
(which usually have just three
leaflets). Allowing more foliage to remain will encourage
strong growth.

Lilliputian lettuce

For a change from large supermarket lettuces, try growing 'Mini Green', a new
variety of head lettuce that
matures at grapefruit size
about 10 weeks after sowing.
Plants are compact enough to
fit into containers and window
boxes. Just one head of 'Mini
Green' makes a salad.

In cool-summer areas, you
can start seed of 'Mini Green'
now, since it resists bolting
in warm weather. In low- to
intermediate-desert areas, order seed now to plant in fall.
In warm-summer, cold-winter
climates, try growing some
under lath now, but save most
of the seed for planting next
spring.

'Mini Green' is available
from W. Atlee Burpee & Co.,
300 Park Ave., Warminster,
PA 18991, (800) 888-1447;
and Stokes Seeds, Box 548,
Buffalo, NY 14240, (716)
695-6980.

Flowers that taste as good as they look

You may have noticed small
flowers such as violas in the
specialty salad mixes sold by
some grocery stores. Restaurants also use flowers, primarily to garnish dishes.

V. J. Billings, owner of
Mountain Valley Growers in
Squaw Valley, California,
suggests that flowers should
be more than merely edible or
attractive—they should have
mouth-watering flavor. Her
best bets include several
varieties of giant hyssop
(*Agastache*).

Giant Mexican lemon hyssop (*A. mexicana*) has incredibly sweet flowers. The 5-foottall plant is somewhat rangy
with few leaves, but the
masses of shocking pink flowers that cover it from spring
until frost make up for the
plant's homely appearance.
The leaves have a lemon
flavor.

'Tutti-Frutti' (a hybrid of
A. barberi and *A. mexicana*)
is similar to giant Mexican
lemon hyssop, but the flowers
are fruitier and the plant only
grows about 3 feet tall.

Mint hyssop (*A. aurantica*)
has the most attractive form

165

RHODODENDRON LEAVES *that look bleached or stippled show signs of attack by greenhouse thrips.*

good chance your plants are infested with greenhouse thrips. These tiny (1/16-inch-long) insects feed on the undersides of rhododendron leaves. They also infest many other widely-planted landscape shrubs, such as mahonia and viburnum.

The yellowish nymphs and black adults are most active during warm weather. The leaf undersides of infested plants are often covered with shiny black excrement. Unless you inspect leaves carefully, the current season's damage usually isn't noticeable until mid- to late summer.

If you suspect your plants are mildly infested with greenhouse thrips, spray leaves regularly with a forceful stream of water. Or thoroughly spray the undersides of leaves with insecticidal soap or a lightweight summer oil. You may need to repeat sprays periodically. More-toxic chemicals, such as acephate, can be used, but these may also kill beneficial natural enemies of thrips.

ROSES CLIMB *over a lor. MeadowView Country C*

THE BEST SUNFLOWERS FOR CUTTING ARE ONES WITH 4- TO 6-INCH FLOWER HEADS, IN COLORS THAT RUN FROM PALE YELLOW TO DEEP RED AND SHAPES THAT RANGE FROM CLASSIC TO UNPREDICTABLE.

BY

LYNN

OCONE

NEW COMPACT
VARIETIES
DELIVER BIG IN
A VASE AND
ARE A CINCH
TO GROW

Sunflowers
that make the cut

THERE'S NO FLOWER QUITE SO IMPRESSIVE AS THE GARGANTUAN 'RUSSIAN Mammoth' sunflower, its 12-inch blooms towering 12 feet above the garden. That's exactly where such a beast belongs—in the garden. Oh sure, there will be those who insist on bringing a bouquet of giant sunflowers indoors. It's not impossible, assuming you own a vase made of lead and a house large enough to contain the flowers' freakish proportions. But for most of us, 'Mammoth' sunflowers, as well as their signature seeds, are for the birds.

Fortunately, giant sunflowers (sometimes called 'Mammoth', sometimes 'Giant'; either name sometimes paired with 'Russian', sometimes not) aren't the only variety on the market. In fact, the trend in sunflowers is toward smaller, more manageable varieties bred for cutting. Although many of these plants can still get quite tall (8 feet is not uncommon), a few varieties never get bigger than 3 feet, making them perfect for small spaces and even containers.

Sunflowers are a cinch to grow and easy to find. Better nurseries sell a half-dozen or so varieties, and catalogs offer even more. Don't be surprised, though, if the sunflowers you grow don't match the printed descriptions of plant height and flower size. The same variety will vary from garden to garden depending on plant spacing, soil fertility, and water.

SINGLE-STEM VERSUS MULTIFLOWERING VARIETIES

Two groups of sunflowers make good cut flowers. The first comprises single-stem varieties such as the new hybrids 'Sunrich Lemon' and 'Sunrich Orange', which produce one great flower per plant, followed by lesser blossoms. Single-stem plants grow and bloom at the same rate, making them a favorite of commercial growers. If you choose a single-stem variety, plant now and successively every two weeks through the summer for continuous bloom.

The second group includes varieties with multiple flowering branches, including creamy yellow 'Valentine' and hardy 'Daisetsuzan'. Unlike single-stem varieties, each plant produces bunches of flowers. These varieties grow best when spaced 18 inches to 3 feet apart.

Ten sunflowers perfect for cutting

BIG SMILE
5-inch flowers, golden yellow petals with brown disks. 12- to 18-inch plants, single stem. From Shepherd's Garden Seeds.

SUNRICH ORANGE
3- to 8-inch flowers, golden orange petals with black disks, pollen-free. 3- to 6-foot plants, single stem. From Shepherd's.

AUTUMN BEAUTY
5- to 8-inch flowers, autumnal shades; brown disks. 5- to 8-foot plants, multiflowering. From Liberty Seed Company.

ITALIAN WHITE
4- to 5-inch flowers, white to yellow petals with chocolate brown disks. 5- to 8-foot plants, multiflowering. From Shepherd's.

Multiflowering plants look great in the garden longer than single-stem plants because they bloom over an extended period, although the first flowers are often the nicest. Since the leaves start to look shabby before the last flowers open, you may want to plant a couple of crops during the summer and pull the older plants as they decline.

Red sunflowers. Choosing which variety to grow is largely a matter of taste. You don't even have to like yellow. One of the most talked-about new varieties is 'Prado Red', touted as the first all-red sunflower, though its petals are actually deep rust and its disks are brown. This multiflowering plant grows 3½ to 6 feet tall with 4- to 6-inch blooms on long stems to 21 inches. A larger reddish multiflowering sunflower is 'Velvet Queen', with 4- to 8-inch flowers on plants that can reach 8 feet.

Double blooms. Another surprising group consists of sunflowers with double flowers, ranging in color from calendula orange to yellow. Because their disks are hidden well inside the blooms, the flowers resemble large chrysanthemums. 'Orange Sun' is a new single-stem variety that grows to 8 feet. Two multiflowering varieties are 'Teddy Bear' (to 3 feet tall) and 'Double Sun Gold' (to 4 feet).

Mixed varieties. Choose a mix if you like to experiment or have limited space. Tall mixes include 'Autumn Beauty', 'Color Fashion Mixed', and 'Inca Jewels'. 'Music Box' is a dwarf mix with 4- to 5-inch blossoms on 28- to 36-inch plants. All have petals in autumnal shades and are multiflowering.

Pollen-free. Perhaps the most house-friendly sunflowers are the pollen-free

NORMAN A. PLATE

COLOR FASHION MIXED
4- to 6-inch flowers, autumnal shades with bicolors; brown disks. 6- to 8-foot plants, multiflowering. From Stokes Seeds.

SUNRICH LEMON
3- to 8-inch flowers, lemon yellow petals with black disks, pollen-free. 3- to 6-foot plants, single stem. From Shepherd's.

ones, including new hybrids like 'Sunbeam', 'Sunbright', 'Sunrich Lemon', and 'Sunrich Orange'. All are single-stem plants, grow to around 6 feet, and won't leave pollen all over the place when flowers are brought indoors.

GROWING TIPS

Depending on the variety you choose and the time of year you plant, sunflowers take 10 to 14 weeks from sowing to cutting. The quick payoff means you can plant throughout the summer.

Sow sunflower seeds in full sun. You can also start them in flats to protect vulnerable seedlings from birds and snails. However you do it, keep birds and snails at bay by using fabric row covers or netting. And remember that sunflowers follow the sun, so place the plants in the garden where you can en-

joy their cheery faces.

Finally, don't pamper sunflowers. They grow fine in most soils, and too much fertilizer results in bushy plants with woody stems and fewer, smaller flowers. Don't overwater, either. To help prevent diseases such as rust, avoid wetting the foliage.

SEED SOURCES

Catalogs are free unless noted. *Ferry-Morse* and *Thompson & Morgan* seeds are available in nurseries.
• *The Cook's Garden*; (802) 824-3400. Catalog $1.
• *Liberty Seed Company*; (800) 541-6022.
• *Shepherd's Garden Seeds*; (408) 335-6910.
• *Stokes Seeds*; (716) 695-6980.
• *Territorial Seed Company*; (503) 942-9547. ■

VALENTINE
5- to 6-inch flowers, lemon yellow petals with dark disks. 5- to 6-foot plants, multiflowering. From Thompson & Morgan.

INCA JEWELS
4- to 5-inch flowers, autumnal shades with bicolors; chocolate brown disks. 5- to 8-foot plants, multiflowering. From Shepherd's.

MUSIC BOX
4- to 5-inch flowers, autumnal shades with bicolors; dark brown disks. 28- to 36-inch plants, multiflowering. From Shepherd's.

DOUBLE SUN GOLD
4- to 7-inch yellow double flowers. 4-foot plants, multiflowering. From Ferry-Morse Seed Co.

CUT-FLOWER CARE

The vase life of sunflowers is typically 5 to 7 days. We got 11 days out of 'Sunrich Lemon', only 3 out of 'Music Box', but your results will vary depending on soil condition, sun exposure, and how you handle the flower once it's cut. For longest-lasting flowers, follow these pointers.

• CUT FLOWERS EARLY IN THE MORNING. DON'T WAIT UNTIL THEY'RE STRESSED BY THE AFTERNOON SUN.

• CUT FLOWERS YOUNG. CHOOSE ONES THAT ARE JUST BEGINNING TO OPEN.

• KEEP STEMS WET. AS YOU CUT, PLACE STEMS INTO A BUCKET OF WATER.

• RECUT. ONCE INDOORS, REMOVE ALL BUT THE TOP SEVERAL LEAVES AND RECUT STEMS AT A SHARP ANGLE UNDERWATER. THE ANGLE INCREASES THE STEM'S EXPOSED, WATER-ABSORBING SURFACE AREA.

BED OVERFLOWS *with yellow perennial helichrysum, creamy Sisyrinchium striatum, pink and yellow linaria, and purple geranium.*

A work of art

A San Francisco Bay Area artist sculpts a fanciful, joyous garden

W ALKING INTO KEEYLA Meadows's garden in Albany, California, is a little like walking into a fairy tale. The imaginative riot of pinks, purples, blues, and yellows, and the cheerful-looking plants, paving, and accessories proclaim this is no ordinary garden—and no ordinary artist.

Meadows's inventive art comes alive in her garden. "I approach the landscape as I do a painting, working with colors, textures, shapes, and composition," she says. "When combining plants, I think about harmonious colors, a slight shifting of hues, and the effect of textures."

In turn, her garden inspires her art. "In the garden, I form an impressionistic look with dappled sunshine and different shades of green—lime-colored feverfew (*Chrysanthemum parthenium* 'Aureum'), variegated liriope, and ground ivy. In my paintings, I achieve the same kind of lacy foliage by cutting out

KEEYLA MEADOWS *displays her "trellis" painting, inspired by her garden's colors and plants. At left, glazed ceramic urn and metal sculpture are foils for lush plants, such as tall foxglove, Lychnis coeli-rosa, and Rehmannia elata.*

shapes and allowing light to filter through them."

Stepping through her back door into the lush garden, you notice immediately that form is as important as function in both design and plants. Each view includes a whimsical art object or sculpture that also performs some practical purpose.

PAINTED BENCH *nestles cozily amid a climbing rose, clematis, and New Zealnd flax.*

Curving raised planters give height, depth, and dimension to the small space. But Meadows didn't leave them bare; she painted the wood bright pink and trimmed it with handmade blue tiles. Blue tiles reappear in the patchwork brick-and-flagstone paving that meanders around the flower beds.

A copper arbor entices visitors to the back of the space, promising a secret garden beyond. But the arbor, with its winding stems topped by giant

morning glory flowers, is far from utilitarian: it comes to life amid greenery and blossoms. Nearby are sprightly benches and handmade urns.

Lush plantings tumble in showers of color from beds and raised planters. And creeping, climbing, and blossoming plants cover every inch of ground. The wonderful jumble of foliage and vivid color reflects the joyous brushstrokes of Meadows's art. ∎

By Lauren Bonar Swezey

NORMAN A. PLATE

WATER FROM BLACK EMITTER LINE *spreads slowly through soil to irrigate grass. Normally hidden inside the tubing is the emitter (below) with its winding chambers.*

Drip irrigation for lawns

Here's what you need to know about the latest developments for watering your grass

MORE THAN A DECADE after its introduction to the gardening world, drip irrigation has become a household term. This system is widely used to water flower beds, vegetable gardens, landscape plants, and container plants. But what about lawns?

Until recently, lawns could be watered only with sprinklers. Reliable equipment for drip-watering lawns didn't exist. But recent developments with more sophisticated emitter lines have changed things.

Emitter lines are made of polyethylene tubing with drip emitters inserted in it at regular intervals. They've actually been around for a while, but their use in lawns was considered experimental by most irrigation specialists.

In recent years, independent researchers, such as those at the Center for Irrigation Technology (CIT) at California State University Fresno, have done enough testing that emitter lines are now recommended for many lawns.

The greatest recent improvement has been the infusion of an herbicide into the emitter plastic. The herbicide prevents root intrusion when emitter lines are buried in soil

(the minute amount doesn't contaminate the soil). Products not protected by a chemical barrier often became clogged with roots.

The treated emitter line, by Geoflow, of Sausalito, California, has a reported life span of 20 years, which equals or surpasses that of many sprinkler systems.

THE ADVANTAGES OF DRIP IRRIGATION

The primary benefit of subsurface irrigation is water savings. Because water delivery is below the soil surface, no water is lost from evaporation, runoff, or overshooting lawn boundaries. Emitter lines are particularly useful with irregularly shaped and narrow strips of lawn, and on slopes. Lack of overshooting also helps eliminate rotting and water stains on fences and house walls, and prevents slippery walkways.

Ali Harivandi, environmental horticulture adviser for UC Cooperative Extension in Alameda County, says a benefit for families is the lack of surface wetting. Because the lawn's surface is never soaked, it can always be used for activities. The incidence of disease—and need for toxic fungicides—is also greatly reduced when grass stays dry.

In addition, with the availability of emitters with different spacings, subsurface systems can be designed for berms and slopes to avoid wet spots at low points and dry spots at the tops.

CIT's research has shown that weed invasion may be significantly reduced in healthy, dense turf that's watered underground, since there is no surface moisture to encourage seed germination. CIT also found no adverse effects from gophers and other rodents, even though they were present in test sites. However, CIT doesn't recommend subsurface drip in lawns that have competition from large trees with many roots, or in soils that are extremely

porous or gravelly. The system costs 1½ to 2 times as much as sprinklers, but drip irrigation specialists believe the advantages outweigh the extra expense, especially for irregularly shaped lawns.

HOW TO SET UP A SYSTEM

Emitter lines have either turbulent flow emitters (with wide channels so debris won't easily clog them) or pressure-compensating emitters (for slopes, hilly terrain, or especially long lines). For most situations, the more durable turbulent flow emitters are best.

The basic design for use in a lawn is sets of parallel emitter lines that run from a supply line to an exhaust line (see drawing on facing page). In most cases, the supply and exhaust lines are made of polyvinyl chloride (PVC). A PVC system is durable and easy to install, since the PVC provides a rigid framework.

You could use black polyethylene (drip) tubing, but "then you're wrestling with two things that curl—the emitter lines and the poly tubing," says Tom Bressan of the Urban Farmer Store in San Francisco. However, for small lawns and narrow planting strips, polyethylene is the simpler solution.

Emitter lines are easiest to install in a new lawn, although they can be installed in existing lawns using a small power trencher (available from equipment rental stores). This machine carves 1-inch-wide, 6-inch-deep trenches. The emitter lines are laid at the bottom, then the trenches are filled in and overseeded.

Layout of the emitter lines will differ according to the shape of the lawn, but the emitter lines always run parallel to one another and should be buried about 6 inches deep—4 inches in very sandy soil. Soil type determines the flow rate of each emitter (½ to 1 gallon per hour), the spacing between emitters on the line, and the spacing between lines.

As a general guideline for

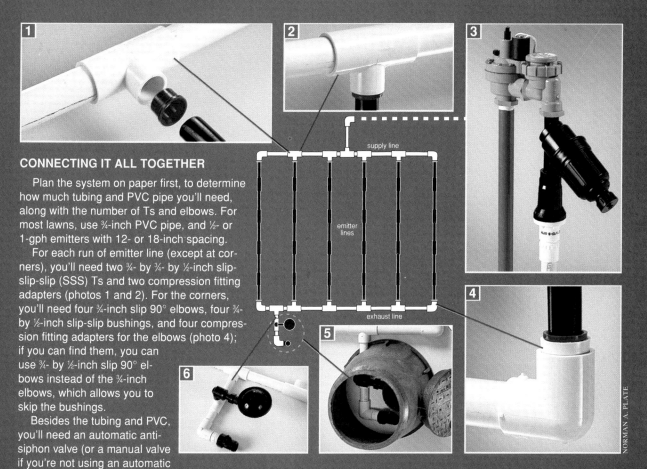

CONNECTING IT ALL TOGETHER

Plan the system on paper first, to determine how much tubing and PVC pipe you'll need, along with the number of Ts and elbows. For most lawns, use ¾-inch PVC pipe, and ½- or 1-gph emitters with 12- or 18-inch spacing.

For each run of emitter line (except at corners), you'll need two ¾- by ¾- by ½-inch slip-slip-slip (SSS) Ts and two compression fitting adapters (photos 1 and 2). For the corners, you'll need four ¾-inch slip 90° elbows, four ¾- by ½-inch slip-slip bushings, and four compression fitting adapters for the elbows (photo 4); if you can find them, you can use ¾- by ½-inch slip 90° elbows instead of the ¾-inch elbows, which allows you to skip the bushings.

Besides the tubing and PVC, you'll need an automatic anti-siphon valve (or a manual valve if you're not using an automatic controller); a 155-mesh filter, a 20- or 30-psi preset pressure regulator (photo 3); a valve box (photo 5); an automatic flush valve, one ¾- by ¾- by ¾-inch SSS T, one ¾- by ¾- by ½-inch slip-slip-thread T, one ¾- by ¾-inch slip-thread 90° elbow, one ¾-inch male pipe thread by male hose thread, and one ¾-inch hose shutoff (photo 6); and PVC pipe glue.

The antisiphon valve must be positioned a foot above the highest point on the system, and the automatic flush valve must be positioned at the lowest point on the system. If you don't use an antisiphon valve, you should install an air relief valve at the system's highest point.

Follow the diagram to put the system together. Use pipe glue to glue PVC pieces together. When glue is dry, insert emitter lines in compression fittings. After installation, flush the lines with the hose shutoff to remove all sediment. If a leak develops, dig down and repair it by splicing in a new section of tubing, using compression fittings; use the hose shutoff to flush the lines after repairs.

clay soil, use ½-gph emitters spaced 18 inches apart with lines spaced 18 inches apart; for loam, use 1-gph emitters spaced 18 inches apart on lines 18 inches apart; for sandy soil, use 1-gph emitters spaced 12 inches apart on lines 16 to 18 inches apart.

At the bottom of a slope, place emitter lines about 25 percent farther apart than is recommended for your soil type; at the top of a slope, set them 25 percent closer.

HOW OFTEN TO WATER

Since the roots of new lawns need time to grow into the soil, it's best to surface-water new sod for the first couple of weeks after installation, and newly seeded lawns until the grass is established.

After that, learning how often to run your system requires some experimentation. Ideally, lawns should be watered according to evapo-transpiration (ET) rates, which are measured in inches per day or week and vary according to climate. This information is available from co-operative extension offices.

For instance, if you live in a mild-summer climate such as that of the San Francisco Bay Area, your lawn needs 1¼ inches of water per week. You can determine how long you need to run your system by using this formula:

$$\text{Application rate} = \frac{231.1 \times \text{Gallons per hr.}}{\text{Emitter spacing} \times \text{Lateral spacing}}$$

Application rate = (inches per hr.)

231.1 (a constant) x Gallons per hr. (emitter rate)

Emitter spacing (in inches) x Lateral spacing (in inches)

Using a 1-gph emitter and 18-inch emitter spacing with lines spaced 18 inches apart (lateral spacing), the application rate would be 0.71 inches per hour. For 1¼ inches total, you need to run your sprinklers 1¾ hours a week. But the underground system should be run more frequently for shorter periods (the soil can't absorb that much moisture at one time), such as for 15 minutes daily or 17 minutes morning and evening three days a week.

WHERE TO GET EMITTER LINE

Treated emitter line from Geoflow is sold at most irrigation supply stores. Or you can order it by mail from the Urban Farmer Store, 2833 Vicente St., San Francisco CA 94116; (415) 661-2204 (catalog $1). The store also provides design assistance; call (800) 753-3747. ∎

By Lauren Bonar Swezey

FLORAL FIREWORKS *burst from baskets hung on lampposts along the Inner Harbour at Victoria, British Columbia.*

Secrets of Victoria's hanging baskets

The fine art of basket planting in British Columbia's capital city

EVERY SUMMER DAY, BOATLOADS of travelers arrive at the Inner Harbour of Victoria, British Columbia. As soon as the visitors hit the street, they invariably glance up, stop cold, and gasp in delight at the baskets hanging from the lampposts.

Victoria has gained horticultural fame with the spectacular hanging baskets the city has been creating for more than three-quarters of a century. The baskets never fail to please resident Victorians, travelers, and visiting British monarchs alike. What's Victoria's secret? We asked, and with typical Canadian generosity, Victoria's horticulturists were quite willing to share the secrets of their aerial magic.

Surprisingly, these baskets are not difficult to make. All the materials are readily available at hardware stores, and the plants (listed on the facing page) or suitable substitutes are sold by many nurseries. Victoria's city horticulturists choose plants for vibrant color and continuous bloom.

MATERIALS

- Sturdy wire basket: 10 inches deep, 16 inches in diameter, 8-gauge (or heavier) galvanized wire
- Sphagnum moss (about 1 cubic foot)
- Potting mix: 4 parts sterile loam, 3 parts peat moss, 2½ parts perlite. Optional: you may want to add 8 ounces of a controlled-release, complete fertilizer (14-14-14) per cubic foot of mix
- Strip of metal: 2 inches wide, 4 feet long, to form a collar around the top of the basket
- Metal pan: 3 to 4 inches deep, 13 inches in diameter, to fit under the basket

PLANTS

6 marigolds: 3 'Lulu', 3 'Gold Gem'
3 variegated nepeta
3 ivy geraniums 'Shirley Claret'
3 schizanthus 'Angel Wings'
6 lobelia: 3 'Blue Fountain', 3 'Sapphire Pendula'
1 Lychnis coeli-rosa (Rose-of-heaven)
3 petunias 'Rose Madness'

ASSEMBLY STEPS

First soak the sphagnum moss in a bucket of water overnight. Remove the moss and squeeze out the excess water. Build the basket in three layers, working from the bottom up, as shown at right.

A strip of metal forms a collar around the top of the basket to hold potting mix in place.

Beneath the basket, a metal pan serves as a catch basin for runoff water (a deep pie pan or oil-changing pan works well for this purpose). To attach the pan, drill three or four holes in the lip of the pan at equal intervals and use steel wire to attach the pan flush to the bottom of the basket.

Use sturdy wire hangers to suspend the basket, then water it thoroughly. For the first two weeks, keep the basket out of direct afternoon sun. Once plants become established, you can move the basket into full sun.

WATER DAILY, FEED REGULARLY

Water the basket daily. Feed plants twice a month with a complete liquid fertilizer. Snip off faded blossoms. You want the plants to become full, even rangy, but if a shoot grows too far out of bounds, snip it back. ■

By Steven R. Lorton

VICTORIA'S 3-LAYER PLANTING SCHEME

BOTTOM LAYER. Insert moss 1 inch thick in the bottom and halfway up the sides of the basket, to just below the middle of the basket. Pack the moss tightly since it will hold the potting soil. Fill in the bottom layer with soil, then plant three nepeta, spaced equidistantly, by gently pushing them through the side of the basket so that the roots extend into the center atop the soil. Repeat the process with three marigolds, placing each of them between two nepeta.

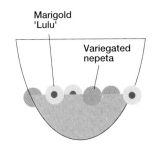

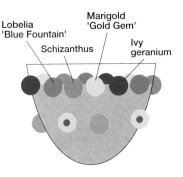

MIDDLE LAYER. Add the next layer of moss and soil; press the soil firmly into place but do not pack it. Then add three ivy geraniums, placing them from the inside so their multiple runners will spread out between the wires. Add three schizanthus, three lobelia, and three marigolds as shown in the center drawing. Add more soil, and continue building up the sides with sphagnum moss until you reach the rim of the basket.

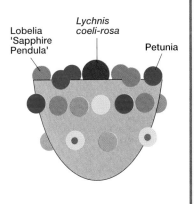

TOP LAYER. Bend the metal strip into a circle and push it down 1 inch between the moss and the soil. Fill the collar with soil, and shape the soil so that it forms a shallow bowl in the center. Plant a single Lychnis coeli-rosa in the center of the basket and surround it with three petunias and three lobelia (stagger plants so that they aren't directly over those in the layer below).

FIERY BLOOMS *of geraniums reach for the sky, while marigolds and lobelia spill down to form a floriferous globe.*

A band of plants for gardeners who dig the blues

10 perennials with blue flowers

BELLFLOWER *(Campanula lactiflora) bears clusters of inch-wide blossoms.*

CORYDALIS *flexuosa 'Blue Panda' bears delicate 1½-inch tubular flowers.*

SALVIA *'East Friesland' bears intense blue flowers on tall spikes.*

DON NORMARK

SEA HOLLY *has thistlelike flower heads that last long when cut for the vase or dried for arrangements.*

A DECADE AGO, gardeners had to search hard for summer-flowering perennials with blue blossoms. That's changed. Nurseries and mail-order catalogs are offering more blue-flowering plants. Here we describe some new introductions and several old-fashioned classics. These perennials thrive in all but the West's coldest and hottest climates.

Agapanthus. New *A.* 'Blue Danube' and *A.* 'Prolific Blue' are hardier varieties developed by hybridizer Don Duncan of Dunford Farms in Sumner, Washington. Plants bear clusters of brilliant blue blooms that reach 2 to 3 feet tall over strappy leaves. Both 'Blue Danube' and 'Prolific Blue' are available only by mail from Wayside Gardens (1 Garden Lane, Hodges, SC 29695; 800/845-1124).

Balloon flower (*Platycodon grandiflorus*). Balloon-like buds pop open to 2-inch-wide star-shaped flowers on stems to 2½ feet tall (dwarf forms reach 1 foot or shorter).

Bellflower (*Campanula lactiflora*). This antique favorite produces clusters of broad bell-shaped, pale blue flowers from early summer into fall. Plants reach 3½ to 5 feet tall.

Centaurea montana bears deep purplish blue blooms resembling cornflowers that reach 3 inches across atop 2-foot stems.

Corydalis flexuosa **'Blue Panda'** bears tubular blue flowers over a 6-inch mound of ferny foliage. It blooms from March into November.

False indigo (*Baptisia australis*). Spikes of sweet pea–shaped, light blue flowers appear in late spring and early summer on 3- to 6-foot plants with grayish green leaves.

Salvia **'East Friesland'.** Masses of dark blue flower spikes appear from early summer through fall on 1½-foot-tall plants.

Sea holly (*Eryngium alpinum*) bears striking thistlelike steel blue to silvery lavender flowers on stout 2½-foot stems.

Spiderwort (*Tradescantia*). You may remember spiderwort from your grandparents' garden where it would flower all summer on stems increasingly long and floppy. 'Zwanenburg Blue' is a new variety that has sturdy, upright 2-foot stems and bears vivid blue flowers over the summer.

Stokes aster (*Stokesia laevis*). The selection 'Blue Danube' is a proven favorite. It bears frilly 3-inch-wide flowers on stems 1 to 2 feet tall. In mild climates, plants will bloom from midsummer through the fall. ■

By Steven R. Lorton

FRAGRANCE FILLS *the summer air as clumps of phlox perfume a border. The 1894 Deepwood House (left) shows off its Queen Anne architecture.*

101 years old—and fresher than ever

Deepwood Estate in Salem invites visitors to stroll through its gardens

I T'S SUMMERTIME AT Deepwood Estate in Salem, Oregon. You're strolling toward the big frame-and-shingle house that looms up among the giant maples. The fragrance of the lush border flowers and the woods nearby is matched in its richness by the sounds of buzzing insects, chirping birds, and rustling leaves.

Little has changed here in the last century. And that's a matter of great pride to the volunteers who planted and pinched, groomed and fussed, to get the place in perfect shape for its 100th anniversary last year.

Inside the 13-room house, stained-glass windows sparkle and hand-carved woodwork gleams, giving the visitor a glimpse of upper-middle-class life in early Oregon.

But from spring through autumn, the real show is outside the house. In the estate's 2 acres of formal gardens, brick paths lead past venerable hedges of boxwood and holly, under arbors, and through fences of lattice. Gnarled old trunks lean over the lawns, vines as big around as your wrist weigh heavily on their support posts, and clumps of daylily, iris, and peony billow out of perfectly edged beds.

One section of the garden is called the Great Room: enclosed by a 10-foot-high hedge is a carpet of lawn upon which stand rectangles and balls of topiary, and at the end of the vista is a fanciful white iron gazebo from the Portland exposition of 1905.

Gardeners will be delighted by the herbaceous borders, which were designed according to the principles of Gertrude Jekyll, who did many of the borders in Victorian England. You'll find no shortage of flowers this month: asters, campanulas, chrysanthemums, cleome, dahlias, delphiniums (in their second flush of bloom), hollyhocks, Japanese anemones, lavender, and lilies. The flowers stand out against the green foliage of earlier-blooming perennials, the blues and celadons of hostas, and the silvers of artemisias and dusty miller.

Spotted through the borders are big, bold cannas that have tropical-looking blossoms and huge green and bronze leaves.

Be sure to see the deciduous vine *Ampelopsis brevipedunculata* with its glistening blue berries, climbing on the lattice fence of the teahouse garden.

Down the slope on the west side of the house, a trail leads through a 2½-acre woodland area with a stream, and shrubs and trees that teem with birds.

To get to Deepwood Estate from Interstate 5, take exit 253 and go west on Mission Street S.E. Turn left (south) on 12th Street and go one block to Lee Street S.E.; turn right into the parking lot. The estate is open noon to 4:30 daily except Saturdays. Admission to the house (including a 45-minute tour) costs $2.50, with discounts for seniors, students, and ages 6 through 12. The grounds are open free of charge. ∎

By Steven R. Lorton

CONTAINER PLANTS *create a leafy screen in Rosalie Ross Sennett's garden, masking views of nearby rooftops and high-rise buildings in downtown San Francisco.*

A rooftop forest... all in pots

Bamboo, shrubs create a secluded courtyard garden

WHEN ROSALIE ROSS Sennett relaxes in her garden, hummingbirds whiz past her ears and bees buzz over the large, colorful blooms she cultivates. While birds and bees are common to many gardens, they are especially welcome in Sennett's rooftop courtyard on a three-story building in downtown San Francisco.

Even if this garden were on the ground, it would still be extraordinary for its variety of plants: more than 130 shrubs, trees, and flowering plants thrive in the 28- by 30-foot courtyard. Perhaps most impressive are the 32 bamboos, some as tall as 15 feet, that help screen out city noise.

All the plants grow in pots—in soil that Sennett carried to the roof in an elevator. Using pots instead of raised beds lets her rearrange the display as she likes.

She bought the first plants nine years ago, when she moved into the townhouse surrounded by high-rises. Eager to counter the starkness of the concrete courtyard enclosed by black wooden walls, she chose bamboo in gallon cans—to add instant greenery.

Next, Sennett bought a carload of plants to help fill the courtyard. "But they made just a tiny dent in the square of concrete," she says. Undaunted, she continued to add more kinds of bamboo, as well as potted trees and shrubs. Today the courtyard is a lush tangle of leaves and flowers.

Of all the plants, Sennett likes the bamboo best: "It's loyal, always green, and always growing." She grows about a dozen kinds, includ-

ing running types such as dwarf whitestripe and giant timber bamboo, and clumping ones like Mexican weeping bamboo.

Growing running types in pots keeps them on good behavior. Left unconfined in a garden bed, their invasive rhizomes (underground stems) pop up wherever they stray.

Japanese maple, ginkgo, pomegranate, and other trees, as well as shrubs such as camellia and jade plant, add texture. For dashes of color, Sennett uses flowers—cosmos, geraniums, salvia—interspersed among the bamboos.

TOPFLIGHT PLANT CARE

Sennett uses a commercial potting soil (a mixture of sandy loam, composted manure, and lava products), adding it whenever she transfers a plant to a larger pot. She fertilizes the plants about three times a year with a 15-30-15 formula.

She had a drip-irrigation system installed, with one main hose that runs around the courtyard and spaghetti tubing that feeds into each pot. Adjustable emitters at the ends of the feeder tubes regulate the water the plants receive. In especially hot weather, Sennett also spot-waters by hand.

She removes dead leaves and blossoms whenever they catch her eye. When it's time to thin older bamboo plants, she uses the culms (stalks) as building material. She created a trellis next to the front door by tying eight bamboo culms together with twine. The trellis directs a lavender starflower (*Grewia occidentalis*) up a wall.

Bamboo culms and twine also help brace the stems of other plants against the wind funneled into the courtyard by nearby buildings. Sennett especially likes the way the bamboos wave gracefully in front of all those high-rises. "That's what makes them glorious," she says. ∎

By Rosalva Welsch

PETER CHRISTIANSEN

heat and drought. This far north, their native heat never comes, and they keep looking good, and often flowering, all summer long. As Evans puts it, "When the native-plant garden is gasping, waiting for fall rains, these are thriving."

Some examples to look for are Baja sage (*Salvia californica*), globe mallow (*Sphaeralcea ambigua*), Guadalupe Island rock daisy (*Perityle incana*), lilac verbena (*Verbena lilacena*), Mexican lobelia bush (*Lobelia laxiflora*), Mexican tulip poppy (*Hunnemannia fumariifolia*), Orcutt's dalea (*Dalea orcuttii*), and San Miquel coral vine (*Antigone leptopus*).

STEPHEN SIMPSON

WHETHER YOU'RE *looking for 4-inch pots of columbine and penstemon, or 5-gallon cans of manzanita and lemonade berry, Tree of Life has a California native for you.*

Home-grown source for native plants goes retail

Tree of Life, in San Juan Capistrano, is now open to the public twice a week

CASPERS PARK

5

TREE OF LIFE

74

San Juan Capistrano

1

Ortega Hwy.

0   5 mi

Pacific Ocean

5

THERE'S NO DENYING it's smart to plant California natives. Most are drought tolerant, many are fragrant, and scores bloom profusely, some through the summer, others even into fall. Yet despite being the most obvious plants for California gardens, California natives are routinely overlooked.

A good way to find out what you've been missing (or, if you don't need convincing, to see one of Southern California's widest selections of native plants) is to visit Tree of Life Nursery in San Juan Capistrano.

This mostly wholesale nursery, long a secret source for some of our best landscape architects and designers, is now open to the public on Fridays and Saturdays. In addition to being able to choose from among the nursery's more than 400 varieties and species of native plants, you can visit its new retail shop, a plastered straw-bale adobe built by owners Jeff Bohn and Mike Evans.

Park near the round adobe. Inside you'll find seeds, gardener gifts, and books. Outside are plants for sale, as well as a native-plant garden (most plants here are labeled).

On the surface, the whole operation appears casual and laid-back, but these guys are serious about their native plants. They even go so far as to introduce mycorrhizal soil fungus, crucial to the successful growth of many natives, to the soil around their plants.

Indeed, for years Tree of Life has specialized in the arcane. Planning on restoring a wetland? The nursery has a good selection of pickleweed and salt grass, two common salt-marsh denizens you're not likely to find growing in any other Southern California nursery. Need arroyo willow, California sycamore, and Western cottonwood for a freeway mitigation project in a riparian zone? You've come to the right place.

Which is not to say that the nursery is too specialized for the home gardener. Two categories of plants deserve special consideration.

BAJA NATIVES

Most California natives look best in spring, but many (with such notable exceptions as lemonade berry and toyon) tend to dry out and look scrubby during the hottest part of summer. Baja California natives, however, laugh at our

ISLAND GIANTS

Plants native to California's Channel Islands have a trait called "island gigantism." Some conspicuous plant parts—leaves, flowers,

A STRAW-BALE ADOBE *houses the nursery's store.*

fruit, or all three—tend to grow larger than those of their mainland counterparts. Ask about island bush poppy (*Dendromecon harfordii*), tree mallow (*Lavatera assurgentiflora*), or island bush snapdragon (*Galvezia speciosa*).

To reach Tree of Life from Interstate 5 in San Juan Capistrano, take Ortega Highway (State 74) east 7½ miles and watch for the sign on the left. Hours are 8 to 4:30 Fridays, 9 to 4 Saturdays. For information, call (714) 728-0685. ∎

By Jim McCausland

TALL FLOWER SPIKES *of 'The Rocket' sparkle in a Kingston, Washington, garden. To launch summer fireworks in your own garden, see page 197.*

JULY

GARDEN
Guide

Let Santa Barbara daisy spill its summer beauty

Have you heard the old joke that the only requirement for perfect grass is a crack in the sidewalk? The same can be said for Santa Barbara daisy (*Erigeron karvinskianus*): it works miracles in tiny pockets of soil, producing a mass of diminutive flowers as long as the weather stays warm. Santa Barbara daisies open white, then turn pink or purplish as they age. The flowers form in drifts atop 10- to 18-inch-tall clumps.

Erigeron karvinskianus is a free-flowering perennial that grows well in *Sunset Western Garden Book* climate zones 8, 9, and 12 through 24. Its toughness, combined with drought tolerance, makes it a good choice for planting in or near stone walls (as shown at right) or among boulders in rock gardens.

Sunset's head gardener, Rick La Frentz, found that Santa Barbara daisy's spilling habit also makes it a good candidate for hanging baskets. Use it alone (three plants for a 12-inch container) or, if you have a larger container (20 inches in diameter or more), plant daisies around the edges to set off a taller plant in the center. Give potted daisies extra water and fertilizer for maximum bloom.

You can buy *E. karvinskianus* at well-stocked nurseries or by mail order from perennial specialists. One source is Digging Dog Nursery, Box 471, Albion, CA 95410; (707) 937-1130. Catalog costs $3.

RUSS A. WIDSTRAND

Asterlike flowers of Santa Barbara daisy turn from white to pink as they age. They drape this garden wall

from midsummer to frost.

TIPS, TRICKS, & SECRETS

Sending your own cut flowers to special friends

It's midsummer, and your garden is overflowing with flowers at their prime for cutting. Wouldn't it be nice to send a bouquet of them to a special friend?

Sunset staff gardener and floral designer Kim Haworth has developed successful techniques for sending cut-flower arrangements across the country using an overnight express service. "I rely mostly on foliage and just a bit of color," says Haworth, "but that's my design style."

In summer, the best flowers to ship are everlasting types, such as statice (*Limonium perezii*) and strawflower. Haworth also likes to include a dahlia or two, but each stem must be inserted in a water pick (available at craft stores or florist markets), which is also necessary for less sturdy flowers. You can experiment to see which flowers hold up by leaving them out of water for 18 to 24 hours.

Haworth's favorite plants for foliage or texture are fern asparagus, bay laurel, broom corn, cast-iron plant, dusty miller (*Senecio cineraria,* woody stems only), ornamental grasses, staghorn fern, and southern sword fern.

Gift bouquet of fern asparagus, broom corn, ornamental grass, statice, strawflowers, sweet bay, and variegated pittosporum is arranged in vase before shipping. At far right, bouquet and vase are carefully wrapped and placed in box.

First, select a box (which you can buy at shipping stores) and a vase that will fit the box. Measure the length of the box, and cut the stems an inch or two shorter.

Arrange the cut stems in the vase. Tie the bouquet together with raffia just above the edge of the vase. Remove it from the vase and wire the stems together at the bottom.

Wrap the arrangement with waxed tissue paper (sold at craft stores or flower markets) or newspaper, reinsert into the empty vase, and then wrap the vase with plastic bubble wrap or newspaper. Line the box with paper and enclose the arrangement, carefully tucking in the foliage.

Pack more paper around the arrangement so it can't rattle around. You may want to add a card advising the recipient to clip stem ends and fill the vase with water upon arrival. Close the box and label it "Fragile" and "Perishable: Open Immediately."

You can ship cut flowers *within* any Western state and *to* most of these states except Hawaii; check with the agriculture department of the destination state. Based on a weight of 3 to 5 pounds, expect to pay about $22 to $32 for overnight morning delivery by a carrier such as Federal Express.

COOK'S CHOICE

Dry herbs at the peak of flavor

In California's Central Valley, July is the prime time to dry fresh herbs. The flavor of most herbs peaks just as the plants begin to bloom, or are in bloom, and when the weather is hot and dry. At this time, the oils in the leaves are most concentrated, and herbs will maintain their flavor when preserved. Hot summer weather also allows the herbs to dry quickly without losing flavor or getting moldy.

The easiest way to dry herbs such as basil, dill, oregano, rosemary, and thyme is to cut twigs or branches, tie them together at the cut ends, and hang them upside down in a warm, dry place. Hang them out of direct sunlight and where air circulation is good. If the area is dusty, hang the herbs in a perforated paper bag (poke several holes in it for circulation).

The herbs should be dry and nicely crisp in about two weeks. To preserve them for kitchen use, strip the leaves from the stems and place them in sealed jars—one for each herb. Store in a dark place.

'Batik', a border bearded iris

Bearded irises are classed by size and height, with tall bearded irises (28 inches or taller when in bloom) getting the lion's share of attention. But a relatively new border bearded iris (shorter than 28 inches) has turned a lot of heads in the past few years. Called 'Batik', this purple-petaled flower with a white spatter pattern looks like, well, batik.

Bred in Nebraska, 'Batik' stands up well to

'Batik' iris has purple petals splashed with white.

harsh winters and has a low enough profile to do well in windy gardens. July and August are prime planting months.

The price of 'Batik' rhizomes, which are offered by many iris growers, has come down to $5 to $10 apiece. Two good mail-order sources are Aitken's Salmon Creek Garden, 608 N.W. 119th St., Vancouver, WA 98685 (catalog $2); and Schreiner's Gardens, 3625 Quinaby Rd., Salem, OR 97303 (catalog $4).

Victorian roses in Arcadia

If you haven't visited the Victorian Rose Garden at the Arboretum of Los Angeles County recently, you should. It's spruced up like new, yet it hasn't sacrificed one whit of its old-fashioned charm.

The Victorian Rose Garden was conceived in the 1950s to complement the Queen Anne cottage and coach house on the arboretum grounds. For authenticity, only roses in cultivation at the turn of the century were planted.

Unfortunately, heritage roses grown on their own

rootstock were rare in the '50s, and the grafted types that were put in didn't do well. Many were replaced by hybrid teas, and the remainder produced few blooms.

Two years ago, arboretum officials asked members of its advanced gardening class, Fanatic Gardeners, if they would be willing to help renovate the garden as a project. They accepted. Instructor Jan Smithen, Bill and Marje Robinson, and Jean Carter did most of the preliminary work. They surveyed the garden and decided which roses could be salvaged; only 10 out of 170 made the cut. Then they compiled a list of suitable replacements, favoring reblooming heritage roses over once-a-year bloomers, and including modern introductions such as those of David Austin, which have a distinctly old-fashioned flower style.

Once the roses were in place, companion plants such as catmint, lamb's ears, Maltese cross, and scabiosa were added. Judy Wigand of Judy's Perennials in San Marcos propagated the majority of these.

The arboretum is just south of Interstate 210, at 301 N. Baldwin Avenue. For more information, call (818) 821-3222.

Jump-start foxglove now

"It can take two years to get foxglove to bloom in New England," says Mary Lou Heard of Heard's Country Gardens in Westminster, "but in Southern California 'biennial' is a misnomer. Plant foxglove in fall of one year, and it will bloom next spring."

Joe Brosius, production manager at wholesaler Magic Growers in Pasadena, agrees and recommends the following procedure:

Starting now, fill flats with a sterile seed-starting mix. Dampen mix thoroughly. Press seeds of biennial foxglove (try *Digitalis purpurea* Excelsior or Shirley strains) gently into the surface. Don't cover with soil; the seeds need light to germinate. Cover flats with a plastic sheet to preserve moisture, then move the flats to a warm, shaded area. Remove plastic when the seeds sprout, but keep soil consistently moist. Thin weaker seedlings so plants are at least an inch apart.

After seedlings have developed their first pair of true leaves, begin feeding with a weak solution of fish emulsion or other plant food. When plants have developed a few more leaves, transfer to 2¼-inch pots. (If you start with a flat at least 1½ inches deep, this intermediate step isn't necessary.) Transplant the seedlings to the garden in September or October when they are 4 to 5 inches tall. You can follow the same plan for Canterbury bells, hollyhocks, verbascum, and other biennials.

"The plants will grow slowly all winter, and burst into bloom in spring," says Brosius.

If you live in an area where summer temperatures

Quick crops for cool summers

If you missed the conventional planting time for short-season summer vegetables, you can still shoehorn a crop into the remaining season. The trick is to start with seedlings, well-developed plants in large containers, or direct-sown seeds, and then push for even, fast growth. Any delay in plant growth could cost you the crop, so from the moment you start vegetables in garden soil, feed and irri-

gate evenly and consistently.

Seed. Don't try anything that takes more than 60 days from planting to harvest. Start by direct-sowing seeds in sifted, well-amended soil in a spot that gets full sun. Plant seeds where you want them to grow; this late, you can't afford to set back growth by transplanting. By choosing only the fastest varieties of different kinds of vegetables, you still have time to plant arugula (roquette), Asian vegetables (mostly Chinese cabbage, broccoli, and mustard), basil, beet, bush bean, cauliflower, kale, kohlrabi, let-

tuce, peppers (both sweet and hot), radish, spinach, squash, and turnip.

Beans, garden cress (peppergrass), and bean sprouts are other fast choices.

Seedlings and plants. Check nurseries and garden centers for vegetable seedlings that are well developed but not rootbound. You should be able to find lettuce and other salad crops. Buy cucumber, pepper, squash, and tomato only if they've already set fruit and grow in large containers (10-inch pots for tomato; 6 inches for cucumber, pepper, and squash).

MICHAEL THOMPSON

regularly get up into the 100s, though, this schedule may not be feasible. In these areas, advises Brosius, either germinate the seeds in an appropriate indoor location, such as a north-facing window, or wait until fall. With luck, you'll still have flowers next year, but a few months later than if you had started the process now.

If you can't find seeds at a nursery, Thompson & Morgan has an excellent selection. For a catalog, call (800) 274-7333.

Launch 'The Rocket' for summer fireworks

One look at *Ligularia stenocephala* 'The Rocket' in bloom (shown on page 192) explains how this perennial got its name. Its flower spires shoot up like skyrockets, and this month they explode with small yellow blossoms. The fireworks last a month.

Tapering flower spires up to 5 feet tall form above big heart-shaped leaves with toothed edges. The leaves, which can reach a foot across, are dark green edged in purple; increased light turns them a bronzy color. The foliage forms a handsome mound from April until frost.

'The Rocket' grows in *Sunset Western Garden Book* climate zones 3–9, 15–17. It likes light shade and damp feet, making it a perfect choice for planting beside a pond or stream. The plant can also be grown successfully in a large container, as long as it's given plenty of water. In the West's coldest climates (zones 1 and 2), you could grow it in a container, moving it into a frost-free location during winter dormancy.

Although 'The Rocket' is relatively new to the retail market, many nurseries now

JOEL ZWINK

Canna grower Rosalind Sarver raises 75 kinds at her nursery in San Diego County.

carry this plant in 1-gallon cans. Plants are also available by mail order from these two sources: Joy Creek Nursery, 20300 N.W. Watson Rd., Scappoose, OR 97056, (503) 543-7474; and Wayside Gardens, Hodges, SC 29695, (800) 845-1124.

Cannas give summer a tropical accent

From summer through fall, fields striped with bold tropical colors brighten Southern California's Deer Springs Road in San Marcos. The flowers are

cannas, more than 75 varieties of them, and the fields belong to Sarver Nursery Co., owned and run by Rosalind Sarver, an octogenarian who says working with plants "and the people who love them" keeps her young.

Catch her at an opportune moment, and Sarver may find time to give you a tour of her 32-acre nursery. She or one of her staff will load you onto a small flatbed truck, and as you bounce over rutted dirt roads, they'll point out rare varieties, including ivory white 'Ermine', a jazzy yellow-red miniature called 'Lucifer', and a two-tone pink named 'Rosalinda' in her honor.

Sarver, who also grows azaleas, ships cannas worldwide. Her most popular variety, she says, is scarlet 'Red President', "the one you see in parks." Her favorite, however, is 'Eileen Gallo', a subtle combination of peach, rose-pink, and cream. Sarver admits that the brilliant 6-foot-tall cannas need some room, but pastel 2-foot dwarfs, ideal for small gardens, are increasing in popularity.

Cannas prefer full sun, ample water, and rich, fast-draining soil. In Southern California, they can be set out year-round, as either plants or dormant tuberous rhizomes.

Bloom season is April

through first frost; August is peak. Plants can become messy-looking, so deadhead spent blooms and trim tired stalks to the ground. Divide after the second or third year and replant divisions just under the soil surface.

Sarver sells potted cannas for $3 to $15; bare-root rhizomes cost $2.50 to $7.50. For a mail-order list, send a self-addressed, stamped envelope to Sarver Nursery Co., Box 905, San Marcos, CA 92079.

Nursery hours are 7 to 4 Mondays through Saturdays, and Sunday afternoons in July and August. For more information, call (619) 744-0600.

COOK'S CHOICE

Sow curly endive now for fall and winter salads

Thrust a fork into one of chef Annie Agostini's salads at Seattle's Crêpe de Paris and you'll spear curly, crunchy, pleasantly bitter

---

endive. Ask her why this green is so uncommon in America and get a dose of French disapproval: "Je ne sais pas...this is the *very best* climate in the world to grow endive. I don't understand Americans!"

If you sow seeds now in the Northwest's milder climates (*Sunset Western Garden Book* zones 4 through 7), you'll be harvesting endive and tossing salads from October well into the winter. A package of seeds is enough to sow a 20-foot row.

Plant seeds in rich, quick-draining soil in a spot that gets full sun. Provide ample water if the summer is dry. Thin plants to 10 inches to a foot apart.

As the plants grow, the leaves will spread out like a giant dandelion. Pull the leaves up into a cone and tie them to blanch the centers.

When you harvest, cut off entire plants at the top of the root, discarding damaged or tough leaves. Sometimes the plants sprout a second crop of leaves.

THE NATURAL WAY

Composting spreads to Sonoma County

Home composting is a hot topic in many California communities, partly out of necessity. In 1989, the California Integrated Waste Management Act (Assembly Bill 939) was passed, mandating that as of January 1, 1995, each California city and county must divert 25 percent of its solid waste from landfill facilities through source reduction, recycling, and composting. By the year 2000, the percentage will climb to 50.

Even without the legal ramifications, home composting simply makes good sense. Compost made from garden waste and kitchen scraps is a great soil amendment and improves plant growth. When used as a mulch, it helps retain soil moisture.

Sonoma County is one of the latest counties to offer

---

a comprehensive home composting program run by UC Cooperative Extension Master Gardeners. Currently, the county has six demonstration sites: Cotati, Petaluma, Santa Rosa, Sebastopol, Sonoma, and Windsor.

A 2-hour compost demonstration class is held at these sites on one weekend of each month. Master Gardeners teach how to compost kitchen and garden waste, and discuss the pros and cons of different composting methods. Demonstration leaders provide technical assistance and tips on troubleshooting.

If you live in Sonoma County, call (707) 527-2608 for dates of demonstrations and for more information. Composting classes are also offered by Alameda County, San Francisco League of Urban Gardeners, and Solano County. To find out if there is a program in your area, call your waste department or sanitation service, or UC Cooperative Extension.

TOOL REVIEW

Quick hose couplers are a snap to use

Like waiting for water to boil, the process of threading hose attachments off and on seems to take forever. A quick coupler can make the job happen almost instantaneously.

Brass and plastic quick couplers work in about the same way: you thread the female part of the coupler onto the male hose end, then thread one male coupler onto each nozzle or sprinkler attachment that fits onto the hose. To connect hose and attachment, you slide back the collar on the female coupler and snap in the male connector.

We've found that brass quick couplers ($7 to $8)

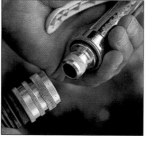

PETER CHRISTIANSEN

last longer than plastic versions ($3 to $4). Brass also allows the water to pass through a ½-inch fitting instead of forcing it through the ⅜-inch fitting common to plastic couplers. (The smaller fitting reduces flow slightly.)

If you choose plastic couplers, avoid those with built-in shutoff valves. Since water passes through them only when they're connected to an accessory, it's impossible to water straight out of the hose end with the coupler attached.

THE NATURAL WAY

Buying butterflies by mail order

For several years, gardeners have been able to buy beneficial insects by mail. Now one source, Brudy's Exotics, is offering eight kinds of butterflies. The butterflies are shipped as eggs or caterpillars in a small deli-style dish. The enclosed instructions tell you how to place them in the garden.

The butterflies available are gulf fritillary, monarch, painted lady, pipevine swallowtail, question mark, red admiral, spicebush swallowtail, tiger swallowtail, and zebra long wing.

Pesticide-free larval food must be provided and should be in the garden when the butterflies arrive. Only the painted lady comes

---

in a kit with larval food.

The firm's catalog lists the butterflies' favorite larval foods. If you want to order some butterflies this summer, it's best to order kinds such as gulf fritillary, monarch, or tiger swallowtail that feed off landscape plants that may already grow in your garden. When the butterflies mature, you will also need to provide nectar plants such as butterfly bush.

A dozen eggs or larvae of a single butterfly variety cost $21.95 to $24.95 (plus $4.95 shipping). You also receive a manual. For a free catalog, write or call Brudy's Exotics, Box 820874, Houston, TX 77282; (800) 926-7333.

By Debra Lee Baldwin, Suzanne Carmichael, Sharon Cohoon, Steven R. Lorton, Jim McCausland, Lauren Bonar Swezey, Lance Walheim

PLANTING

❑ **PLANT ANNUALS.** There's still time to perk up your garden with summer annuals. Choices include geraniums, marigolds, petunias, salvias, verbena, and zinnias. Plant them in beds and pots as soon as you can, water them well, and begin fertilizing in a week or two.

❑ **PLANT VEGETABLES.** You can still direct-sow seeds of beets, broccoli, bush beans, carrots, chard, Chinese cabbage, kohlrabi, lettuce, peas, radishes, scallions, spinach, and turnips.

❑ **START SHOPPING NOW FOR BULBS.** Catalogs from bulb suppliers will start arriving soon packed with choices for fall planting. Order early.

MAINTENANCE

❑ **CARE FOR GROUND COVERS.** After blooms fade, shear back plants to keep them compact, then scatter a complete granular fertilizer over the beds and water it in well.

❑ **DIG SPRING BULBS.** In all Northwest climate zones, dig, divide, and replant daffodils. In zones 1, 2, and 3 (see map), dig hyacinth and tulip bulbs when foliage has faded completely; put them in open boxes or mesh bags where plenty of dry air can circulate around them. In zones 4–7, bulbs can stay in the ground.

PACIFIC NORTHWEST
CHECKLIST
JULY

❑ **FEED MUMS.** Fertilize chrysanthemums every three weeks until buds show color, then feed blooming plants on a weekly schedule.

❑ **GROOM STRAWBERRIES.** Clean out dead leaves and stems. Fertilize and water plants thoroughly.

❑ **MULCH SHRUBS.** Azaleas, camellias, and rhododendrons benefit from a 3- to 4-inch layer of organic mulch spread over their root zone. Mulch helps maintain soil moisture, which in turn helps keep these shrubs healthy as they set next spring's flower buds.

❑ **SOAK HANGING BASKETS.** Wind and sun dry them out quickly. During hottest weather, you may have to water twice daily.

❑ **TEND FUCHSIAS.** Water plants regularly and thoroughly. Snip off faded blossoms before seed pods can develop. Feed plants monthly with a complete liquid fertilizer (12-12-12 is a good choice).

❑ **TEND ROSES.** When you cut hybrid tea blossoms, snip them off just above a five-leaflet leaf. Water plants well during the hot, dry months, and feed them regularly to encourage repeat bloom.

❑ **WATER WISELY.** To reduce the amount of water lost to evaporation, irrigate in the early morning.

❑ **WORK THE COMPOST PILE.** Toss spent flowers, grass clippings, and most pulled weeds on the compost pile (put noxious plants like morning glory and deadly nightshade in the trash). Turn the pile, and if it's dry, soak it well. If decomposition is slow, toss a handful of high-nitrogen fertilizer into the pile as you turn it.

In my country garden in Washington's Skagit Valley, the great feast of summer starts in July when I spy the first ripe 'Early Girl' tomato—the chief ingredient in my secret vegetable sandwich. I pull a young onion, pick a cucumber, and head to the kitchen. Between two slabs of grainy bread, I place fat slices of tomato, thin slices of onion and cucumber, slivers of dill pickle from the jar, dashes of salt and pepper, and—if no one is looking—a large slather of mayonnaise. Heaven!

To keep my tomatoes, cukes, and other row crops coming, I feed plants in early July and again in mid-August with a low-nitrogen (5-10-10) granular fertilizer. I apply it by side-dressing: I drag a shovel along each side of the row 4 to 6 inches from the base of the plants to form a wide furrow about 4 inches deep. Then I lay down a thin line of fertilizer, cover it with soil, and water it in well.

•

Most summer-blooming clematis will produce a second flush of bloom if you cut back the old flower heads just as soon as the first flush is over, then fertilize plants well. Last summer, *Clematis lanuginosa* 'Candida' and *C.* 'Niobe' both rewarded me with a fine second round of flowers.

•

PACIFIC NORTHWEST
Garden Notebook
BY STEVEN R. LORTON

Recently I was reminded of an ugly truth: Matilija poppy (*Romneya coulteri*) is invasive. A couple of years ago, I smugly planted it in a perennial border to enjoy its big crepy white flowers with yellow centers. Now, after two years of restrained behavior, the poppy is sending shoots out 5 feet in every direction. I'm going to dig it out in November.

THAT'S A GOOD QUESTION

Q: Why are Northwest gardeners going crazy over bamboo? Which varieties grow tall? Which kinds stay low?

A: I've seen giant or Japanese timber bamboo as tall as 35 feet, while dwarf bamboos can stay under 2 feet. If you're bewitched by bamboo, you should meet the American Bamboo Society's Pacific Northwest Chapter. Members receive newsletters and notification of plant sales and events. For $10, you can join the chapter. Send a check payable to the society to Phillip B. Davidson, Pacific Northwest Chapter, 10416 107th St. Court S.W., Tacoma, WA 98498; (206) 588-0662.

PLANTING

❏ **PLANT SUMMER COLOR.** Nurseries still have a wide variety of summer flowers that will bloom into fall. Choices include ageratum, celosia, dahlias, marigolds, petunias, portulaca, salvia, sweet alyssum, and zinnia.

❏ **PLANT IRISES.** Plant new rhizomes or dig up and divide overcrowded clumps six weeks after flowers fade. Cut apart healthy rhizomes, and trim leaves back to about 6 inches; discard dried-out or mushy rhizomes. Plant new or just-divided irises in fast-draining soil in a spot that gets full sun.

❏ **SET OUT MUMS.** To add bright color to the fall garden, plant garden chrysanthemums now. If plants haven't formed flower buds yet, pinch growing tips to keep growth compact.

❏ **PLANT FALL CROPS.** Zones 1 and 2 (see map): for harvest in fall (except in highest altitudes), plant beets, broccoli, bush beans, cabbage, carrots, cauliflower, green onions, peas, spinach, and turnips. Below 5,000 feet, plant winter squash among spinach; it will cover when you harvest the spinach.

MAINTENANCE

❏ **CARE FOR LAWNS.** Mow high during the heat of summer; mow when the grass is about a third taller than the rec-

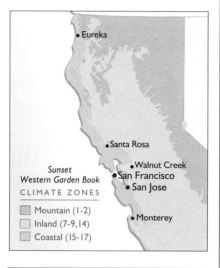

Sunset
Western Garden Book
CLIMATE ZONES

▨ Mountain (1-2)
☐ Inland (7-9,14)
▨ Coastal (15-17)

• Eureka
• Santa Rosa
• Walnut Creek
• San Francisco
• San Jose
• Monterey

ommended height. For bluegrass and fescue, mow when the grass is 3 to 4 inches tall, with your mower set at 2 to 3 inches. Cut Bermuda grass when it's not quite 2 inches, with the mower set at 1 inch. If your lawn is full of crabgrass and it has set seed, collect the clippings after mowing to keep it from spreading.

❏ **WATER WISELY.** If you water with an automatic controller, make sure it runs often enough so plants get ample water, but not so often that the soil stays overly wet. As a test, check soil moisture just before the system is due to come on by digging down with a trowel or using a soil probe. If the soil seems too dry or too moist, adjust the irrigation time.

❏ **COAX BOUGAINVILLEA BLOOMS.** Bougainvillea blooms best if kept on the dry side, so allow the top several inches of soil to dry out between waterings.

❏ **TEND FRUIT TREES.** Zones 1 and 2: On trees with heavy fruit set, thin plums 2 inches apart and apples, nectarines, and peaches no closer than 4 inches apart.

PEST CONTROL

❏ **CONTROL WORMS.** If geraniums, nicotiana, penstemons, and petunias appear healthy but have no flowers, budworms are probably eating the flower buds before they open. Look for holes in buds and black droppings. Spray every 7 to 10 days with *Bacillus thuringiensis* (BT).

Inspect tomato plants for chewed leaves and black droppings, then hunt through foliage and handpick and destroy tomato hornworms. If hornworms are still small, you can control them by spraying with BT, but it's less effective against large ones.

By July, just about everyone, including me, is ready to get away for a vacation. Last summer, I started imagining the fate of the new perennial bed in my Palo Alto, California, garden if I took off. I'd been watering the bed by hand—my favorite way to irrigate plants because I can closely analyze what's happening in the garden. Through past experience, I'd found that good plant-sitters are hard to find, so I could visualize all my young plants shriveling up in the summer heat.

That's when I decided to put in a low-tech drip system, which actually oozes rather than drips water. It was simple to set up: lengths of ooze tubing snake through the bed, and the tubing is connected at the hose bibb to a filter, pressure regulator, and backflow preventer. It took only part of an afternoon to install the system (it cost about $90). A battery-powered controller operates the system while I'm away. The perennials are doing fine, but I still keep a hose in the garden so I can water by hand when I'm back home.

•

I always make a trip to the nursery this month. It's a great time to look for summer-blooming treasures, such as purple coneflower

NORTHERN CALIFORNIA
Garden Notebook
BY LAUREN BONAR SWEZEY

(*Echinacea purpurea*). This 4- to 5-foot-tall perennial produces masses of 3- to 4-inch-wide purple daisies with dark purple centers. The coneflowers look fantastic blooming with bright yellow coreopsis or orange-scarlet Mexican sunflower (*Tithonia rotundifolia*).

THAT'S A GOOD QUESTION

Q: Why are my marigolds and other summer annuals small and wimpy-looking?

A: Stunted annuals are a fairly common sight in gardens. Too often, I've seen plants from sixpacks set out in clay soil with no compost or fertilizer. The hard soil and lack of nutrients inhibit root growth, so the plants languish. Apply a liquid fertilizer to give plants a boost.

The same sad result occurs when seriously rootbound plants are set directly in the ground without first loosening their root mass. The coiled roots just keep winding around and around instead of growing out into the surrounding soil.

PLANTING

❏ **PLANT FOR LATE-SUMMER COLOR.** Your choices include ageratum, celosia, cosmos, dahlias, marigolds, petunias, portulaca, salvia, and zinnia. In light shade, plant begonias and impatiens.

❏ **PLANT VEGETABLES.** You can still plant warm-season vegetables, including beans, corn, squash, and tomatoes. It's also time to start seeds of the cabbage family, such as broccoli and cauliflower.

MAINTENANCE

❏ **CARE FOR FRUIT TREES.** To prevent breakage, support fruit-laden limbs of apple, peach, pear, and plum trees. Discard any fallen fruit, which may harbor insects or disease.

❏ **CARE FOR LAWNS.** Mow a bit higher during summer's heat. For bluegrass and fescue, set your mower at 2½ to 3 inches; hold off fertilizing cool-season lawns until September. Mow Bermuda grass to a height of ¾ to 1 inch; continue your feeding program. Check with your water department for watering restrictions, and ask for ET (evapotranspiration) guidelines.

❏ **CUT BACK CANE BERRIES.** After harvesting June-bearing blackberries

CENTRAL VALLEY
CHECKLIST
JULY

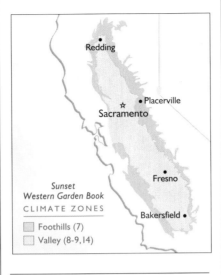

Sunset Western Garden Book
CLIMATE ZONES

❏ Foothills (7)
❏ Valley (8-9, 14)

and boysenberries, cut spent canes to the ground. Tie up this year's new canes; they'll bear fruit next year, if not this fall.

❏ **FERTILIZE.** Keep vegetables and summer-blooming annuals growing vigorously with regular applications of

nitrogen fertilizer. Container plants need more frequent feeding with a complete liquid fertilizer.

❏ **MULCH.** To conserve soil moisture, keep plant roots cool, and discourage weeds, cover the soil around plants with a 2- to 3-inch layer of organic mulch, such as compost, wood chips, or redwood bark.

❏ **WATER.** If necessary, rebuild furrows or soil basins around plants to direct water to their roots. Conserve water by using drip-irrigation tubing or soaker hoses.

PEST & WEED CONTROL

❏ **CONTROL WORMS.** If your geraniums, nicotiana, petunias, and penstemons appear healthy but have no blooms, budworms are probably eating their flower buds. To control them, spray every 7 to 10 days with *Bacillus thuringiensis* (BT), a biological control. BT can also help control young tomato hornworms; handpick adult worms.

❏ **WEED.** Hand-pull or hoe weeds before they starve beneficial plants of nutrients and rob them of water. For really tough invaders such as Bermuda grass, you may have to spot-spray with an herbicide such as glyphosate.

The longer I garden in the Central Valley, the more I come to appreciate July, even though it has a split personality. July rolls in with a blast of heat and a cloud of dust. Twice-a-day waterings make me swear never to plant anything in containers ever again. Spurred by the hot weather, Bermuda grass runs rampant, and I must battle it for every inch of open ground around my garden in Exeter, south of Fresno.

But late in the day, as I stand with a cool drink in one hand and my trusty hose in the other, July inevitably reaches out to me. The crape myrtles are blooming with rare intensity, and my 'Iceberg' roses are shining. The day only gets better as I pick a fresh 'July Elberta' peach—maybe the best-tasting variety grown in what is widely considered the world's finest peach-growing climate. 'July Elberta' is a heavy-bearing freestone variety developed by Luther Burbank. I have to thin my tree judiciously, but the extra effort rewards me with a bumper crop of medium-size fruit.

•

A good way to learn first-hand which fruit and vegetable varieties taste the best is to visit a Certified Farmers' Market. Most of the farmers love to talk about what they grow, and they'll usually give you a taste. Most larger cities have farmers' markets. To find the market

CENTRAL VALLEY
Garden Notebook
BY LANCE WALHEIM

nearest you, call your county agricultural commission or cooperative extension office.

•

One flowering perennial that soothes me in July is mealy-cup sage (*Salvia farinacea*). Though it's usually grown as an annual, I leave mine in the ground. The plants die back in winter, and I all but forget about them until summer, when their deep blue flowers add a refreshing coolness to the garden.

THAT'S A GOOD QUESTION

Q: Recently, I spread a heavy dose of dry fertilizer around my fruit trees, then went out of town for a few weeks, hoping that rain would water the trees. When I returned, the leaves were turning brown and falling off. What did I do wrong?

A: When nitrogen fertilizer is applied to a moisture-stressed plant, its roots tend to absorb the nitrogen too quickly, often causing the plant to suffer foliage burn, especially in hot weather. So always water the root zone thoroughly *before* applying fertilizer. The reason to water well *after* fertilizing plants is to ensure that nutrients are spread throughout the root zone. If the fertilizer remains concentrated in the upper soil, it may cause root damage and foliage burn.

CHECKLIST

PLANTING

❏ **ADD SUMMER COLOR.** Coastal, inland, and high-desert gardeners (*Sunset* climate zones 22–24, 18–21, and 11, respectively) can still plant heat-loving annuals such as globe amaranth, Madagascar periwinkle, marigolds, portulaca, salvia, verbena, and zinnias.

❏ **STRETCH THE HARVEST.** If you are prepared to water diligently, you can plant for a late harvest of summer vegetables. Start beans, carrots, corn, cucumber, and summer squash from seed. Coastal gardeners can add peppers. Inland gardeners can still plant summer melons early in the month.

MAINTENANCE

❏ **FERTILIZE SELECTIVELY.** Summer annuals should be fed monthly. Many vegetables will benefit from the same treatment. (Not tomatoes, though, or you'll get lots of leaves but not much fruit.) Subtropicals, such as bird of paradise, and warm-season lawns should also be fertilized now. Give azaleas and camellias their last feeding of the year. Water plants thoroughly a day or two before feeding, then deep-water again immediately afterward.

❏ **ADJUST MOWING HEIGHT.** Cool-season grasses are slowing down now. To keep their roots shaded and to conserve soil moisture, leave these grasses tall—1½ to 2 inches for rye grass, 2

Sunset
Western Garden Book
CLIMATE ZONES

1–3 ⬜ 11
13 ⬜ 14–24

inches or more for tall fescues. Warm-season grasses such as Bermuda, St. Augustine, and zoysia, on the other hand, are growing rapidly. Mow frequently, keeping below 1 inch to lessen thatch buildup.

❏ **CARE FOR CYMBIDIUMS.** Next year's flower spikes are developing now. To ensure proper development, inland and coastal gardeners should water weekly and feed plants with a high-nitrogen fertilizer this month and next. Follow label directions.

❏ **MOVE HOUSE PLANTS OUTDOORS.** Give them a summer vacation. Many grow faster and look healthier if they spend all or part of the summer outdoors. Protect from strong winds and bright light. Spray foliage with water occasionally to wash off dust, and watch for whiteflies and other pests.

❏ **PRUNE HYDRANGEAS.** After flower clusters fade to brown or green, cut back each stalk that has bloomed to two or three buds from the base of the plant. They'll quickly spring back with vigorous new growth. Don't prune stems that haven't bloomed; they'll bear flowers later this year or next.

❏ **WATER CITRUS.** Shallow-rooted citrus need to be watered more frequently than other fruit trees. To prevent fruit drop, irrigate thoroughly at regular intervals—2 to 3 weeks apart depending on soil conditions. Avoid wetting tree bark, however, as citrus are susceptible to a fungus disease that can infect their trunks.

❏ **SHOP FOR SEEDS.** Browse through nursery seed racks or seed catalogs for cool-season annuals and vegetables and spring-flowering perennials. Start seeds in flats next month, set out in the garden in early fall, and get a head start on the winter-spring growing season.

Y ou know how your hair can be at the top of its form one day and completely shapeless the next? And you get so disgusted with it you just want to hack it all off? Well, I used to treat the summer plants in my Huntington Beach garden the same way. I'd let my Mexican bush sage and French lavender go past lush extravagance to seedy disgrace before I'd bring out the shears. Then I'd overreact and give them crew cuts.

Here's what I do now. In July, I cut back artemisias, lavenders, salvias, and other bushy summer perennials lightly—by no more than a third of their height. I repeat the process periodically throughout the growing season, and stop pruning when the weather cools off. That way, my garden's summer favorites will have enough foliage left to look handsome throughout the winter, instead of like oversheared poodles.

•

Speaking of plants, this spring I saw a charmer for containers at Weidners' Gardens in Encinitas. It's called *Bacopa* 'Snowflake'. It has tiny heart-shaped leaves, is blanketed in five-petaled white flowers,

SOUTHERN CALIFORNIA
Garden Notebook
BY SHARON COHOON

and has a cascading habit that's ideal for planters or hanging baskets. It likes lots of water but is otherwise care-free. Mine has bloomed nonstop for months. For more information, call Weidners' at (619) 436-2194.

•

Garden Gems are a decorative twist on the practice of using pottery shards to cool soil surfaces of container plants. The terra-cotta ornaments come in leaf, butterfly, and other imprints. Prices range from $8 for a box of 5 to $16 for a box of 20. I saw them for the first time at Hortus in Pasadena; (818) 792-8255. For a brochure, call (714) 650-6232.

THAT'S A GOOD QUESTION

Q: Can you suggest a native plant that flowers in the summer?
A: Here are three. California fuchsia (*Zauschneria californica*) blooms steadily from now until well into fall. Though the plant is a bit sprawly for some tastes, I find its fiery red-orange tubes as irresistible as hummingbirds do. Tamer summer-blooming natives include white, pink, and sulfur-flowered buckwheat (*Eriogonum*) as well as *Salvia greggii* and its cultivated varieties.

ANYWHERE IN THE WEST

❏ **CARE FOR ROSES.** After each round of bloom, cut off faded flowers just above a node with five leaflets (nodes closest to the flower have three leaflets). Fertilize and water deeply to encourage the next round of bloom.

❏ **HARVEST CROPS, FLOWERS.** As vegetables mature, pick them often to keep new ones coming, and to keep ripe ones from becoming overmature (cucumbers, zucchini) or rotten (tomatoes). Pick flowers before they go to seed to encourage continued bloom.

❏ **MULCH.** Put a 3-inch organic mulch around permanent plants to conserve soil moisture, keep roots cool, and control weeds. Use leaves, shredded garden waste, or lawn clippings as mulch.

❏ **PRUNE CANE BERRIES.** In all but the coldest parts of the West, cut out drying old raspberry canes after the harvest, and cut off blackberry canes that have fruited. In cold-winter areas, cut canes in August.

❏ **TEND CYMBIDIUMS.** To help promote bud formation for next year's bloom, apply quarter-strength liquid fertilizer every time you water.

❏ **WATER.** Water annual flowers and vegetables only after the top inch of soil has dried out. Soil basins and furrows

CHECKLIST
JULY

help direct water to the roots. Deep-rooted permanent plants can be watered less often, but irrigate deeply when you do.

INTERMOUNTAIN WEST

❏ **PLANT VEGETABLES.** Plant pumpkins early in the month (so they'll be ready for Halloween), preferably from seedlings. Sow tomato seeds right away: plants will come up and flower by September and will fruit through frost.

❏ **POLLINATE MELONS, SQUASH.** When high temperatures inhibit fruit set on squash, dab pollen-bearing male flowers with a small artist's brush, then paint the pollen onto female flowers; you can identify female flowers by their swollen bases.

❏ **SOLARIZE SOIL.** Clean weed seeds out of your soil now, during the hottest part of the year, by tilling the soil, raking and watering it, then covering it with clear plastic weighted down along the edges. After three weeks, turn the soil again and repeat the process. Trapped heat will kill weed seeds and seedlings near the soil surface, reducing the

number of weeds you'll have to control after planting.

❏ **THIN TREES.** Open up top-heavy trees like firs and pines to protect them from strong winds. Prune out suckers; dead, diseased, or injured wood; and closely parallel branches.

SOUTHWEST'S LOW AND INTERMEDIATE DESERTS

❏ **PLANT VEGETABLES.** Plant beets, broccoli, cabbage, carrots, cauliflower, green onions, leaf lettuce, peas, spinach, and turnips for fall harvest. Plant winter squash among the spinach: as you harvest spinach, the squash will fill in the gaps.

❏ **TIP-PRUNE PERENNIALS.** To make them bushier, pinch out the tips of chrysanthemums, fuchsias, and recently planted marguerites.

❏ **WATCH FOR WORMS.** Budworms destroy geranium, nicotiana, penstemon, and petunia buds before flowers even have the chance to open. If that's happening in your garden (look for holes in the buds), spray plants every 7 to 10 days with *Bacillus thuringiensis* (BT). If you see chewed tomato leaves spotted with black droppings, look for tomato hornworms, which can eventually reach the size of cigars. You can control small ones by spraying with BT; handpick the large hornworms.

Hot days have their good points. They give me a reason to rise at dawn and work in the coolest and, to my mind, the most beguiling part of the day. As birds sing, I hoe off young weeds, leaving their tender roots to dry and die as the day warms up. I pull larger weeds and throw them onto a garden path, where they "cook" all day, leaving only limp leaves to collect and add to the compost pile at day's end.

●

Mornings are my favorite time for watering. In the still-cool air, less moisture is lost to evaporation, and leaves dry out fairly quickly, minimizing the risk of diseases like mildew. Once the plants are watered, top off the birdbath. In the evening, look at it again to see how much water is gone: it's a graphic gauge of how much evaporative moisture loss your plants have suffered during the day. Over time, you'll be able to tell whether your plants need water just by looking at the birdbath.

●

Evenings are perfect for setting out nursery seedlings (if your garden's not too hot for transplanting). Set them out an hour before sun-

INLAND WESTERN STATES
Garden Notebook
BY JIM McCAUSLAND

set, and water them well. They'll have the night to recover before they have to face the sun. It also helps to put shadecloth or lath over new transplants for their first week or two in the garden.

THAT'S A GOOD QUESTION

Q: Recently, I spread a heavy dose of dry fertilizer around my fruit trees, then went out of town for a few weeks, hoping that rain would water the trees. When I returned, the leaves were turning brown and falling off. What did I do wrong?

A: When nitrogen fertilizer is applied to a moisture-stressed plant, its roots tend to absorb the nitrogen too quickly, often causing the plant to suffer foliage burn, especially in hot weather. So always water the root zone thoroughly *before* applying fertilizer. The reason to water well *after* fertilizing plants is to ensure that nutrients are spread throughout the root zone. If the fertilizer remains concentrated in the upper soil, it may cause root damage and foliage burn.

Inspirations &

Three landscape architects share their

PETER CHRISTIANSEN

What happens when you ask three designers with diverse backgrounds and from different regions of the West to renovate the same suburban front yard? The results are inspiring, as you see in the range of redesigns on these six pages.

Sunset selected a site with problems typical of many mature landscapes: an oversize lawn in poor condition, a lack of color or interest, and space not put to good use. The front of the house, dominated by a 1,500-square-foot lawn, has a Japanese maple near the front door, a large 'Modesto' ash in the parking strip, and a driveway wide enough for three cars. The owners enjoy flowering plants but are occupied with work and two children and have little time for gardening.

We gave each landscape architect a photograph of the garden, its dimensions, and descriptions of the neighborhood and family. Each was given the same guidelines: the cost of the project should run between $15,000 and $25,000; the garden should be fairly low-maintenance and water-thrifty, but should not have an arid look; and the lawn should be reduced in size or eliminated. We worked with the landscape architects as if we were the homeowners, discussing and making changes as they might.

BY LAUREN BONAR SWEZEY

A casual, bungalow garden

When Jana Ruzicka of Laguna Beach, California, works with clients, her goal is to reconnect them with their surroundings.

Ruzicka wanted a garden that would look as if it belonged with a traditional California bungalow. So that the family would have a place to sit and relax in the garden, she removed the front porch railing to give a more open, welcoming feel, then expanded the porch. She kept the garden open to the street so the family could still interact with neighbors.

She also beefed up the size of the porch posts, took off the screen door, painted the front door magenta to set off the colors of the potted flowers, painted the trim a dark green to blend with the garden, and used a neutral gray-brown color for the house.

Ruzicka designed low, curving walls to surround the front garden. "I decided they shouldn't look too perfect," she says, "but should be made of rammed earth, with rocks or bricks inserted into them here and there." In the tops of the walls, depressions with drainage holes would hold *Sedum spathulifolium.*

The front walk's rustic look comes from rough concrete shapes. Ruzicka even proposes that the driveway edge be chiseled away to give an imperfect appearance.

Ruzicka prefers indigenous plants appropriate to the climate—taller near house and walls, lower near the gravel path across the center of the garden. Her choices are simple and understated: a single-petaled climbing rose on the walls; foxgloves, geraniums, yarrows, and grasses along the gravel path; and bulbs popping up in spring.

Renovations

plans for making over a typical front yard

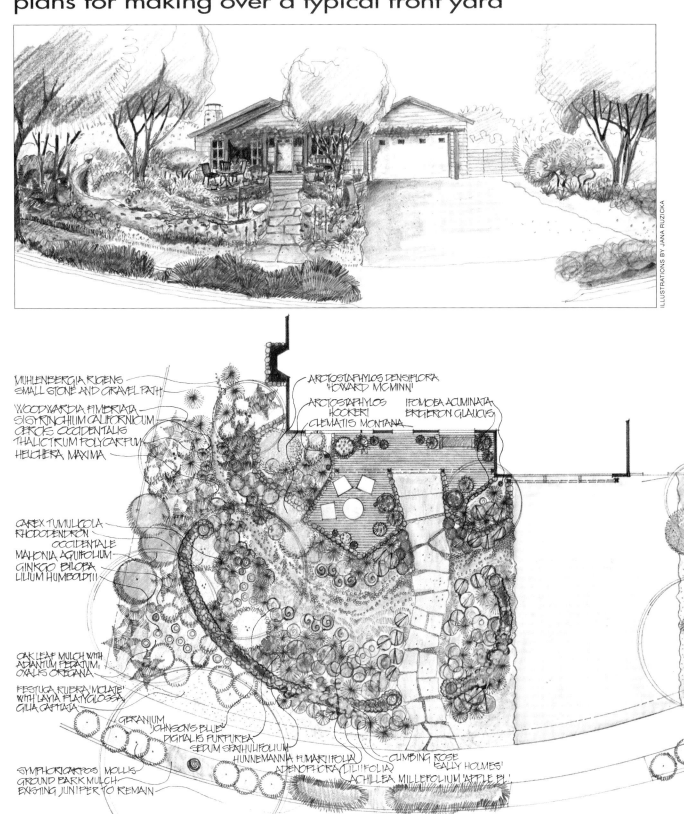

MUHLENBERGIA RIGENS
SMALL STONE AND GRAVEL PATH

ARCTOSTAPHYLOS DENSIFLORA
'HOWARD MCMINN'

WOODWARDIA FIMBRIATA
SISYRINCHIUM CALIFORNICUM
CERCIS OCCIDENTALIS
THALICTRUM POLYCARPUM
HEUCHERA MAXIMA

ARCTOSTAPHYLOS
HOOKERI
CLEMATIS MONTANA

IPOMOEA ACUMINATA
ERIGERON GLAUCUS

CAREX TUMULICOLA
RHODODENDRON
OCCIDENTALE
MAHONIA AQUIFOLIUM
GINKGO BILOBA
LILIUM HUMBOLDTII

OAK LEAF MULCH WITH
ADIANTUM PEDATUM
OXALIS OREGANA

FESTUCA RUBRA 'MOLATE'
WITH LAYIA PLATYGLOSSA
GILIA CAPITATA

GERANIUM
'JOHNSON'S BLUE'
DIGITALIS PURPUREA
SEDUM SPATHULIFOLIUM
HUNNEMANNIA FUMARIIFOLIA
ADENOPHORA LILIIFOLIA

CLIMBING ROSE
'SALLY HOLMES'

SYMPHORICARPOS MOLLIS
GROUND BARK MULCH
EXISTING JUNIPER TO REMAIN

ACHILLEA MILLEFOLIUM 'APPLE BL.'

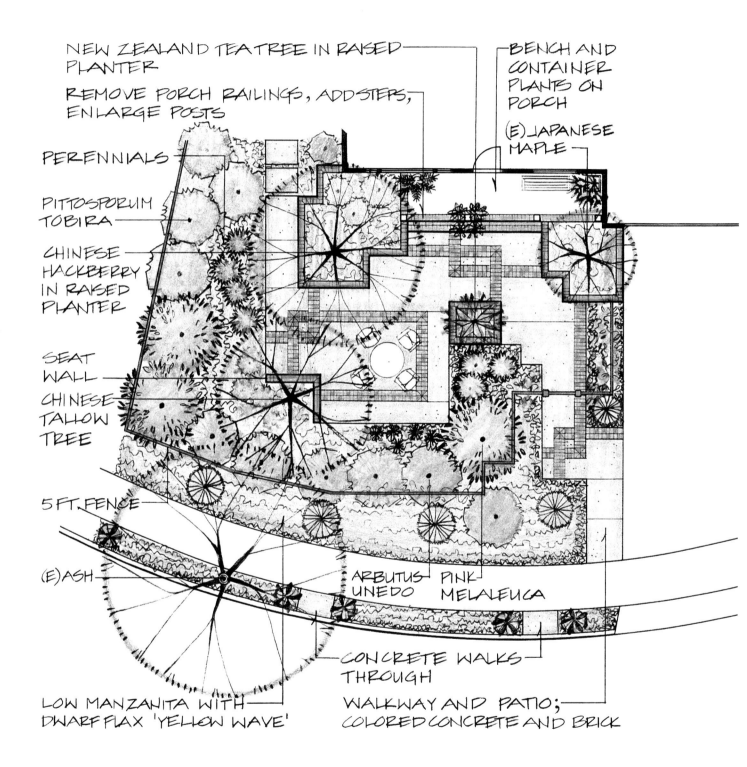

NEW ZEALAND TEA TREE IN RAISED PLANTER

REMOVE PORCH RAILINGS, ADD STEPS, ENLARGE POSTS

PERENNIALS

PITTOSPORUM TOBIRA

CHINESE HACKBERRY IN RAISED PLANTER

SEAT WALL

CHINESE TALLOW TREE

5 FT. FENCE

(E) ASH

LOW MANZANITA WITH DWARF FLAX 'YELLOW WAVE'

BENCH AND CONTAINER PLANTS ON PORCH

(E) JAPANESE MAPLE

ARBUTUS UNEDO

PINK MELALEUCA

CONCRETE WALKS THROUGH

WALKWAY AND PATIO; COLORED CONCRETE AND BRICK

Front entry yields to private patio space

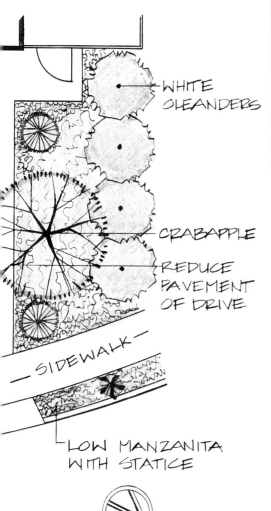

WHITE OLEANDERS

CRABAPPLE

REDUCE PAVEMENT OF DRIVE

— SIDEWALK —

LOW MANZANITA WITH STATICE

Lisa Moulton of Redwood City, California, created a private space by combining two functions: a front entry and a patio surrounded by a fence. "I love the psychology of designing front yards," she says. "The transition from the hectic outside world into the home is complex—it's comforting to have a series of transitions."

The first is at the gate, where you go from a public space to a private world. The next is in front of the steps, which Moulton has identified with a brick pattern. There, visitors have the choice of entering the private seating area or continuing to the door.

The key to Moulton's design is the use of brick—a traditional material already on site—in a less traditional way, with a woven pattern set in colored concrete. "It gives the garden a more contemporary feel," she says.

Moulton widened the front steps, faced them with brick, and removed the old railings. Posts were enlarged to give the house a more substantial look. Raised planters and a low wall provide extra seating for parties. To meet city codes, the 5-foot-high fence is open across the top, with vines weaving in and out.

Plants also help the transition from outside world to home. Says Moulton, "Anyone sitting in the patio will feel surrounded by plants and lushness. The space also will feel larger than it does now, when you see it all at once." Two new trees on the southeast and southwest sides of the garden shade the patio for morning brunch and from afternoon sun. Perennials along patio edges provide seasonal color.

Moulton narrowed the driveway by 8 feet, gaining room for a planting bed to the right of the driveway.

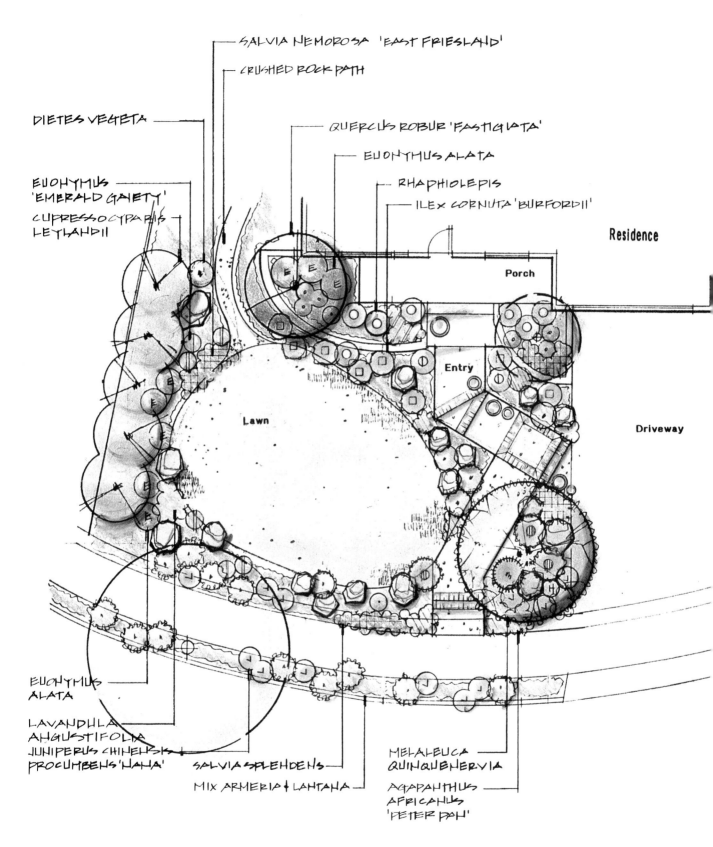

SALVIA NEMOROSA 'EAST FRIESLAND'

CRUSHED ROCK PATH

DIETES VEGETA

QUERCUS ROBUR 'FASTIGIATA'

EUONYMUS ALATA

EUONYMUS 'EMERALD GAIETY'

RHAPHIOLEPIS

CUPRESSOCYPARIS LEYLANDII

ILEX CORNUTA 'BURFORDII'

Residence

Porch

Entry

Lawn

Driveway

EUONYMUS ALATA

LAVANDULA ANGUSTIFOLIA
JUNIPERUS CHINENSIS
PROCUMBENS 'NANA'

SALVIA SPLENDENS

MELALEUCA QUINQUENERVIA

MIX ARMERIA & LANTANA

AGAPANTHUS AFRICANUS 'PETER PAN'

Street

A computerized view of a low-maintenance garden

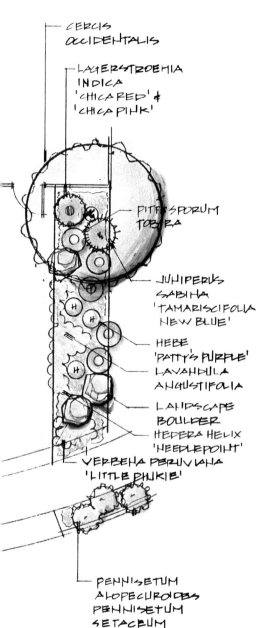

CERCIS
OCCIDENTALIS

LAGERSTROEHIA
INDICA
'CHICA RED' &
'CHICA PINK'

PITTOSPORUM
TOBIRA

JUNIPERUS
SABINA
'TAMARISCIFOLIA
NEW BLUE'

HEBE
'PATTY'S PURPLE'
LAVANDULA
ANGUSTIFOLIA

LANDSCAPE
BOULDER
HEDERA HELIX
'NEEDLEPOINT'
VERBENA PERUVIANA
'LITTLE PINKIE'

PENNISETUM
ALOPECUROIDES
PENNISETUM
SETACEUM

Alan Burke, of Preview, in Seattle, designs his plans in the traditional way but also uses digital imaging, which lets him show garden concepts as "photographs."

A computer rendering (above) shows a casual, low-maintenance garden of ornamental grasses, shrubs, and natural boulders. To create a welcoming transition from both street and driveway, he designed a 6-foot-wide walk accented with brick steps and clusters of 24- and 36-inch-diameter terra-cotta pots.

"It's challenging to create an interesting transition in such a short span," he explains. "By adding a jog and accenting the path with pots or other sculptural elements, you create a sense of a journey. But you still want easy access to the car, especially when it's raining."

Pots of blooming plants seem to diminish the expanse of walk, making it more friendly and providing color. Where the walks from street and driveway join, brick creates a central meeting point. Burke says it's important to match this new brick with existing brick on the chimney and raised beds.

For low maintenance, he chose broad-leafed evergreen shrubs, accented with deciduous shrubs for fall color. Boulders and ornamental grasses punctuate the beds and complement the Craftsman-style architecture. Burke planted Leyland cypresses along the southwest side of the garden to create a sense of enclosure.

He reduced lawn size by more than half, and suggested a dwarf fescue, such as 'Bonsai', that needs less water than many other grasses. Well-prepared soil is as important as grass selection. Burke says, "I rototill in at least 4 inches of amendments with fertilizer, then come back six weeks after planting the sod and give it more nitrogen." ∎

ARTEMISIA, *lion's tail, penstemon, and salvia grow along a pathway that runs from the patio off the boys' rooms through the chaparral below the house.*

CHAD SLATTERY

Bringing the garden inside

A Laguna Beach house was designed to show off the garden—even from indoors

ETSY AND GARY JENKINS OWN A breathtaking piece of property. Naturally, it's on top of a hill. Just as naturally, below their house, a triangle of virgin chaparral plunges sharply to the sea. On a clear day, the eye can't help but follow this plunge, sailing on past the triangle's tip and across the water to Santa Catalina and San Clemente islands offshore.

Yet the ocean breezes that clear the air also stunt the native vegetation—and can chill the bones, even on a summer day. Conversely, without shade anywhere for relief, the glare of the sun can be oppressive. Despite the view, you feel an urge to retreat indoors.

Step into the cool, gray fortress the Jenkinses call home, however, and your eye is immediately drawn back outside. From indoors, the planted garden looks so at home with its surroundings you can hardly tell where it ends and the chaparral begins. For that matter, it's sometimes difficult to tell whether you are indoors at all.

Inside or out? It's a delightful dilemma. And it didn't happen by accident.

To begin with, the property found the right owners. The Jenkinses, who are active in local environmental groups such as Laguna Greenbelt, appreciated the undisturbed native vegetation on the site almost as much as they did the view. Jeff Powers, of Earthscaping Designs in Laguna Beach, shared their sentiments. Not surprisingly, the garden he designed for the Jenkinses looks very much at home in the midst of the chaparral below their house.

But it was architect Mark Singer, also from Laguna Beach, who gave Powers something unique to work with—a building that pushes at and retreats from the edges of its site, creating a setting in which boundaries between interior and exterior are fluid, unlike those of a traditional boxy house with clearly defined interior spaces sandwiched between front and back yards.

AN ATRIUM, AN AERIE, A WILDLIFE HABITAT

A central two-story entryway and a skylit atrium divide the house into two wings. This is where the fun begins. A two-story wall of glass is all that separates the entryway from an informal-looking patio, giving the interior space the feeling of being part of the exterior. "In a warmer climate, we would have eliminated the glass and left the house open to the outdoors," says Singer. "It's too cold here for that, but that's the feeling we wanted."

Similarly, glass wraps around the atrium. When you walk through the glass door leading into it, you feel as if you are stepping outside.

Gray slate tile is also part of the illusion—it is used as flooring in the entryway and atrium, as well as on an adjacent patio, where it is broken into rough-edged pieces. A waterfall trickling down one stone wall in the entryway further blurs the distinction between inside and out. So do the reedy grasses and red-barked dogwood planted just beyond the atrium door. "They relate to the waterfall because you'd find both in moist environments in nature," says Powers. "Plus, this cool, shady area is a perfect micro-climate for them."

The view from the entryway across the patio encompasses a band of shore-line and Palos Verdes Peak to the north. Even more awe-inspiring, though, is the view west from the large, undivided room that contains the Jenkinses' kitchen, dining room, and family room. The window wall culminates in a mas-sive curve of glass.

Looking down on this great room, one feels like an eagle in an aerie. The leaves of recently planted sycamore trees will eventually fill in, providing summer shade and further enhancing the feeling of being in the treetops, says Powers.

On the opposite side of the atrium is the house's bedroom wing. The Jenkins boys, Christopher and Kyle, think they have the best location. Being on a lower level and facing a retaining wall on one side, their rooms could have had the least attractive views in the house. But Powers gave the boys an intimate wildlife habitat centered around a fish pond just outside the floor-to-ceiling glass walls of their adjoining bedrooms.

"This is the boys' private garden, and they love it," says Betsy. "They're always out there studying something."

The area above the retaining wall—planted with toyon, ribes, manzanita, and other native plants—is a continuation of the boys' outdoor science lab. The plants are attractive as food or habi-tat to birds, insects, and other animals. Not coincidentally, their presence also helps blur the distinction between gar-den and chaparral.

The boys have a second playground on the other side of the house, a large oval of lawn that serves as a soccer field for the neighborhood—that is, when their parents aren't hosting parties on it.

IMPATIENS *around a fish pond add color outside the boys' rooms.*

A band of indigenous grass (*Stipa*) around the lawn's edge looks at home against the chaparral backdrop, but the tough-leafed, clumping grass has a prac-tical purpose—keeping the boys' soccer balls in bounds.

A path below the lawn switchbacks down the hill through an exuberant mix

THE IRREGULAR *footprint of the house creates inviting pockets for plants. Its gray color was chosen to echo the hues of the surrounding chaparral.*

of drought-tolerant plants, including lion's tail, penstemon, salvia, and verbe-na. The path, in some places also paved in gray slate, connects to the patio and fish pond off the entryway.

"I love walking this pathway," says Gary. "It feels like I'm on a hiking trail somewhere far away from everything."

Maybe it's the *Artemisia arborescens* that creates the feeling. Not only is this silvery white shrubby perennial the common thread that weaves the bends and curves of this section of the garden together, but it's also a link to the gray hues in the surrounding chaparral. It may look sublimely natural, but like everything else about this project, it didn't happen by accident.

"The gray ties in with the gray of the building, which of course also ties in with the chaparral," says Powers. "Architecture and landscaping can con-nect in hundreds of ways when they're planned together. But it's not often we have the chance." ∎

By Sharon Cohoon

Cultivate your garden photo skills

Easy but effective techniques for better photos of flowers and gardens

A DEW-KISSED ROSE unfurls in the misty morning light, and you want to capture its beauty in a photograph. You get your camera, aim, and shoot, expecting a picture-perfect shot. When the photos are processed, they're too light, too dark, too contrasty, or blurry.

Many of us are so proud of our gardens that it's a big disappointment when the photographs we take don't measure up to our expectations. But taking consistently good pictures is not unlike cultivating a rose: to get the best results, you have to know a few techniques.

We followed professional photographer Russ Widstrand around a Southern California garden to learn about the techniques he uses when he shoots home landscapes and flowers for *Sunset.* Here we share some of his tips that any gardener can use. Many of them work with all types of cameras, although some apply only to cameras with interchangeable lenses and manual controls.

Shoot when the light is right. Many people believe that bright, sunny days are the best for photography. On the contrary, says Widstrand: "The radical colors, textures, and patterns of the garden go wacko in bright daylight." In a sunlit scene, your eye can see details in the highlights and shadows that the film won't record. To see what the film will capture, squint at the scene before you shoot.

The best times to shoot gardens, especially overall views, are the early morning and late afternoon, when the sun is low in the sky, and on overcast days, when the light is even and details are not obscured by contrasty shadows.

Shade the lens. If you do shoot in the sunshine, prevent direct sunlight from hitting the lens and causing light streaks and hot spots in photos. Attach a screw-on shade to the lens. Or shade the lens with your hand or a hand-held card—just be sure that it doesn't intrude into the field of view.

Control light in close-ups. When you photograph subjects such as flowers close up, some basic tools can help you improve the quality of the light. Widstrand often places a translucent white umbrella above flowers to diffuse the hard light and reduce contrast. He also uses a folding white reflector to bounce light into dark shadows in order to enhance detail.

Warm up blue light. At prime shooting times such as early morning or on overcast days, the light often has a bluish cast. This can produce pleasing effects if you're photographing delphiniums and want to accentuate their blue flowers. If, however, you want more accurate color rendition, use a screw-on 81B series warm-up filter to correct the blue cast.

PHOTOGRAPHER RUSS WIDSTRAND *(left) uses an umbrella to diffuse harsh overhead light and a reflector to bounce light into shadows. The beardless iris above was shot in diffused light using an umbrella and reflector; the contrasty photo below was taken in direct sunlight.*

SHOT IN BRIGHT MIDDAY LIGHT, *the garden scene at left is marred by contrasty shadows and hot spots. The scene looks more pleasing in the photo at right, which was taken later in the day, when the sun was lower in the sky.*

Choose film carefully. Each film type has its own color qualities and sensitivity to light, and a unique grain pattern. If you keep an album of garden photos, color print film can give you satisfying results. Like many professional photographers who shoot for *Sunset*, Widstrand exclusively uses color transparency (slide) film. Why? "It's better in its ability to capture color than print film, giving a more accurate rendition of the subject," he says.

Consider film speed. An advantage of medium or fast films (ASA/ISO 200, 400, and higher) is that they can be used in low-light situations such as shade. A disadvantage

of faster films is that they have a coarser grain pattern, which shows in enlargements. Slow films (ASA/ISO 25 or 100) require more exposure but are less grainy and have better color saturation.

Frame your shot. Think of the camera's viewfinder as a picture frame, and compose the subjects within it for desired emphasis. Be aware of how objects relate to each other and to the edges of the frame. Use the frame to highlight central elements or crop out unwanted details.

Move in on the subject. Get close to the subject and make it fill the frame. This adds impact and eliminates distracting details. Consider

using a close-up lens or a macro lens; either enables you to focus closer to the subject, giving you a larger image.

Keep backgrounds simple. Don't let the subject get lost against a cluttered background. Even if the subject is stationary—a flower bed, for example—you can often move around it to find a simple background such as a patio wall or the shade cast by a tree.

Eliminate camera movement. Whenever possible, use a tripod. It minimizes camera movement, which causes blurred photos.

Use a cable release. This enables you to trip the shutter

without touching and possibly moving the camera. Cable releases usually screw into the shutter button.

Shoot several exposures. To ensure that you get the best exposure, make a series of "bracket" shots. Start by making the exposure indicated by the camera's light meter, then make another exposure a half f-stop over the indicated exposure and another one a half f-stop under.

Vary camera position. Experimenting with different camera levels, angles, and points of view can help you add interest to even a simple photograph. ■

By Lynn Ocone

ORIGANUM LIBANOTICUM *cascades along path. Design: Wendy Wilde, Berkeley.*

The other oreganos

*Nine varieties to grow
for showy bloom*

ORNAMENTAL OREGANOS ARE RARE in nature. But there are plenty of cultivated varieties well suited to milder Western climates. These ornamentals, related to culinary oreganos, are grown for their pink or purplish flower clusters or their sprays of showy chartreuse, pink, or purplish bracts (modified leaves that form part of the flower head).

For years, dry-climate rock gardeners have been tucking some of the low-growing species, such as dittany of Crete (*Origanum dictamnus*), into nooks and crannies, but lately, many more species and hybrids have become available through nurseries and mail-order catalogs. They add handsome texture and summer color to raised beds, retaining walls, rock gardens, and perennial borders. Many are attractive in containers.

CHOOSE PLANTS FOR THEIR FLOWERS OR HOPLIKE BRACTS

Because flowers and plant forms vary considerably, choosing an ornamental oregano depends on personal taste. All plants described here (except 'Kent Beauty' and *O. rotundifolium*) are evergreen in mild-climate areas and about 1 foot tall when not in bloom (except where noted). Plant heights and appearances change when flower spikes form.

Blooms appear in summer and make long-lasting cut flowers. When they're dried, their color holds indefinitely. Plants thrive in conditions similar to those of their Mediterranean habitat— good drainage, minimal water, full sun. All of these oreganos except dittany of Crete are hardy into *Sunset Western Garden Book* Zone 2 (Denver), but too much moisture can be a limiting factor in wet climates such as Seattle's.

Oreganos with flower clusters. Two new varieties are *O. laevigatum* 'Herren-hausen' and *O. l.* 'Hopley's'. Rather than hoplike flower structures, these varieties produce long stalks topped with clusters of small flowers. 'Herren-hausen' stalks reach 1½ to 2 feet, topped by lilac pink flowers set in dark purple calyxes; foliage is tinged reddish purple. 'Hopley's' has darker purple flowers, and stalks reach 2 to 2½ feet. They look best when planted among other tall perennials that support their stalks.

Oreganos with hoplike flower bracts. Dittany of Crete and *O. calcaratum* both have round, woolly, silvery green leaves and produce 18-inch flower sprays covered with purple-tinged bracts. The flowers and leaves of *O. calcaratum* are a bit larger, but the plant may produce fewer flowers than dittany of Crete. Both need well-drained soil.

Origanum libanoticum (*O. pulchellum*) produces large, showy, pink-tinged bracts on 2-foot arching branches; the plant spreads to 3 feet. Bracts elongate to several inches during the season.

Origanum rotundifolium has attractive round leaves and large (1 inch), round, bright green bracts that form on 18-inch sprays. Variety 'Green Flowering' has narrower, lime green bracts, with tiny pink or white flowers; *O. r.* 'Kent Beauty' has large, purple-tinged bracts, and its foliage is 8 to 10 inches tall.

Origanum sipyleum is a 2-foot-tall shrublet that reaches 3 feet when in bloom. Leaves are smooth, and wiry-looking flower stems have purple-tinged bracts.

Many perennial and herb nurseries sell a selection of ornamental oreganos. You can also order them by mail.

Canyon Creek Nursery, 3527 Dry Creek Rd., Oroville, CA 95965. Catalog costs $2.

Mountain Valley Growers, 38325 Pepperweed Rd., Squaw Valley, CA 93675; (209) 338-2775. Catalog free. ∎

By Lauren Bonar Swezey

CLOSE-UP *of O. rotundifolium shows its round, bright green bracts.*

RIDDLED WITH TRAILS, *apple at left is infested with apple maggots. The fruit at right shows marks of codling moth (apple worm) damage: one tunnel in, one tunnel out.*

DOUG WILSON

The nastiest apple pest in the West

Choose your weapons to fight the apple maggot before it ruins your fruit

ONCE UPON A SUMMER, APPLE trees had one principal insect problem: the codling moth, or common apple worm. In most cases, even infested trees often bore plenty of edible fruit.

Then, around 1980, the apple maggot was discovered in Oregon, and since then it has been gradually found in much of the Northwest and Northern California. Apple maggot can do serious damage to apples. Unlike traditional apple worm (codling moth larva), which just tunnels in and out of the fruit, apple maggot riddles the fruit with brown trails. There's nothing left to save. The photograph above tells the tale.

Eric LaGasa, state entomologist in Washington, calls it the nastiest pest backyard apple growers can face. Bad as it is, however, apple maggot can be controlled.

Apple maggot covers most of the territory between the Pacific Ocean and the Cascades and Sierra Nevada from Seattle to the San Francisco Bay Area, including all of western Oregon. Its northern boundary is the Olympic Peninsula and roughly the King County–Snohomish County line. On the south end, the maggot follows the California coast to Marin County, though in the Sacramento Valley it doesn't go far

south of Chico. A few maggots have shown up in Alameda County.

East of the Cascades, there's a small population of apple maggots in northeast Spokane. In the Columbia Gorge, the pest's range extends to Goldendale on the Washington side and to The Dalles on the Oregon side.

If you live outside these areas and see apple maggot damage similar to that shown in the photo, you should notify your county agricultural commissioner or farm adviser in California, or your county extension agent in Washington or Oregon.

Early apples suffer the most, followed by midseason apples. Hard late apples are least susceptible; some even have enough internal pressure to kill the maggots before they develop. Although the maggots do most of their damage to apples, crabapples and hawthorns can get high infestations and be carriers of the maggots.

COMBAT STRATEGIES

These three methods to control apple maggot can also be used to control codling moth.

Apple bags. To completely protect apples from insects and guarantee near-perfect fruit, bag your apples around July 1 (see "The secret to perfect apples is in the bag," on page 161).

Traps. For fairly good control (and a lot less work), set out sticky traps in July to catch apple maggot flies. (Specialized traps are also sold for codling moths.) You can buy inexpensive commercial traps coated with stickum and a chemical attractant. Hang two to six traps in each tree, more if you catch many flies, and recoat or replace the traps as they become covered with insects.

Organic gardening suppliers sell commercial traps. One good source is Peaceful Valley Farm Supply, Box 2209, Grass Valley, CA 95945; call (916) 272-4769. The catalog is free. To find local suppliers of one brand of trap (Pherocon AM), call the manufacturer, Trécé, at (408) 758-0204; ask for customer service.

Pesticides. Apply diazinon or malathion every 7 to 10 days from mid-July to the preharvest time specified on the label for apple maggot control. These pesticides also control codling moth, but only if you start spraying earlier (consult label directions). *Bacillus thuringiensis* is the preferred biological control for codling moth larva in home gardens, but it doesn't control apple maggot. ∎

By Jim McCausland

IT'S HARD TO BEAT TREE MALLOW *for an almost continuous summer flower show. For details on Lavatera thruingiaca 'Barnsley,' the variety shown here, see page 222.*

AUGUST

GARDEN
Guide

Russian sage is a perennial Western winner

It's no wonder that Russian sage (*Perovskia atriplicifolia*) is popping up in more Western gardens. Consider the plant's attributes: It's hardy, adapts to all Western climates, withstands summer heat and drought, and actually enjoys winter chill. It's a summer-blooming beauty, with arching flower spikes that form a pale blue haze over silvery gray-green foliage. And it's fragrant, with a sagy aroma that becomes most pungent by late summer.

This deciduous semi-woody plant awakes from dormancy in spring by sending up 3- to 4-foot-tall stems that sprout 9-inch to foot-long bloom spikes filled with small lavender blue flowers. Snip off faded flower spikes to encourage the plant to keep on blooming.

Russian sage makes an excellent filler in perennial borders. Plant in a place that gets full sun. It tolerates poor soil but does best in well-drained soil. Fertilize it lightly when you do other woody plants.

Many nurseries carry Russian sage (often sold as *Perovskia* 'Blue Spire') in 1-gallon cans or 4-inch pots. You can also order dormant roots from perennial specialists for planting in fall or spring, depending on your garden's climate. Occasionally you'll find *P. abrotanoides* for sale, or a hybrid between this and *P. atriplicifolia*; all are similar in appearance and have the same virtues.

Blue spires of Russian sage rise beside a garden path flanked by other flowering perennials.

AUGUST '95

DON NORMARK

A misty arbor for potted plants and for people

Hot, dry August days can make gardening a challenge if you grow many plants in containers, especially in hanging baskets, which dry out quickly and require diligent watering.

Dodo Wood of Yuba City, California, who gardens in moss-lined hanging baskets, transformed a concrete patio into a nurturing habitat for her plants. To filter sunlight and protect plants from the drying winds, she built a redwood arbor and covered it with translucent plastic. Then she rigged the arbor rafters with a double-purpose system to water and mist plants. One line of PVC pipe runs along the rafters to feed a sprinkler system for watering the containers. Another PVC pipe is studded at 2-foot intervals with 40 low-water-volume misters. The sprinkler and misting functions operate independently.

Among the plants that thrive under Wood's arbor are impatiens, saxifrages, staghorn and sword ferns, and tuberous begonias. The baskets are watered twice daily in warm weather, and plants are fed monthly with half-strength liquid fertilizer. When it gets really hot, Wood runs the misters to

NOARMAN A. PLATE

Soothing blanket of fog, spewing from mister-laced pipes mounted to the rafters, cools and humidifies the air beneath the arbor.

increase the humidity and lower the temperature under the arbor by more than 10°. This also makes the patio more comfortable for people.

Look for misters where drip-irrigation supplies are sold. One source is the Urban Farmer Store, 2833 Vicente St., San Francisco, CA 94116; (800) 753-3747. Catalog is free.

THE NATURAL WAY

New ways to attract good bugs

Beneficial insects such as ladybird beetles and lacewings are the garden's good bugs: they feed on plant-damaging pests, including aphids, mites, scale, and whiteflies.

One way to attract good bugs to your garden, and possibly reduce the amount of chemical spraying needed, is to set out plants whose nectar or pollen provides beneficial insects

with a good food source. Especially attractive to beneficial insects are plants of the Umbelliferae family, including carrots, celery, coriander, dill, fennel, and parsley.

A new method of attracting beneficials is to spread or spray a sugar-protein combination on or around infested plants. This new treatment not only attracts beneficials, but also keeps them in the garden longer to breed and feed on pests. These alternative insect food sources—with names such as BugPro and

Predfeed—are becoming increasingly available in nurseries and mail-order catalogs.

Another new attractant is called Lady Bug Lure. It includes a chemical that simulates the scent of aphids, attracting ladybird beetles and several other types of beneficial insects that feed on aphids and other pests.

If you can't find these products in a nursery, write to Peaceful Valley Farm Supply, Box 2209, Grass Valley, CA 95945; call (916) 272-4769.

'Firetail', a knotweed from England

Plants of the genus *Polygonum,* or knotweed, are perennials admired for their delicate flower spikes and clumps of broad leaves. Now *P. amplexicaule* 'Firetail', a new variety imported from England, is winning admirers in the Northwest.

'Firetail' produces masses of rosy red blooms on 4- to 6-inch-tall flower spikes above bushy 2- to 4-foot-tall plants. Blooms keep coming from mid-June until frost. In full sun, the leaves take on a maroon tint that complements the flowers.

'Firetail' is currently being grown in the perennial border at the Bellevue Botanical Garden and in the demonstration bed at Wells Medina Nursery in Bellevue, which also sells it.

'Firetail' should do well in climate zones 4 through 7. It prefers full sun but will tolerate light shade and does best in rich, well-drained acid soil, with ample summer water. 'Firetail' is most commonly available in 1-gallon cans. You can plant it out immediately.

'Firetail' is named for its fuzzy red flower spikes.

DON NORMARK

How much life is in your soil?

Elaine Ingham of Oregon State University, in Corvallis, tests soil to determine its microbial biomass, then builds tables on computers from the results. In time, she plans to develop a map of soil life all over the world.

Ingham will test your soil for a fee and send you an analysis of its health (and suggest what you might do to improve it if it isn't up to par). Cost is $30 for a basic test of total and active bacteria and fungi, or $95 for a test of the whole food web, from microbes to nematodes. It takes about two weeks for the basic test, four weeks for the comprehensive test.

Send a cupful of soil in a sealed plastic bag by overnight mail to Elaine Ingham, Department of Botany and Plant Pathology, Cordley Hall 2082, Oregon State University, Corvallis, OR 97331.

Dutch elm disease is spreading in the Northwest

Dutch elm disease, which devastated the American elm *(Ulmus americana)* in the East and Midwest, is slowly spreading in the Pacific Northwest. First identified in Portland in 1977, then in Spokane and Vancouver, Washington, in 1990, the disease was diagnosed last year in Bellevue and Tacoma.

Unlike the Midwest, Northwest communities did not plant American elm as the dominant street tree. But the elms are still common, growing on private property, in city parks, and in rows along streets, including parts of Seattle's Washington Park, south Tacoma, and several old Portland neighborhoods.

The disease, which affects both American and European elms, is a fungus that invades, then clogs the tree's water-delivery system, effectively casuing death by dehydration. Bark beetle larvae spread the disease by burrowing into elm bark and sloughing off fungus spores. Infected trees can also transmit the disease to adjacent elms through interconnected root systems.

The first sign that Dutch elm disease (DED) may be present is wilted branch tips. Leaf yellowing and premature drop often follow. If you suspect the disease, contact your county extension office, which may be equipped to give a diagnosis if you submit a sample according to their specifications.

If DED is diagnosed, there are very few options. In most cases, the tree must be removed. Once removed, it is important to strip the bark off the tree to prevent beetles from continuing to burrow beneath the bark, breed, then infect other elm trees.

In rare cases, if a DED infection is caught very early, radical pruning by an arborist may save the tree. If less than 3 percent of the tree is infected, annual injections of fungicide may keep the disease from doing further damage. The injections, however, are expensive and must be repeated yearly or the disease will return.

Preventative options are equally limited. Although it's always wise to keep elms healthy and fertilize them regularly, even healthy trees can become infected. The only effective way to slow the spread of Dutch elm disease is constant vigilance through community-wide programs that identify, treat, and carefully dispose of infected trees.

'Touch of Red' calendula

Few flowers warm up a cool-season garden as well as the bright orange and yellow blooms of *Calendula officinalis*. Now a handsome new selection called 'Touch of Red' has petal edges that are touched with red, giving them a burnished look. Started from seed this month, this calendula will bear flowers from late fall through spring.

'Touch of Red' grows 16 to 18 inches tall and makes good cut flowers. The mixture comes in white, yellow, and orange, but at *Sunset*'s gardens in Menlo Park, California, the yellow and orange shades seem to predominate. The orange one (pictured here) has the most intense color; it seems to glow in the sun.

Order seeds as soon as possible and sow them in

NORMAN A. PLATE

Faceup flowers show off new calendula's rosy tips.

flats for transplanting outdoors in September. Choose a spot with full sun much of the day, and plant in well-amended soil with good drainage. Water regularly.

Seeds are available from Thompson & Morgan, Box 1308, Jackson, NJ 08527; (800) 274-7333. A packet of 150 seeds costs $2.95 plus shipping; catalog is free.

A watering plan for young trees

Established trees should be able to take some summer drought without irrigation. However, young trees need summer water for their first two years. Normally, 15 gallons of water a week is ample, though trees planted in sandy soils may require more.

Jerry Clark, Seattle's city arborist, suggests that each young tree be given 5 gallons of water three times a week. Form a shallow saucer-shaped basin in the soil around the trunk, and slowly run water into the basin so that it soaks directly down to the root mass. If rain doesn't fall, water the young trees until they go into dormancy.

Horticultural society is the talk of San Diego

It was love of plants and a thirst for knowledge that inspired a group of gardening enthusiasts to create the San Diego Horticultural Society in 1994. They wanted an organization that would appeal to professional gardeners and novices alike, as well as be a meeting place that would let people share information on plants.

"No one realized how popular such an organization could be," says society president Don Walker, who is also a member of the Southern California Horticultural Society. The first meeting last September attracted about 80 people who packed into a room at Quail Botanical Gardens in Encinitas.

Before long, the society had outgrown Quail, and the nonprofit club moved to a 500-seat auditorium in the

How to divide iris like a professional

Dividing tall bearded iris clumps every three to four years prevents overcrowding and ensures healthy plants. Mary Hess, owner of Bluebird Haven Iris Garden in Somerset, in California's Gold Country foothills, ought to know. Over the past 14 years, she has raised nearly 100,000 plants in her garden.

You can dig and divide irises from six weeks after blooms until two months before frost. The following techniques are based on the ones Hess uses.

First, with miniature spade or potato fork, dig around each plant about 4 inches from the base. Pry the clump up and gently knock dirt from the roots.

Break the rhizomes (horizontal underground stems) apart at knucklelike joints, leaving roots and leaf fan attached. Or cut rhizomes with a knife or clippers disinfected with a household disinfectant such as Lysol. Rhizome pieces will be 3 to 4 inches long, depending on variety, and should appear firm and white inside.

Trim leaves of the fan to 8 to 12 inches. Shaping leaves into a point improves their appearance.

Grasp the roots at the base of the rhizome so they dangle from the bottom of your closed fist. Clip hanging roots, leaving about 4 inches of newer, whitish root growth. Set plants in dry shade for a day or two to allow cuts to heal.

Choose a planting site with well-drained soil in full or part sun.

Loosen soil to a depth of 8 inches, and amend with well-aged compost. Remove the top 4 inches of amended soil, and work a high-phosphorus fertilizer 4 inches into the remaining soil. Using some of the removed soil, shape mounds about 3½ inches high to support each rhizome, spacing rhizomes 18 to 24 inches apart. Set the rhizome on the soil mound so the roots can spread out evenly. Cover the rhizome with not more than ½ inch of soil. Fill in around mounds with soil, and tamp firmly.

Water immediately, then mulch around the plant with a loose material such as straw. Continue to water about once a week (more often if temperatures top 80°) until fall rains begin.

Satellite Wagering Facility at the Del Mar Fairgrounds, rent-free thanks to the 22nd District Agricultural Association. Meetings are held from 7 to 9 P.M. on the second Monday of the month. Average attendance has been close to 200.

"You can get really intimidated by all the plants that can grow in San Diego," says Steve Brigham, a nursery manager and horticulturist who is the society's vice president. "At our meetings, though, we're all real friendly and passionate about gardening. We make things nonthreatening for new members."

At each meeting, an invited lecturer talks for about an hour. Past subjects have ranged from roses to South African bulbs to formal English gardens. Following the presentation, a panel of experts fields questions from the audience, or talks about plant specimens (as many as 100) that members bring to the meeting.

The annual membership fee of $25 includes garden tours and a monthly newsletter. To get more information, call (619) 630-7307.

Clifftop park in Newport Beach

Not many places along San Diego's developed coast let you smell salt spray and sagebrush in the same whiff. Now, thanks to a successful city and community partnership, there's one more.

Cliff Drive Park, in Newport Beach, is just a block inland from Pacific Coast Highway and minutes from the beach. Yet the sage-perfumed air at this newly planted park makes you feel as if you're deep in the hills.

The idea behind this 2-acre native-vegetation project was to restore the hillside to the way it might have looked when Tongva and Acagchemem people regularly trekked it on their way to the asphalt mine at the hill's base. The Indians used the mine's tar there for glue, for trade, and to waterproof their canoes.

A parking lot that would have paved over the spring-fed creek at the base of the hill was the impetus for the project. Jan Vandersloot and other neighborhood residents who were fond of the

modest riparian habitat rallied an opposition force. Their team included Newport Harbor High School (biology classes had used the site for field trips for more than 30 years), historians familiar with the hill's importance to indigenous tribes, and members of California Native Plant Society. The opposition prevailed, the parking lot proposal died, and the notion of replacing the non-native ice plant with sages, toyon, willows, and other plants more appropriate to the site's history rose in its place.

Though the battle of the weeds hasn't been totally conquered—abundant 1994–1995 winter rainfall made *everything* grow—the hillside now looks, and smells, native. Stop by and have a whiff of California the way it used to be.

To reach Cliff Drive Park, turn inland off Pacific Coast Highway at Riverside Drive and then, after two blocks, left at Cliff Drive. Park at the top of the bluff and walk down to Avon Creek. The native plant section of the 10-acre park is the 2-acre slope at the west end of the park, between Avon Street and Cliff Drive.

Indigenous plants fit for a museum

The climb schoolchildren make from the bus parking lot to the Southwest Museum's entrance is called the Hopi Trail. Kids probably wouldn't want that changed. But now that this Los Angeles museum's new Ethnobotanical Garden is firmly established, the trail could just as easily be named after the Gabrielino. The Hopi would recognize many of the plants in the garden, but the Gabrielino, who lived in this area, would feel right at home among the manzanita, ceanothus, and pungent sage that again grace this site.

Though the new garden is a vast improvement visually over the weedy hillside it replaced, beautification is not its main role. The museum's mission is to preserve the history and culture of Native Americans, and this garden is designed to help visitors understand the importance of indigenous plants to those cultures.

Plants typical to chaparral, desert, tule bog, and dry riverbed terrains are represented; additional sections are devoted to medicinal, dye, and basket-making plants. Each significant plant is identified, and a brochure explains its uses. You'll find out, for instance, that the roots of a modest-looking plant called amole are used for soap, and that its fibers, when bound together, make a dandy broom.

The Southwest Museum is located at 234 Museum Drive in Los Angeles. It's open 11 to 5 Tuesdays through Sundays. For more information, call (213) 221-2164.

By Suzie Boss, Sharon Cohoon, Dayna Lynn Fried, Steven R. Lorton, Jim McCausland, Lynn Narleskey, Lauren Bonar Swezey, and Lance Walheim

Handy gauge tells when to water

Evapotranspiration (ET) is the amount of water that evaporates from the soil plus the amount that transpires through the leaves of a specific plant, such as grass. By irrigating according to ET rates, you can maintain acceptable plant growth without overwatering. But most gardeners find the ET concept difficult to follow.

Now a simple device called Moisture Smart Watering Gauge can tell you when to water your

When the gauge's water level drops, it's time to irrigate.

lawn. You insert the gauge in the lawn and fill it with water to the "zero-line" as

directed in the instructions, then wait until the water level falls to a certain level that indicates it's time to irrigate. For example, when the water level drops about ¾ inch, it's time to irrigate lawns in loamy soil. To provide adequate soil moisture, turn on the sprinklers long enough to refill the gauge to the original zero-line.

The gauge can also be used in any other irrigated areas of the garden. It's available from Gardener's Supply Company, 128 Intervale Rd., Burlington, VT 05401; (800) 955-3370. Cost is $24.95 plus shipping charges.

PLANTING

❑ **SOW FALL AND WINTER CROPS.** Anytime this month, sow cilantro, cress, endive, lettuce, radishes, scallions, Swiss chard, and turnips (for greens). Late in the month, sow arugula, cabbage (for spring harvest), corn salad, mustard, and onions.

MAINTENANCE

❑ **HARVEST HERBS.** For maximum flavor, cut herbs in the morning just after the dew has dried. If you aren't going to use them immediately, lay them out on a window screen in a dry, shady place and allow them to air-dry. They should be dry and nicely crisp in about two weeks.

❑ **DIVIDE EARLY PERENNIALS.** Dig and divide bearded irises and Oriental poppies now. When you dig up clumps, inspect the roots, discard old, worn-out pieces, and remove any clinging grass and weeds. Replant divisions and water them well.

❑ **PROPAGATE SHRUBS.** Now is the time to take tip cuttings of many shrubs: camellia, daphne, elaeagnus, euonymus, hebe, holly, hydrangea, magnolia, nandina, rhododendron, and viburnum are all candidates. Snip the terminal bud off a 4-inch-long cutting. Strip leaves off the lower end of the cutting (leaving three to five leaves at the top), and dip the cut end into rooting hormone. Put the cuttings in pots

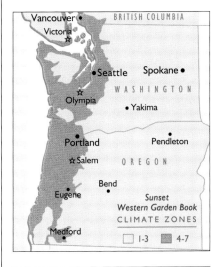

containing equal parts of potting soil and sand. Place the pots in strong light (not direct sun), and water often enough so that the soil stays moist but not soggy. Misting cuttings daily or covering them with a clear plastic tent helps keep them moist. Move plants into a protected area before frost.

❑ **DEADHEAD FLOWERS.** Snip off faded blooms on annuals to keep flowers coming. If you don't plan to use seeds

from perennials and they don't have attractive seed pods that you want to enjoy, cut blooms as soon as they fade.

❑ **FERTILIZE.** Annuals, container plants, and long-blooming perennials can still benefit from a good feeding. Use a complete liquid food monthly into October, or apply it half-strength every two weeks.

❑ **MAKE COMPOST.** August generates a big batch of material for the compost: spent flowers, inedible vegetable parts, prunings, grass clippings, pulled weeds. Put all these on the compost pile. Hot, rainless weather will dry the pile out, so water it well, and turn it once more before fall arrives.

❑ **PRUNE CANE BERRIES.** Remove canes that bore fruit in June. On everbearing plants, prune off the half of the cane that has already produced fruit.

PEST & WEED CONTROL

❑ **BAIT FOR SLUGS.** In hot August weather, you'll find slugs in the cool spots—under rocks, among ground covers, next to house foundations. Continue to bait, but keep children and pets (especially dogs) away from the poisonous bait.

❑ **WEED.** Before they bloom and scatter seeds around your garden, pull weeds. Put seed-free weeds onto the compost pile.

I can't imagine August without perennial sunflower (*Helianthus multiflorus*). I came to admire this flower as a child growing up in Ohio, where the climate is not unlike that of Spokane. So when I started my Seattle garden in the early 1970s, I ordered a plant from White Flower Farm in Litchfield, Connecticut. Divisions of that plant are thriving now in my Skagit Valley garden. This sunflower reaches up to 6 feet tall, producing masses of 3-inch-wide, sunshine yellow blooms from early July into October. Through the years, I've probably cut enough flowers to fill the Kingdome. A few nurseries carry this sunflower in cans. You can also order it from a perennial specialist.

•

Like sunflowers, fuchsias are at their blooming best in August. If you want to see some prize plants, head for the Oregon Fuchsia Society show at Beaverton Mall, August 25, 26, and 27. More than 150 plants will be on display. Hours are 10 to 9 Friday, 10 to 7

PACIFIC NORTHWEST Garden Notebook
BY STEVEN R. LORTON

Saturday, and 11 to 6 Sunday. The mall is at 3205 S.W. Cedar Hills Boulevard. Admission is free.

THAT'S A GOOD QUESTION

Q: Is August too late in the year to fertilize evergreen shrubs?

A: In a word: no. Evergreen shrubs still have time to take up the nutrients before they go into dormancy, and they'll benefit from a dose of a complete fertilizer this month.

Because I'm forgetful, I devised my own timetable for fertilizing evergreens and other plants in the ground. I feed plants on holidays: On Valentine's Day, I lightly broadcast granular 20-20-20 fertilizer, then on April Fools' Day, Memorial Day, and the Fourth of July, I apply 12-12-12 fertilizer. And if I feel like it, I give plants another light feeding on my birthday, August 5. Container plants need more prodigious fertilizing (see the checklist item above).

CHECKLIST
AUGUST

PLANTING

❏ **PLANT OR SOW FALL ANNUALS.** Coast, Inland: Start seeds of fall- and winter-blooming annuals, such as calendula (see item on page 225), pansy, Iceland poppy, primrose, stock, and viola. If you need instant color, nurseries should still have a good supply of warm-season flowers in 4-inch pots.

❏ **SOW SWEET PEAS.** Coast, Inland: To get a crop of early flowers, sow an early-flowering kind, such as Winter Elegance, available from Shepherd's Garden Seeds; (408) 335-6910. Colors include cream, lavender, pink, salmon, and white. This type will bloom when days are short. Protect new growth from slugs and snails, and provide support for the vines.

❏ **SOW PERENNIALS.** Coast, Inland: For bloom next spring and summer, sow seeds (in containers) of carnations, columbine, coneflower, coreopsis, feverfew, gaillardia, hardy asters, hollyhock, lupine, penstemon, phlox, Shasta daisy, statice, and yarrow.

❏ **START COOL-SEASON CROPS.** Coast, Inland: Start seeds of broccoli, brussels sprouts, cabbage, and cauliflower; they need six to eight weeks to reach transplant size. Sow seeds of carrots, chard, lettuce, peas, and radishes directly in the ground. Mountain:

Eureka

Redding

CALIFORNIA

NEVADA

Mendocino

Sacramento
Santa Rosa

San Francisco

San Jose

Fresno

Monterey

Sunset Western Garden Book
CLIMATE ZONES

☐ Mountain (1-2)
☐ Valley (7-9)
☐ Inland (14)
☐ Coastal (15-17)

Where frosts aren't expected until late October, sow seeds of beets, carrots, radishes, and spinach for harvest by fall.

❏ **ORDER SPRING PLANTS.** Browse catalogs and order spring-flowering bulbs and perennials this month. Mountain: Be sure to specify that you need plants in time for September planting (in coldest, highest-elevation areas, wait until spring to plant).

MAINTENANCE

❏ **HARVEST FLOWERS FOR DRYING.** For dried arrangements, harvest flowers that keep well, such as celosia, English lavender, globe amaranth, hydrangeas, roses, statice, strawflowers, and yarrow. Cut with as long a stem as possible, strip off large leaves you don't want, fasten in small bunches, and hang upside down in a dark, dry, well-ventilated area.

❏ **SHAPE PLANTS.** After a summer of growth, some ground covers, shrubs, and vines may need minor trimming. Snip out wayward shoots or awkward growth, but don't do any major pruning. Avoid shearing shrubs into gumdrops and other unnatural shapes.

❏ **PREPARE BEDS FOR FALL PLANTING.** Cultivate the soil at least 12 inches deep (if possible), then turn in a 2- to 3-inch layer of organic matter (such as compost)

PEST CONTROL

❏ **CONTROL POWDERY MILDEW.** For a nontoxic control, mix 2 teaspoons baking soda and 2 teaspoons lightweight summer (horticultural) oil in a gallon of water, then spray plants thoroughly. You can also buy ready-mixed fungicides such as triforine and benomyl, but they are more toxic to mammals.

By the time August rolls around, I'm getting a good harvest off my lone tomato plant: just one 'Early Girl' serves my family well. I used to wait until the medium-size fruits were picture-perfect red and slightly soft to the touch before picking them. I'd set the tomatoes I couldn't use that day on the kitchen counter, but by the time I was ready for the rest, a few had rotted and others had that over-the-hill taste.

Then I had a chat with Marita Cantwell, a post-harvest specialist at UC Davis. I learned that if you leave a ripe tomato on the plant too long, acid declines and flavors change. If you want a great-tasting tomato with shelf life, Cantwell suggests that you harvest just before the red-ripe stage, while the fruit is turning from orange to red. Tomato ripening is a dynamic process, she explains, and an orange tomato will continue to develop full flavor on the kitchen counter (away from direct sun). When the tomato turns fully red, it's ready to eat. If you prefer to harvest tomatoes at the red stage, pick them just when they turn fully red, and don't wait until they soften. And don't store tomatoes in the refrigerator: temperatures below 50° destroy their flavor and texture.

•

Speaking of tomatoes, one of the greatest organic vegetable gardens I've ever visited is the 5-acre Valley Oaks Garden Project at Fetzer Vineyards in Hopland, California. August is a great time to

NORTHERN CALIFORNIA
Garden Notebook
BY LAUREN BONAR SWEZEY

visit. Jeff Dawson and his crew grow not only some 115 varieties of tomatoes, but 40 sweet and hot peppers, 30 eggplants, 50 melons, and 18 basils. You'll also see an herb crescent, an espaliered apple fence, and 25 varieties of table grapes. In a separate area of the garden, you can view Dawson's seed-saving project, where he allows crops to mature and then harvests the seeds. Free tours are offered at 11 and 3 daily. For details, call (707) 744-1737.

THAT'S A GOOD QUESTION

Q: This past spring I grew cauliflower, but the plants never produced heads. What did I do wrong? Should I try again this fall?

A: To produce the best heads, cauliflower plants should grow rapidly and then mature in cool weather. That's why fall planting is generally considered best in mild-winter areas. Vince Rubatzky, professor emeritus of vegetable crops at UC Davis, says that all cauliflower benefits from exposure to cold (below 50°) after seedling stage. Autumn's warm soil and air temperatures give plants a fast start, then the heads mature in late fall when it's cool. If seedlings or developing plants are moisture-stressed at any time, they may not develop a head or will produce one that is only button-size. Keep seedlings growing vigorously by planting them in rich soil. Water often enough that the soil stays constantly moist, but not wet.

PLANTING

❏ **PLANT OR SOW ANNUALS.** Start seeds of fall- and winter-blooming annuals, such as calendula, Iceland poppy, pansy, primrose, snapdragon, stock, and viola. If you're having a summer party and need instant color, nurseries still have many warm-season flowers in 4-inch pots.

❏ **PLANT VEGETABLES.** Early in the month, start from seed. Sow beets, broccoli, brussels sprouts, cabbage, carrots, cauliflower, endive, kale, kohlrabi, onions, parsnips, and turnips. About midmonth, start cole crops from transplants instead of seed. Wait until next month to start lettuce and peas.

❏ **PREPARE BEDS FOR FALL PLANTING.** Cultivate the soil at least 12 inches deep (if possible) and then work in a 2- to 3-inch layer of organic matter such as compost and a complete fertilizer. Rake planting beds smooth.

MAINTENANCE

❏ **CARE FOR ROSES.** Cut off faded flowers and water as necessary. Feed lightly to encourage repeat bloom. Remove any suckers and unwanted branches.

CENTRAL VALLEY
CHECKLIST
AUGUST

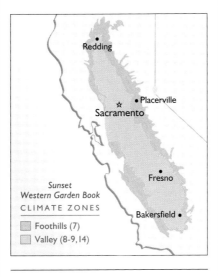

Sunset Western Garden Book
CLIMATE ZONES

▨ Foothills (7)
▨ Valley (8-9, 14)

❏ **CUT BACK PERENNIALS.** When flowers have finished, cut back to 6 inches to encourage repeat bloom on strong stems.

❏ **FERTILIZE.** This month is your last chance to fertilize tender fruit trees such as citrus and avocado. Camellias and azaleas are setting next year's flower buds; apply an acid fertilizer now to boost bloom. Keep using liquid fertilizers on container plants. If plants have yellow leaves with green veins, apply chelated iron.

❏ **MULCH.** Add fresh mulch as needed to keep soil and roots cool, save moisture, and discourage weeds. Lay down at least 2 to 3 inches, as much as 5 to 6 inches around large plants. Keep mulch several inches away from tree and shrub trunks so they stay dry.

❏ **WATER AS NEEDED.** Keep a close eye on maturing vegetables; letting them dry out now could cost the harvest. Also watch newly planted seeds and container plants. They'll need frequent watering in hot weather. Re-form soil basins around fruit trees as needed.

Large trees and shrubs may need a deep soaking now if they depend for their water on rain instead of irrigation. Water with soaker hoses, a slow-running sprinkler, a deep-root irrigator, or a hose running slowly until the soil is well soaked at least to the plant's drip line. Check moisture penetration by digging down with a trowel.

CENTRAL VALLEY
Garden Notebook
BY LANCE WALHEIM

No matter how busy I am, two things always get done in my garden: in March I plant tomatoes, and in August I plant broccoli. Even though I have a degree in botany and have been gardening for more than 20 years, I still think there's a bit of hocus-pocus about planting a cool-season crop such as broccoli in the hottest part of summer. It would seem to make more sense to plant my broccoli when I plant my tomatoes. But I guarantee that if I did that, it would bolt (go to seed) long before I could harvest it. Sometimes gardening is a matter of faith, so trust me on this.

Planted this month, my broccoli matures to perfection every time. I like 'Green Comet'. By the end of October, I'm harvesting the tightest, most beautiful heads you've ever seen. Even after I cut the main stalk, the side shoots keep yielding bite-size florets through winter.

•

With memories of springtime watery eyes and runny nose, I recently stopped by the allergy-free demonstration garden at Cal State Fresno. I was amazed to see the many great flowering plants— including rhaphiolepis, spiraeas, and verbena—that won't contribute to airborne pollen. Before the fall planting season arrives, visit the garden to note which of the allergy-friendly plants you'd like to add to your garden. The garden is near the main campus entrance, at Scott and Keats avenues. It's open during daylight hours and admission is free.

•

My kids laugh at me when I inspect our tomato plants for hornworms. I learned my technique by watching a hungry scrub jay hunt: I nod my head up and down as I run my eyes along each branch and under leaves in search of the chubby green hornworms. Handpicking is the only way to control the big ones without sprays, and no hornworm is going to beat me out of my tomatoes.

THAT'S A GOOD QUESTION

Q: Some of the landscape plants I put in last year are drying out, even though they are watered regularly by a drip system. What could be wrong?

A: To find out, first clean the filter. Then check your system while it's operating. Open the ends of the main lines and let them run for 15 minutes to flush out debris. Check for clogged emitters and unclog them with a pin or replace them if they're broken. If each plant has only one emitter, it may be time to add one or two more to increase drip coverage of the expanded root zone. Install the new emitters farther from the trunk. Also make sure that the spray patterns of minisprinklers haven't been disrupted by new growth. Once the system is operating well, adjust the frequency or duration of the watering cycle.

CHECKLIST
AUGUST

PLANTING

❑ **ADD SUMMER VEGETABLES.** Coastal gardeners (zones 22–24; see map) can still add transplants of cucumber, eggplant, pepper, squash, and tomato. Look for fast-maturing varieties. Inland and low-desert gardeners (zones 18–21 and 13, respectively) can sow or transplant a final crop of beans or corn.

❑ **BEGIN WINTER CROPS.** Coastal, inland, and high-desert (zone 11) gardeners can sow cool-season vegetables in flats midmonth and transplant the seedlings to the garden in six to eight weeks. Good candidates include anything in the Brassica family—broccoli, cabbage, cauliflower, kale, mustard; root crops such as beets, carrots, onions, and turnips; head and leaf lettuces; and edible-pod peas.

❑ **BUY AND PLANT BEARDED IRIS.** Iris rhizomes begin arriving in nurseries this month. Shop early for best choice. Plant 1 to 2 feet apart in an area that gets at least a half-day of sun. In hot inland areas, bury rhizome tops slightly to prevent sunburn. Closer to the coast, plant so rhizome tops show slightly above soil surface. Water thoroughly immediately after planting.

❑ **START ANNUALS FROM SEED.** Calendula, Iceland poppies, nemesia, pansies, snapdragon, stock, sweet peas, and many other cool-season annuals can be sown in flats starting midmonth.

Sunset *Western Garden Book* CLIMATE ZONES

1-3 7-9 11 13 14-24

(This is often the only way to obtain tall-stemmed varieties or a large quantity of a single color.) Keep flats in partial shade. By October—prime fall planting time—the seedlings will be ready to transplant into the garden.

MAINTENANCE

❑ **FEED TURF.** Give warm-season turf grasses such as Bermuda and St. Augustine a light feeding with a high-nitrogen fertilizer.

❑ **HARVEST VEGETABLES.** Pick summer vegetables frequently, whether you use them or not, to encourage plants to continue producing well into fall. Fast-growing cucumber, squash, and zucchini plants can be harvested almost daily. Check to see if heavy-producing tomato vines need additional support.

❑ **PRUNE FOR FALL BLOOM.** Trim marguerites by a third to encourage a fresh crop of fall flowers. Fuchsias pruned now may also produce a second bloom.

❑ **RENEW MULCH.** Check mulch you applied in spring. If it's less than an inch deep, add compost or shredded bark to a depth of 3 inches. Keep mulch away from bases of trees and plant stems.

❑ **CARE FOR ROSES.** Remove dead twigs, spent flowers, and hips; prune very lightly to stimulate fall flowering. Gardeners in hot inland locations should wait another month, until temperatures slacken. Water deeply and regularly.

❑ **SHOP SEED CATALOGS.** Explore seed catalogs for unusual cool-season annuals, vegetables, and spring-flowering perennials to order now.

PEST CONTROL

❑ **PROTECT HOUSE PLANTS.** Spider mites, scale, and thrips may attack during summer months. Spray infestations with insecticidal soap or horticultural oil according to label instructions.

By late summer most of my plants look as if they want to join me in the shade. Don't yours? Mulch and water all you want, but they still look pooped and parched. Not my dear old grays, though. Santolina, catmint, and lavender are as impervious to heat as men in seersucker suits in magazine ads.

At the moment, the coolest gray in my garden is *Artemisia* 'Silver King'. It billows over the rocks edging my sunniest border. My temperature drops just looking at it.

•

Speaking of grays, *Plectranthus argentatus,* which I admired in several shade gardens in Del Mar this spring, is one nonstandard silver to look for. This Australian native quickly matures into a 3- by 3-foot mound of plush leaves the color and texture of dove gray suede. Though grown mostly for its foliage, it also has small blue flowers with deeper-toned dots. The Huntington Botanical Gardens in San Marino (818/405-2141) and Quail Botanical Gardens in Encinitas (619/436-3036) propagate it regularly for their sales.

•

Southern California Gardens, An Illustrated History, by Victoria Padilla, has been reissued in a hardbound limited edition by Allen A.

SOUTHERN CALIFORNIA
Garden Notebook
BY SHARON COHOON

Knoll of Santa Barbara. Though written nearly 40 years ago, this gardening classic is anything but dry or dusty. Its tale of how succeeding waves of newcomers to the area transformed Southern California into one of the richest plant environments in the world is a real page-turner. To order (about $40 plus shipping), call (800) 777-7623.

THAT'S A GOOD QUESTION

Q: "I can't keep culinary sage alive more than a season or two. "It's beautiful one day, and dead the next. What am I doing wrong?"
A: *Phytophthora,* soil fungi that cause root rot, are the likely culprits, according to Jerry Turney, plant pathologist at the Huntington Botanical Gardens. When we water, these water molds release spores that swim to plant roots and infect them. Sage has little resistance to these fungi, so anything you do to improve the plant's drainage will help. Try raised beds and lots of soil amendments. Pine bark mulch, which has been shown to inhibit phytophthora, is a particularly good additive, says Turney. "Use up to 50 percent and add another ½ inch or so above the soil." Forgoing tricolor and purple sage for less sensitive golden or garden sage will help, too, adds Shirley Kerins, curator of the Huntington's herb garden.

CHECKLIST
AUGUST

PLANTING

❏ **PLANT CROPS.** Zones 1-3 (see map): If your garden doesn't get frost until October, sow seeds of beet, carrot, lettuce, radish, and spinach. All should mature by then.

Zones 12 and 13: Plant beans, corn, cucumbers, squash, and tomatoes. Late in the month, set out transplants of beets, broccoli, cabbage, carrots, cauliflower, chard, and spinach. Mulch and shade the transplants to protect them from late summer heat.

❏ **PLANT AUTUMN CROCUS, IRIS.** Zones 1-3: Buy and plant corms of autumn crocus (*Colchicum*) and rhizomes of bearded iris. Autumn crocus should bloom within a month; iris blooms next spring.

MAINTENANCE

❏ **CARE FOR ANNUALS.** Encourage long-blooming annuals to flower through the summer by shearing or pinching off faded flowers, then watering and fertilizing plants.

❏ **CARE FOR LAWNS.** Zones 12 and 13: Cut common Bermuda at about 1½ inches, hybrids at ¾ inch, zoysia and St. Augustine at 1½ to 2 inches. If you have fescue, Buffalo grass, or Kentucky blue grass, cut it at 2 to 3 inches.

❏ **CHECK FOR CHLOROSIS.** Yellowish leaves with green veins are signs of iron deficiency chlorosis. Apply chelated iron to correct the problem.

❏ **DIVIDE PERENNIALS.** Zones 1-3: Divide bearded iris early this month.

Sunset Western Garden Book CLIMATE ZONES
☐ 1-3
☐ 10-11
☐ 12-13

Dig and divide Oriental poppies at any time during August. Before you replant the divisions, remove any grasses and weeds clinging to rhizomes or roots.

❏ **FEED ROSES.** Zones 12 and 13: Apply soluble sulfur (Disper-Sul) to roses to acidify the soil, fortify soil with a complete fertilizer, and add iron chelate to correct chlorosis. Water everything in thoroughly.

❏ **FERTILIZE STRAWBERRIES.** Zones 1-3: Feed them now for best berry production next year.

❏ **HARVEST HERBS.** They have the most flavor if you pick them just after morning dew has dried. Use them fresh or lay them on a screen to air-dry in a shady place.

❏ **PICK FLOWERS FOR DRYING.** Strip leaves off long stems, bundle them together, and hang upside down indoors to air-dry.

❏ **PREVENT FRUIT SPLIT.** Zones 12 and 13: Citrus, melons, pomegranates, and tomatoes can split when monsoon rain or heavier-than-usual irrigation gives them too much water after summer drought, causing the fruits' skins to stretch and split. To minimize fruit split, keep the soil evenly moist around plants as crops near maturity.

❏ **PRUNE PEPPERS, TOMATOES.** Zones 12 and 13: Prune spring-planted peppers and tomatoes to encourage a fall crop. Cut back tomatoes by about a third, and lightly prune peppers. Protect both with shadecloth to prevent sunburn on newly exposed stems.

❏ **WATER TREES AND SHRUBS.** Permanent landscape plants that rely mostly on rain for irrigation may need a deep drink now. Water with a soaker hose, deep-root irrigator, or hose running slowly into a watering basin built around the plant.

PEST & WEED CONTROL

❏ **CONTROL CORN BORERS.** Zones 12 and 13: When translucent patches skeletonize corn leaves, corn borer larvae are likely to blame. Spray plants (especially where leaves join the stalk) with *Bacillus thuringiensis*.

Summer nights have their own magic. After dark, stroll down the sidewalk and you'll breath in the fragrances—perhaps carnations, heliotrope, honeysuckle, lavender, lilies, roses, or in wilder places, the mellow scent of cottonwood leaves. Sometimes the scents are hard to track, so let your nose lead you to find your favorites, then bring their aroma into your garden. Recently, I fell in love with a sweet-smelling honeysuckle growing in a friend's entry court. I bought a plant, then trained the vine over my front porch, where it's never far out of nose range.

•

Keeping a sharp edge on tools like spades and hoes can make garden work go much faster. Most tools are unsharpened when you buy them. I usually use a mill bastard file: it takes 20 or 30 minutes to put the first edge on, then just 1 or 2 minutes to touch it up after each use. A bench grinder makes the job go faster, but don't hold the metal to the wheel so long that it gets too hot and changes color; it can become hard and brittle.

•

INLAND WESTERN STATES
Garden Notebook
BY JIM McCAUSLAND

If you garden in the Southwest's high desert or in any other cold-winter climate, especially through New Mexico, look for a new book that's just appeared this summer. *Best Plants for New Mexico Gardens and Landscapes,* by Baker Morrow (University of New Mexico Press, Albuquerque, 1995; $24.95), is an encyclopedia of sorts, listing plants by common name according to category. It also includes tips about soil preparation and Southwestern-style landscaping.

THAT'S A GOOD QUESTION

Q: When should I pick my apples?

A: Wait until two or three healthy apples drop (wormy apples ripen and drop ahead of the main crop). Taste one: If it's sweet and not too starchy, start to pick by gently lifting and pulling fruit off the tree. If the apples don't pull free easily, leave them on the tree and try them again a week later. Some kinds of apples, such as 'Yellow Transparent' and most other early ones, tend to ripen all at once. Others, like 'Gravenstein', tend to ripen over a longer period of time. And many late apples don't ripen until after frost, so be patient.

The colorful magic of koi

A guide to help decide if koi can live with you

$20,000 for a single prize specimen, you can also buy one a few months old for as little as $3 and watch it grow.

Where do you begin? A koi dealer can introduce you to fish that gleam like the purest gold or silver, and perhaps let you hand-feed salmon-size creatures with diaphanous fins and tails. Most dealers are free with pond-building advice, and can supply hardware and hook you up with landscape professionals who specialize in koi ponds.

Dealers can also recommend koi whose size, color, and conformation will fit your budget and fish-rearing experience. Chris Moore, a koi dealer in Everett, Washington, says: "We sell beginners inexpensive fish, usually in the $3 to $5 range, then let them trade up to bigger fish as they progress." Not all dealers make trade-ins, but most will bend over backward to see that you succeed with the fish they sell.

Many dealers ship fish for overnight air delivery by placing koi in containers filled with superoxygenated water (fish losses are very small). Dealers carry

SCHOOLING KOI *gleam in the dark-bottomed pond (left) of Dick and Mary Glassberg, designed by Steve Rose of Perkiss-Rose Associates, Fullerton, California. Below, an indoor-outdoor pond allows fish to swim under a glass wall and into the house at feeding time.*

W HEN I OWNED A COCKATOO, I WAS delighted with her beauty and surprised by her obvious affection for me. But I never expected to encounter a beautiful *fish* with personality. Then I met the koi.

Koi swirl through the water, displaying shades of red, gold, platinum, white, orange, yellow, gray, black, and blue. When you appear, they'll swim up and eat food out of your hand, and even nuzzle your fingers.

There are 14 classes of koi, all bred to be seen from above. Many are bred in the United States, while others come from Japan, China, Israel, and Singapore. Some grow fast, some slowly. While you can spend as much as

STEPHANIE RAUSSER

PRIZE-WINNING SANKE KOI *is held by breeder Fred Tonai of Golden State Fisheries in Sacramento. The 5-year-old, 30-inch female is valued at $6,000.*

aquatic plants and preformulated koi food, and they can supply information about feeding schedules for your climate and local water quality: whether, for example, your water contains koi-killing chlorine, chloramines, and ammonium, and what to do if it does.

CREATING KOI HABITAT

If you have an underused swimming pool, or an 8- by 10-foot free space in a fenced, secured part of the garden, you have enough room for koi. Here's how to create the right habitat.

Convert a swimming pool. There's powerful logic behind the notion that a koi-filled pool serves a higher purpose than a rarely used pool. Pools are easy to convert. Cosmetically, it pays to give the pool bottom a dark coat so the fish show up better. The pool's mechanical filter should be converted to (or supplemented with) a biological filter.

Install a prefab pond. Though koi originated in Japanese rice paddies flooded with water just a few inches deep, it's best to choose a pond at least 3 feet deep. Shallower ponds make koi fishing too easy for predators (see "Protecting koi," above right). A 7- by 10-foot, 600-gallon free-form plastic pond costs $400 to $500; one that's half that size costs $275.

Build a pond. The easiest way is to dig an 8- by 10-foot pond at least 3 feet deep (as much as 5 feet deep where winters are very cold), then seal it with a flexible plastic liner (25 to 50 cents per square foot). Put landscaping fabric, old

carpet, or sand down first to keep tiny rocks from puncturing the liner. Sides should be vertical: a sloped, concave bottom can cause a wrinkled liner and make it too easy for herons to wade in after the fish. Cover the bottom of the pond with pea gravel, and put a wooden rim around the top to protect exposed plastic from sunlight. An 8- by 10- by 2-foot pond with liner, pump, and filter costs $500 to $1,000.

You could also line the pond with concrete, but leaks through hairline cracks in concrete are difficult to find.

HEALTHY WATER, HEALTHY FISH

Both biological and mechanical filters can keep water pure and fish healthy. Most koi fanciers favor biological filters that use bacteria or water plants to remove impurities from the water.

Most people install biological gravel filters in small, separate ponds so the filters can be cleaned without removing the koi. The same is true for water plant filters, though many people put water plants in with the koi as well.

A koi dealer can provide more specific information on the merits of biological and mechanical filters. Size and construction details depend on the size of your pond, your climate, and the size and number of your fish.

Simple filters cost $100 to $300, basic pumps $60 to $250 and up, depending on the volume of water you need to move and purify.

Whatever kind of filter you use, you can expect algae to cloud your pool for a

month or so in late spring. The algae don't hurt the fish.

PROTECTING KOI

Koi were originally bred for the cooking pot, effectively turning each rice paddy into a two-crop plot. These days, koi have far more to fear from cats, raccoons, and herons than from humans. Border your pond with a 2-foot-tall fence to deny both raccoons and herons a water-level perch to fish from.

If you're opposed to a water-side fence, install a low, single-strand electric wire to stop raccoons, and put bird netting over the pond to foil herons. A plastic statue of a heron may help keep the real ones away. Move the statue frequently to fool the birds.

KOI SOCIETIES AND SOURCES

For information about koi societies, write or call Associated Koi Clubs of America, c/o Bob and Joan Finnegan, Box 1, Midway City, CA 92655; (800) 646-1685.

Koi dealers are scattered all over the West; following are 10 of the many excellent ones. Unless noted, dealers sell koi as well as koi food, water plants, pumps, filters, and liners, both on site and by mail.

California. *Asahi Fancy Koi, Inc.,* 1051 W. 190th St., Gardena 90248; (310) 532-2020.

California Nishikigoi Center, 2159 East Ave., Hayward 94541; (510) 881-8629.

Del Mar Aquarium, Pond & Water Garden, 1101-B Camino Del Mar, Del Mar 92014; (619) 259-0780.

Golden State Fisheries, 10190 Florin Rd., Sacramento 95829; (916) 689-3474.

Laguna Koi Ponds, 20452 Laguna Canyon Rd., Laguna Beach 92651; (714) 494-5107.

Nishikigoi, 11364 Lott Point, San Diego 92126; (619) 689-8079. By appointment only (ask for Stanley Yiu); no plants.

Hawaii. *Hawaii Koi Farm,* 73-4425 Paiaha St., Kailua-Kona 96740; (808) 325-7022. By appointment; no plants.

Oregon. *Willamette Koi and Water Lilies,* 1710 45th Ave. N.E., Salem 97305; (503) 363-0603. No mail order.

Washington. *Golden Pond, Inc.,* Box 251, Oakville 98568; (360) 273-9858. Fish, medication, and food.

Moorehaven Water Gardens, 3006 York Rd., Everett 98204; (206) 743-6888. ■

By Jim McCausland

WATER-LOVING PLANTS *float in pots and sprout from ponds. The tall arrow-leafed plant at left center is Thalia dealbata. At right, Iris laevigata 'Variegata' shows off its cream-striped leaves. At rear, pink-flowered Lavatera 'Barnsley' grows on terra firma.*

JAMES FREDERICK HOUSEL

They flood the garden with aquatic plants

In this liquid landscape, water plants grow in pools and pots

TO BORROW A LINE from Coleridge, there's water, water, everywhere in this unconventional garden created by sculptors George Little and David Lewis of Bainbridge Island, Washington. Aquatic plants in pools and in pots—set in the ground and in the air—occupy almost every nook and cranny.

Altogether, the garden has nearly 20 water features. Aquatic plants grow in big ceramic containers or rise from 2-foot-deep pools, the largest of which is 5 by 12 feet. Some of the pools were dug in the ground and sealed with reservoir liners. Other pools are raised rectangles built of pressure-treated 2-by-6s, then lined.

A number of the pools and pots spout water or incorporate fountains fed by small recirculating pumps. Tall sculpted columns serve as pedestals for plants in pots.

Water is pumped up through pipes in the columns, then spills over the plants and dribbles back down into the pools below.

Plants grow in a variety of wide, shallow pots. Most of the pots measure 8 inches to a foot deep and 28 inches or more in diameter. Little and Lewis favor black plastic pots because they don't show up in the dark pools and they tend to attract less algae.

Little and Lewis mix and match the aquatic plants just as they would terrestrial plants in borders. For big, bold leaves, they use plants like *Thalia dealbata* and arrow arum (*Peltandra virginica*); for vertical punch and flowers, they add water-loving irises (*I. ensata* and *I. laevigata*). Assorted water lilies (*Nymphaea*) float on the surface in the ponds and the big pots, providing greenery splashed with gorgeous, fra-

grant blooms. The grassy foliage and tiny seed heads of dwarf cattail (*Typha minima*) sprout here and there, often coupled with water forget-me-not (*Myosotis palustris*) and baby's tears (*Soleirolia soleirolii*).

In each of the pools, a few goldfish keep the mosquito population under control. Periodically, if the water becomes unusually murky, the owners empty the containers and drain the pools, scrub the liners and pots, and then add fresh water.

Two sources for aquatic garden plants and materials supply much of what Little and Lewis use: Moorehaven Water Gardens, 3006 York Rd., Everett, WA 98204, (206) 743-6888; and Lilypons Water Gardens, 81-900 Johnson St., Box 1130, Thermal, CA 92274, (800) 365-5459. ■

By Steven R. Lorton

DENSE CLUSTERS *of 1- to 2-inch-wide blooms and glossy leaves distinguish 'Flower Carpet' roses.*

Knee-high roses all summer

A new disease-resistant variety makes its Western debut this summer

MOST KINDS OF ROSES require a trade-off: to enjoy the beauty and fragrance of their flowers, you have to be willing to nurse plants that are susceptible to foliar diseases such as black spot and powdery mildew. This summer, a new landscape rose called 'Flower Carpet' offers a better return: it bears a mass of lightly fragrant pink blooms, and the plant is remarkably resistant to disease.

'Flower Carpet' is already well known in Australia, New Zealand, South Africa, and Europe. In foreign competitions, it has won three gold medals, including one at the All Deutschland Rose trials in 1990. To qualify for that award the rose went three years without spraying; then it also won the highest rating for natural disease resistance ever given.

This spreading shrub grows slightly larger than 2 feet tall and 3 to 5 feet wide. Its small leaves have a glossy sheen. The iridescent pink double flowers look something like informal floribunda or polyantha roses. After bloom, pea-size reddish hips may appear, but they tend to drop off in warmer climates.

The plant should grow and flower well throughout the West. In *Sunset*'s test garden in Menlo Park, California, 'Flower Carpet' roses bloomed best in full sun. Because of its relatively small size, this rose takes well to a container. Give it a pot at least 16 inches wide and deep, and repot occasionally to freshen the soil and keep the plant from becoming rootbound. Or try growing it as a ground cover, setting out plants at 3-foot intervals in a diamond pattern and letting them fill in the gaps.

Once plants are well established in the garden, they need only annual winter shearing (not conventional pruning) to keep their shape. Fertilize plants about every six months to keep blooms coming.

Because 'Flower Carpet' is being sold as a landscape shrub, it is not currently available through conventional rose suppliers. That means you won't be able to buy it through most mail-order rose sources, and it won't be sold bare-root in winter. Look for it in nurseries and garden centers now. Expect to pay $14 to $18 for a plant in an 8-inch pot. If your nursery doesn't carry 'Flower Carpet', ask it to order from a wholesale supplier such as Monrovia or El Modeno.

'Flower Carpet' is the first in a series of roses expected to have similar growth habits and relative disease resistance. A white-flowered variety is due out in 18 months, to be followed by other colors. ∎

By Jim McCausland

ANTHONY TESSELAAR

Mints for every taste

Peppermint and spearmint, of course. But also pineapple, basil, even chocolate

GINGER

CHOCOLATE

APPLE

8ASIL

PINEAPPLE

IT CAN TAKE SERIOUS stretching of the taste buds to identify a culinary mint in a blind tasting. When you sample basil mint, ginger mint, or pineapple mint, for instance, you might think, "Hmm, the flavor seems familiar, but I just can't put my finger on it." Then someone tells you the name and you say, "That's it!"

Twenty-two or so flavored mints are now available through mail-order catalogs. Regardless of whether their flavors truly reflect their given names, many of these mints go way beyond traditional spearmint (*Mentha spicata*) and peppermint (*M. piperita*). Their refreshing qualities add punch to aïoli, fish, fruit salads, jellies, lamb, lemonade, poultry, and tea. Order this month for late summer and fall use.

Keep in mind when selecting mints that confusion reigns in their naming. Some may actually be known by several names. Blue balsam mint and candy mint, for instance, are thought to be variants of *M. piperita* 'Mitcham', also called black peppermint. But Arthur O. Tucker, a professor of agriculture and natural resources at Delaware State University and an expert on herbs, doesn't believe that they warrant separate names.

TASTING WINNERS

Last summer we grew and tasted 17 varieties in *Sunset*'s test gardens in Menlo Park, California. These are some we especially enjoyed.

Apple (*M. suaveolens*): fuzzy grayish leaves with delicate apple fragrance. Grows 2½ feet.

Basil (*M. gracilis*): heart-shaped, highly aromatic leaves that emit a spicy fragrance. Grows 2 feet.

Black peppermint (*M. piperita,* sold as peppermint from black 'Mitcham' stock): dark green leaves with dark red stems. More intense than standard peppermint. Grows 1 to 2 feet.

Chocolate (*M. piperita*): shiny, dark green leaves with a tingling aftertaste—and, yes, a hint of chocolate. Grows 1½ to 2 feet.

Curly (*M. spicata* 'Crispa'): wavy, spearmint-flavored foliage with stiff stems. Makes good drink swizzle sticks. Grows 2 feet.

Ginger (*M. arvensis*): soft, pointed, grayish leaves with a fruity flavor. Grows 2 feet.

Lemon bergamot (*M. aquatica,* sold as *M. piperita*; not pictured): soft, fuzzy foliage with lemony, floral flavor. Grows 2 feet.

Pineapple (*M. suaveolens*): fuzzy, variegated green-and-white leaves with fruity, pineapple-like flavor. Grows 2 feet.

PLANT IN CONFINED AREAS

Mints spread rapidly by underground stems, so plant them where they can be controlled—in tall, wide pots (so runners don't touch the ground and root) or in a bed confined by paving. "Mints are like stray cats," says Tucker. "You take them in, give them

NORMAN A. PLATE

TO KEEP MINTS *under control, grow in pots. Above are curly (top right), peppermint (front), and spearmint.*

some food, and they're yours forever."

Mint flavors develop best if plants are given full sun, plenty of water, and a fertilizer high in nitrogen. For a large batch at maximum flavor, cut when plants are just at full bloom. Otherwise, harvest mint as you need it, and cut off flowers when they form. Mints look best if cut back completely twice a year—in summer and fall.

WHERE TO BUY MINTS

Many nurseries carry a small selection of flavored mints, but for the less common ones, order by mail.

Dabney Herbs, Box 22061, Louisville, KY 40252; (502) 893-5198 (catalog $2). Sells 17 culinary mints.

Mountain Valley Growers, 38325 Pepperweed Rd., Squaw Valley, CA 93675; (209) 338-2775 (catalog free). Sells 22 culinary mints.

Nichols Garden Nursery, 1190 N. Pacific Highway, Albany, OR 97321; (503) 928-9280 (catalog free). Sells 11 culinary mints. ■

By Lauren Bonar Swezey

CURLY   **BLACK PEPPERMINT**   **SPEARMINT**

CORN IS RIPE FOR PICKING
and zinnias are ready for cutting in this Yelm, Washington, garden. To learn how the owner copes with her bountiful harvest, see page 244.

DOUG WILSON

SEPTEMBER

GARDEN
Guide

River of grass weaves through their meadow

After enduring years of drought and dead lawns, landscape designers Brigitte Micmacker and John Denning decided to make their California garden more ecologically appropriate. They wanted to create a native meadow, but also needed a cool carpet for their teenage daughter, Shoshana, and friends to sit on. Their answer? A path of lawn through a meadow of native grasses and flowering perennials with big rocks as accents.

"We didn't consciously create a river of grass," says Micmacker, "but it turned out to look just like one, especially when the late afternoon sun hits it, because of the special quality of light at that time."

The river of grass is a turf-type tall fescue. The meadow is planted primarily with clumps of *Festuca* 'Pt. Molate', a native California grass. *Achillea millefolium*, clover, and *Iris douglasiana* are planted among them. Perennials such as purple catmint and yellow yarrow add color beyond the meadow.

Since the lawn is so small, Micmacker and Denning can mow it with a push mower. "And we don't have to smell exhaust," says Micmacker. They never fertilize the meadow or lawn because the clover, which was planted into the lawn, is a nitrogen-fixer and provides some nutrients. They use only organic fertilizers on the perennials.

PETER O. WHITELEY

Long narrow lawn is turf-type tall fescue. Grassy clumps on either side are *Festuca* 'Pt. Molate'. Purple

flowers (lower right) are catmint.

WORTH A TRY

Cool blues for a hot-summer garden

What do you do for blue flowers when agapanthus have finished their moment of glory? That question has many gardeners gazing longingly at catalog photos of bluebeard (*Caryopteris clandonensis*), a favorite perennial-like dwarf shrub for the West's cool-summer areas but seldom recommended where hot summers are the rule. Still, some gardeners have decided to give bluebeard a shot, and their gamble has paid off.

In Rolling Hills on the Palos Verdes Peninsula, in Pasadena, and in Redlands (*Sunset Western Garden Book* climate zones 23, 21, and 18, respectively), we've seen bluebeards thriving in garden beds on moderate to no summer water. While purists may point out that bluebeard's flowers are a shade or two more violet than agapanthus, nobody is complaining about its long bloom period, which can span the entire warm season. Plants begin flowering along with daylilies and bearded irises in May and can linger until November, when they make a show with wine red asters.

A mounding deciduous plant to 2 feet tall, bluebeard bears flower clusters above silvery or gray-green

Clusters of sky blue flowers cover bluebeard from spring through summer in this Redlands garden.

foliage. In a moderately watered border, bluebeard is an especially fine companion for gray-leafed, yellow-flowered perennials such as basket-of-gold (*Aurinia saxatilis*), yellow yarrow (*Achillea* 'Moonshine'), or lavender cotton (*Santolina chamaecyparissus*). It also makes a beautiful companion to shrub roses in mixed borders.

Bluebeard is becoming more available in nurseries throughout the West. Named varieties you are likely to find include 'Dark Knight' (silvery leaves and darker flowers), 'Kew Blue' (sil-

very leaves and lavender-blue flowers), and 'Longwood Blue' (silvery leaves and sky blue flowers). A handsome gold-leafed variety called 'Worcester Gold' is being grown in Riverside in full sun without suffering scorched leaves.

In Southern California, plants tend to be short-lived (although bluebeard has thrived for nearly five years in the Redlands garden pictured above). Set out plants in fall in well-drained soil; in winter when they're dormant, cut them back to 6 to 8 inches tall. To prolong bloom, cut off spent flowers.

NEW PLANT REPORT

From Hawaii, five new plumerias

Hawaii's favorite lei flower now comes in five new varieties. The new plumerias, introduced from Hawaii just last month by Marilynn's Garden, a wholesale-only nursery in Orange County, California, bear large (3 to 4 inch diam-

eter), sweetly fragrant flowers. Collectively sold as the premium Blue Ribbon Line, these varieties come in unusual colors: 'Angus Gold' bears butterscotch flowers streaked with raspberry; 'Kimo', apricot-gold flowers; 'Mary Moragne', delicate pink flowers; 'Puu Kahea', vibrant yellow flowers with pink and white stripes; and 'Sally Moragne', large hot pink flowers tinged with tanger-

ine. Availability is limited, so expect to pay more for these varieties; gallon-size plants start at $30.

Plumerias grow best in sunny courtyards near the coast. Where frost is likely in winter, grow them in pots to move to a protected spot. Though plumerias grow to the size of small trees (15 to 20 feet tall), they have small root systems and are content to remain in the same pots for years. In fact, because good drainage is their primary requirement, most people find them easiest to grow this way.

If you can't find plants at your nursery, ask to have them ordered from Marilynn's Garden.

COOK'S CHOICE

Instant salad in a pot

Here's a quick weekend project that keeps on yielding greens for your salad bowl for months. All you need is a large container (18 inches wide or larger), a 2-cubic-foot bag of potting soil, and seedlings from the nursery.

The pot shown below took about 10 minutes to plant (shopping for the plants takes the most time). Many nurseries now carry gourmet varieties of lettuces and greens; we chose calendula (an edible flower), curly and Italian parsley, endive, 'Lollo Rosso' lettuce, mizuna, and 'Red Giant' mustard.

If you can't find the plants you want at nurseries, you can start them from seed or order seedlings through the mail.

'Red Giant' mustard (top center) and calendula add color to salad pot.

Grape hyacinth and candytuft—a cool combination

Some plants make perfect partners: their flower colors look smashing together, they bloom at the same time, and their growth habits complement each other. That's the case with grape hyacinth (*Muscari armeniacum*) and candytuft (*Iberis sempervirens*), shown at right in an Atherton, California, garden. Both plants bloom in early spring. Grape hyacinth's grassy leaves and deep blue flowers are just tall enough to rise above candytuft's bright white flowers. In low borders or clustered in a rock garden, these two plants look as cool as a spring breeze. Add some white or light blue pansies and the effect is stunning.

All these plants should be available in nurseries by midmonth. Plant them in full sun or partial shade. Set the grape hyacinth bulbs about 2 inches deep and 2 to 3 inches apart. The more you plant, the better the show. Plant the candytuft and pansies from sixpacks. Set them among the bulbs (but not right on top), at least 6 inches apart.

After bloom is through,

Grape hyacinth's grassy leaves and deep blue flowers poke through blooming evergreen candytuft in early spring.

cut off spent flowers. Use hedge shears for large plantings.

In mild climates, the candytuft stays good-looking all year; it forms mounds of deep green foliage, about 8 inches to a foot tall. It's also amazingly tough.

Grape hyacinth is among the easiest bulbs to naturalize, and will quickly multiply to give you an abundance of slightly fragrant flowers. As its leaves die back after bloom, you can tuck them beneath the candytuft's foliage.

KNOW YOUR ENEMY

Eugenias make a comeback

Eugenia, or brush cherry (*Syzygium paniculatum*), is the shrub that made the Disneyland topiaries famous. It's widely planted in *Sunset Western Garden Book* zones 16 and 17 and often in zone 15. Unfortunately, it is also the only host of a pest called eugenia psyllid (*Trioza eugeniae*), which arrived in the United States from Australia (eugenia's native home) about seven years ago and began damaging plants so badly

that many nurseries stopped selling eugenia.

The psyllid, which resembles an aphid, feeds on the undersides of new leaves, causing pitting and distortion. It also excretes honeydew, which nourishes the growth of sooty mold, a dusty black coating on the leaves. Until recently, the only method of controlling the pest was to spray insecticides every few weeks, especially in winter and spring. Yet this wasn't always adequate. The psyllids bred faster than the chemicals could kill them. Also, repeated sprays damaged foliage and caused outbreaks

of other insect pests.

Fortunately, Don Dahlsten of University of California Center for Biological Control in Berkeley discovered a parasitic wasp in Australia that controls the psyllid. The wasp has been released in Northern and Southern California, and appears to be doing its job.

Nurseries such as Yamagami's in Cupertino are now carrying eugenia again, and this month is a good time to plant it. If you already have eugenia in your garden, don't spray it with insecticides—the chemicals will also kill the beneficial wasps.

A bold palette of autumn hues

Unlikely blends of colorful flowers and foliage can wake up a landscape. Pink and orange, for example, are colors that would seem to clash. But Seattle landscape designer R. David Adams, who is known for his bold plant combinations, found a way to bring the hues together successfully. When Adams planted his bed of pink impatiens, he knew that before their bloom season was over the *Enkianthus campanulatus* behind it would turn a rich orange, creating a potential color clash. He tied their seemingly disparate colors and textures together with the weeping, white-tipped foliage of Canada hemlock (*Tsuga canadensis* 'Albospica').

When the first hard frost hits, the impatiens will die back and the enkianthus will drop its leaves to display a handsome bouquet of naked branches. The hemlock will continue to light up a dark corner of the garden through the winter.

Impatiens and white-tipped Canada hemlock are backed by fiery orange enkianthus.

Plants that take the Central Valley's heat

Droughts come and go, and you can be sure another one will come. So water conservation, especially in areas with hot, dry summers like California's Central Valley and surrounding foothills, should always be a prime consideration when planning your garden.

Water-thrifty plants not only save water, but in many areas they are the only plants that look like they belong. The McConnaugheys of Exeter, 10 miles southeast of Visalia, know this well. When they built a new house on a dry, rocky hilltop with little topsoil, they knew it would be a challenge to grow anything. But they did their homework, researching California and Southwest natives and other plants that thrive with little water. Their garden, which won a xeriscape award, is pictured at right.

The McConnaugheys brought in large rocks to complement the existing terrain. They built small ponds for koi and a waterfall to add the soothing sounds of

Fountain grass (*Pennisetum orientale*) complements early California–style courtyard.

moving water. Grasses, including various types of fountain grass (*Pennisetum*) and Moor grass (*Molinia caerulea*), link the house to the grassy hilltop. Flowering perennials such as Santa Barbara daisy (*Erigeron karvinskianus*) and sea lavender (*Limonium latifolium*) punctuate the ground cover planting of dwarf coyote brush (*Baccharis pilularis* 'Twin Peaks'). Trees planted include 'Burgundy' desert willow (*Chilopsis linearis*), Mescal bean (*Sophora secundiflora*), and Texas mesquite (*Prosopis glandulosa*).

'Fuji' for late crops of apples in the Northwest

If you enjoy the sweet flavor and crisp texture of 'Fuji' apples, consider growing your own. There are really two types of 'Fuji'—one has red skin, the other green or yellow. The flesh of both types, however, is identical in flavor and texture.

'Fuji' is a late-ripening apple; it doesn't produce the bumper crop in cool, moist climates that it does in hotter, drier climates. It's at its best in the inland Northwest's apple-growing regions east of the Cascades. But it also does well in Seattle, Portland, and the Willamette Valley. It's least successful in the chilly damp climates found along the coast.

Standard trees grow to 35 feet. Trees grafted onto a dwarfing rootstock will stay at 10 to 12 feet and take well to espalier.

'Fuji' is not a reliable self-pollinator, so you need to plant it near a good pollinator such as any of these: 'Gala', 'Granny Smith', 'Jonagold', 'McIntosh', or 'Yellow Delicious'.

A tree planted now will yield its first crop in a year. In hot dry climates, the harvest starts in late September. In milder climates, the season extends into November. 'Fuji' apples have a long storage life.

Plants in containers can be set out immediately. Two good Northwest sources for 'Fuji' trees are Bear Creek Nursery, Box 411, Northport, WA 99157; and Northwoods Retail Nursery, 27635 S. Oglesby Rd., Canby, OR 97013; (503) 266-5432.

Stop hoses from jaywalking

Garden hoses tend to have one bad habit: they cut corners. You tug them toward you, and like frightened snakes they slither sideways, swiping at flower beds or vegetable rows in their path.

Sunset's test gardener, Bud Stuckey, solved the case of the errant hose by installing the device pictured at right, a rotating plastic collar mounted on a stationary shaft, at the corners of his planting beds. The collar keeps the hose gliding smoothly. It has a broad "mushroom" cap to keep the hose from slipping over the top. The sharp end of the sturdy shaft resembles an oversize hypodermic needle; you just push it into the ground.

Garden supply centers

NORMAN A. PLATE

Toadstool-shaped caddy keeps a hose gliding smoothly.

and nurseries sell many kinds of hose guards. The one Bud uses, called the Hose Caddy, sells for $5 to $6. You can order it from Fast Forward Concepts, Box 711, Trabuco Canyon, CA 92678; it costs $6.95 including shipping.

Look, listen for zebra and porcupine grass

Tall and stately zebra grass (*Miscanthus sinensis* 'Zebrinus') is a spectacle in September and October. The clumps produce grassy stalks that stretch as tall as 7 feet. The rich green leaves with yellow stripes arch up and droop down. The seedheads, which appear about mid-September, look like short, stiff tassels of gold-braided rope atop long stems; they open up into fluffy plumes.

The grass holds its color well in cold weather, but it dies and dries to a rich straw color after a prolonged cold snap. It stands up well through the winter, even in snow, and is as handsome in the winter garden as it is in the summer garden. It's also a musical plant—throughout the year, you can hear this grass rustling in the slightest breeze.

Porcupine grass (*M. sinensis strictus*), an almost identical plant, is often sold as zebra grass. The differences are slight but important. Porcupine grass is a bit shorter-growing (rarely reaching above 5 feet), and its leaves don't arch but stay stiff and jut up at an angle, which is why this grass makes less noise in the wind than its cousin.

Both grasses grow in all Western climate zones. You can plant them from nursery cans this month. Water plants well until rains start. By next spring they should be well established and quite drought tolerant. The clumps expand gradually but do not run. If you let dried foliage stand through winter, cut it to the ground in February or March, before new growth emerges.

Reaping the Western vegetable harvest

It's like winning the lottery: for every seed, seedling, or young potato you put in the ground, you reap many pounds of beans, corn, squash, tomatoes, potatoes, and other crops. But harvesting can be a challenge if your crops all ripen at once.

We asked Nita Jensen of Yelm, Washington, how she copes with the harvest from her 5,000-square-foot country garden not far from the slopes of Mount Rainier (pictured on page 238). Much of her harvest is eaten fresh and shared with relatives. For the rest, she employs various strategies for processing different crops.

Jensen grows snap beans, picking them as soon as the pods are filled out but before the beans inside start to harden. The beans are blanched and frozen, then cooked like fresh green beans as needed.

Ripe tomatoes are used fresh or given away (Jensen and her husband, Dillard, don't like the acid flavor of frozen tomatoes). At season's end, green tomatoes are canned as chowchow relish.

Jensen picks corn (supersweet 'Kandy Korn') when the kernels are milky inside. To preserve the harvest, she strips kernels from the cob with a corn cutter and processes them as creamed corn to stock in the freezer.

Winter squash ('Buttercup' and 'Sweet Meat') are picked after their skins harden and the leaves start to die. The squash are stored with potatoes in the root cellar, a cold but frost-free concrete basement. To prevent rot, Jensen washes the squash in a solution of 1 cup bleach mixed with 3 gallons water, then dries and stores them on racks. Stored this way, the squash can last all the way through May. If a squash shows any sign of softening around the stem (a precursor to rot), it's immediately cut up, cooked, and frozen.

Beets are pickled. Kale is picked after frost, which sweetens it. Carrots are harvested all through winter.

'Curlew' daffodil has intense scent

When *Sunset*'s head gardener, Rick La Frentz, tested a number of new daffodils last year, a clear favorite emerged—'Curlew'. It's a winner on two counts: beautiful two-tone flowers, each with creamy white petals behind a pale yellow cup, and intensely sweet fragrance.

You can buy bulbs of 'Curlew' this month for planting immediately. Pot them up for flowers on foot-tall stems next spring. Set the pots out along an entry walk or on a patio table during peak bloom, or bring them indoors for a few hours to perfume a room.

If you live in the cold-winter West (zones 1, 2, 3, and 10), keep potted bulbs in a chilly, relatively frost-free place like a garage or unheated but enclosed porch. In Arizona's intermediate and low deserts (zones 12 and 13), keep potted bulbs in the coolest place you have, then set them out when new foliage emerges.

You can buy 'Curlew' from nurseries and garden centers, or order it from the Daffodil Mart, 7463 Heath Trail, Gloucester, VA 23061; (800) 255-2852.

By Sharon Cohoon, Kevin Connelly, Steven R. Lorton, Jim McCausland, Lauren Bonar Swezey, Lance Walheim.

PLANTING

❑ **PERMANENT PLANTS.** Perennials, shrubs, and trees can go in the ground this month. Shop nurseries for plants displaying handsome autumn berries; set them out immediately.

❑ **SPRING-BLOOMING BULBS.** After Labor Day, nurseries and garden stores will have bulbs for sale. Shop early to get the best selection. Plant bulbs soon after you buy them so they don't wither and lose vigor.

MAINTENANCE

❑ **CARE FOR LAWNS.** After mowing the lawn, rough up bare spots, generously scatter grass seed over the area, and cover it with a thin layer of soil, mulch, or compost. Water the area well, and keep it moist until rains begin. Fertilize established lawns with about 1 pound of actual nitrogen per 1,000 square feet of turf.

❑ **DIVIDE IRISES.** Zones 4–7 (see map): dig and divide species and hybrids of Pacific Coast irises this month. Cut rhizomes apart with a sharp knife, and replant them immediately. They'll bloom next spring.

❑ **GROOM ROSES.** Cut flowers to take

PACIFIC NORTHWEST
CHECKLIST
SEPTEMBER

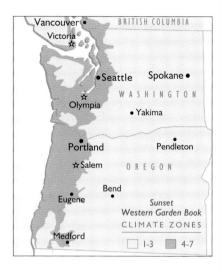

Vancouver
BRITISH COLUMBIA
Victoria ☆
● Seattle   Spokane ●
WASHINGTON
☆
Olympia
● Yakima
● Portland
Pendleton ●
☆ Salem
OREGON
Bend ●
● Eugene
*Sunset
Western Garden Book*
CLIMATE ZONES
Medford ●
❑ 1-3   ▨ 4-7

indoors, shaping the plants as you cut. Later in the month, allow a few of the flowers to form hips; this encourages the plant to head into dormancy. Hips are beautiful and the smaller ones will attract birds.

❑ **FUSS WITH FUCHSIAS.** Snip back errant shoots and remove faded blossoms. Water and continue to feed plants on a regular schedule.

❑ **MAKE COMPOST.** Start a new pile with prunings, clippings, spent annuals, and vegetable refuse you take out of the garden this month. Turn the existing pile. The compost you create may be ready to spread on beds in late winter.

❑ **WATER.** Plants in pots and under eaves need special attention. In a dry Setemper, if local water-use ordinances allow, irrigate deeply to reduce stress on plants during fall and winter.

❑ **CLEAN GREENHOUSES.** Before moving plants into the greenhouse for the winter, give it a complete cleaning. Move everything out, rake and sweep, and hose it down well. Take the old soil out of seedbeds and flats. Replace broken glass and cracked weather-stripping. Check the vents and heating and watering systems.

PEST CONTROL

❑ **BAIT FOR SLUGS.** Continue to spread bait around their favorite hiding places. Take care to keep bait away from children and pets.

Eupatorium maculatum will be in full bloom this month in my Skagit Valley garden. Commonly called Joe-Pye weed and sometimes sold as E. purpureum, it's a statuesque plant that has wine-red stems and dark green leaves with a burgundy blush. The flowerhead is a large, wide dome made up of thousands of tiny coral-rose blossoms. Unfortunately, this plant has caused a bit of a rift between me and my neighbor and fellow gardener, Ingrid Meyer.

Several years ago, I gave Ingrid a division of my plant. Last summer I paid a visit to her garden—and there was the offspring of *my* Joe-Pye growing more than 15 feet tall and sporting the biggest blooms I'd ever seen. Ingrid responded to my ruffled sense of plant parenthood by saying, "Oh, I don't know what happened—it's just happy here."

"Horse manure!" I thought. Then the light bulb went on: horse manure. The Meyers' horse, Skittles, produces lots of the stuff, and Ingrid gathers buckets of it to use everywhere. So last winter, I put some well-rotted horse manure around the crown of my Joe-Pye. It hasn't hit 15 feet yet, but it's getting taller and the flowers are bigger and brighter. Here we come, Ingrid.

•

Dahlias are at their blooming peak now. My friend Mii Tai, a blue-ribbon dahlia grower in Spokane, says September is the perfect month to shop for them. Keep an eye out at nurseries for varieties

PACIFIC NORTHWEST
Garden Notebook
BY STEVEN R. LORTON

you want to add to your garden. But don't look at the blooms alone; notice that the foliage of dahlias can make an important contribution to a mixed border.

•

Because I've been trying to raise a school of koi in my garden pond, I'm looking forward to the Washington Koi and Water Garden Society Koi Show, September 9 and 10 at Country Village Shopping Center, 23730 Bothell-Everett Highway in Bothell. The show is open 10 to 4 Saturday and Sunday; admission is free. You'll see 30 ponds filled with koi, and fish will be for sale.

THAT'S A GOOD QUESTION

Q: The leaves of my vine maple have been showing red since July. What's going on?

A: Vine maple (*Acer circinatum*) is one of the Northwest's most garden-worthy natives. Sometimes as early as July, vine maple leaves can develop a strong reddish cast—a natural response to summer heat and drought. True autumn color doesn't start to appear until September, when the leaves turn orange, scarlet, and brilliant yellow.

If you want to add a vine maple to your landscape and be certain you get the autumn color you prefer, go shopping this month. Nurseries sell plants in 5- and 15-gallon cans as well as balled-and-burlapped stock. Set plants in the ground immediately, and water them well.

CHECKLIST
SEPTEMBER

PLANTING

☐ **PLANT ANNUALS.** To get cool-season annuals off to a good start so they'll bloom this winter and early spring, plant cool-season annuals after mid-month in cooler coastal areas, at the end of the month in warm inland areas. If the weather is hot, shade new seedlings temporarily. Keep the soil moist. Set out calendula, forget-me-nots, Iceland and Shirley poppies, larkspur, ornamental cabbage and kale, pansies, primrose, snapdragon, stock, sweet peas, toadflax, and violas. In coastal areas, plant cineraria, nemesia, and schizanthus.

☐ **PLANT PERENNIALS.** Coast and inland: When the weather cools a bit, plant campanula, candytuft, catmint, coreopsis, delphinium, dianthus, diascia, foxglove, gaillardia, geum, Japanese anemone, penstemon, phlox, pincushion flower, salvia, scaevola, and yarrow. Nurseries should have a good selection.

☐ **SET OUT PERMANENT PLANTS.** Coast and inland: September marks the beginning of the fall-planting season. Nurseries should be well stocked with a good variety of trees, shrubs, vines, and ground covers (wait until spring to plant frost-tender plants such as bougainvillea and citrus).

☐ **SHOP FOR BULBS.** To get the best selection of healthy bulbs, shop soon. Choose firm ones without soft or moldy spots. Plant anemones, crocuses, daffodils, Dutch iris, freesias, homeria,

Eureka
Redding
CALIFORNIA
NEVADA
Mendocino
Sacramento
Santa Rosa
San Francisco
San Jose
Fresno
Monterey

Sunset Western Garden Book
CLIMATE ZONES

☐ Mountain (1-2)
☐ Valley (7-9)
☐ Inland (14)
☐ Coastal (15-17)

hyacinth, ixia, leucojum, lycoris, oxalis, ranunculus, scilla, sparaxis, tritonia, tulips, and watsonia. (In mountain areas: some of these bulbs, such as freesias, homeria, and watsonia, are not hardy; choose from what's available at nurseries.) In mild climates, chill tulips and hyacinths as directed on page 268.

MAINTENANCE

☐ **CARE FOR CITRUS.** Coast and inland: To prevent citrus fruit from drying out as they mature, give trees regular deep soakings during warm fall weather. To

avoid stimulating new growth that can be susceptible to winter damage, do not prune trees now.

☐ **CARE FOR LAWNS.** Coast and inland: Late September is a good time to plant new lawns or renovate old ones. To renovate, dethatch, aerate, fertilize with a complete lawn fertilizer, and water well. In mountain areas, plant new lawns early in September (at highest elevations, wait until October to plant seed; it will germinate in spring when snow melts).

☐ **HARVEST.** Check crops daily, so you can be sure to harvest fruits and vegetables at their optimum ripeness. Mountain: If frost is forecast, pick or protect eggplant, peaches, peppers, plums, tomatoes, and other tender produce; light frost won't damage most apples and pears.

☐ **STORE SUMMER BULBS.** Mountain: When foliage dies down, lift begonias, cannas, dahlias, and gladiolus. Let them dry for a few days, then store at 35° to 50° in a place where they'll get good air circulation. Store cannas and dahlias in sand, peat moss, or vermiculite. Leave begonia tubers in their containers (store at same temperatures).

☐ **WATER.** Coast and inland: September is often one of our hottest months. Keep an eye on plants, watching for signs of moisture stress, such as wilting during the early morning or evening. Mountain: Winds can dry out plants even when weather is cool.

When fall arrives, bulbs are on my mind. I'm always dazzled by catalogs with color photographs of tall elegant tulips such as 'Apricot Beauty' and 'Magier' (white edged with purple), two recent favorites of mine. I still like to plant a few of these in my garden, but lately I've turned my attention to species tulips for the same reason I've gotten into perennials: they keep coming back.

Between working and caring for my 2-year-old, I don't have time to devote several days every fall to planting a couple of hundred bulbs like I used to. So now I plant mostly the more diminutive (6 to 8 inches tall) but still showy *Tulipa batalinii* ('Apricot Jewel', 'Bright Gem', 'Bronze Charm', 'Yellow Jewel'), *T. kaufmanniana* varieties and hybrids, *T. saxatilis*, and *T. sylvestris*. Varieties and hybrids of *T. greigii* also come back reliably every year, and some of them grow 14 to 16 inches tall. Every year I just add a few dozen to what I already have, and the show keeps getting better.

•

I trained as a horticulturist in the Pacific Northwest and became acquainted with the Northwest plant world first. So even though I

NORTHERN CALIFORNIA Garden Notebook

BY LAUREN BONAR SWEZEY

was born and raised in the Bay Area, I'm often perplexed by the native flora when I'm out hiking in our local hills. A handy new field guide I just discovered should help; it's called *Plants of the San Francisco Bay Region: Mendocino to Monterey*, by Eugene N. Kozloff and Linda H. Beidleman (Sagen Press, Box 51042, Pacific Grove, CA 93950, 1994; $35 including tax and postage). Although the plant key is technical, the 227 line drawings and 457 color photographs make visual identification easy.

THAT'S A GOOD QUESTION

Q: What annuals can I plant now that will give me color starting in late fall or early winter?

A: You can choose from a large selection of annuals to plant in fall, but only some of them will give you early winter color. For earliest bloom, you need to get the plants in the ground and established while the weather is mild and the soil is still warm. If planted too late, the annuals just sit and pout until spring. Good choices for early color are calendula, *Chrysanthemum multicaule*, *C. paludosum*, fairy primrose (*Primula malacoides*), pansies, snapdragon, stock, and sweet alyssum.

PLANTING

PLANT ANNUALS. Take advantage of summer's last warm days to get winter flowers going. After midmonth, sow seeds of California poppy, clarkia, and *Dimorphotheca*. Or buy nursery transplants. Set out calendula, Iceland poppy, larkspur, pansy, primrose, snapdragon, stock, and viola. If weather is hot, shade new seedlings temporarily.

PLANT PERENNIALS. After summer heat subsides, plant campanula, candytuft, coreopsis, delphinium, dianthus, foxglove, gaillardia, geum, Mexican evening primrose, penstemon, phlox, salvia, and yarrow. Nurseries will have sixpacks, 4-inch pots, and gallon cans.

PLANT VEGETABLES. There's still time to plant most cool-season vegetables. Set out transplants of broccoli, cabbage, cauliflower, chard, kohlrabi, and lettuce. Sow seeds of beets, carrots, lettuce, onions, peas, radishes, spinach, and turnips.

PREPARE TO PLANT. If you're planning to relandscape or add to an existing landscape, get ready now. Clean planting areas and till soil, adding amendments and complete fertilizer if necessary. You can also install the irrigation system. Before planting, water to sprout weed seeds, then hoe or spray with herbicide to eliminate weeds.

SHOP FOR BULBS. Buy early to get top-quality bulbs. Plant anemone, crocus, daffodils, Dutch iris, freesia, homeria, ixia, leucojum, lycoris, oxalis,

CENTRAL VALLEY
CHECKLIST
SEPTEMBER

Sunset
Western Garden Book
CLIMATE ZONES
- Foothills (7)
- Valley (8-9,14)

ranunculus, scilla, sparaxis, tritonia, and watsonia. Buy hyacinths and tulips now and chill them as directed on page 268.

MAINTENANCE

CARE FOR LAWNS. After a dry summer, renovate cool-season lawns such as bluegrass, fescue, and rye to remove thatch, improve water penetration, and invigorate the turf. Dethatch, aerate, and apply a complete fertilizer. If you don't use the lawn, think about replacing all or part of it with plants that require little water.

COMPOST. As summer flowers and vegetables give way to fall plantings, add debris to a new pile for building the soil next spring. Wherever you'll be planting this fall, work the compost you made this summer into the soil.

CONTROL PESTS. Mites are a likely problem this month. Control them by keeping plants clean and free of dust (a strong spray from a hose works well). Or spray with a summer oil or sulfur (don't mix the two; read labels carefully). You can also try releasing predatory mites, available from suppliers of beneficial insects.

DIVIDE PERENNIALS. Now through October is a good time to divide many perennials that are overgrown or not flowering well. Dividing is also a good way to increase plants.

Use a spading fork to lift and loosen the clumps. With a sharp knife, cut sections through soil and roots of plants such as agapanthus, coreopsis, daylilies, Mexican evening primrose, ornamental grasses, and penstemon.

FERTILIZE. Flowering annuals, perennials, and fall-planted vegetables should be fertilized for a strong start. Incorporate a complete fertilizer at planting time, and follow up in three to four weeks.

WATER. September can be one of the year's hottest months. Watch plants for signs of water stress, especially rootbound container plants, which dry out quickly.

In September, I visit lots of gardens to see how certain plants have stood up to the Central Valley's summer. And often, the ones that still look fresh at summer's end are those partly shaded by big trees. As I drive through some of my favorite neighborhoods, such as Fig Garden in Fresno and Land Park in Sacramento, I can't help but think that our parents and grandparents appreciated shade trees a great deal more than we do. It's the large, enduring trees that give these neighborhoods character and distinction, and make them cooler and more inviting. I just don't see the same kind of planting going on in new subdivisions.

As we head into planting season in the Central Valley, think about setting out a large shade tree if you have room. According to scientists at Lawrence Berkeley Laboratory, planting trees and using light-colored, more reflective building materials throughout a Central Valley city like Sacramento could cut summer cooling costs by 30 to 50 percent. Some of my favorite shade trees include our native valley oak, Chinese pistache, Chinese tallow tree, hybrid sycamores, sour gum, and zelkova. Your city or county parks department can usually provide information about planting trees on city streets. Or contact a tree planting group like the Sacramento Tree Foundation (916/924-8733) or Tree Fresno (209/226-8733).

CENTRAL VALLEY
Garden Notebook
BY LANCE WALHEIM

The graceful, feathery blooms of my ornamental grasses really start to shine this month. One of my favorites is Eulalia grass (*Miscanthus sinensis*). Its large, stringy plumes sway nicely in the breeze and last well into winter. My yellow-striped 'Zebrinus' gets big—up to 8 feet tall—but what a show! If you can't find it locally, send for a catalog ($3) from Kurt Bluemel, 2740 Greene Lane, Baldwin, MD 21013.

If you live or garden around California native oaks, note that California Oak Foundation has moved from Sacramento to Oakland (1212 Broadway, Suite 810, Oakland, CA 94612; 510/763-0282). This nonprofit organization is a valuable source of information on preserving oaks—some of the Central Valley's most treasured trees.

THAT'S A GOOD QUESTION

Q: Why is it always recommended to plant trees and shrubs 1 or 2 inches higher than the surrounding soil?

A: After planting, most trees settle a little. If the plant's crown (top of the rootball) sinks lower than the surrounding soil, water will settle up against the trunk and the soil may stay overly wet, promoting disease. This can be a serious threat to plant health, especially in heavy soils. Even if the plant is a little high after settling, it's all right. Water will drain away from the trunk and keep it dry.

PLANTING

❑ **BUY AND PLANT BULBS.** Spring-flowering bulbs begin arriving in nurseries this month. Shop early while stock is fresh and selection is ample. Choices include babiana, daffodils, freesia, ixia, ornamental oxalis (also called shamrock), ornithogalum, sparaxis, spring star flower (*Ipheion uniflorum*), and watsonia. In the high desert (zone 11), plant immediately. In all other zones, wait until the soil cools in late October or early November before planting for most bulbs.

❑ **CHILL BULBS.** For best performance in all areas except the high desert, chill tulips, crocus, and hyacinth for six to eight weeks before planting (see page 268). Plant after Thanksgiving.

❑ **PLANT FOR WINTER-SPRING COLOR.** Set out cool-season annual seedlings starting mid-September near the coast and in the low desert (zones 22–24 and 13, respectively). Choices include calendula, Iceland poppy, snapdragons, pansy, nemesia, and stock. Inland (zones 18–21), wait until October to plant.

❑ **PLANT (OR SOW) COOL-SEASON VEGETABLES.** Coast and inland: after midmonth, set out seedlings of broccoli, brussels sprouts, cabbage, cauliflower, celery, chives, kale, and parsley. Sow seeds for beets, chard, chives, collards, kale, kohlrabi, parsnips, peas, radishes, spinach, and turnips. Plant garlic, onions, and shallots. High desert: plant lettuce, radish, and spinach.

SOUTHERN CALIFORNIA
CHECKLIST
SEPTEMBER

Sunset
Western Garden Book
CLIMATE ZONES

1-3 7-9 11 13 14-24

❑ **PLANT SWEET PEAS.** For sweet peas by December, plant seeds now. Look for varieties designated "early-flowering." To speed germination, soak seeds overnight before planting. Provide a wall or trellis or several 6-foot poles for vines to climb.

MAINTENANCE

❑ **PROTECT AGAINST BRUSHFIRES.** Dead vegetation adds fuel to flames. In fire-prone areas before onset of Santa Ana winds, cut and remove all dead leaves and limbs from trees and shrubs, especially those that grow near the house. Clear leaves from gutters, and remove woody vegetation growing against structures.

❑ **ENCOURAGE ROSE BLOOM.** For a second flush of bloom in fall, cut spent flowers back to just above a five-leaflet leaf. Fertilize, mulch, and water well.

❑ **FEED PERMANENT PLANTS.** Feed established trees, shrubs, ground covers, and warm-season grasses such as Bermuda now. Repeat in a month. Coastal gardeners (zones 22–24) can also fertilize tropical plants with a fast-acting product one last time if needed. Don't feed California natives or drought-tolerant Mediterranean plants, and wait three to four weeks to fertilize new transplants.

❑ **GROOM FLOWERS.** To prolong bloom, pick faded blossoms from begonias, dahlias, Felicia daisies, geraniums, marguerites, penstemon, and other summer-blooming flowers.

❑ **FORCE WEED SEEDS.** When preparing a new bed for planting, water to start weeds growing. As soon as weeds germinate, pull them out or remove them with a hoe. New plants will have less competition.

❑ **SPREAD MULCH.** Hot fall days are hard on heat-sensitive azaleas, camellias, and gardenias. Protect these and other plants by renewing organic mulch in a layer as deep as 3 inches. Keep mulch away from the trunks of trees and shrubs.

Luscious 'Ace' has been a peach—my best tomato yet. (Thanks to the Orange County Organic Gardening Club for healthy starter plants.) But two vines don't yield enough fruit for tomato sauce or chutney. And two vines are all I have room for in my postage-stamp backyard.

My lettuce patch, however, will be another story. The yield I typically get from seeds, which I'll sow again next month in my 3- by 4-foot raised bed, never fails to astound me. This little plot keeps my husband and me in lettuce, arugula, and endive from winter through late spring. And dinner guests go home with surplus.

The secret is choosing cut-and-come-again kinds that can be sown thickly and harvested early and often. Shepherd's California Mesclun Mix, my introduction to this technique, is still my blend of choice.

•

It's hard to fathom for a gardener, but there are actually people out there willing to give away compost, horse manure, wood chips, broken concrete, nursery flats, PVC drip tubing, and other items I usually have to pay for. CALMAX, a material exchange program run by the California Integrated Waste Management Board, can put you in touch with these resources through a bimonthly catalog or their on-line computer services. For details, call (916) 255-2369.

SOUTHERN CALIFORNIA
Garden Notebook
BY SHARON COHOON

•

Succulents are survivors. But toughness isn't their only asset: they're also "user-friendly" plants.

A new book called *Dry Climate Gardening with Succulents,* by James Folsom and John Trager (Pantheon, 1995; $25, softcover), is chock-full of design ideas and growing tips, and it's available at the Huntington Botanical Garden gift shop. To find out more about succulents, attend the Huntington's 12th Annual Succulent Plants Symposium on Saturday, September 9. Call (818) 405-2160 for details.

THAT'S A GOOD QUESTION

Q: "Why did my fern get silvery-looking all of a sudden?"
A: Thrips are the likely culprits. They can siphon off the plant's juices for weeks, or even months, before you notice the silvery or tan cast. You'll need an 8- to 10-powered hand lens to identify them; brown spots—fecal pellets—on the reverse of the leaves are telltale signs.

Wade Roberts, director of Sherman Library Gardens in Corona del Mar, where the ferns are notoriously luxuriant, suggests trying insecticidal soap first to combat thrips. And if that fails, apply half-strength malathion. "If you spray, keep the plant watered to decrease the chances of burning the plant," says Roberts.

PLANTING

❏ **BUY BULBS.** Throughout the West, shop for spring-flowering bulbs in nurseries just after Labor Day. Shop early for the best selection, and to avoid bulbs that have been picked over and thrown back into the wrong bins by careless shoppers.

In zones 1–3 and 10–11 (see map): bulbs can go into the ground this month.

In zones 12 and 13: before planting, prechill bulbs of crocuses, hyacinths, and tulips as directed on page 268. Set the bulbs out in late October or November.

❏ **PLANT CROPS.** Zones 12 and 13: If you plant beans and corn by Labor Day, you'll be harvesting by Thanksgiving. You can sow beets, carrots, celery, chard, endive, green onions, kale, kohlrabi, leeks, parsley, parsnips, peas, potatoes, radishes, spinach, and turnips as soon as temperatures drop below 100°. Sow broccoli, brussels sprouts, cauliflower, and lettuce in flats for transplanting into the October garden.

❏ **PLANT PERENNIALS.** Moderate temperatures and, in most places, approaching winter rainy season make this a good time to plant perennials such as campanula, candytuft, catmint, coreopsis, delphinium, dianthus, diascia, foxglove, gaillardia, geum, penstemon, phlox, salvia, and yarrow. Set them out in well-prepared soil and water well. In zones 1–3 and 10–11, mulch around plants to keep ground from heaving.

INLAND WESTERN STATES
CHECKLIST
SEPTEMBER

Sunset Western Garden Book CLIMATE ZONES
- 1–3
- 10–11
- 12–13

MAINTENANCE

❏ **HARVEST CROPS.** Zones 1–3: Cantaloupes are ready when skin is well netted and the fruit slips easily from the vine. Corn is ready when kernels are milky inside. Pick watermelons when tendrils near the fruit start to turn brown; pick winter squash when rind colors up and hardens.

❏ **FEED LAWNS.** Apply about 1 pound of actual nitrogen per 1,000 square feet of turf. After application, water in well.

In zones 12 and 13, stop feeding your Bermuda lawn before you overseed it.

If you don't plan to overseed, apply high-nitrogen fertilizer now and water it in well to keep the Bermuda actively growing for as long as possible.

❏ **WATER.** Pay special attention to plants growing under eaves, trees, patio overhangs, and in containers.

In zones 1–3 and 10–11: irrigate trees and shrubs thoroughly after they drop their leaves. Continue deep-watering lawns.

❏ **MAKE COMPOST.** Make a pile about 4 feet in diameter, putting down alternating layers of green matter (grass clippings, vegetable remains) and brown matter (dried leaves). Water the pile enough to keep it as moist as a squeezed-out sponge, and turn the pile with a pitchfork weekly. Compost will be ready in about six weeks.

❏ **MULCH PLANTS.** Zones 1–3 and 10–11: Lay down a 3- to 4-inch layer of organic mulch around perennials and shrubs, and over bulb beds to protect roots from freezing. You can use straw, shredded leaves (run them through a lawn mower or shredder to keep them from matting when they get wet), or rough compost.

❏ **WINTERIZE GREENHOUSES.** In cold-winter areas, attend to the greenhouse before hard frosts come. Scrub out seedbeds and flats with a weak dilution of bleach and water. Then check and replace weather-stripping, broken glass, and torn plastic. Finally, check vents, filters, and heaters, replacing or repairing broken parts.

Lots of months seem interchangeable—a day from one could be swapped with a day from an adjacent month with no one the wiser—but not September. The heat usually breaks sometime this month, and thunderheads signal a battle between colliding warm and cold fronts. When rain showers come, often on a hot day, I try to be as skeptical as I am thankful, digging into the soil with my fingers to see how deeply the rain penetrated. Subsurface dust often tells the tale, and I must drag out the garden hose to give plants the deep watering they need.

•

I used to sow wildflower seeds in spring, broadcasting them into prepared, weed-free beds. Then I noticed that the same kinds of wildflowers I was planting would sprout and bloom in other gardens well before they appeared in mine. The difference was that those wise gardeners were sowing in fall. Try it and see the difference.

•

If you don't have much experience growing wildflowers, one of the following books may help. For mountain gardeners, The

INLAND WESTERN STATES
Garden Notebook

BY JIM McCAUSLAND

Wildflower Gardener's Guide, one in a series by Henry W. Art (Garden Way Publishing, Pownal, VT, 1990; $14.95), recommends 33 of the best wildflowers. For California and Southwest gardeners, How to Grow the Wildflowers, by Eric A. Johnson and Scott Millard (Ironwood Press, Tucson, 1993; $14.95), offers information on 89 garden-worthy wildflowers.

THAT'S A GOOD QUESTION

Q: What is the best planting season for trees and shrubs—spring or fall?

A: In any region, the idea is to give a new transplant as much time as possible to become established before it has to face the year's most extreme weather, be it heat (as in the desert) or cold (as in the mountains). If you garden in a cold-winter climate, set out container plants as early in spring as the soil can be worked; fall is the second-best time. If you garden in the low or intermediate desert, plant after the soil and air cool in fall. Bare-root stock is best planted in winter or earliest spring, just before it leafs out.

'MARVEL STRIPE'

'BRANDYWINE'

'GREAT WHITE'

'GOLDIE'

'CHEROKEE PURPLE'

'EVERGREEN'

'AMISH PASTE'

'COSTOLUTO GENOVESE'

'ORANGE CHERRY'

'GREEN GRAPE'

'STUPICE'

'RED CURRANT'

'YELLOW CURRANT'

HEIRLOOM

Ruby color, round shape, and rich, herbaceous flavor once defined that glory of summer, the ripe tomato. These days, the color may be vibrant green, near white, or chocolate. The size can be that of a pea or a baseball, and the form can be lumpy, pear-shaped, or ruffled. And the taste? Intensely sweet to tangy, tropical, or earthy. Yet despite such novel qualities, these "new" tomatoes go back centuries.

Where have they been all our lives? Until recently, they were only in home gardens and specialty seed catalogs. Now they're popping up at farmers' markets, top restaurants, even supermarkets.

Heirloom is the term given to many of the tomatoes, an appropriate term for something that connects us to earlier times. They're varieties that have passed from generation to generation among families and friends. Today they're locally grown, picked ripe, and raised commercially by small specialty farms.

By buying and growing heirlooms we keep their heritage alive, encourage a diverse selection of tomatoes in the marketplace, and enjoy the excitement of discovery.

THE NEWEST TOMATOES IN THE MARKETPLACE ARE SEVERAL GENERATIONS OLD. HERE ARE THE TOP 12 FOR GROWING AND COOKING

This is peak harvest season, the best time to discover heirloom tomatoes. Of hundreds of varieties, the ones pictured at left get the most votes from our survey of expert growers for memorable flavor, good looks, and adaptation to the West's climates.

ENJOYING TOMATOES AT THEIR BEST

For best flavor, select or harvest tomatoes fully colored. Choose while still firm (they will last several days on the counter), or pick or buy them slightly soft to use in a day or two. But don't wait until they turn extra-soft with translucent flesh, or you'll get an off-taste.

Never refrigerate a tomato that isn't completely ripe (fully colored); flavor development will stop, though color may continue to change. As for chilling fully ripe tomatoes, some experts say flavor declines; some insist it doesn't. All agree that tomatoes are tastiest at room temperature.

With tomatoes this good, you don't need to do much to get great results. Jan Blüm, owner of Seeds Blüm (an heirloom seed company near Boise), suggests the simplest recipe of all. "They're best if

ROASTED TOMATO SOUP
For intensely flavored orange soup, purée roasted 'Goldie' tomatoes with broth; add sour cream swirls.

TOMATOES

BY ELAINE JOHNSON & LAUREN BONAR SWEZEY

eaten right off the bush, with tomato juice running down your wrist. I keep a salt-shaker on a post in the garden."

THE EXPERTS' PICKS

Look for their selections at farmers' and specialty markets. Kinds vary by area, and some sources label tomatoes more by color than name. A few tomatoes are more difficult to find, but you can grow these at home.

Diverse flavors are one of the charms of heirloom tomatoes. Partly, differences are a matter of perception; some palates are more tuned to sweet or acidic tastes. But climate, soil, and growing methods also affect flavor.

Unless noted, plants are indeterminate (vinelike, need support, and generally bear over a longer period than determinate plants, which are compact and bushy).

'AMISH PASTE'. Dates to the turn of the century. Oblong, paste-type fruit with solid flesh, few seeds, sweet flavor; also used for slicing. Large for a paste tomato. Less available in markets than some.

'BRANDYWINE'. An Amish Beefsteak with pink-red color "like Gamay Beaujolais," says Jeff Dawson, garden director of Fetzer Vineyards Valley Oaks Garden Project in Hopland, California. Large; rich flavor, firm-soft texture, thin skin.

'CHEROKEE PURPLE'. Said to have originated with the Cherokee. Pink-chocolate with handsome green stripes on shoulders, round to oblong, medium size. Sweet, earthy, complex flavor; soft texture. Big producer; disease tolerant.

'COSTOLUTO GENOVESE'. An Italian variety with an unusual fluted profile. Deep red color; intense, full, sweet flavor; meaty texture. Size varies. Good fresh or cooked. Vigorous, heavy yield.

'EVERGREEN'. Yellow-green with vivid green interior. Medium to large, with irregular shape; sweet-tart flavor; firm texture; delicate skin. Vigorous plant.

'GOLDIE'. May have been around for 150 years. Large, with beautiful golden orange color, sweet flavor, good acid balance. Vigorous plant.

'GREAT WHITE'. Actually a light yellow. Large Beefsteak with mild, melonlike flavor, low acidity. Vigorous plant.

'GREEN GRAPE'. Cherry-type tomato. Yellow-green when ripe. Very sweet and juicy taste with some acidity; seeds are

Fireworks Tomato Salad

Cooking time: About 10 minutes

Prep time: About 30 minutes

Notes: This rainbow-colored salad with the lively flavor of salsa shows off the smaller tomatoes' shapes. Serve on its own, spooned over slices of larger tomatoes, or with steak or chicken.

Makes: 4 servings

- ¾ pound (3 to 4) fresh pasilla or Anaheim chilies
- 1 large fresh jalapeño chili
- 5 cups small, ripe, multicolored heirloom tomatoes (or 1-inch chunks of larger tomatoes)
- 2 tablespoons lime juice
- ⅓ cup coarsely chopped fresh cilantro, plus sprigs

  Salt and pepper

1. Place pasilla and jalapeño chilies on a 10- by 15-inch baking sheet. Broil 2 to 3 inches from heat until black and blistered all over, turning as needed, 6 to 10 minutes.

2. Let chilies cool, then peel, seed, and rinse. Coarsely chop pasillas and mince jalapeño.

3. For small tomatoes, leave any tiny ones whole; quarter or halve somewhat bigger ones. In a bowl, combine tomatoes, chilies, lime juice, and chopped cilantro. Season to taste with salt and pepper. Garnish with cilantro sprigs.

Per serving: 76 cal., 11% (8 cal.) from fat; 3.3 g protein; 0.9 g fat (0.1 g sat.); 17 g carbo.; 27 mg sodium; 0 mg chol.

Four-in-One Roasted Tomatoes

Cooking time: About 1½ hours

Prep time: About 15 minutes

Notes: Baking intensifies tomatoes' flavor and sweetness. Use this basic recipe to roast tomato halves to go with meats (as noted here) or to turn into marinara sauce, a richly flavored appetizer spread, or a deceptively simple soup (directions are on page 254).

For plain roasted tomatoes, large slicing kinds taste very good but hold their shape less well than smaller slicers or paste or currant types.

Makes: 8 servings plain roasted tomatoes

- 1 onion (6 oz.), peeled and cut into lengthwise slivers
- 2 tablespoons extra-virgin olive oil

  Salt and pepper

- 4 to 5 pounds ripe tomatoes
- 1 tablespoon minced garlic

1. In an 11- by 17-inch roasting pan, combine onion and 1 tablespoon oil. Sprinkle generously with salt and pepper, then stir. Cut enough tomatoes in half horizontally to fill pan, placing cut side up over onions. (If using tiny cherry tomatoes, don't cut; simply scatter over onions.)

2. Brush tomatoes with remaining oil, sprinkle generously with salt and pepper, and pat garlic on top. Bake, uncovered, in a 450° oven until juices in pan have evaporated and onions just begin to caramelize, 1¼ to 1½ hours; as needed for even cooking, move tomatoes and onions gently with a spatula from edges to center of pan. Do not let mixture scorch.

3. Serve tomatoes and onions hot to accompany grilled meats, polenta, or other foods. Or use as directed in one of the ways outlined on page 254.

Per serving plain roasted: 88 cal., 44% (39 cal.) from fat; 2.2 g protein; 4.3 g fat (0.6 g sat.); 13 g carbo.; 21 mg sodium; 0 mg chol.

NOEL BARNHURST

FIREWORKS TOMATO SALAD
Low-calorie, salsa-flavored salad combines roasted chilies with small, multicolored tomatoes.

Roasted Tomato Soup

Cooking time: About 5 minutes
Prep time: About 15 minutes
Makes: 5 to 6 cups, 4 servings

1. To pan with **roasted tomatoes and onions** (from Four-in-One Roasted Tomatoes, page 252), add 1 cup boiling **chicken broth**, and stir to loosen browned bits.

2. Whirl half of mixture in a blender into a smooth purée, then add ¾ cup more boiling broth. Repeat with remaining tomato mixture and ¾ cup more boiling broth. If a thinner texture is desired, add additional broth. Pour into wide bowls.

3. Combine ¼ cup **reduced-fat sour cream** and ⅛ teaspoon **salt**. Drop several small spoonfuls into each bowl, then pull a knife tip through sour cream into soup to form designs.

Per serving: 206 cal., 48% (99 cal.) from fat; 6.3 g protein; 11 g fat (2.4 g sat.); 27 g carbo.; 140 mg sodium; 5 mg chol.

Roasted Tomato Marinara

Cooking time: About 20 minutes
Prep time: About 15 minutes
Notes: If desired, add warm chunks of cooked Italian sausage (¾ lb.) to cooked sauce.
Makes: 3 to 3¾ cups, 8 servings; enough for 2 packages (12 oz. each) dried pasta, cooked

1. Coarsely chop **roasted tomatoes and onions** (from Four-in-One Roasted Tomatoes, page 252), then return to pan.

2. Stir in ¾ cup **dry red wine** such as Zinfandel if using red tomatoes (use dry white wine with other tomato colors), ¾ cup **vegetable broth**, and ½ cup chopped **fresh basil**.

3. Bake in a 450° oven, stirring occasionally, until slightly thickened, about 20 minutes. Add 1 teaspoon **sugar** if sauce is too tart. If sauce gets too thick, add more broth.

4. Use sauce hot or let cool, then chill airtight up to 2 days or freeze.

Per serving (sauce only): 108 cal., 37% (40 cal.) from fat; 2.4 protein; 4.4 g fat (0.6 g sat.); 14 g carbo.; 116 mg sodium; 0 mg chol.

Roasted Tomato Spread

Cooking time: About 10 minutes
Prep time: About 10 minutes
Notes: Serve at room temperature with raw vegetables such as red bell peppers, cucumbers, or carrots; slender baguettes; or crackers.
Makes: About 3 cups, 12 servings

1. Coarsely chop **roasted tomatoes and onions** (from Four-in-One Roasted Tomatoes, page 252). Mixture should equal about 3 cups and be thick and fairly dry; if it's too wet, return to roasting pan and bake in a 450° oven 10 to 20 minutes longer, stirring often.

2. In a bowl, combine tomato mixture with 2 teaspoons minced **fresh marjoram leaves** or ½ teaspoon dried marjoram leaves. Garnish with **fresh marjoram sprigs**.

Per serving (spread only): 58 cal., 43% (25 cal.) from fat; 1.5 protein; 2.8 g fat (0.4 g sat.); 8.5 g carbo.; 14 mg sodium; 0 mg chol.

NOEL BARNHURST

Grilled Pesto-Tomato Sandwiches

Cooking time: About 5 minutes
Prep time: About 20 minutes
Notes: Grower Stuart Dickson of Stone Free Farm in Watsonville, California, contributed this sandwich idea. His favorite tomato choice is 'Marvel Stripe', but fluted 'Costoluto Genovese', as well as deeply colored 'Evergreen' and 'Goldie' look beautiful, too.
Makes: 4 servings

1. You'll need 8 to 10 ounces **bread** cut into ½-inch-thick diagonal slices about 6 inches long. Use a flat loaf like francese or ciabatta and cut 12 slices; or cut 8 slices of French bread (not a skinny baguette). Cut enough slices of your favorite **heirloom tomatoes** (about 1 lb.) to cover bread. Rinse and crisp 2 cups lightly packed **arugula leaves**.

2. Place bread (without tomatoes) on a 12- by 15-inch baking sheet and broil 2 to 3 inches below heat until golden, about 3 minutes. Turn bread over and spread with ⅔ cup homemade or purchased **pesto**. Broil until bread edges are golden, about 2 minutes.

3. Arrange arugula and tomatoes on bread. Season generously with **salt and pepper**; serve open-face.

Per serving: 389 cal., 51% (198 cal.) from fat; 10 g protein; 22 g fat (3.8 g sat.); 38 g carbo.; 658 mg sodium; 6.7 mg chol.

small. Often sold as an heirloom, though is a more recent open-pollinated variety. Compact, determinate plant; a prolific producer.

'MARVEL STRIPE'. Originally from Oaxaca, Mexico, from seed saved for five generations. Large bicolored Beefsteak-type yellow tomato with red stripes. Mildly sweet, good tomato flavor, low acidity. Vigorous plant; a prolific producer.

'ORANGE CHERRY'. Large (1½ inches) for a cherry-type tomato, with intense orange color and exceptionally sweet tomato taste. Rarely available in markets.

'RED CURRANT'. A species from South America with clusters of pea-size fruits. Sweet-tart, fruity flavor. Vigorous, prolific plant. 'Yellow Currant' is similar. (Some tomatoes sold as currants aren't the true species and may be larger.)

'STUPICE'. All-around favorite, from Czechoslovakia. Small; rich red color; sweet, nicely balanced, regular tomato taste. Slightly tough skin. Excellent fresh or roasted. Occasionally available in markets. Early, heavy producer; easy to grow.

HOW TO SAVE YOUR OWN SEEDS

If you've discovered an heirloom tomato you'd love to grow next season, you can save the seed. In most cases, the seeds will produce exactly the same kind of tomato. (By contrast, seed from a hybrid tomato—a cross of two varieties—will never produce the same tomato.) Even though tomatoes are self-pollinating, a few kinds cross-pollinate with other tomatoes nearby. If the grower didn't isolate the plants or protect the flowers, you may not get the same tomatoes next season. You won't know until you grow the seeds.

Tomato seeds are encased in a gel sac. Allowing seeds to go through a fermentation process that removes the sac helps destroy seed-borne diseases.

1. Choose thoroughly ripe, soft fruit. Wash, and cut open across the middle (not through the stem end).

2. Into a labeled container, gently squeeze tomatoes to extract seed, pulp, and juice. Cover with plastic wrap.

3. Set the container at room temperature out of sun. Stir twice a day until covered with mold; it will smell foul. This takes about three days (less in warmer weather). Don't let fermentation go beyond this point or seeds may germinate.

4. Pour everything into a fine strainer; rinse clean with water. Blot seeds dry and finish drying on a dish (seeds stick to paper or cloth) out of sun; stir twice a day. This takes one to three days, depending on the temperature.

5. Store seeds in an airtight container, and set in a dark spot that's cool and dry.

A good reference for learning more about seed saving is Suzanne Ashworth's *Seed to Seed: Seed Saving Techniques for the Vegetable Gardener* (Seed Saver Publications, Decorah, IA, 1991; $19.95).

HOW TO GROW HEIRLOOMS NEXT SPRING

Sow seeds in flats or containers six to eight weeks before danger of last frost is past; set them on a water heater or use a heating coil to keep between 75° and 90°. Keep soil moist. Right after germination, set plants in bright, indirect light.

After several sets of leaves form, transplant into 4-inch pots. Water only enough to keep roots from drying out; fertilize weekly with fish emulsion or half-strength liquid fertilizer.

A week or so before transplanting into the ground, set tomatoes outside in partial shade (protect from frost), and gradually introduce them into full sun.

Plant in full sun in well-amended soil. Growers prefer compost, manure, or an organic fertilizer (such as 7-10-7) plus kelp, and cover crops (such as fava beans) planted in fall. Soils high in phosphorus are important for fruit production.

In cool or short-season climates, cover planting bed with black plastic, plant through it, and then cover with row covers. Set determinate types about 2 feet apart, indeterminate types 3 feet apart.

Water regularly to get plants established, then water deeply but less frequently to develop deep rooting. Stuart Dickson of Stone Free Farm in Watsonville, California, says, "Don't pamper them—make them work for their water." This is especially important when they are fruiting. Most growers prefer drip irrigation.

Diseases and insects don't seem to be a major hindrance to growing heirlooms. David Cavagnaro, a writer and photographer who works with Seed Savers Exchange, says most heirlooms are vigorous plants that often outgrow foliage diseases. To avoid soil-borne diseases, rotate crops so they don't grow in the same bed for three to four years. Small tomato hornworms can be controlled with *Bacillus thuringiensis* (BT); hand-pick large ones. ■

WHERE TO FIND SEEDS AND SEEDLINGS

You can buy heirloom tomato seeds or seedlings by mail. Also, a few retail nurseries carry seedlings. Catalogs or listings are free unless noted.

FETZER VINEYARDS VALLEY OAKS GARDEN PROJECT,
Box 611, Hopland, CA 95449. Offers seeds of 65 tomatoes, many of which are heirlooms, some in limited quantities (write for a list of seeds).

NATURAL GARDENING COMPANY,
217 San Anselmo Ave., San Anselmo, CA 94960; (707) 766-9303. Sells seeds and organically grown seedlings of 12 heirloom tomatoes.

SANTA BARBARA HEIRLOOM SEEDLING NURSERY,
Box 4235S, Santa Barbara, CA 93140; (805) 968-5444. Call or write for a free list of 35 organically grown heirloom seedlings.

SEED SAVERS EXCHANGE,
3076 N. Winn Rd., Decorah, IA 52101; (319) 382-5990. Preserves heirloom varieties and is an exchange for seed savers (members write directly to each other). Membership ($25) includes a list of more than 1,780 tomatoes, the majority of which are heirloom. Call for a brochure.

SEEDS BLÜM,
HC33, Idaho City Stage, Boise, ID 83706. Catalog $3. Sells seeds of 40 heirloom tomatoes.

TOMATO GROWERS SUPPLY CO.,
Box 2237, Fort Myers, FL 33902; (941) 768-1119. Sells seeds of 75 heirloom tomatoes.

Great gardens, great ideas for fall planting

Designers at three public gardens combine plants for spectacular effects in beds and pots. Now's the time of year to follow their leads

SOME OF THE BEST PLANTING ideas can be gleaned from gardening professionals who work their magic in public places.

At the Arizona Biltmore in Phoenix, where the garden is at its most colorful in winter, Don Dickerman turns garden beds into floral tapestries. At Stanford Shopping Center in Palo Alto, California, Jackie Gray mixes annuals, bulbs, and perennials to create extravaganzas in pots and beds. And just up the road at Filoli in Woodside, Lucy Tolmach creates dazzling displays by interplanting bulbs with annuals.

These experts share some of their special design tips and planting techniques—suitable to any home garden—just in time for the fall planting season, which starts now in mild-winter areas. (In the desert and inland Southern California, wait a few weeks until the weather cools down.)

THE ARIZONA BILTMORE'S *formal European garden (left) is planted with red and white geraniums, 'Blue Crown' and 'Gold Crown' pansies, and white sweet alyssum. The bed at top features red geraniums and white petunias. Don Dickerman (above) pauses in front of 'Lilac Cascade' petunias and rhaphiolepis. Below, silver lace (Chrysanthemum ptarmiciflorum) sets off 'Lilac Cascade' petunias and pink geraniums.*

ARIZONA BILTMORE: TAPESTRIES OF ANNUALS

Expansive displays of colorful annuals and green lawns surround the Biltmore, a historic Frank Lloyd Wright–style hotel on 39 acres in the middle of Phoenix. Don Dickerman, along with a crew of 30 gardeners, is responsible for planting and maintaining the hotel gardens. "We plant 300,000 plants a year in 2½ to 3 acres of flower beds," he says. "The Biltmore is one of the only places in the Southwest where you'll see a formal European garden."

In this mild low-desert climate, gardeners can plant warm-season flowers such as petunias and geraniums for winter bloom. For Dickerman and his team, winter planting season begins October 1, when the weather has cooled off from summer but is still mild enough to give

plants a fast start. Before planting, the gardeners amend the beds with a blend of peat moss and chicken manure. Then they mix in slow-release fertilizer (14-12-14). "The soil preparation really pays off," says Dickerman. Every six weeks, plants are fed with an all-purpose fertilizer. On frosty nights, Dickerman's team shields the beds with row covers. In April, gardeners start changing over to warm-season plants.

Dickerman's tips for tapestry gardens

•Gardeners here use no more than three colors in one bed, and often use only two. "I like yellow and white, red and yellow, red and white, and pink, blue (or lilac), and white."

•Petunias are planted 12 inches apart, pansies 4 to 5 inches apart. Geraniums are planted in a triangular pattern 16 inches apart. Sweet alyssum spreads nicely if plants are spaced 6 inches apart in a single or double row.

•"Liberty series and 'Yellow Sprite' snapdragons are more tolerant of rust than other types."

•" 'Crystal Bowl' pansies don't hold up to heat as well as other types."

•Fibrous begonias prefer early morning sun. They can last two years. "I like 'Vodka' (bronze-red leaves, red flower), 'Linda' (green leaves, pink flower), and 'Viva' (green leaves, white flower). In the cool shade I use cyclamen."

•His favorite warm-season plants include bush bougainvillea, Dahlberg daisy, dwarf lisianthus, new dwarf blue and white star clusters (*Pentas lanceolata*), as well as Tropicana and Cooler series of Madagascar periwinkle (*Catharanthus roseus*), which are disease resistant.

STANFORD SHOPPING CENTER: ARTFUL LIVING BOUQUETS

Compared with most shopping malls in the United States, Stanford Shopping Center is a breath of fresh air. Walkways between stores are open to the outdoors and get plenty of sunshine and gentle breezes, so plants and flowers thrive. This is where garden designer Jackie Gray creates her magic.

Gray is an artist whose medium is plants. She combines the flower colors of annuals, bulbs, and perennials in containers and planting beds as carefully as a painter who works on canvas. Her designs are an inspiration to any gardener. Her artistry begins in fall, when she plans her color combinations carefully so she can order her tulips accordingly. "At other times of the year, I can be more spontaneous and plan as I shop for plants," she says.

She plants all of her annuals in September and October to take advantage of the warm weather, which helps plants root and get going. Fall planting is especially important for Iceland poppies and pansies. "I plant primroses at the end of October when the weather is cooler—and always from 4-inch pots," she says. "Then I come back in November and December and plant tulip and daffodil bulbs among the annuals. And in January, I plant anemones and ranunculus from cell-packs."

Because the plants are watered often,

feeding is especially important. Gray uses a timed-release fertilizer at planting time and then a water-soluble 20-20-20 formula every six weeks or so.

The most serious pests during the warm season are whiteflies, particularly around plants where air circulation is limited. To control them, Gray finds that yellow sticky cards work better than chemicals. *Bacillus thuringiensis* (BT) controls budworms on petunias.

BIG ROUND POT *shows off delphinium and hydrangea surrounded by lower-growing impatiens with flowers in pale pink to rose. Pink Diascia vigilis and lobelia trail over the edges.*

AT STANFORD SHOPPING CENTER, *colorful plants in containers are changed with the seasons. The fall-planted container at far left holds pansies, pink stock, 'Ice Follies' daffodil, and 'Golden Parade' tulip. In November, Gray randomly shakes tulip bulbs among the plants (left) and buries the bulbs where they drop.*

Gray's tips for big living bouquets

• "Every garden needs something bright—a little yellow, lime green, or iridescent white—to catch the eye. I might put a lime green helichrysum in a pot with purple heliotrope and pink petunias, for instance."

• "My color tastes change from season to season. A few years ago, I would have been aghast at using red with yellow. Then I saw red and yellow 'Flaming Parrot' tulip and thought that it would be so pretty in the right situation—maybe combined with bright red primroses, soft yellow 'Cream Crown' pansies, and *Chrysanthemum paludosum*."

• "I experiment with new flowers every season. Some combinations work well, others don't. This year, I was pleased with the pink peony poppies (from Paeony Flowered Mixed). I also liked pink petunias, Pastel Mixed asters, and *Convolvulus tricolor* 'Blue Ensign' and 'Rose Ensign' (all but the petunia are from Thompson & Morgan seed catalog). I was disappointed with 'Danebrog Laced' poppy. It was supposed to be a traffic-stopper, and it flopped. It grew 5 feet tall and fell over."

• "In late fall I pull out and discard delphiniums, geraniums, and heliotrope. Delphiniums do so well from cellpacks that I just buy new ones, geraniums get too woody, and heliotrope doesn't come back well. All other perennials get cut back in late fall. Then I transplant woody, deciduous ones such as Russian sage into cans, and replant them when they leaf out again. Others, like phlox or diascia, I leave in the pots."

• "A lot of perennials that you expect to bloom only once will bloom two or three times in our mild weather if you cut them back; the bloom stalk might be shorter. Examples are perennial phlox and delphiniums."

• "We deadhead constantly, but I'm not shy about coming in at midseason and cutting down annuals like petunias to just a few leaves to get them to bush out again."

AT STANFORD, *summer bouquets are planted when spring bloom is through. Packed into the container above are Salvia farinacea 'Victoria' (center), white dwarf cosmos, Gaillardia grandiflora 'Goblin', dwarf gloriosa daisy, 'Cambridge Blue' lobelia, and white sweet alyssum. In the container below, mixed colors of coleus, white and lime green nicotiana, and purple heliotrope combine to create a cool white and green arrangement highlighted with burgundies and purples.*

RENEE LYNN

AT FILOLI, *'Pink Diamond' tulips are underplanted with 'White Perfection' violas. Their midseason bloom coincides with nearby weeping cherries.*

FILOLI: BULBS AND BEDDING PLANTS TEAM UP

The 654-acre Filoli estate, south of San Francisco in Woodside, California, is a well-known horticultural jewel. Starting in early spring, its 16 acres of formal gardens come alive with color.

For 18 years, garden superintendent Lucy Tolmach has been combining tulips in single colors with drifts of a flower in a contrasting or complementary color such as forget-me-nots, pansies, violas, and wallflowers. She also stuffs single colors of narcissus, hyacinth, and muscari in containers.

Tolmach plans her garden around three overlapping bloom periods. The early spring bloomers (mid-February to March) are the hyacinths and daffodils. "When daffodils, such as 'Pink Charm', are planted in containers, I get close to four weeks of display," says Tolmach. She then moves the containers out of view and naturalizes the bulbs in a field.

Next come the late daffodils and early to midseason tulips. Single late tulips carry the show into April. "After the bulbs finish, we snap off the stems and let the flowers planted below them grow up and cover the old foliage," she says.

She and her crew plant the bulbs and flowers from October through mid-December. Tulips go in rows 6 inches deep and 8 inches apart; bedding plants are set between them. The beds are kept moist. "Tulips can't be allowed to dry out," says Tolmach. "If it's dry in winter, you need to water." ∎

By Lauren Bonar Swezey

Tolmach's tips for teaming bulbs with bedding plants

•"I keep records of every plant combination and even take videos (the color seems truer than in photographs) of everything that's blooming. It's difficult to remember shades of colors, so this sparks my brain when I'm ordering bulbs."

•"I love 'Pink Charm' daffodil, with its bright coral cup and white perianth. It's wonderful with our creamy white magnolias. So is 'Mount Hood' (a large white Trumpet daffodil)."

•Tolmach's favorite new hybrid pansy is Silhouette Mix—a beautiful pastel yellow and pale lavender mix. "I use it with 'China Pink', a lily-flowered tulip, or 'Blushing Bride', a pale yellow tulip with a red rim fading to cream with pink stains."

•For late-season color, Tolmach combines 'Angelique' tulips with 'Tall White Bouquet' forget-me-nots.

•"I don't mix different kinds of bulbs together in containers," she says, "because it's difficult to match the bloom time. It's less risky to plant them in separate pots and cluster the pots together."

CONTAINERS HOLD *'Blue Parrot' tulips and white forget-me-nots. Beside steps, long-stemmed 'Maureen' tulips rise elegantly above Siberian wallflowers; bulbs were spaced out in a diamond pattern rather than clumped together.*

ON DISPLAY *in the garden, various pots of bonsai are moved off growing and grooming tables (above) as each comes into its prime or when the garden's mood is in need of a change.*

Japanese design ideas flourish in a Walla Walla garden

ECHOES OF JAPANESE DESIGN: *bamboo ladle, stone basin atop rock, plus gravel, ferns, ground cover (Equisetum scirpoides), and a yellow calendula for color.*

EVEN THOUGH IT'S A BIT DIFFICULT TO DEFINE, THIS one-of-a-kind garden in Walla Walla, Washington, is a treasure chest of landscaping ideas. Its creator, Ikune Sawada, explains, "It's not a Japanese garden. It's an inland Northwest garden by a Japanese American."

After moving to Walla Walla 2½ years ago, Sawada, a native of Okayama, Japan, applied Japanese horticultural techniques to design a garden that drew from the palette of inland Northwest plants.

He started almost from scratch, with just a patch of lawn (80 by 90 feet) and a few plantings along the property's edge. He decided to leave a number of large, old trees-of-heaven (*Ailanthus altissima*). These aggressive, fast-growing trees, with their big seed clusters in midsummer, are often considered weed trees in the Northwest. But Sawada says he admires the trees for their winter form and for the privacy and shade they provide.

Next, he hand-dug an irregularly shaped pond, measuring roughly 20 by 30 feet and 5 feet deep. He piled some of the

BONSAI TABLES *were made from pressure-treated lumber. Plants are clustered together nursery-style. Gravel below drains excess water. Lath overhead diffuses sun.*

COMBINED ELEMENTS *give garden Japanese serenity with hardworking American livability.*
Big rocks, decking, masonry, and plants surround pond, where water lilies grow in sunken plastic pots.
Simple, weathering fence screens and provides background for bonsai display.

soil from the excavation along the pond's sides and to the rear of the hole to make mounds and a waterfall. A professional firm poured the wire-reinforced concrete floor and edges of the pond. He stocked the pond with a school of koi and added several water lilies sunk in 5-gallon plastic pots.

Native granite boulders were then craned into place. Next, a wooden deck and garden wall went in. The pondside deck serves both as a space for entertaining and as a place where Sawada can display his extensive collection of bonsai.

He put down steppingstones and gravel, then interplanted with creeping plants like alyssum and Kenilworth ivy (*Cymbalaria muralis*) for summer color and thyme for year-round greenery. Perennials were planted where they would soften a deck edge or add a touch of foliage and color between the stones.

Sawada selected plants as much for their structure as for their flowers. Among the perennial plants he chose were balloon flower (*Platycodon grandiflorus*), iris (*Iris ensata, I. sibirica,* and *I. tectorum*), spiderwort (*Tradescantia andersoniana*), and

yarrow (*Achillea filipendulina* 'Coronation Gold').

Pines (*Pinus nigra*) and Japanese and fullmoon maples (*Acer palmatum* and *A. japonicum,* respectively) were spotted around the garden and shaped to show off their trunk and branch structure, to provide bursts of foliage, or to grow tall and open, forming lacy canopies or delicate screens.

Wherever there was shade, Sawada dotted the area with ferns and left open spaces for wild mosses to establish themselves.

During the growing season, he fertilizes at four regular intervals between March and mid-July by lightly broadcasting granular 12-12-12 fertilizer. During the hot months, he makes the rounds early each morning, spot-watering each plant with a wand. Bonsai are watered twice or more daily.

He keeps plants in shape by continual snipping and pruning. After the first hard frost, he gives the garden a general cleanup. But beyond that, says Sawada, "it's pretty much just a puttering labor of love." ∎

By Steven R. Lorton

SEPTEMBER   263

Perennials that put
on a late-summer show

*Here are 10 that brighten the West's gardens
from now into autumn*

W HEN YOU THINK ABOUT IT, gardeners are a bit like show-biz directors. We stage our big production numbers in spring and midsummer. Most of us wouldn't consider September a big month for a flowering perennial show. But look around: just when it seems the curtain is coming down on summer, a whole cast of perennials is ready to step on stage and dazzle the audience.

Here we list 10 of September's top performers. All of these plants are hardy throughout the West.

Most of them are easy to find at nurseries. Buy them in bloom in gallon-size cans. You can plant them immediately or

ASTER BLOOMS *(at left) appear in late summer and last well into autumn. Sedum telephium 'Autumn Joy' (above) forms dense clusters of coral flowers that turn a handsome brown when frost hits; you can leave the dry flower heads on the plant for winter interest or cut them for indoor display.*

JAMES FREDERICK HOUSEL

BOLTONIA *bears daisylike flowers on branching stems. The plants, which grow up to 6 feet tall, give an airy look to a late-summer garden.*

slip the cans into decorative pots until blooms fade, then set them in the ground. Water newly set-out plants well until temperatures cool and fall rains begin. Plants will have the winter and next spring to get established. Feed them lightly next spring and summer (granular 12-12-12 fertilizer is a good choice).

Aster. Masses of old-fashioned daisy-like flowers in shades of lavender to deep violet characterize *Aster frikartii*. Plants grow to 3 feet tall. *A. tataricus* blooms on 5- to 8-foot-tall stems so sturdy they need no staking (this aster is available from White Flower Farm, 20 Irene St., Torrington, CT 06790; 203/496-9600).

SEPTEMBER

WHEELBARROW CORNUCOPIA *includes long-necked calabash and spiky 'Crown of Thorns' gourds, acorn-shaped squash, and miniature pumpkins. For details on this colorful harvest, see page 276.*

OCTOBER

GARDEN
Guide

Autumn beauty in Spokane's Japanese garden

It's difficult to imagine the lush and lacy splendor of a Japanese garden in Spokane's dry, cold-winter climate until you see the Spokane-Nishinomiya Japanese Garden. It artfully employs the principles of Japanese gardens using plants that are hardy and in many cases native to the inland Northwest. This month, the deciduous plants will be at their peak of autumn color. If you visit, bring a camera and a notebook to record planting ideas you can adapt in your own landscape.

Look for displays of vivid foliage by several varieties of Japanese maple (*Acer palmatum*), the dark red leaves of *Euonymus alata,* the golden yellow leaves of 'Kwanzan' cherries (*Prunus serrulata* 'Kwanzan'), and an assortment of willows. The deciduous plants show their colors against an evergreen backdrop of black and ponderosa pines.

The 1½-acre garden was opened in 1974 and named for Spokane's sister city—Nishinomiya, Japan. It is graced by two handsome stone lanterns, a pair of bridges, and a waterfall that spills into a pond. The garden is at the corner of 21st Avenue and Bernard Street, on the central west side of Manito Park. It is open from 8 to dusk daily through October, then closes until April. Admission is free.

ROBERT BARROS

Japanese maples blaze behind ceremonial bridge over pond stocked with koi (some over 2 feet long).

OCTOBER '95

- Spokane's Japanese garden
- Garlic planting time
- Snow crocus
- Vines for hummingbirds
- Grow a row for the hungry
- Harvest surprises— gourds and squash

Willow branch trellis keeps annual vines upright

A garden is never quite complete without a handsome vertical focal point, such as a trellis. The tepee-type trellis shown here in *Sunset*'s Menlo Park test garden is made of corkscrew willow (*Salix matsudana* 'Tortuosa').

It was simple to put together. Test garden coordinator Bud Stuckey used 8-foot-long pieces of willow and sunk them 1 foot into the ground. You can make the trellis as he did, tall and narrow with willow branch ends set close together in the soil, or you can position the branches a bit farther apart to make the trellis shorter and wider at the base.

For vines that don't twine, like sweet peas, you need to wrap the base of the trellis with a foot-wide piece of pea netting to give the peas something to hold onto. Plant seeds around the base of the netting.

For twining vines like scarlet runner bean (a spring-planted vine), plant beans about 2 inches apart in a circle around the base of each branch.

Corkscrew willow is available from florists, flower markets, and craft stores (if you can't find it, ask a store to order it for you). For a slightly different look, make your trellis from prunings of fruit and other types of trees.

NORMAN A. PLATE

Corkscrew willow branches form a tepee for sweet peas.

Don't forget the garlic

Nothing hones the appetite like garlic, and few plants are as easy to grow. The only difficult thing about garlic is remembering to plant it in fall, since so few vegetables are started then.

One of the widest selections of garlic is offered by Filaree Farm of Okanogan, Washington. The farm's price list covers more than 100 kinds, but if you don't see what you want, ask (Filaree grows more than 450 strains).

For *Sunset Western Garden Book* cold-winter climate zones 1, 2, 3, 10, and 11, excellent garlics include 'German Red', a favorite with gourmet cooks; potent 'Romanian Red', which makes just four large cloves per bulb; and 'Chesnok Red', an all-around favorite. In mild-winter zones, try 'Inchelium Red', which has done well in taste tests, and 'Silverwhite', which has a more refined flavor.

October is late in the shipping season for Filaree, so you should order as soon as possible and plant garlic cloves as soon as they arrive. Plant garlic in good garden soil about twice as deep as the clove is high, base down, in a place that gets full sun. If the ground freezes where you live, cover the planting bed with 6 inches of an organic mulch such as chopped leaves or straw. (Don't use hay; the seeds will fill your garden with weeds next summer.)

For a price list, send $2 to Filaree Farm, 182 Conconully Highway, Okanogan, WA 98840. Filaree has also published a book called *Growing Great Garlic* ($12.95), by owner Ron Engeland.

Tomatoes— not too cold, not too hot

More than most plants, tomatoes have fairly precise climate tolerances at both the hot and cold ends of the thermometer. Specifically, tomatoes grow best at temperatures between 65° and 80°.

If this month is late in the tomato season where you garden, you're probably thinking about frost. But if tomatoes had minds, they'd be thinking more about 55°, the temperature at which both plants and fruit start to suffer chilling injury. Such injury isn't always visible, but it does make ripe fruit go bad quickly after harvest.

To circumvent or minimize chilling injury, cover tomato plants with plastic

SANTA BARBARA GARDEN *sits above a canyon cloaked with wild vegetation. Lawn is a fire buffer. Tipu trees are pruned for fire safety.*

Landscaping for wildfire safety

Two replacement gardens in burned-over Santa Barbara and Oakland offer valuable landscape lessons for wildfire country

A FEW DAYS AFTER THE DEVASTATING Oakland hills fire of 1991, all that remained of gardens among the still-smoking piles of ash that had once been houses were the blackened skeletons of trees. But now, four years later, gardens are finally starting to overtake the scorched earth. Among them are ones that reflect a new fire-savvy design approach.

Fires like the one that destroyed homes and landscapes in the Oakland hills aren't new to the West. About a year before the Oakland fire, a similar blaze swept through chaparral in the Painted Cave neighborhood of Santa Barbara, destroying many homes in its path. And two and a half years after

when fires break out. And in a hospitable growing climate like Santa Barbara's, it doesn't take the native chaparral long after a fire to regenerate and become a hazard once again.

Now that gardens are coming to life in the burned areas of Oakland and Santa Barbara, we decided to look at how two homeowners—one in each area—approached the task of relandscaping. What approach was best for their areas? What lessons did they learn?

A RIDGETOP GARDEN
IN SANTA BARBARA

"The Painted Cave Fire turned into an event of opportunity. Many homes have been rebuilt in a much more firesafe way, with noncombustible roofs, stucco walls, and plantings that are less dense and more fire-resistant."

> —Charlie Johnson, public information officer for Santa Barbara County Fire Department

Perched above a canyon in the Santa Barbara foothills 7 miles from the fire's origin sits the home of Mary and John Wiemann. The Wiemanns bought the lot— only ¾ mile from their former house—after the fire destroyed the house that had occupied it.

The doomed house was ranch-style with a wood shake roof. Behind it was a wild hillside covered with untamed bougainvillea. Winds propelled the fire through the canyon behind the house, where it fed on brush and jumped onto roofs.

When the Wiemanns purchased the property, fire safety was on their minds. "I can't imagine rebuilding without thinking of fire safety," says Mary. "The fire was just so devastating. I knew the architects would take care of the building because of the new codes. But it was up to us to do something with the landscape."

Fire safety wasn't the only issue on the Wiemanns' minds. They also had to think of water conservation because of the many previous years of water rationing. And the area gets hot, dry winds in summer, so the plants had to be tough.

To design the garden, the Wiemanns hired landscape contractor Adam Graham. In the front yard, Graham used

a combination of fire-resistant and low-fuel-volume plants such as agapanthus, desert spoon, and *Limonium perezii*. *Senecio mandraliscae* is the primary ground cover. Graham intentionally stayed away from highly flammable plants such as junipers and eucalyptus.

Because the front-yard plants require so little supplemental water once established, the Wiemanns were able to justify a large lawn in the backyard. Besides serving as a play area, it acts as a green buffer against fire that might encroach up the canyon. Fire-resistant jade plants and low-fuel-volume perennials grow around its perimeter.

An annual addition of a 3-inch layer of mulch throughout the property inhibits the growth of weeds; grasses and weeds down the back slope are controlled by spraying when necessary.

OAKLAND HILLS GARDEN *combines low-fuel-volume and fire-resistant plants with multilevel patios that create a buffer zone against fire.*

OAKLAND HILLS
MEDITERRANEAN GARDEN

"Relandscaping in the Oakland hills is a balancing act between revegetating the area, restoring the character of the neighborhoods, and fire safety. We encourage the holistic approach—considering the whole site up front, where the house will be placed, and the use of open space, as well as where trees and other plants will be situated."

> —Arnold Mammarella, design review supervisor for the City of Oakland

On October 20, 1991, a contemporary three-story wood house on a steep slope in a well-developed residential area several miles from the start of the fire burned to the ground. The house wasn't surrounded by eucalyptus and pine trees,

Oakland, wildfires swept across the hills of Laguna Beach and Malibu.

"Every square inch of hillside from Northern California to the Mexican border has burned 500 times in the last 10,000 years. That's once every 20 years," says Warner R. McGrew, assistant fire chief and fire marshal for Santa Barbara City Fire Department.

Fire is part of nature's cycle of life in such wild plant communities as chaparral, oak woodland, and forest. Burns clean out dead and diseased plants, help some plant seeds germinate, and play a key role in the evolution of most native plants. But suburban sprawl has intruded on these natural ecosystems, and inevitably, some houses will burn

CURVED TERRACE *with seat walls acts as firesafe buffer zone between the house and the hillside.*

but one large oak was close enough to touch the house.

Landscape architect Robert Koch, who designed the home's original garden, speculates that the fire sped from tree to tree in the neighborhood, and when it reached the house, it ignited the oak and then the structure. Most of the

landscaping—primarily Mediterranean and California native plants—was then only a year old.

"I thought the rosemary would go like a powder keg because of the aromatic oil, but it didn't," says Koch. "French lavender and five kinds of salvia also survived." But not one live tree was left.

When it came time to redesign the garden, Koch worked closely with architect Chris Lamen, who created a much more firesafe house—a rosy Mediterranean stucco villa with a copper roof.

Multilevel terraces covered with cast-stone pavers and surrounded by stucco seat walls create a transition from the stucco house to existing brick terraces.

Koch designed a Mediterranean hill-

side to complement the house. The garden of contrasts blends low-fuel-volume, fire-resistant plants—ceanothus, cistus, echium, euphorbia, lavender, myrtle, and salvia—with lusher, edible plants, such as artichokes, herbs, and peppers.

Koch also brought in large boxed trees—all of which are maintained to reduce fuel volume—and placed them well away from the house for safety. At the top of the slope are four native oaks. Along the south side of the property are half a dozen fruiting olive trees. Across the hill are citrus and strawberry trees (*Arbutus unedo*).

The garden is watered by two parallel drip-irrigation lines: one waters the drought-tolerant plants, the other the thirstier kinds. A third line irrigates the trees. An automatic controller regulates the system. ■

By Lauren Bonar Swezey

How to make your property firesafe

"Surviving a fire is an equation. Defensible space + safe home construction + safe landscaping + easy access for firefighters + residents preparing themselves for fire = survival."
—Warner R. McGrew, assistant fire chief and fire marshal for the City of Santa Barbara

When you make your home more firesafe by changing to fire-resistant roofing materials and boxing in eaves, the changes are permanent. But a safe landscape must be maintained.

Create an area of defensible space (a cleared area where firefighters can safely stand to protect a house threatened by fire) around your house. State laws vary on how much clearance around the house is required. California law specifies a 30-foot clearance around each house in high-fire-hazard areas. But researchers have found that fewer homes would be lost to fire if owners cleared a space of 100 feet for homes on level ground or as much as 400 feet for those on steep slopes, especially if the houses have fire-resistant roofs. In cities such as Santa Barbara, 100 feet is the minimum clearance required.

Such clearances don't mean that the property has to be devoid of plants. You can have a firesafe landscape by altering the arrangement of plants—thinning or sculpting plants and creating distance between them. If you live on a slope, it's important to consider slope stability (consult with a geologist, if necessary).

Step 1: Rearrange your landscape

▶ Within 30 feet of the house, establish and maintain a greenbelt. Give it regular maintenance and adequate water; well-watered plants are less likely to burn. Keep vegetation next to the house shorter than 1½ feet. Trees are a greater risk to homes than shrubs and ground covers.
▶ Eliminate fire ladders—plants of different heights that provide a continuous fuel supply from the ground up into the tree canopy. Prune tree limbs, lower shrubs and thin them, and cut back ground covers.
▶ Eliminate fire pathways—horizontal paths of foliage that allow fires to move quickly from plant to plant—by separating plants.
▶ 30 to 50 feet from the house, create a transition zone. Space clumps of shrubs at least 18 to 20 feet from other shrubs, brush, or structures (leave enough plants to stabilize a slope). Leave only a few well-spaced trees. Plant low-fuel-volume herbaceous perennials such as common yarrow, gazania, and poppy, or low-growing ground covers (as tall as 18 inches) and keep them well watered.
▶ 50 to 200 feet from the house, arrange plants into islands. Make the

distance between shrubs three to five times plant height.
▶ In heavily wooded areas, cut out weak or diseased trees. Remove some healthy ones if necessary to space trees 10 feet apart on level ground and 30 feet apart on steep slopes (41 to 60 percent slope). Control stump sprouting.
▶ Anywhere on the property, avoid planting highly flammable plants such as acacia, California buckwheat, California sagebrush, cedar, chamise, cypress, dry annual grasses, dwarf coyote brush, *Eucalyptus camaldulensis, E. globulus, E. rudis, E. viminalis,* fir, juniper, pampas grass, pine, Scotch broom, scrub oak, Spanish broom, spruce, and yew. Whenever possible, use low-fuel-volume ground covers, perennials, and plants that are reluctant to burn, such as barberry, bush morning glory, *Coprosma kirkii,* cotoneaster, daylily, dwarf pittosporum, gaura, jade plant, myoporum, sedum, vinca, and white trailing ice plant.
▶ Young plants are less likely to burn than mature ones. And low-growing plants inherently have a lower fuel load (the amount of leaves, bark, twigs, and branches—dead or alive—that accumulates in a plant) than tall shrubs and trees.

Step 2: Provide regular landscape maintenance

As needed:
• Clean up leaves and other litter.
• Cut grasses to about 4 inches when they turn brown.
• Remove brush.
• Clean all vegetation from the roof, and clean gutters several times during the year.
• Keep plants near the house watered.
• Work with neighbors to clear common areas and prune heavy vegetation between houses.
Every few years:
• In early spring, prune or mow down low-growing ground covers such as ceanothus. Fertilize and water afterward.
• Periodically cut back native chaparral plants severely.
• Thin crowns of clustered trees to 10 feet apart (don't remove more than 25 percent of foliage, 15 percent for oaks).
• Trim limbs up off the ground at least 10 feet, but preferably 20 feet.
• Cut branches or raise the lower canopy to provide at least a 15-foot clearance from the roof or chimney.
• Prune all dead branches; remove dead plants. All plants are flammable if not pruned periodically. A well-maintained plant has a high live-to-dead fuel ratio, which makes it more firesafe.
• Along driveways, clear out overhanging tree branches and prune bush shrubs for fire truck access.

SHERBET-COLORED GODETIAS *and Sprenger asparagus fern fill vase.*

NORMAN A. PLATE

Glorious godetias

For borders or bouquets, these choice annuals are easy to grow. And they now come in single colors

SATIN SERIES *godetias bloom in foreground; behind is taller Grace Series. In bloom, godetias are dazzling; avoid planting them near flowers in competing colors.*

O LD-FASHIONED FLOWERS LIKE the ones we see in pictures of old cottage gardens are gaining favor once again. Among the most flamboyant of these old-time annual bloomers is godetia (*Clarkia amoena*), also called farewell-to-spring.

You may already know the wild species, a sprawling plant with wiry stems that's native from California to British Columbia. But two much-improved hybrids, called Grace Series and Satin Series godetia, are now available. They produce clusters of vibrantly colored 2-inch-wide flowers on bushy, uniform plants. And unlike older types sold as mixes, these godetias come in individual colors.

We grew them for two seasons in *Sunset*'s Menlo Park, California, test garden and found them to be outstanding performers. Like all godetias, they prefer cool temperatures, so plant them in fall or late winter for late-spring bloom.

GROW TALL ONES FOR CUTTING, SHORT ONES FOR EDGINGS

Plants in the Grace Series were developed for cut flowers; each plant grows 2½ feet tall and produces 15 or so strong flower stems. The numerous flowers on each stem start opening from the top. Cut stems when the first flowers open; other flowers along the stem will open successively.

In our tests, the outer stems tended to flop over. If you want the entire planting to grow upright, stake up the outer stems. Flower colors include lavender, rose pink, shell pink, red, and salmon; you can also buy mixed colors.

Dwarf godetias make up the Satin Series. As pot plants, they grow 7 to 8 inches tall. In *Sunset*'s garden, they grew 10 to 14 inches tall. The stems aren't as long as those in the Grace Series, but you can still get cut flowers. Colors include deep rose, lavender, pink, red with white edge, salmon, white, and mixed.

EXPECT A BRIEF BURST OF COLOR

Sow godetias in the garden in fall, or start seeds in flats between December and February for transplanting to beds in early spring. Because godetia is supposedly difficult to transplant from containers, we tried both methods at *Sunset*. Both plantings were successful. However, when we sowed the seed, germination was spotty. We found godetia easy to transplant, provided that the plants don't become rootbound in the containers and that the rootball is handled gently.

Grow godetias in full sun and well-drained soil (sandy soil is ideal, but not necessary); keep the soil moist. Godetias prefer soil that hasn't been enriched with fertilizers or compost.

Unlike many other annuals that bloom over a long period, godetias spend several months developing green growth. Then, come May, they burst into glorious bloom for about eight weeks. Because of the long period with no bloom, you may want to plant godetias in a border between other flowering plants.

WHERE TO BUY SEEDS

Seeds are available by mail from *Park Seed Co.,* Cokesbury Road, Greenwood, SC 29647; call (800) 845-3369. Packets cost $2.90 plus shipping. ∎

By Lauren Bonar Swezey

Fall is prime time to plant columbines

Choose from more kinds and colors than ever

F ROM SONGBIRDS TO SHOOTING stars, columbines have been compared to all sorts of aerial wonders. When the spring breeze rustles their stems, columbine blooms do seem to flutter like birds and streak like stars.

And now, riding high on the wave of perennial-plant popularity, more kinds of columbines are more widely available than ever. With their lacy, scalloped leaves and nodding flowers, columbines lend a woodland accent to any garden. Plant them to enliven a spring border or to add bursts of color under tall trees.

Columbines grow in all Western climate zones; most kinds do best in filtered sun. Nurseries and seed catalogs give you plenty of choices. Set out plants this month or start seeds now for spring bloom. Columbines are short-lived perennials, but because they self-sow freely, they keep coming back year after year.

WESTERN COLUMBINES
WEAR LONG SPURS

Gardeners first started using columbine in the Old World, where European columbine (*Aquilegia vulgaris*) grows all over the continent and the British Isles. And pretty blue alpine columbine (*A. alpina*) is native to the Alps.

When botanists reached the New World, they struck columbine's genetic mother lode. Unlike the European columbines, which have short spurs, the plentiful native North American species have long spurs and come in a range of rich colors.

From the Southwest comes golden columbine (*A. chrysantha*), whose large yellow flowers grow on 4-foot-tall plants that tolerate drought. If you'd rather have white flowers on the same plant, try 'Silver Queen', one of the longest-flowering columbines. From

CHARLES MANN

LAURIE E. DICKSON

BALANCING ATOP *tall, wiry stems, the long-spurred flowers of hybrid American columbines (above) wave gently in the lightest breeze. At right, pristine white petals of Rocky Mountain columbine stand out against purple-blue sepals.*

Texas and Mexico comes the similar *A. longissima,* whose yellow flowers have drooping 4- to 6-inch spurs (try 'Maxistar', with its extra-large flowers).

In the Rockies, the blue-and-white-flowered Rocky Mountain columbine (*A. caerulea*) is Colorado's state flower. This 12- to 16-inch-tall plant likes filtered sun and moist soil. It comes in a large-flowered version called 'Blue Jay'. For a similar but much smaller Colorado native, try *A. saximontana.*

Western columbine (*A. formosa*), which grows from California and Utah north to Alaska, produces red-and-yellow flowers with red spurs on 1½- to 3-foot plants. For orange-and-yellow flowers, try *A. f. truncata* (also sold as *A. californica*).

Breeders have also produced outstanding long-spurred strains like the 2- to 3-foot-tall McKana Giants, which come in many colors and bloom over a long season, 12-inch-tall Dragonfly, 18-inch Music, 18- to 30-inch Songbird,

30-inch Star, and 3-foot Harlequin. 'Robin', with white-and-rose-pink flowers, is one of the Songbird columbines that is most often sold separately.

If you want to grow short-spurred flowers, try European columbine. Breeders have come up with flowers in whites, reds, bicolors, improved violet shades, and double-flowered forms, and even one with no spurs at all. Look for improved forms such as 'Nora Barlow' (double, spurred).

SEXUAL PECULIARITIES

If all columbines in the garden are from one strain, like McKana Giants, the seed they form will produce offspring pretty much like the parents. All you need to do is cull out poor-quality flowers or those colors that start to dominate the mix.

When more than one kind of columbine grows in the garden, interbreeding complicates the picture. "In no

genus do the species cross more easily," notes the 1956 edition of the *Royal Horticultural Society Dictionary of Gardening.* When different kinds of columbine cross, the children don't usually resemble their parents: they might be better, they might be worse. If you grow American and European columbines together, they'll cross and the European genes will tend to dominate, so over time the long spurs of the American parents will probably shrink, and the flower colors will become washed out.

PLANTING OPTIONS AND SOURCES

Many nurseries and garden centers sell columbine plants in fall and spring. One mail-order specialist that sells them for fall planting is White Flower Farm, Box 50, Litchfield, CT 06759; (800) 503-9624. Its free catalog lists varieties of *A. caerulea, A. chrysantha,* and *A. longissima,* and the hybrids 'Blue Butterflies' and 'Robin'.

Seed companies also offer a variety of columbines. If you scatter seeds over cultivated soil this month, seedlings will come up early next spring. Two seed sources that sell a good selection of columbines are J. L. Hudson, Seedsman, Box 1058, Redwood City, CA 94064 (catalog $1), and Thompson & Morgan, Box 1308, Jackson, NJ 08527, (800) 274-7333 (free catalog).

Once plants are established, give them regular water and light fertilizing after spring growth starts, then again after flowering. When blossoms have faded, you can sometimes force another round of bloom later in the season by cutting back flower stems.

Mildew can be a problem on aging leaves, but there isn't much you can do about it beyond providing good air circulation.

If leaf miners wreak havoc on foliage, try *A. canadensis,* whose graceful red-and-yellow flowers rise on 2- to 3-foot stems. This plant resists the miners. ∎

By Jim McCausland

NORMAN A. PLATE

YOU CAN SEE THE DIFFERENCE *between large-flowered, long-spurred American species and the small-flowered, short-spurred Europeans. The top two flowers are 'Nora Barlow', the three biggest are Dragonfly, the center one is A. alpina, and the two at lower right are A. vulgaris 'Michael Stromminger'.*

BONSAI SPECIMENS *sit on cedar tables and stone columns. A tile-roofed fence gives the garden the look of an old Japanese village.*

JAMES FREDERICK HOUSEL

Stagecraft lessons from a bonsai master

Artful techniques for displaying plants in containers

A PONDEROSA PINE *bows among assorted Japanese maples showing fiery autumn colors.*

HAVING MASTERED BONSAI, THE Japanese art of growing dwarfed plants in containers, Terry Welch of Woodinville, Washington, displays his potted plants using stagecraft worthy of high Kabuki. The techniques Welch uses can be adapted by any gardener who likes to grow plants in containers.

Welch has more than 100 specimens of bonsai, including conifers, Japanese maples, ornamental crabapples, fruiting apples, and rhododendrons.

He showcases plants individually or in groups, placing them at various focal points in the garden or on large display tables. The display tables are made of cedar 4-by-4s and 2-by-4s topped by 1-by-4 planks.

"I move plants around a lot," says Welch, "and bring them forward at their showiest time." This month, for example, he will feature Japanese maples as they blaze with fall color.

To vary the heights of grouped plants, Welch places them on pedestals—large ceramic kiln posts, stone columns, and rounds of weathered wood.

When he arranges bonsai plants in groups, Welch places the small ones up front and the large ones with solid masses of leaves in the back. Plants with contorted shapes or clusters of stems go on higher pedestals and are placed so that their forms don't conflict with those of nearby plants.

Welch places his plants against simple, dark backgrounds, including weathered cedar fences, evergreen hedges like the Japanese holly (*Ilex crenata* 'Convexa') pictured above, and stands of deep green Douglas fir, which make the intricate shapes of bonsai and pots stand out like sculpture against the stark walls of an art gallery.

To keep his plants looking their best, Welch repots them each year in mid-March. He carefully pulls plants from their pots, prunes their roots, and grooms them. He then scrubs the containers and replants, adding some new soil mix from his own potting blend of loam, compost, and pulverized granite.

Welch feeds his plants twice monthly from April through October using water-soluble fertilizers. At the start of each feeding month, he uses an organic fish fertilizer (5-2-2); at midmonth he switches to a complete fertilizer (20-20-20). Plants that produce flowers are fed only a low-nitrogen fertilizer (0-10-10), twice each month in September and October. Conscientious watering is essential. Welch uses a long watering wand with the nozzle set for a soft spray. ■

By Steven R. Lorton

289

A STEEL-JAWED CRANE *hoists a 3,500-pound slab onto a delivery truck at the Marenakos quarry, east of Seattle.*

Bring home a boulder

How to choose and use big rocks for your garden

WITH ALL OF ITS geologic faults, volcanoes, and glaciers, the West is full of rocks. Yet they seldom occur naturally in urban landscapes, so we bring them into our yards—to create rock gardens, to use as strong accents among our plants, and to build walls, paths, and benches.

Quarries and rock yards can provide a surprising variety of decorative rocks, from small flagstones and cobbles to huge boulders and columns.

Put a plant in the wrong place, and you can move it later. Put a 2-ton rock in the wrong place, and you're in big trouble. That's why it's wise to work with a landscape architect, designer, or contractor with plenty of experience in installing rock. And if you live on a sloping lot, you may need to consult a landscape contractor or architect to ascertain the abil-

AT THE QUARRY, *shoppers stalk a pile of boulders weighing between 900 and 1,800 pounds apiece.*

ity of the slope to hold the rocks securely.

SHOPPING FOR ROCKS

To find a rock yard or quarry, or dealers in decorative or landscape rock, look in the yellow pages under Quarries or Rock. At a rock yard, selection is easy: roam

through the yard, flagging the rocks you want with pebbles or colored ribbon. Figure out exactly where each will go in the garden—and which side will go up (taking snapshots of the rocks can help you place them at delivery time). If a rock won't work one way, imagine it with another side up. One of the most beautiful landscape rocks we've seen was stacked in the rock yard alongside the vertical columns, but was used in the garden as a horizontal ledge covered with ornamental thyme.

Most rock is sold by the ton, though some is also sold by shape (slabs and columns, for example). There are also one- and two-man rocks: rocks one or two men can push using 8-foot poles for leverage. A one-man rock weighs 300 pounds or less, a two-man rock as much as 900 pounds. Anything bigger must be handled by machine.

Prices vary widely from city to city. Local fieldstone or slab rock might run $125 per ton, granite boulders $50 to $200 a ton. Basalt or granite columns are usually in the $150 to $300 range for those as tall as 6 feet, more for taller ones. If you want rocks covered with moss or lichen, expect to pay an extra $10 to $20 a ton, but beware: moss doesn't always survive the move from high-mountain canyons to backyard patios, especially when sun exposure and air quality are significantly changed.

Quarries that sell only one kind of rock often have much better prices per ton, but variety is limited.

Many rock yards can grind, cut, polish, and drill rocks to order. They have machines to form birdbaths in the tops of boulders or to drill holes through basalt columns so that they can be used as fountains. Cost depends on the kind and amount of rock involved and the time it takes to do the job.

If you have a sturdy vehicle and need only a modest amount of rock, you can save money by hauling it yourself. Just weigh your vehicle when you go in, then reweigh with the load and pay on your way out.

Any yard can deliver rock in a dump truck, leaving it for you to put in place. Minimum orders (10 tons is common) are often delivered free within a few miles. For bigger rocks, find a yard that has a boom-equipped truck that can not only deliver the load but also dig holes and use the boom to set each rock in place. You'll pay more for this service and about $100 per hour extra for the truck.

IN THE GARDEN, *a landscaper uses a backhoe (above) to place slabs and boulders in predetermined positions. Shovel work (below) finishes the job.*

USING ROCKS IN THE GARDEN

As a general rule, don't put larger rocks on top of smaller ones: unless you do it very artfully, the larger rocks will look unstable. Rocks with flat top surfaces are useful as informal benches or for holding container plants.

Bury the bottoms of rocks in soil to make them look as if they're native and not imports dumped into the landscape. Allow for the settling of large rocks; since the amount of settling can be significant, it takes expertise to know how much to expect—another good reason for working with a landscaping professional.

Rocks look better with time. Scars from transport and handling disappear, and lichen grows if you live where the air is relatively unpolluted. After the lichen has formed a wash over the rock and roughed up its surface, moss may move in if it's native to rocks in your part of the West. ∎

By Jim McCausland

LIGHT UP YOUR GARDEN *with fall-blooming perennials. Clockwise from lower right are diascia, aster, society garlic, Salvia leucantha, Japanese anemone, Salvia azurea grandiflora, and gaura. For details, see page 295.*

NORMAN A. PLATE

292

NOVEMBER

GARDEN
Guide

Fiery foliage and berries for fall bouquets

When clipped and brought indoors, blazing autumn leaves can team up with red or orange berries to create bouquets that celebrate the season. *Sunset* gardener and floral designer Kim Haworth makes casual arrangements like the one pictured at right. She starts with a dark container to set off the foliage. She clips a few branches and berries from the garden, then groups the clippings by color.

The darker colors—from either a bunch of orange leaves or berries—form the bouquet's center. (A V-shaped branch wedged into the container can help support floppy foliage and make floral foam unnecessary.) Haworth surrounds the foliage or berries with clusters of yellow leaves and adds a clump of dark leaves, such as red oak, for an accent.

The following plants yield handsome material for fall bouquets. *For foliage:* Chinese pistache, many grasses (bunch golden seed stalks together like a sheaf of wheat), Japanese maple, *Liquidambar styraciflua*, oakleaf hydrangea, Persian parrotia, persimmon, pin oak, *Pyrus calleryana*, red oak, scarlet oak, and sour gum (tupelo). *For berries:* cotoneaster, holly, pyracantha, and roses that have attractive hips. *For foliage and berries:* Japanese barberry, nandina, and some deciduous cotoneasters.

Casual arrangement lasts about five days in water.

NOVEMBER '95

- Display autumn leaves and berries indoors

- Harvest art from recycled plant scraps

- Moving big rhodies

- New green 'St. Patrick' rose

- Medieval gargoyles for modern gardens

PETER CHRISTIANSEN

PLANTING
OPPORTUNITIES

Spice up the garden with choice fall bloomers

This month, when gardening in other parts of the country is shutting down, perennial gardens throughout much of the West can still be full of colorful flowers—if you grow the right plants. Last November we visited a half-dozen nurseries to find out which plants were still blooming, and we were pleasantly surprised at the large number available (see the photo on page 292).

Some of the color makers listed below put on their best show in the cool fall months. Others start blooming in spring or summer and continue nonstop. To prolong flowering, regularly clip off spent blooms.

Anemone hybrida (Japanese anemone). Maple-like leaves and branching stems 2 to 4 feet tall. White, pink, or rose flowers appear in fall. Partial shade.

Asters. Many kinds. *Aster frikartii* hybrids bloom the longest, from late spring to fall. Plants grow 2 feet tall. Sun.

Diascia vigilis. Spreading perennial to 1½ feet tall with shiny green foliage and light pink flowers. Bloom starts in spring. Sun.

Gaura lindheimeri. Branching flower spikes 2¼ to 4 feet tall bear pink buds that open to white. Sun.

Scabiosa. Starting in spring, *S.* 'Butterfly Blue' and *S.* 'Pink Mist' bloom almost all year, growing 1 to 1½ feet tall. Sun.

Salvia. Many species bloom over a long period. Heights and flower colors vary. Sun.

Tulbaghia violacea (society garlic). Grasslike foliage with pink-lavender flower clusters on foot-long stems through fall. Sun.

THE NATURAL
WAY

Citrus spray controls ants, roaches, and flies

Many homeowners have never had to contend with roaches, but ant invasions seem to be a universal problem. When rains or very hot days come, ants seek shelter indoors. Kitchens are a prime destination.

Many products that claim to stop ants dead in their tracks just don't measure up. Either they don't work as advertised or they're toxic to humans and pets and can't be used around food. If the first rains of winter have brought ants into your house, a new nontoxic insecticide called Bugs 'R' Gone may help to eradicate them.

The active ingredient in this unique product is natural orange peel oil. The citrus oil and the other food-grade ingredients are considered by the Environmental Protection Agency to be safe for use around food, people, and pets, and can even be sprayed around barbecue and picnic areas.

Bugs 'R' Gone works as a contact insecticide: it kills any ant, roach, or fly it hits. The citrus aroma also has some residual effect, so pests won't return.

The product is available in pump sprays at major drugstores, home-improvement centers, and some natural-food stores. Cost ranges from $3 for 8 ounces to $15 for a gallon.

PLANTING
TECHNIQUES

Tips for growing Japanese maple in Northern California

When Japanese maple leaves blaze with fall color, it's tough to resist taking one of these glorious trees home from the nursery. But once you have a tree, where will you plant it? If in the right location, Japanese maple (*Acer palmatum*) grows well in Northern California. If not—especially in hotter areas (zone 14 and parts of 15)—the tree may be plagued with problems, including leafburn and verticillium wilt.

Nurseries sell two types of Japanese maple. Seedling trees are usually tougher and better able to withstand heat and strong sunlight. Named varieties, usually ones with finely cut leaves or distinctly colored foliage, are a little more delicate.

Seedling trees can withstand the most sunlight, but all Japanese maples really prefer filtered sun for at least some of the day, ideally in the afternoon. Many named varieties will develop scorched leaves if given anything more than a few hours of morning sunlight.

Which conditions increase your chances for success with a Japanese maple? Planting near a lawn, where frequently run sprinklers increase humidity, helps reduce chances of leafburn. If the light is right and plants still get leafburn, salts from your irrigation water may be building up. Leach them out with an especially heavy irrigation every three or four waterings.

Japanese maples also need good drainage and prefer soil on the acid side. Fill the planting hole with water, let it drain, then repeat. If water remains in the hole after 24 hours, plant in containers or raised beds. Otherwise, verticillium wilt—a soilborne disease—can set in.

Once the trees are established, water regularly, and never allow the soil to dry out completely.

Recycle plant scraps to art

Using dry vines, leaves, berries, and greens that most gardeners consign to the compost heap, Nita Jensen concocts extraordinary decorations for display in and outside her house in Yelm, Washington.

The artful recycling started one fall as she was trying to figure out how to get rid of tough old pumpkin vines. She formed the vines into wreaths and dried them, and everybody who saw them wanted one. This initial success led Jensen to experiment with other vines and plant parts.

Her simple techniques have as much to do with seeing the beauty in natural things as in arranging them. Here are her favorite materials and the techniques she uses to arrange them.

Grassy leaves and vines. The best of these include bean vines, Siberian iris leaves, and daylily leaves, all of which are brown and stringy now. They form best when they're wet. Rinse them in warm water, then twist them into a kind of vegetable twine for tying into bows. They dry to the form they were in while wet. These are perfect for tying off bunches of berries, woody stems, and green leaves.

Scotch broom also fits loosely into this category. Collect its soft green stems, then rinse and form them.

Woody vines and twigs. Grapevines wind well into wreaths and swags that go over windows, fireplace mantels, or mirrors. The woody vines are stiff enough to hold a shape by themselves. Red first-year maple twigs and small branches look best bunched, tied off, and put into vases for vertical tabletop arrangements.

Fruits and berries. Cranberry-colored barberries and hawthorn (both wild and domestic kinds), orange-red rose hips, and white snowberries all add color to arrangements and hold up well. No work is involved beyond cutting branches that are thick with berries and occasionally watering the containers that hold them.

Greens. The leaves of Oregon grape (*Mahonia aquifolium*) hold their fresh, glossy, hollylike look well. Gray dusty miller leaves are a good, long-lasting contrast. To keep these fresh, Jensen puts sprigs into miniature vases filled with water.

For a green background, nothing beats moss brought in from the Jensens' riverbank. The moss can be used in arrangements with plants or formed into wreaths. To make moss wreaths hold their shape, Jensen starts with wire wreath blanks from a florist. Baby fern leaves poke out of the moss, which conceals the water-filled small glass containers that keep the ferns fresh.

A bean-vine wreath and a swag on the windowsill (bottom left) are accented by bright rose hips. A ceramic pot (above) features dusty miller, rose hips, and Oregon grape.

THE NATURAL WAY

This vine maple has earned a name for itself

The Pacific Northwest's native vine maple (*Acer circinatum*) displays an amazing range of forms, varying in height, leaf color and size, and bark color and texture. Surprisingly, though, only one named variety of vine maple is available: *A. c.* 'Monroe'. This small tree grows to 15 to 25 feet high (occasionally taller if grown in deep shade). Its deeply lobed leaves are reminiscent of those of fernleaf fullmoon maple (*A. japonicum* 'Aconitifolium'). With its open form and lacy branches, *A. c.* 'Monroe' makes an attractive canopy for ferns and other plants that do well in light shade. Grow this maple in rich, acid soil with good drainage.

You'll find *A. c.* 'Monroe' is sometimes sold at arboretum and plant society sales as well as specialty nurseries. A good mail-order source is Forestfarm, 990 Tetherow Rd., Williams, OR 97544-9599; (503) 846-7269. Plants in 1-gallon cans cost $19 each, plus shipping; catalog is $3.

Antifreeze for roses

Milo Ball of Spokane loves growing hybrid tea roses, and even in Spokane's cold, harsh climate, he's never lost one to freeze. His trick will work anywhere in the cold-winter Northwest (*Sunset Western Garden Book* climate zones 1–3), with any size rose bed.

Ball grows his roses in a large, circular bed. In early November, when temperatures start to drop, he has a load of topsoil dumped at his garden. After cutting back the plants to a height of about 19 inches, he mounds the topsoil over the bed until an 18-inch-deep layer covers the roses.

The plants stay buried through the winter. Then, beginning in late March, when night temperatures are unlikely to dip much below 25°, Ball gradually shovels off the soil over a two-week period, removing about one-third of the layer at a time, so that the plants acclimate slowly. He spreads the soil over other beds throughout his garden. With the soil removed, he finishes the pruning job on the roses, cutting them back to 6 to 8 inches in height. This pruning, coupled with the plants' exposure to light and warm temperatures, causes them to zoom into active growth.

Apple canker: it's payback time

Rotting out patches of trunk bark and girdling twigs and branches, various apple cankers weaken and often kill apple trees. If your trees have canker, now is the time for treatment.

Start by pruning cankered branches, cutting a few inch-es below (toward the trunk from) the cankers. Make each cut about ¼ inch above a side branch. Then burn or dispose of all infected prunings.

Next, go to work on large branches—those whose cankers cover less than a third of the branch's diameter. Cut away the bark over the cankered area with a good knife, scraping down to clean, light-colored sapwood. Finally, burn the scraped area lightly with a small propane torch. As an alternative, use the torch to do the whole job, burning through the infected bark and down to sapwood.

Spray the tree with fixed copper before fall rains set in. It will stop new canker spores from entering the tree through fresh leaf scars and places where the bark has been broken or injured. (If it rains before the spray has dried on the tree, spray again as soon as the weather clears.) Spray one last time when leaf drop is mostly complete.

Moving a big rhody to a new home

If there is a big, cherished rhododendron in your garden but it's in the wrong place, this is the month to move it. You may be able to do this job by hand (with a hardy team), or you may want to rent a backhoe and forklift or even hire a professional service to do it. Whatever strategy you choose, the transplanting techniques are the same.

Dig the new hole first. It should be at least 1½ times larger than the projected rootball but only deep enough so that the top of the rootball will be even with the surrounding ground after the hole is backfilled with soil.

Keeping the rootball intact, gardeners use an aluminum skid to slide this large rhododendron into a new location at Hendricks Park in Eugene, Oregon..

MICHAEL THOMPSON

Next, dig around the drip line of the plant; then start excavating under the rootball. You may have to rock the plant back and forth gently as you dig. Once the ball is free, lift and move it gingerly to the new hole. It's often a good idea to set the rootball on a heavy canvas tarp so you can slide it along. A soft rope tied around the base of the trunk may help you with the pulling.

Set the plant in the new hole. Fill the space around the rootball with good, loose, organically rich soil. Water the plant deeply by setting a sprinkler under its canopy and letting the water run until the soil is thoroughly soaked. Do not fertilize the plant for a year. A layer of mulch, several inches thick over the surface of the soil, will help protect the roots from freezing and conserve moisture. Keep the plant well watered for at least two summers until it is established.

Newsletter for native-plant lovers

"**W**e Californians don't have the water, the time, or the money to continue the horticultural pretense that we live in northern Europe," says Louise Lacey, publisher of the newsletter *Growing Native.* "Using California native plants in our gardens would create savings in all those categories. Plus, it provides the gratification that comes from healing a piece of the earth."

But native plants are still a tough sale with gardeners. "People are intimidated by natives because they don't know how to use them or care for them," says Lacey.

Lacey is changing all that. Her newsletter covers such basic topics as pruning natives, growing ceanothus, and sources for native bulbs, plants, and seeds, as well as offbeat subjects such as bonsai natives and naturalizing natives around a pool.

A subscription costs $30 a year for six issues. First-time subscribers receive a free 20-page booklet packed with information on natives, as well as a packet of California wildflower seeds to grow for cutting. For details, write or call *Growing Native,* Box 489, Berkeley, CA 94701; (510) 232-9865.

Catproofing house trees

If you have both an indoor tree and a house cat, you'll come to dread a certain *scratch-scratch-scratching* sound. But if you cover the bare soil around the base of the tree, you're not likely to hear that sound again.

The best soil cover is polished river rock (fist-size stones are best).

For living ground covers, there are two approaches. Plant the soil surface with trailing house plants like ivy (English, Swedish, or grape), pothos, or creeping Charlie. Keep them off the crown of the tree (the place where the trunk emerges from the soil)

or you may set up conditions that encourage crown rot.

A second approach is more popular with interior plantscaping companies: when you pot your house tree, leave about a 4-inch clearance from the soil surface to the top of the pot's rim. Fill the space by setting potted kalanchoes or other potted flowering house plants atop the soil. This keeps roots of tree and ground covers apart, so you can repot or replace either without affecting the other.

Gargoyles in the landscape?

In medieval times, grotesque figures of animals and humans were thought to repel evil spirits. That's why gargoyles have embellished the walls, balconies, and buttresses of such majestic cathedrals as Notre-Dame de Paris for centuries. In their latest reincarnation, gargoyles have become landscape art.

Spitting gargoyle, 17 inches tall, perches pensively.

A 4-year-old American firm, Design Toscano, sells reproductions of European gargoyles in plaster (for indoor use), marble, and resin-based synthetics that will stand up to sun, frost, and rain.

Prices run from about $20 for a dwarf gargoyle (6 inches tall) to $1,075 for a giant gargoyle (47½ inches tall). For a free catalog, write or call Design Toscano, 17 E. Campbell St., Arlington Heights, IL 60005; (800) 525-0733.

'St. Patrick' rose bears yellow flowers flushed with green.

A new blushing green rose

They wouldn't name you 'St. Patrick' if you didn't wear a shade of green, now would they? And sure as there are shamrocks, the 1996 All-America Rose Selections winner bearing this name wears this hue— or comes close anyway. The large, pointed buds of this new hybrid tea are bright chartreuse. The open flowers are more of a yellow-gold, especially early in the season. But they too can take on a greenish cast when temperatures rise, particularly in areas with torrid summers. Its cool gray-green foliage is a handsome foil for the vivid flowers.

Another distinction of 'St. Patrick' is that it was hybridized by an amateur, Frank Strickland of Riverside, California, from 'Brandy' and 'Gold Medal'.

'St. Patrick' will start appearing in retail nurseries this month. If you can't find it, ask your local nursery to contact Weeks Roses, the wholesale growers who introduced the variety, at (800) 992-4409.

Choose roses when they're blooming

The best way to shop for roses is to see them in bloom. And in Southern California, the late fall flush

of bloom in public gardens lets you "window shop" before bare-root planting season arrives.

Good places to see large, well-labeled rose collections include A. C. Postel Memorial Rose Garden, Mission Historical Park, adjacent to Old Mission Santa Barbara in Santa Barbara; the Victorian Rose Garden, Arboretum of Los Angeles County, 301 N. Baldwin Avenue, Arcadia; International Rosarium, Descanso Gardens, 1148 Descanso Drive, La Cañada–Flintridge; and the Rose Garden at the Huntington Botanical Gardens, 1151 Oxford Road, San Marino.

By Sharon Cohoon, Steven R. Lorton, Jim McCausland, Lauren Bonar Swezey, Lance Walheim

PLANTING

❏ **BULBS.** If you haven't planted spring-flowering bulbs yet, there's still time to get them into the ground. In addition to such obvious choices as crocus, daffodils, and tulips, consider planting ornamental allium, anemones, freesias, and scilla.

❏ **EVERGREENS.** Now that most deciduous leaves have dropped, it's a good time to add evergreens to the landscape. Nurseries sell a wide assortment of evergreen trees and shrubs in containers. Put them in the ground immediately if the soil isn't too soggy to dig.

❏ **HARDY FLOWERS.** Sow seeds of hardy annuals like candytuft, clarkia, larkspur, and linaria, as well as wildflower mixes. Fall-sown seeds will germinate and flower earlier than the same seeds sown in spring.

❏ **PEONIES.** In zones 4–7, herbaceous and tree peonies can go into rich, well-amended soil now for bloom next spring and summer.

MAINTENANCE

❏ **CUT BACK MUMS.** When the last flowers fade, cut back chrysanthemum plants to within 6 inches of the ground. They'll send up new shoots in spring.

❏ **DIG SUMMER BULBS.** Dig dahlias, glads, and any other summer bulbs you don't plan to leave in the ground all win-

Vancouver • / BRITISH COLUMBIA
Victoria ☆
Spokane •
● Seattle
WASHINGTON
☆
Olympia
● Yakima
Portland ●
Pendleton ●
☆
Salem
OREGON
Bend ●
Eugene ●
Sunset
Western Garden Book
CLIMATE ZONES
Medford ●
❏ 1-3   ■ 4-7

ter. Remove the excess dirt, then store them in a frost-free place.

❏ **GROOM LAWNS.** Take advantage of the few dry, warm days this month to cut and groom the lawn.

❏ **MAKE COMPOST.** As you clean up the garden for winter, put *almost* everything on the compost pile (put garden monsters like morning glory and deadly nightshade in the garbage can). Chop up large or coarse prunings and corn-

stalks. Turn plant debris into the pile, and wet it down well.

❏ **MULCH.** At month's end, after you've pruned and groomed perennial and shrub beds, spread a 3- to 4-inch layer of mulch around plants. Use a thicker layer over tender-rooted plants.

❏ **PRUNE SHRUBS, TREES.** Remove dead, diseased, and injured wood first, along with closely parallel and crossing branches. Before proceeding, step back and eye the plant for form. Don't get carried away—you can always take more branches off later, but you can't put them back on.

❏ **ROOT-PRUNE POTTED PLANTS.** As most house plants and outdoor container plants head into dormancy this month, it's a good time to knock plants out of their pots, untangle the roots, and cut back the big ones. In most cases, you can trim large roots back by a third. Use pruners or a sharp knife. Massage the rootball with your fingers to loosen it and remove some of the old soil. Then repot the plant with fresh potting mix, and water it well.

PEST CONTROL

❏ **CONTROL CANKER.** If your apple, apricot, peach, or pear trees had canker problems last year, rake up fallen leaves and twigs, and send them out with the trash. Then apply fixed-copper spray. See page 297 for more information.

My conscientious son, John, had scolded me a hundred times: "Dad, wear safety glasses when you mow." But I didn't. Then last fall, while I was giving the lawn its final clip, I heard a screech and saw a round, brown something rocketing at me. The next thing I remember is sitting in the emergency room of Skagit Valley Hospital unable to see with my left eye. A stick about 4 inches long and big around as a broom handle had directly struck my eye. Mercifully, my eyelid closed before the stick hit, and there was no puncture. I was bandaged, given pain pills, and sent home to bed. My sight began to return the next morning. It was a frightening and thoroughly humbling experience.

I've learned my lesson: whenever I mow now, I reach for one of the pairs of safety glasses that fill a bucket in my storage shed—clear goggles with straps, wraparound glasses in clear plastic, black-framed spectacles with safety lenses. They cost between $3 and $6 a pair, sometimes less, depending on the style. I feel naked without them now.

•

The magic and mystery of orchid growing comes to life when the Oregon Orchid Society puts on its annual Fall Orchid Show and Sale in

PACIFIC NORTHWEST
Garden Notebook
BY STEVEN R. LORTON

the Cloverleaf Building of the Washington County Fair Complex in Hillsboro. After viewing the profusion of orchids on display, you may find it hard to leave empty-handed. If you're a beginner, you will find that no orchid is easier to grow than the cymbidium. If you buy plants now, they will produce their bold flower spikes indoors during late winter and early spring.

THAT'S A GOOD QUESTION

Q: Why are garden tools often made in such hideous fluorescent colors?

A: I used to think the same thing, so I bought a couple of trowels with handsome natural wood handles. And like any gardener, I'd be working with a trowel, then lay it down to do something else. I've spent hours looking among plants for my elegant trowels. But no problem with the red-, yellow-, and blue-handled tools. I can spot them a hundred yards off. On some rainy winter day, I'll sand the wooden handles of my stylish tools and give them a couple coats of red paint. It will preserve the wood, and I won't have any trouble finding them next year.

CHECKLIST
NOVEMBER

PLANTING

☐ **PLANT GARLIC.** Choose a site in full sun with well-drained soil. If your soil is heavy and poorly drained, plant in raised beds. Mix in plenty of compost. Plant cloves of artichoke (the common white type), elephant, and rocambole garlic about 2 inches deep.

☐ **PLANT FOR PERMANENCE.** Zones 14–17: November is a good time to plant cold-hardy ground covers, shrubs, trees, and vines. Wait until spring to set out tender plants, such as bougainvillea, mandevilla, and princess flower. Bare-root roses and trees start appearing in nurseries next month: plan ahead and determine what your garden needs. Make sure to choose a tree that will fit your garden space.

☐ **PLANT PERENNIALS.** Zones 14–17: Nurseries have a wide assortment in sixpacks, and in 4-inch and 1-gallon containers. Choices include artemisia, campanula, catmint, columbine, coral bells, dead nettle (*Lamium*), delphinium, Oriental poppy, penstemon, perennial foxglove (*Digitalis mertonensis*), phlox, salvia, and species geraniums.

☐ **SOW WILDFLOWERS.** Zones 14–17: For spring bloom, choose a mix suited to your climate (available in many seed catalogs) or buy individual kinds and develop your own color combinations. You can also buy mixes for specific purposes, such as attracting butterflies or beneficial insects. Scatter seeds in well-prepared soil; lightly rake them in.

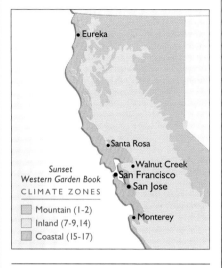

Sunset Western Garden Book
CLIMATE ZONES
☐ Mountain (1-2)
☐ Inland (7-9,14)
☐ Coastal (15-17)

MAINTENANCE

☐ **COMPOST.** Start a simple compost pile by layering greens (grass and weeds without seedheads) with browns (straw, dried leaves). Or build a simple wire bin: bend a 4-foot-high piece of 12- to 14-gauge wire fencing into a cylinder about 4 feet across and hook the cut edges together. To fill, alternate 1- to 1½-foot layers of garden debris with 2- to 3-inch layers of soil. Sprinkle nitrogen fertilizer every 1½ feet. Keep the pile evenly moist, and aerate it by turning it every two weeks or so.

☐ **DIVIDE DAHLIA TUBERS.** Withhold water to allow plants to go dormant. Then dig them carefully with a spading fork; trim away brown foliage and most of the stems, and brush off soil. Allow to dry for a few hours before storing or dividing. To divide, use a sharp knife to cut each clump into sections; include an inch of stem and an eye with each division. Discard soft or diseased tubers. Store in peat moss or sand.

☐ **FEED CITRUS.** Zones 14–17: During winter, apply citrus food monthly. Nonstressed, well-watered trees are hardier, according to Don Dillon, a nurseryman who specializes in citrus.

☐ **FEED LAWNS.** Zones 14–17: If you haven't already done so this fall, or if the fertilizer you're using requires a second application (check label), feed lawns now with a granular lawn food formulated for use in winter (nutrients are released in small amounts while growth is slow).

☐ **STAKE TREES.** Trees grow stronger trunks if left unstaked, but trunks with leaning tops and those planted in very windy areas need support. To determine how high to place ties, move your hand up the trunk until the treetop straightens (if it's not bent, place tie about two-thirds up the trunk). Tie tree to stakes with commercial ties, or use wire or rope covered by hose or tubing. Check ties periodically to make sure they're not digging into the trunk; loosen if necessary. Remove when the tree can support itself.

W hen it comes to gardening, I'm a strong believer in the adage "Cleanliness is next to godliness." That sounds extreme, but when you avoid spraying toxic pesticides, as I do, sanitation is especially important.

Many garden troublemakers, such as codling moth and brown rot, spend the winter on crop debris or on alternative hosts such as weeds. Unless you clean up the debris, they can attack next year's crops. For instance, if your peach tree has shown signs of brown rot (sunken cankers on twigs, sticky brown droplets oozing from bark and dead flowers, and rotted fruit covered with gray spores), clean up the tree and the soil around it before the first fall rains. This will make the disease less likely to spread, so you may not need to spray.

This fall, make it a priority to clean up garden debris everywhere. Rake up leaves, clear out weeds, clean out dead plants from the vegetable garden, and remove prunings from the garden. All of this material can be composted if the pile gets hot enough (160°) to kill the pests. If not, bag and discard the debris.

•

One of my favorite shade plants for foliage texture is *Brunnera macrophylla*. The 1½-foot-tall plant produces dark green heart-

NORTHERN CALIFORNIA
Garden Notebook
BY LAUREN BONAR SWEZEY

shaped leaves that can reach 9 inches across. In spring, blue flowers similar to those of forget-me-nots appear on long stems. Because brunnera self-sows readily (but is easily controlled), plant two or three plants and soon you'll have a lovely large-textured ground cover. If you don't want the seedlings, dig them up and pass them along to gardening friends.

THAT'S A GOOD QUESTION

Q: Why do all the experts say that fall is supposed to be the best time to plant trees and shrubs?

A: Fall is the best time to plant hardy (not frost-tender) trees and shrubs because summer heat is past and plants have enough mild weather ahead to become established. The soil temperature is still warm, which encourages root growth. As cold air and short days arrive, top growth slows, but roots continue to grow. Winter rains should arrive to irrigate plants. By the time spring comes, the plants, supported by strong root systems, are ready to burst into growth.

When a shrub or tree is planted in spring, roots get off to a slow start because of cool soil, and top growth is limited until roots can supply the plant with moisture and nutrients.

MAINTENANCE

☐ **CLEAN UP.** Pull up what's left of summer's annuals and vegetables. Rake leaves. Except for weeds that have gone to seed, add all plant debris to the compost pile. Prune dead or broken branches from shrubs and trees. Thorough cleanup will eliminate hiding places for earwigs, slugs, snails, and sowbugs, as well as overwintering spots for fungus diseases.

☐ **DIG CORMS AND TUBERS.** If you haven't already, lift dahlia and begonia tubers and gladiolus corms. Trim remaining dead stems or leaves, brush off soil, and store in a cool, dry place.

☐ **FERTILIZE.** Feed cool-season annuals and vegetables that you set out last month; use a high-nitrogen fertilizer. If ground covers, shrubs, or trees didn't grow well last summer, or had poorly colored foliage, fertilize with a high-nitrogen food. Fertilize bluegrass, fescue, or rye grass lawns if you haven't already done so this fall, or make a second application now if one is necessary (check the fertilizer package).

PEST AND WEED CONTROL

☐ **CONTROL DISEASES.** To avoid peach leaf curl, rake fallen leaves and remove old fruits from peach and nectarine trees. Then thoroughly spray with fixed copper (with the highest percentage of copper you can find) or lime sulfur.

PLANTING

☐ **FIGHT EROSION AND FLOODING.** On slopes and hillsides, especially

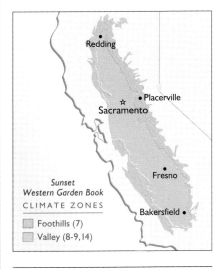

Redding

• Placerville
Sacramento ☆

• Fresno

Bakersfield •

*Sunset
Western Garden Book*
CLIMATE ZONES
☐ Foothills (7)
☐ Valley (8-9,14)

where wildfires struck this year, sow seed of annual and perennial rye grass.

☐ **PLANT ANNUALS.** This is the last opportunity to set out winter annuals. Choices include African daisy (*Dimorphotheca*), calendula, English and fairy primroses, Iceland poppy, pansies, snapdragon, stock, sweet alyssum, sweet William, violas, and wallflowers.

☐ **PLANT FOR PERMANENCE.** It's not too late to plant most ground covers, shrubs, and trees. In fact, if you're looking for plants with fall color, this is a great month to shop; many will be at

their peak. But wait until December for bare-root roses, trees, and vines to arrive in nurseries; wait until spring to plant cold-tender plants, such as citrus.

☐ **PLANT BULBS, CORMS, AND TUBERS.** Many nurseries still have the most common spring-flowering bulbs.

☐ **PLANT LAWNS.** There is still time to sow seed or lay sod of cool-season grasses. Keep in mind that this winter's new lawn will be next summer's water guzzler. Consider reducing turf areas to conserve water. Or replace lawn altogether with unthirsty ground covers.

☐ **PLANT PERENNIALS.** Nurseries have a wide assortment in sixpacks and pots. Selections include alyssum, basket-of-gold, campanula, columbine, coral bells, coreopsis, delphinium, dianthus, English daisy, gaillardia, gloriosa daisy, oriental poppy, penstemon, phlox, and salvia.

☐ **PLANT VEGETABLES.** Wait until January to plant most cool-season vegetables. But you can sow peas and spinach, and plant garlic and onions.

☐ **SOW HARDY ANNUALS.** For spring bloom, start seeds of bachelor's button, clarkia, forget-me-not, Johnny-jump-up, linaria, pansy, and sweet alyssum.

☐ **SOW WILDFLOWERS.** Sow wildflower seed now and let winter rains bring up plants. First, prepare the soil by watering to bring up weed seeds, then kill the weeds by hoeing or using a contact herbicide. Then broadcast the wildflower seed and lightly rake it into the soil. Wait for rains to water it in.

November brings great weather for lingering outdoors, so this is the month I work hard to grow my soil. I'm a firm believer that soil is a living thing, teeming with earthworms, microbes, and insects, good and bad. Together with mineral particles and remnants of living plants, they create a complex biology crucial to the health of all plants growing in it.

I start by adding the food—organic matter. My compost pile is ripe for harvest after a summer of adding garden debris. But that runs out quickly, so I buy a few bags of steer manure and maybe get a load of compost from a recycling specialist or landscape supply yard.

I throw down several inches of compost wherever there's space. In open beds, I work it in deep with a shovel. Around existing plants, I lightly cultivate it in with a trowel. Once in place, the organic matter has the winter to break down and replenish the ground that has worked hard for months, yielding wonderful color and a bountiful harvest.

November is also the best month to plant cover crops in open beds, another way to pay back the soil. I prefer a mixture of plants, usually some fava beans, a vetch, and maybe some clover. They add nutrients to the soil through nitrogen fixation and provide organic

CENTRAL VALLEY
Garden Notebook
BY LANCE WALHEIM

matter when I rotary-till them into the ground in spring.

•

Consider anything vertical as a possible support for sweet peas. Planted from seed early this month, they'll need little care until spring. Plants need to hold onto something narrow, such as string or wire. So tie strings to the tops of light posts, fences, or other elevated points. Then tie the other ends of the strings to small stakes and plant beside them. Spring will have never smelled so good.

THAT'S A GOOD QUESTION

Q: Can I fertilize my trees and shrubs this month, or should I wait until spring?

A: It depends on the kinds of plants. The roots of most plants, including hardy deciduous trees and shrubs, continue to absorb nutrients even when the tops have begun to go dormant. So if you fertilize the first week or two of November, the plants will absorb the nutrients needed for a healthy burst of growth in spring.

It's probably better to wait to feed less hardy plants such as citrus and bougainvillea. The late nitrogen can cause an early flush of tender growth that could be especially frost sensitive.

CHECKLIST
NOVEMBER

PLANTING

☐ **CONTINUE TO PLANT BULBS.** Plant any spring-flowering bulb that doesn't require prechilling now. Choices include anemones, daffodils, grape hyacinth, ranunculus, scilla, and species tulips. South African bulbs such as freesia, ixia, sparaxis, and watsonia are well suited to our climate and naturalize readily here. Hustle to plant them, though, if you garden in the high desert (zone 11).

☐ **CHILL BULBS.** Put bulbs of Dutch hyacinth and tulips in the refrigerator crisper six weeks or more before planting (see page 268).

☐ **PLANT COOL-SEASON VEGETABLES.** Try arugula, beets, bok choy, broccoli, brussels sprouts, cabbages, carrots, cauliflower, chard, collards, garlic, kale, leeks, lettuce, onions, peas, radicchio, radishes, spinach, and turnips.

☐ **PLANT WINTER, EARLY-SPRING ANNUALS.** Coastal, inland and low-desert gardeners (zones 22–24, 18–21, and 13, respectively) can set out calendula, Iceland and Shirley poppies, larkspur, nemesia, pansies, snapdragon, stock, and other early-blooming annuals. For shady areas, try cineraria, primrose, and cyclamen.

☐ **SHOP FOR BIENNIALS.** Showy cottage-garden favorites—foxglove, Canterbury bells, hollyhock, and Queen Anne's lace—do best if planted in late fall. They will establish roots before soil temperatures drop, and be ready to bloom on schedule come spring.

Sunset
Western Garden Book
CLIMATE ZONES
☐ 1-3   ☐ 11
☐ 13   ☐ 14-24

☐ **SOW WILDFLOWER SEEDS.** Broadcast seeds by hand over weed-free soil. Rake the area lightly to cover seeds with soil. Wait for rain, or water seeds yourself. Keep the soil consistently moist until seeds germinate and winter rains take over.

MAINTENANCE

☐ **CLEAN UP.** As summer annuals and vegetables decline, pull and toss them into the compost bin. Remove decaying flowers and leaves from beneath perennials and shrubs to eliminate hiding places for slugs, snails, and sowbugs.

☐ **TUNE UP TOOLS.** Get hardworking shovels, hoes, and cultivators back in shape by cleaning and smoothing the steel parts with fine-grade sandpaper or steel wool. Rub with a well-oiled rag to ward off rust.

☐ **TEND CHRYSANTHEMUMS.** Support still-blooming plants with stakes and ties. After bloom, cut back plants, leaving 6-inch stems. Lift and divide old clumps; cut roots apart and discard woody centers, then replant.

☐ **PRUNE CANE BERRY PLANTS.** Old canes of blackberry, boysenberry, and loganberry should be cut back to the ground. Leave the new, smooth-barked canes that grew this year to bear fruit next year. Wait until December or January to cut back the canes of low-chill raspberries.

PEST AND WEED CONTROL

☐ **MANAGE CABBAGEWORMS.** The white butterflies flitting through your cabbage patch are laying eggs that will hatch into leaf-chomping caterpillars. Control damage by using floating row covers to exclude the butterflies. Or spray the uncovered plants with *Bacillus thuringiensis*, focusing the spray carefully on the cabbageworm larvae.

☐ **CONTROL SNAILS AND SLUGS.** Handpick snails in the early evening or morning. Or use barriers (row covers or copper stripping), baits, or traps. Pay special attention to seedlings and tender-leafed plants; these are favorite foods for snails.

November used to be a dull, between-seasons period in my garden, but now that I've seen gardens of the masters, I know what mine's been missing. What theirs have and mine doesn't—and yours may lack, too—is an abundance of fall bloomers. These plants are not as easy to find as spring bloomers, but they're well worth the search.

One I'm going to add this year is *Aloysia virgata*. Picture a tall (up to 12 feet), narrow shrub covered with white panicles that look like Veronica 'Icicle' but smell like Johnson's baby powder. I've seen it. I've inhaled it. I must have it.

Other fall-blooming temptations: pumpkin-orange *Gladiolus primulinus* (*G. dalenii*), *Salvia* 'Costa Rica Blue', white-flowered, freesia-scented *Buddleia asiatica*, magenta-flowered *Hypoestes aristata*, and *Ruellia macrantha*, a compact shrub covered from fall through spring with bright pink flowers.

●

The Gardening Angels, a group of volunteers dedicated to educating children about gardening, have put in 82 garden projects in Los Angeles County schools. But a lot more schools are on the waiting list, and more volunteers are sorely needed. Gardening expertise isn't necessary. All potential Angels need is a love for children and a will-

SOUTHERN CALIFORNIA
Garden Notebook
BY SHARON COHOON

ingness to commit 1 to 2 hours a week for 12 to 14 weeks. Call (213) 744-4341 for details.

●

Once leather gloves get wet or muddy, they become too stiff for comfort. Cotton gloves don't last. Mud Gloves—cotton gloves coated with latex rubber—are just right. They keep your hands dry, your fingernails don't pop through them after two wearings, you can wash them, and they're only $7.95 a pair. If you can't find them locally, call Gardener's Supply Company at (800) 444-6417.

THAT'S A GOOD QUESTION

Q: Do I dig up my dahlias now or not?

A: If dahlias have excellent drainage, you don't have to dig and divide them until they become overcrowded, unless the ground freezes. But tubers left in heavy soil can rot during winter rains. Merle Robboy of Corona del Mar, a dahlia enthusiast for 30 years, digs and divides his dahlias in late November. He finds that blossoms are usually more spectacular if he replants the tubers every year. Other growers lift dahlias now but wait for eyes to sprout in February before dividing. Each dahlia division needs at least one eye, and eyes can be difficult to identify on dormant tubers.

CHECKLIST
NOVEMBER

PLANTING

❑ **BULBS.** In cold-winter zones 1–3, 10, and 11, plant spring-flowering bulbs immediately. In zones 12 and 13, prechill crocus, hyacinths, and tulips for six weeks in the refrigerator (see page 268).

❑ **ANNUALS.** In sunny places in zones 12 and 13, plant ageratum, aster, bells-of-Ireland, calendula, candytuft, clarkia, cornflower, foxglove, larkspur, lobelia, painted daisy, petunia, phlox, snapdragon, stock, sweet alyssum, and sweet pea. In shady places, set out dianthus, English daisy, pansy, primrose, and viola.

❑ **HARDY TREES, SHRUBS.** Zones 12 and 13: plant acacia, cassia, *Cordia boissieri*, desert spoon, fairy duster, mesquite, oleander, palo verde, *Salvia greggii*, and Texas ranger.

❑ **VEGETABLES.** Zones 12 and 13: put in asparagus, beets, broccoli, brussels sprouts, cabbage, carrots, cauliflower, celery, endive, garlic, kale, kohlrabi, leeks, lettuce, mustard, oriental vegetables, parsley, peas, radish, spinach, Swiss chard, and turnips.

❑ **OVERSEED BERMUDA LAWNS.** Zones 12 and 13: mow Bermuda grass at about ½ inch, then overseed with 10 to 20 pounds of annual or perennial ryegrass per 1,000 square feet.

❑ **WILDFLOWERS.** Sow seeds of spring-flowering wildflowers in cultivated beds, water well, and pull weeds.

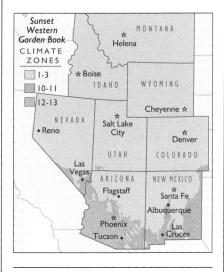

Sunset Western Garden Book CLIMATE ZONES

1-3
10-11
12-13

MAINTENANCE

❑ **CULL SPLIT CITRUS.** Zones 12 and 13: pick off and discard split fruit, which attract fungi and insects.

❑ **DIG AND DIVIDE DAHLIAS.** Zones 1-3, 10, and 11: stop watering a few days before digging, then unearth tubers with a spading fork. Discard tops, brush off dirt, and let tubers cure for a few days in a frost-free, dry place. Then store them in boxes of peat, sand, or vermiculite.

❑ **CONTROL PESTS.** In zones 12 and 13, pests arrive as plants put out tender new growth. *Aphids:* Blast them off with a hose, then spray with insecticidal soap. *Snails, slugs:* Put out bait or hand-pick snails and slugs when you see them.

❑ **PRUNE ROSES.** Zones 1–3, 10, and 11: prune roses anytime after frost. Remove dead, diseased, crossing, and injured canes, then prune for shape. Zones 12 and 13: prune plants lightly as you remove fading flowers. Fertilize and water for a flush of winter bloom.

❑ **PRUNE TREES, SHRUBS.** After leaves fall, prune deciduous trees and shrubs on a day when the temperature is above freezing. Remove dead, diseased, and injured branches, water sprouts, and crossing or closely parallel branches, then prune for shape.

❑ **MULCH.** Zones 1–3, 10, and 11: put a 3- to 4-inch layer of organic mulch around half-hardy plants, bulb beds that might heave during hard winter frosts, and around trees and shrubs.

❑ **MAKE COMPOST.** Chop up plants to make them decay faster. If you don't have a compost grinder, go over weeds and fallen leaves with your mower before adding them to the pile.

❑ **MAINTAIN TOOLS.** Put an edge on hoes, shovels, and pruning shears, then wipe them down with machine oil. Wipe wooden handles with linseed oil.

I'm a great believer in biological calendars, marking down the date of the first mosquito I slap in spring, the first night I hear frogs croak (usually a couple of days after the first mosquito), the first daffodil I see, and so forth. But in autumn the calendar loses its crisp certitude, since things aren't starting with a bang but tailing off slowly. Oh, there's the first killing frost to mark down, all right. But last leaf to drop, last apple harvested—it's tough to develop much enthusiasm for such things.

Instead I spend more time tracking storms and weather, so when somebody says, "Sure has been dry this winter, hasn't it?" I can answer, "Well, we're just ³⁄₁₀ of an inch under average." It's so satisfying—and it really does keep me more in tune with natural cycles, which is what gardening is all about.

●

There's been much discussion about whether you should rotate indoor plants every week to give all leaves equal light during the dark days of winter. I've tried it, always with the same result: the plant gets steadily thinner until the days lengthen again in spring. Instead of rotating light-starved indoor plants, it makes more sense to install a good plant light on the dark side of the plant.

●

Every fall I hear from concerned readers whose pines are dropping needles faster than a dog sheds hair. All the needles don't come off,

INLAND WESTERN STATES
Garden Notebook
BY JIM McCAUSLAND

but you wonder how an evergreen can lose so much of itself and remain healthy. Yet it's a normal seasonal process. Evergreens don't keep their needles forever—just for three to five years. That means they lose a third to a fifth of their needles every year, and these usually drop in fall when the first autumn winds roar through.

●

Concern about autumn storms leads some people to try to protect themselves by disfiguring their trees in the most horrible ways, usually by topping. It's a barbaric practice that accomplishes nothing: the top regrows but without the strength it had before it was cut. A better way to protect yourself is by simply opening the tree up so that the wind passes through instead of hitting the canopy as though it were a sail. A friend of mine climbed his 60-foot Douglas fir and took out roughly every third branch from bottom to top. The process didn't disfigure the tree but made it safer in storms.

THAT'S A GOOD QUESTION

Q: When should I cut back my hybrid tea roses and by how much?
A: It depends on your climate. In cold-winter areas (*Sunset Western Garden Book* climate zones 1, 2, 3, 10, and 11), cut rose bushes back by about two thirds as soon as leaves fall. In coldest areas (zones 1 and 2), completely cover pruned shrubs with a leaf mulch until spring. In intermediate and low deserts, you can hold off pruning until January.

Ground covers that make sense for the '90s

12 diverse choices for problem areas in shade or sun

I T TOOK AN EARLY snow to show me how well ground covers could define space in my Port Orchard, Washington, garden. Looking out over the fresh powder, one saw an arrangement of trees, shrubs, and fences emerging from a flat, white field. It was easy to imagine how a drift of variegated Japanese spurge could illuminate a dark space beneath a pine, and how one of the new selections of kinnikinnick could carpet a swath of sandy ground where no healthy grass would grow.

While recarpeting my garden with ground covers, I found that the trick is putting the right plant in the right place. And a well-chosen ground cover not only defines and beautifies a space, but also can drastically reduce maintenance and water use, especially if you're replacing a lawn. And your choices go beyond commonplace plants like English ivy, ice plant, and star jasmine.

Some of the 12 ground covers we recommend here are virtual unknowns with great promise, while others are new varieties of more widely known plants. In general, these ground covers require low to moderate maintenance.

November is a good month to plant ground covers in the West's mild-winter areas—places where the ground doesn't freeze for long in winter. Plants spend the winter sending out roots to prepare for a burst of spring and summer top growth. In the West's coldest areas (*Sunset Western Garden Book* climate zones 1, 2, and 3), wait until spring to plant.

A ground cover can't thrive if its roots have to struggle through compacted soil or hardpan. If your garden soil isn't easily crumbled loam, till in a 3- to 4-inch layer of well-rotted manure,

A SOFT, LOW CARPET *of blue star creeper (above) flowers all summer as it flows around steppingstones. Lush mounds of Bolax gummifera (right) border a lawn at the Bloedel Reserve on Bainbridge Island, Washington.*

peat moss, or other organic amendment, water well to settle the soil, then plant.

Set out plants in a diamond pattern. Spacing depends upon variety: for variegated Japanese spurge, it might be 8- or 10-inch intervals (closer plantings fill in faster); for *Bolax,* it might be 24-inch intervals or more. Mulch can help conserve water, keep down weeds, and prevent soil from heaving if

the ground freezes.

With luck, rain takes care of most of the first season's watering. In warm weather, newly set out plants may need a little extra water, but by the second summer many of them can get by with normal garden irrigation, and the most drought-tolerant varieties can make it on rainfall alone. Drip irrigation can be used with ground covers (especially using low-volume spray heads), but many gardeners find drip tubing too difficult to maintain once plants have filled in.

Feed plants by spreading a complete fertilizer in spring after new growth begins, then again in early summer.

GOOD CHOICES FOR THE SHADE

Shade is a relative term: although many plants can't handle much direct sun, even shade lovers need a fair amount of light to survive. Light filtered through high-arching trees is often about right, though plants that need shade inland may handle full sun near the coast.

Blue star creeper (*Laurentia fluviatilis*), zones 4, 5, 8, 9, 14–24. Grows like baby's tears, but with pale blue flowers in summer. It needs regular fertilizer and water to thrive.

Dwarf periwinkle (*Vinca minor*), all zones. This periwinkle is less likely to become a pest than its aggressive cousin, *V. major,* but it needs more water and fertilizer to thrive. Standard

SELECT YOUR FAVORITE *from this array of ground covers, each with different foliage textures and some with fruits or flowers.* **Top row from left:** *variegated Japanese spurge; cotoneaster; and Bolax gummifera.* **Center row from left:** *salal; ophiopogon; and creeping St. Johnswort.* **Bottom row from left:** *kinnikinnick; dwarf periwinkle 'Atropurpurea'; and wintergreen.*

flowers are blue (for a better shade of blue, try 'Bowles'); you can also get it in wine ('Atropurpurea'), white ('Jekyll's White'), and variegated ('Ralph Shugert' and 'Variegata').

Dwarf plumbago (*Ceratostigma plumbaginoides*), zones 2–10, 14–24. Grows as a low carpet of fresh green leaves in spring, topped by pretty blue flowers in summer and fall. Deciduous leaves turn red in autumn. Mow it back in winter.

Epimedium rubrum, zones 1–9, 14–17. Spreading by creeping roots, this perennial produces red flowers. It dies back in cold-winter climates.

Ophiopogon planiscapus 'Nigrescens', zones 5–10, 12–24. Greenish black, grassy leaves grow in clumps and look quite black in shade.

Variegated Japanese spurge (*Pachysandra terminalis* 'Variegata'), zones 1–10, 14–21. Distinguished by its cream-edged leaves, this variegated pachysandra has the toughness and weed-defeating denseness of its all-green counterpart.

SUN LOVERS

In areas with very hot summers, filtered sunlight often serves these ground covers better than full sun.

Bolax gummifera (*B. glebaria*), zones 4–7, 14–17. Clambering over the landscape on arching stems, this plant spreads 3 feet in four years; *B. g.* 'Nana' grows more slowly to half that size, and is easier to find (check with nurseries that specialize in rock-garden plants).

Cotoneaster, all zones. Plants come in evergreen and deciduous forms and bear showy berries (usually red) that birds love. For an evergreen, try bearberry cotoneaster (*C. dammeri*). For deciduous plants with good fall color, try *C. adpressus praecox* or—in all but desert zones 12 and 13—rock cotoneaster (*C. horizontalis*).

Creeping St. Johnswort (*Hypericum calycinum*), zones 2–24. Evergreen leaves, topped with yellow flowers in summer. Takes shade or poor soil; spreads fast. It drops some leaves in cold climates.

Kinnikinnick (*Arctostaphylos uva-ursi*), zones 1–9, 14–24. An outstanding native evergreen for sandy soil, with pink flowers in early summer, red berries in fall. Stems of all kinnikinnick root as they spread. 'Vancouver Jade', with jade green leaves, spreads quickly; 'Wood's Compact' has a thick cloak of dark green leaves over red branches.

Salal (*Gaultheria shallon*), zones 3–7, 14–17, 21–24. Grows less than 2 feet tall in the mild Northwest's full sun; give it partial shade farther south. Pink or white summer flowers form dark, edible fruit. It likes acid soil. Shear it back if it gets too tall.

Wintergreen (*Gaultheria procumbens*), zones 2–7, 14–17. Low-growing foliage is dotted by red, wintergreen-scented berries. Give it acid soil. It needs shade in hot-summer areas.

SOURCES

You can buy many of these ground covers at nurseries and garden centers, but some may be hard to find. Two good mail-order sources for plants are Forestfarm, 990 Tetherow Rd., Williams, OR 97544, (503) 846-7269; and Greer Gardens, 1280 Goodpasture Island Rd., Eugene, OR 97401, (503) 686-8266. Each company's catalog costs $3. ■

By Jim McCausland

PUSS A. WIDSTFAND

Perennials forever ...free

You can increase the number of perennials in your garden by dividing them in fall

A SHOVEL IS PERFECT *for digging and dividing daylilies (left); it easily slices through compacted roots of red-hot poker (center). For smaller divisions, wash away soil and tease apart clumps (top right) into smaller units (bottom right).*

ONE QUICK WAY TO DOUBLE—OR even quadruple—the size of your perennial garden at no cost is to divide overgrown and crowded clumping perennials and bulb-like plants. Not only do you get new plants to fill the gaps in existing beds or to start an entirely new border, but dividing improves the health of an established plant so it will grow vigorously and bloom profusely.

In mild-winter climates, fall is the best time to divide spring- and early-summer-blooming perennials (in cold-winter climates, divide plants earlier in fall so the roots can get established before cold weather sets in). Late-summer- and autumn-blooming plants such as aster and purple coneflower can be divided in late fall or spring.

WHEN IT'S TIME TO DIVIDE

As clumping or bulblike perennials grow, they put out new growth around the center clump. Some plants—aster and astilbe, for instance—eventually turn woody in the center; this old growth becomes less vigorous or even dies. Divide such clumps into sections, then discard unproductive growth and save only the healthiest parts of the plants.

Most perennials, however, don't develop a woody clump; you can simply divide the entire plant into sections and replant each section.

To survive, each division must have

roots and at least one stem or sheaf of leaves and a growing point. While you can often divide a plant into dozens of sections, remember that the smaller the section, the longer it will take to mature and put on a good show of bloom. For best results, divide plants into fewer, larger pieces—unless you have a very overgrown plant (typical of agapanthus or red-hot poker) or you need a lot of plants to start a new garden.

How often you divide perennials depends on how fast the clumps expand. Some vigorous growers, such as bee balm *(Monarda)* or lamb's ears *(Stachys byzantina),* often need dividing every two to three years. Slower growers, such as bleeding heart *(Dicentra),* need dividing only every five years or so.

If a plant is blooming poorly, has a lot of dead material in the center, or is cramped and pushing out of the soil, it's time to divide. If the plant appears vigorous and is blooming, then wait.

THE HARDEST PART: DIGGING UP PLANTS

The day before dividing a plant, moisten the soil thoroughly so you can dig up the plant more easily. Use a shovel or spading fork to cut a circle into the soil around the plant—6 to 12 inches beyond the plant's perimeter. Getting large, overgrown plants out of the ground is often the toughest part of the job. With more delicate plants, be care-

WHICH PLANTS NEED DIVIDING? HOW OFTEN? BEST METHOD?

ICONS INDICATE the best tools for dividing each plant: clippers, hand, saw (or knife), shovel, ax, or spading fork.

EVERY 2 TO 3 YEARS

Achillea (yarrow), *Chrysanthemum*, *Tulbaghia violacea* (society garlic)

Aster, Geranium (species), *Monarda* (bee balm), *Primula* (primrose), *Stachys byzantina* (lamb's ears)

Kniphofia (red-hot poker)

Nepeta

Salvia leucantha (Mexican bush sage)

EVERY 3 TO 5+ YEARS

Agapanthus

Armeria (thrift), *Bergenia, Dicentra* (bleeding heart), *Echinacea* (purple coneflower), *Heuchera* (coral bells), *Veronica*

Astilbe

Campanula

Clivia miniata

Dietes

Hemerocallis (daylily)

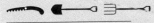

Phlox

Rudbeckia (large types)

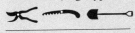

HAND AX EASILY DIVIDES *tough clump of Mexican bush sage (top left); yarrow (bottom left) needs the more surgical touch of a knife. Soil from brittle-rooted clivia (right) is washed away with a garden hose.*

ful not to damage the roots.

Once the plant is out of the ground, gently tease some soil from the rootball (hose it from fragile roots). Bulbous- or tuberous-rooted plants such as clivia and daylily are easier to divide if you remove all the soil from their roots.

Check the plant for natural dividing points between clumps of stems or leaves where you can cut or pull it apart.

CHOOSE YOUR METHOD

Plants can be divided with a shovel, spading fork, knife, saw, ax, or pruning shears (clippers), as well as by hand. How you divide a plant depends on the plant's growth habit, which tool you have on hand, how much time you have, whether you want to save all parts of the plant, and, most important, the type of roots the plant has.

Plants that have tough, sturdy roots (daylily) usually need prying or chopping apart. Fibrous-rooted plants (yarrow) are easy to cut apart with shears or a knife. Brittle or delicate roots (clivia) need gentle handling.

"Red-hot poker is a tough plant," says Brad Carter, assistant director at UC Irvine Arboretum. "I just want to get it done and go on to something else. When I use a shovel, I know I'll lose about 20 percent of the plant (some of it gets chopped up). But we have so much red-hot poker here and it comes back so vigorously, it doesn't matter if I lose

some of the plant." If you don't want to lose anything, use a pruning saw instead.

Mexican bush sage is another tough plant. It grows so vigorously that Carter can make 100 little plants from one 2-year-old clump. But a shovel won't work on it. "I tried to use a shovel by jumping on it with all of my weight, and I just bounced off! Now I use an ax."

With expensive, slow-growing plants like clivia, you'll probably want to save all divisions. Because clivia has brittle roots that separate easily, Carter simply washes the soil from the roots, then gently pulls sections from the main clump by hand. "This way, I don't lose any of the plant," he says.

Once the plant is divided, you can cut its foliage back to 4 inches (except on plants like clivia, or divisions with little foliage). Some gardeners leave foliage of evergreen plants intact, but Carter says the plants look neater when trimmed. "The foliage tends to decline after dividing, anyway."

Mix organic matter into the new planting area, and replant the divisions right away so they don't dry out. To allow for settling, plant the divisions about 1/2 inch higher than the level at which they were originally growing. Water well, then keep the soil moist. You can also replant divisions into containers and wait until the plants are established before transplanting them into the ground. ∎

By Lauren Bonar Swezey

TWINKLING WHITE LIGHTS *and vine prunings wound around humble wire tomato cages create these festive "trees." For details, see page 313*

DECEMBER

GARDEN

Guide

Light up the garden with golden winter blooms

Tagetes lemmonii is not a dainty little plant. Depending on how happy it is in its location, and how little it gets pruned, this shrubby perennial marigold can take up as much as 36 square feet in a garden. And—despite its finely textured, pungent foliage—most of the year you'd probably begrudge it that much space. In summer, the small golden orange flowers start appearing sporadically. But in winter, it's a different story: they completely blanket the plant.

"No other plant gives you quite the same abundance of yellow just when you really need it," says Darwin Black, who designed and maintains this garden in Laguna Beach, California, for Don Clurman. "That's why I try to talk every client into using it. It's my winter garden mainstay."

"When the days get cooler and the sun is lower in the sky, *T. lemmonii* creates this absolute golden glow," he continues. "It lights up the whole garden. Whether you're working outdoors or sitting inside looking out, it brightens up a dark day."

Ease of care also endears *T. lemmonii* to Black. It's pest-free, needs little or no fertilizer, and tolerates almost any type of soil. Best of all, it requires no dead-heading. "New growth covers spent flowers, so why bother removing them? I just shear the whole thing back in late January."

Black's favorite compan-

Masses of blooms cloak billowing mounds of *Tagetes lemmonii* in this Laguna Beach garden.

ion plant for *T. lemmonii* is purple-spiked Mexican bush sage (*Salvia leucantha*). It gets the same treatment as the marigold. By December, the sage begins to bow a bit from the weight of its blooms, but under leaden skies, the effect seems romantic rather than bedrag-gled. Bronze-hued flax and sedges add autumnal tones to this border, red-leafed cane begonias add richness, and the glaucous blades of

- The winter-blooming marigold
- "Trees" of vine prunings
- A prolific asparagus
- White blooms for a white Christmas
- Decorative strawberry tree
- Garden globes

RUSS A. WIDSTRAND

blue oat grass add contrasting coolness. But they are only the supporting cast. *Tagetes lemmonii* is this winter garden's golden star.

GARDEN DECORATION

Spin a little holiday magic with vine prunings

Not even Ebenezer Scrooge could quibble with the cost of the handsome outdoor decorations shown in the photo on page 310, designed by gardener Charlcie Kaylor. Using materials recycled from her garden, Kaylor forms imaginative Christmas "trees" from tomato cages turned upside down atop large terra-cotta pots.

To begin, Kaylor anchors the rim of each cage with four 24-inch lengths of aluminum rod bent into a hairpin shape—pushing each staple into the pot's soil. She then ties together the wire prongs that are normally sunk into the ground with twine to make a pointed top.

Once the cages are anchored in place, Kaylor weaves grapevine and honeysuckle prunings in and around the wire. You could also use any other vine or long, flexible branches pruned from plants such as redtwig or yellowtwig dogwood, willow, wisteria, or woody clematis.

Finally, Kaylor strings the lights, carefully weaving the electric cords around the cage and between branches so that the cords aren't readily visible and are also not deeply entangled. At night, the decorated cages twinkle by the front entry to her house.

After the holidays, Kaylor disassembles the cages, removes soil from the pots, and scrubs them. She then fills the pots with fresh soil and plants primroses for a colorful cool-season display. And the cages wait until it's time to support next summer's tomatoes.

CONTAINER
CULTURE

CONTAINER CULTURE

Flax teams up with kalanchoe

For a surprising display of colors and textures, Jean Manocchio of Belli Fiori in Redwood City, California, combined New Zealand flax (*Phormium tenax* 'Sundowner') and deep pink 'Eternity' kalanchoe in an 18-inch Mexican pot. Manocchio chose the kalanchoe to play off the flax's coral pink blush.

The flax is permanently planted in the container, with the kalanchoe as seasonal color. (Cyclamen and flowering cabbage are other handsome winter companions.)

For this display, Manocchio planted a dozen 4-inch kalanchoes around the flax. When their bloom is done, she replaces them with other low-growing plants, such as primroses or Imperial Antique Shades pansies.

During warm weather, the pot needs water every other day. Fertilizer is applied monthly.

NORMAN A. PLATE

Kalanchoe flowers echo rosy blush of New Zealand flax leaves.

FOR THE VEGETABLE GARDEN

UC 157: A perfect, prolific asparagus

Traditional asparagus varieties have always been longer-lived and more productive in cold-winter climates than in mild-winter ones. A hybrid developed by the University of California changes all that. Half of the spears produced by UC 157 are male and spend less energy producing seed. The deep green spears are tender and plump, and the plants send out a lot of them.

Asparagus is a perennial; established plants produce for years. Plant them as soon as bare-root crops are available this month or next. Set in full sun where they won't be disturbed—in a long row in the back of the vegetable garden, for example. Dig a trench about a foot wide and 10 inches deep. Work organic material such as compost into the soil at the bottom of the trench, then water. Set the bare-root crowns into the bottom of the trench with roots down; space them about 12 inches apart. Cover them with a few inches of soil, then water again.

As the spears grow, gradually fill in the trench with soil, leaving the tips uncovered. Water and fertilize plants regularly during the growing season.

Don't harvest any spears the first year. Instead, allow the foliage to unfurl, producing energy to go down to the roots. Harvest a few spears the second spring, but always leave plenty to keep the plant healthy. The third spring, you'll have a good harvest.

UC 157 should be available bare-root in nurseries later this month. Most mail-order vegetable catalogs also sell it.

313

NORMAN A. PLATE

Medley of white-flowering plants includes violas, primroses, camellias, and paperwhite narcissus.

To give the pots a festive look, stuff pine or fir branches around the pot edges and add a bow of silver, metallic green, or gold.

NEW PLANT REPORT

A dogwood with a dark bark

Any gardener who has ever grown dogwoods with red or yellow twigs (various species of the genus *Cornus*) knows how beautiful the bare branches look in the winter garden. Now gardeners in the West (outside of desert zones 10–13) can expand the color scheme with a dark-stemmed dogwood that's new to the U.S. market. *Cornus alba* 'Kesselringii' has very dark purple, almost black stems.

It grows like other shrub dogwoods, fountaining to a height of around 7 feet. In summer, it's covered with oval leaves 3 to 5 inches long and half as wide, in shades of green, greenish yellow, or green edged in white. White clusters of flowers appear in May, followed by small white fruits.

This easily grown dogwood does best in loose, rich soil with ample water. It looks good when interplanted with dogwoods that have yellow or red stems, or planted alongside the glistening green branches of *Kerria japonica*. If you buy a plant this month, you can enjoy it in a pot on a deck or set it in a bed immediately.

One mail-order source for *C. alba* 'Kesselringii' is Forestfarm, 990 Tetherow Rd., Williams, OR 97544; catalog $3. An 18- to 30-inch plant costs $7 plus shipping.

CONTAINER CULTURE

White flowers for a white Christmas

Snow isn't likely to fall in Northern California's lower elevations in winter. But you can create your own white Christmas on your front porch.

Large containers filled with white-blooming plants offer a sophisticated alternative to red poinsettias. They go together in minutes.

All you need are containers in several different sizes, each at least 18 inches in diameter, and enough potting soil to fill the contain-

ers. Then look for white-blooming plants in 4-inch pots (6- to 8-inch-wide pots work, too, but are more expensive).

Some of the choices in December are azaleas, camellias (sold in 1-gallon or larger containers), candytuft, cyclamen, pansies, paperwhite narcissus, and primroses (*Primula obconica*, fairy primrose, and English primrose). To set off the white flowers, also choose a few foliage plants, such as

variegated ivy. Buy enough plants to fill each pot with rootballs just touching.

Fill the container with potting soil to within about 6 inches of the top. Arrange plants so tallest ones are at the rear of the pot (for one-sided viewing) or in the middle (if pots will be viewed from all directions). Cluster medium-size plants around the tall ones, and save the shortest plants and trailers for the edges. Fill in with soil, then water well.

Strawberry tree for fruit, greenery

When we think of holiday greens, conifers naturally come to mind. But in mild-winter areas of the Southwest, broad-leafed evergreens are also candidates for seasonal greenery. One excellent choice is strawberry tree (*Arbutus unedo*). This shrub or small tree has glossy green 2- to 3-inch leaves with serrated edges, and its flaky bark is a rich red-brown. In fall, it bears clusters of puffy fruits—each between the size of a marble and a table-tennis ball—that turn from yellow to strawberry red as they ripen. In a mild winter, the fruits dangle from the tree at Christmastime.

This native to southern Europe and Ireland grows in a handsome irregular form to an eventual height of 8 to 35 feet. *Arbutus. unedo* is hardy in *Sunset Western Garden Book* climate zones 4 through 24, although it may be damaged during a severe winter.

Buy a tree this month in a 5- or 15-gallon can, slip it into a decorative container (make sure it provides good drainage), and display it on a deck or patio or next to an entry. Set out plants in the garden whenever soil is workable. Give them a sunny location and well-drained soil.

A strawberry tree may bear fruit and small white flowers at the same time.

Secrets to growing great nandina berries

Every now and then, you run across a *Nandina domestica* laden with bright red berry clusters like the ones shown at right. Why don't all nandinas produce such great crops?

No one is quite sure. Even though this obliging plant with delicate bamboo-like leaves produces male and female flowers, they appear to be somewhat self-sterile. Avid gardeners have observed that the plants produce the best berries when planted in groups.

Robert Boddy, owner of Descanso Nurseries in Fort Bragg, California, says nandinas never produce berries in his cool, wet coastal climate, but they do inland in Santa Rosa and Ukiah. He speculates that nandinas need more warmth to produce berries than they get directly on the coast.

Audrey Teasdale of Monrovia Nursery in Azusa, California, advises gardeners not to expect any berries from the globe-type nandinas such as 'Nana Purpurea'. But *N. d.* 'Compacta' and 'Moyer's Red' should produce as much fruit as the species does.

Barrie Coate, horticultural consultant in Los Gatos, California, finds *N. d.* 'Compacta' the most dependable berry producer of all

Hefty clusters of bright red berries can be a nandina's crowning glory in winter.

nandinas he has grown. "They always bloom and always fruit," says Coate. And there are no guarantees that a particular plant of *N. domestica* will fruit because they're grown from seed and are extremely variable.

Cactus for the holidays

Thanksgiving cactus, Christmas cactus, and Easter cactus are among the most successful winter-blooming house plants, and they come in more colors than ever. The plants look much alike, and because they've been so heavily hybridized, growers often market them as holiday cactus. But there are differences.

Thanksgiving and Christmas cactus hybrids are the most closely allied. Both produce flowers in white, yellow, orange, red, pink, salmon, purple, violet, and combinations of those colors. Different varieties can come into flower anytime from now through February.

You can encourage these cactus to set flower buds by giving them cool nights (50° to 55°) or 12 to 14 hours of darkness daily for six weeks starting in early autumn. To promote regular flowering, keep plants on the moist side and feed them every week during bloom with quarter-strength liquid fertilizer.

Easter cactus bears large flowers in shades of pink, orange, purple, lavender, and red; white appears in bicolors. Expect blooms during spring.

Holiday cactus is sold at garden centers or by florists. One mail-order source that offers a wide variety of hybrids is Rainbow Gardens, 1444 E. Taylor St., Vista, CA 92084, (619) 758-4290; catalog $2.

A beauty of a book about rhodies

Among the many books about rhododendrons, a new one stands out: *The Book of Rhododendrons,* by Marianna Kneller (Timber Press, Portland, 1995). This oversize (10- by 13½-inch) hardbound volume is the perfect gift for the gardener who loves rhododendrons or simply appreciates beautiful botanical paintings.

Kneller, artist-in-residence at Exbury Gardens in England (home of the Rothschild rhododendrons), has spent 15 years documenting the genus with her paintings. Each of the 73 full-page paintings illustrates the eight-month growing cycle (buds, flowers, leaves, seeds) of one species in a subsection of rhododendrons.

Each painting is accompanied by text written by one of 50 of the world's leading rhododendron experts. It discusses the discovery of the particular plant in the wild, aspects that make the plant garden-worthy, and advice on growth and care of rhododendrons.

The book also lists the world's greatest rhododendron gardens, including Meerkerk Rhododendron Gardens on Whidbey Island and Rhododendron Species Botanical Garden in Federal Way, Washington. If you can't find this title in local bookshops, call Timber Press at (800) 327-5680. The book costs $45 plus $6.50 shipping and handling.

Corral those invasive roots

Many plants, such as Bishop's weed and numerous bamboos, spread by underground rhizomes—creeping stems that send up growing shoots—until they threaten to take over the garden.

Now you can solve the problem with plastic root barriers, which can contain invasive rhizomes. Sold in rolls as wide as 3 feet, the plastic is thin enough to be cut with scissors. To install, just trench around or alongside the problem plant, set the collar vertically in the trench, and fill in with dirt. The top of the collar should be 1 inch above soil level.

The collar's depth depends upon the plant you're trying to contain. Most rhizomes don't go more than a foot deep unless the soil is very sandy. (Invasive tree roots, such as those of willows, can go much deeper, so in most cases there isn't much use in trying to contain them.)

One source of root barri-

ers is Bamboo Gardens of Washington, 5016 192nd Place N.E., Redmond, WA 98053; (206) 868-5166. A 2-foot-wide strip costs $1.50 per foot plus shipping.

Ornamental pears that stand tall— yet strong

'Bradford' pear, a variety of *Pyrus calleryana,* has been a popular street tree in Northern California because of its dense, upright branching, full canopy, and orange-red fall color. As trees have aged, nurseries and arborists have discovered that 'Bradford' doesn't live up to its promise.

When the tree is young, its long, upright branches form narrow crotch angles. As it matures, the branches start opening up, so that by the time the tree reaches 20 feet tall, the branches might spread 25 feet. The full canopy strains the branch joints, resulting in major breakage during windy weather (or icy weather in colder climates). Fall color can be iffy, too. The leaves

often don't color up until December, and early cold snaps can cause them to fall without coloring.

Keith Warren of J. Frank Schmidt & Son Co. nursery in Oregon suggests two better varieties: 'Aristocrat' and 'Chanticleer' ('Chanticleer' is also sold as 'Cleveland Select' and 'Stone Hill').

'Aristocrat' is a pyramidal tree to 40 feet tall and 28 feet wide with an informal, open habit and more horizontal branching than 'Bradford'. Because of its branching habit, it forms wider crotch angles, which are less prone to breakage. Also, fall color develops earlier, in a dependable dark red to yellow-orange.

'Chanticleer' makes an upright, narrowly pyramidal tree to 40 feet tall and about 15 feet wide. Branches are shorter than on 'Bradford', so there is less weight on the narrow crotch angles and much less problem with breakage. Again, fall color develops earlier and is a handsome orange-red to reddish purple.

Trees are available at many nurseries. If you can't find them, ask your nursery to order one for you.

Squirrelproof birdseed

As colder weather sets in, the competition for food between birds and squirrels starts to heat up. Squirrels will perform any acrobatic maneuver and chew through any material softer than iron to get their paws on the goodies you put in a bird feeder.

One way to foil these enterprising gluttons and help birds get the food they need is to use birdseed treated with hot pepper. Squirrels can't stand the pepper taste, but birds don't seem to mind it at all.

One source of pepper-treated bird food mix is Dancing Squirrel, Box 8000, Buffalo, NY 14267; (800) 450-7631. Cost ranges from $1.25 to $1.81 per pound, plus $3 shipping and handling, depending upon the quantity you buy. (There is a 16-pound minimum order; 24- and 48-pound units are also available). The mix includes millet, sunflower hearts, black oil sunflower seeds, cracked corn, peanuts, and red pepper.

Giant ornaments for the garden

Great glass globes with mirror coatings are garden ornaments you just can't miss. Placed among plants, they reflect leaves and sky (and you, if you get close enough) in their shimmery surface.

Victorian gardeners called them gazing balls and placed them on pedestals. Now gardeners are rediscovering them. And well-stocked nurseries are selling them in sizes from 6 to 12 inches in diameter, and in myriad colors—gold, orange, red, violet, deep green. (Colors other than silver are more

Gazing ball rests in low birdbath amid flowering perennials.

difficult to place tastefully in the garden.)

What's the best way to display a gazing ball? San Francisco landscape architect Topher Delaney suggests

placing it in a shady area, on the ground among, say, tree ferns and baby's tears to attract light and sparkle; in a stone urn surrounded by blue delphiniums or pink roses;

or in a birdbath (though the ball's 2-inch stem will show on one side). For dramatic effects in a roof garden overlooking San Francisco Bay, Delaney placed a row of blue gazing balls among black stones.

Prices range from $30 for a 6-inch-diameter globe to $65 for a 12-inch one. If you can't find them at a nursery, try one of these Bay Area suppliers: Lumbini, in San Francisco, (415) 896-2666; Bluestone Main, Petaluma, (707) 765-2024; or Roger Reynolds Nursery, Menlo Park, (415) 323-5612. ■

By Sharon Cohoon, Steven R. Lorton, Jim McCausland, Lauren Bonar Swezey, Lance Walheim, Hazel White

PLANTING

❏ **TREES, SHRUBS.** Zones 4–7: All but marginally hardy shrubs and trees can go into the ground this month. Shop for broad-leafed evergreens to fill vacant spots in your landscape.

❏ **HOLIDAY PLANTERS.** Nurseries will be bursting with plants—cyclamen, forced narcissus, poinsettias—in 6-inch pots. Group several plants in a large container filled with fresh potting mix, tie on a bow, and you've got a gift.

❏ **PROPAGATE HARDWOODS.** Zones 4–7: Take cuttings of aucuba, barberry, forsythia, holly, honeysuckle, hydrangea, rose, rose of Sharon, spiraea, and weigela. Make pencil-size tip cuttings, dip the ends in rooting hormone, and put them in potting mix. Give cuttings strong light, but keep them out of direct sun. Make sure the rooting medium stays constantly moist. A cool greenhouse, coldframe, sunporch, or windowsill is a good place for them.

❏ **PROPAGATE EVERGREENS.** Start new evergreen shrubs by ground layering. Scrape away a fingernail-size bit of bark on a small lower limb. Treat the wound with rooting hormone. Bend the limb into a shallow trench in the ground with the wound touching the soil. Cover the limb with a thin layer of soil. Stake it down or lay a rock on top of it to hold it in place. By next fall, the

PACIFIC NORTHWEST
CHECKLIST
DECEMBER

Sunset Western Garden Book CLIMATE ZONES
❏ 1-3 ■ 4-7

branch will have developed a self-sustaining network of roots, and you will be able to cut it from the parent plant and transplant it.

MAINTENANCE

❏ **CARE FOR CHRISTMAS TREES.** To prolong the freshness of a cut tree, saw an inch off the bottom of the trunk, and keep the tree in a bucket of water in a shady area outdoors until you're ready to bring it in the house. Before setting

the tree in a stand, saw another inch off the bottom of the trunk. Use a stand that holds water, and keep the reservoir full (check daily the first week). Keep the tree away from heaters, and avoid hot-burning tree lights.

❏ **ROTATE HOUSE PLANTS.** To keep potted plants from growing lopsided toward a light source, give the plants a quarter turn each week. A chalk mark or insignificant scratch on the pot helps you keep track of how far to turn the plant each time.

❏ **TEND AFRICAN VIOLETS.** Clip back shriveled leaves and faded flowers. Feed plants early in the month with a commercial fertilizer made for African violets. Plants may reward your attention by ushering in the New Year with a flush of bloom.

❏ **TEND GIFT PLANTS.** Place flowering gift plants in a cool spot with bright, indirect light. Don't let them sit in water; remove any decorative foil from the pot, or perforate the foil, and set the pot in a saucer.

PEST CONTROL

❏ **BATTLE SLUGS.** Even in winter, slugs wake up when the weather warms. Put bait at the base of large pots, near rocks and stonework, and in other places where slugs go to escape the cold. Keep children and pets away from bait.

Just about the time the ornaments go up on the tree in my home, the first red blossom of a hybrid camellia called 'Freedom Bell' appears in my Seattle garden. Years ago, while shopping at Wells-Medina Nursery in Bellevue, the plant caught my eye, and nurseryman Ned Wells coaxed, "Get this. You'll love it."

I got it. I love it. (Thank you, Ned.) 'Freedom Bell' has given me years of pleasure. Its first flower opens in December; then other buds mature and open, putting on a vigorous bloom show through March. The semidouble flowers measure about 2½ inches across. They are bell-shaped and face upward. As the blooms fade, they drop from the plant. The branches are upright, and the leaves are shiny and leathery. If you can't find 'Freedom Bell' camellia locally, you can order it from Nuccio's Nurseries, Box 6160, Altadena, CA 91003; (818) 794-3383. A 30- to 36-inch plant costs $22.50 plus shipping.

•

My neighbor Mary Williams has a great system for recycling her Christmas tree. After she takes the tree down, she hauls it outside and cuts off the branches, then uses the boughs to cover tender plants, protecting them during the cold snaps that typically come in January and February. The needle-laden branches provide enough insulation to keep plants like delicate ferns and sedums from freezing to death. A blanket of boughs has even helped a gardenia make it

PACIFIC NORTHWEST
Garden Notebook
BY STEVEN R. LORTON

through many winters in her garden. In spring after the needles have fallen off (they add a bit of organic matter to the soil), she breaks up the branches and puts them on the compost pile. She saws the trunk into fireplace-size logs for the wood pile.

•

If you're fresh out of gift ideas for gardening friends, consider giving a personalized certificate good for one garden clean-up (by you) or a pad of vouchers, each worth an hour of your horticultural handiwork or one lawn-mowing.

THAT'S A GOOD QUESTION

Q: Every Christmas we get florists' cyclamen. By mid-February the flowers have stopped and foliage is leggy. Is it worth keeping them?
A: If you have a greenhouse or a bright sunroom, florists' cyclamen (*C. persicum*) will thrive indoors year-round in well-drained pots. Water plants and fertilize them as you do other blooming house plants. If you live in one of the Northwest's mild-winter areas (*Sunset Western Garden Book* climate zones 4–7), you can also try growing these plants outdoors (wait until around April 1 to set them out). I've been growing two plants for about six years on the south side of my Seattle garden, where they're nestled close to the house foundation. Although my plants don't produce as many blooms as the ones you get from the florist, they have good-looking leaves and some flowers.

CHECKLIST
DECEMBER

PLANTING

☐ **SELECT A LIVING CHRISTMAS TREE.** Most nurseries carry the following kinds: Aleppo pine, Colorado blue spruce, dwarf Alberta spruce, giant sequoia, and Monterey pine. Before bringing the tree indoors, water it thoroughly and hose it down. Indoors, set the pot in a cool location in a plastic saucer. Check soil moisture daily.

☐ **SHOP FOR BARE-ROOT PLANTS.** Zones 14–17: Late this month, nurseries begin selling bare-root cane berries, fruit trees, grapes, and roses, and perennial vegetables such as asparagus, horseradish, and rhubarb. Ask nursery personnel to recommend varieties suitable for your climate (some fruits may require more winter chilling than your area gets). Plant as soon as possible after bringing them home. If soil is too wet to plant, temporarily cover roots with moistened mulch, or plant in containers.

MAINTENANCE

☐ **CLEAN UP.** Coast and inland: If you didn't get around to it earlier, remove dead foliage and stems from dormant perennials now. Rake up fallen leaves. Chop garden refuse into small pieces with loppers or a shredder for compost. Toss diseased plants into the garbage.

☐ **FILL HUMMINGBIRD FEEDERS.** Zones 14–17: These birds stay in Northern California through winter. Because flowers are scarce at this time

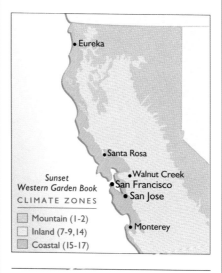

• Eureka

• Santa Rosa

• Walnut Creek
• San Francisco
• San Jose

Sunset Western Garden Book
CLIMATE ZONES
☐ Mountain (1-2)
☐ Inland (7-9,14)
☐ Coastal (15-17)

• Monterey

of year, it's important to keep your feeder filled; clean and refill it regularly.

☐ **KEEP CUT CHRISTMAS TREES FRESH.** To prolong freshness of a cut tree, saw an inch off the bottom of the trunk, then store the tree in a bucket of water in a shady area outdoors until you're ready to bring it indoors. Before setting the tree in a stand, saw another inch off the bottom of the trunk. Use a stand that holds water, and keep the reservoir full (check daily the first week). Keep the tree away from heaters, and avoid hot-burning tree lights.

☐ **PRUNE FOR HOLIDAY GREENS.** Long-lasting choices include evergreen magnolia, juniper, pine, and redwood.

☐ **TEND GIFT PLANTS.** Place flowering gift plants in a cool spot with bright, indirect light. Don't let them sit in water; remove any decorative foil from the pot, or perforate the foil and set the pot in a saucer.

☐ **WATCH FOR COLD WEATHER.** Zones 14–17: Keep an eye on the weather report. If cold weather is predicted, move tender container plants under the eaves, and suspend covers over plants in the ground using four tall stakes (don't allow the cover to touch the leaves).

☐ **WATER.** Zones 14–17: If fall and early winter rains have been light, check soil moisture periodically and water when the soil is almost dry to the touch. Also, water plants growing under eaves where rain can't reach. Make sure plants are adequately watered if a freeze is predicted; drought-stressed plants are more susceptible to freeze damage.

PEST CONTROL

☐ **APPLY DORMANT SPRAY.** Zones 14–17: To smother overwintering insect eggs and pests such as aphids, mites, and scale, spray deciduous flowering and fruit trees as well as roses with dormant oil after leaves have fallen. For complete coverage, spray the branches, branch crotches, trunk, and ground beneath the tree's drip line.

W hen December rolls around, I'm ready to get into the holiday shopping mode. But the only time I have to shop is on weekends—just like 10 zillion other people. And where do I find most holiday shoppers? Competing for parking spaces at shopping malls. But in the past few years I've found great places to shop away from the crowds: at botanical garden gift shops and some full-service garden centers. There, I always discover wonderful handmade gifts for gardeners.

Shops vary in the extent of their offerings. The two-year-old UC Santa Cruz Arboretum gift shop offers a handsome array of natural ornaments and wreaths, as well as many other garden and nature-related gifts. On a smaller scale, UC Berkeley Botanical Garden gift shop, the Strybing Arboretum Society Bookstore in Golden Gate Park, and the Mendocino Botanical Garden gift shop in Fort Bragg have great selections of books, along with small gifts.

Orchard Nursery in Lafayette and Alden Lane Nursery in Livermore create full-fledged winter wonderlands with lights, gifts, and decorated trees. Roger Reynolds Nursery in Menlo Park offers a good collection of handmade gifts, ornaments, and gift plants.

•

NORTHERN CALIFORNIA
Garden Notebook
BY LAUREN BONAR SWEZEY

Since I've been writing this new feature, I've been using a journal to keep track of what goes on in my garden. To help, I use *Garden Notes Through the Years,* by Betty Mackey. It's not fancy (plastic comb binding, recycled paper with black line drawings), but in it I can make week-by-week observations for four years on facing pages, so it's easy to compare notes. For a personalized copy, send a check for $12.20 to B. B. Mackey Books, Box 475, Wayne, PA 19087.

THAT'S A GOOD QUESTION

Q: I would like to plant a peach tree but have a small garden. Are dwarf varieties available?

A: Yes. Ron Ludekens of L. E. Cooke Co., one of the leading developers of genetic dwarf peaches that grow to about 5 feet tall, says that 'Empress' is one of his favorites for flavor. Two drawbacks: it's a clingstone (the pit doesn't separate from the fruit), and it fruits best where winters are colder than in the San Francisco Bay Area. 'Golden Glory', his second choice for flavor, does well in all zones but 17. 'Southern Sweet', 'Southern Flame', and 'Southern Rose' do well everywhere and produce good-flavored fruit. Ludekens suggests planting all three varieties for a succession of fruit all summer.

PLANTING

❑ **DECORATE FOR THE HOLIDAYS.** Make the front porch or entryway of your home say a festive welcome. Decorate it with potted plants blooming in shades of red and white. Nurseries offer many options, including cyclamen, kalanchoe, pansies, poinsettias, and primulas. And don't forget to place a wreath on the front door.

❑ **PLANT BARE-ROOT FRUITS, VEGETABLES, ROSES.** Bare-root season starts late this month, so you'll have a wide range of fruit trees, berries, and roses from which to choose. Set out roots of perennial vegetables such as artichoke, asparagus, and rhubarb. If soil is too wet to plant, heel in the bare root plants (cover their roots with soil) or plant them temporarily in containers. Roots must stay moist.

❑ **PLANT FLOWERS.** For instant color, set out blooming calendulas, Iceland poppies, pansies, primroses, and violas. Seedlings planted now will bloom in spring. Also consider planting bare-root perennials such as astilbe, Oriental poppy, and peony.

❑ **SHOP FOR CAMELLIAS.** Choose plants while they are in bloom. Most nurseries will be well stocked with sasanquas and early-blooming japonicas.

MAINTENANCE

❑ **CARE FOR CHRISTMAS TREES.** To prolong freshness of a cut tree, trim an inch or so off the trunk's base when you

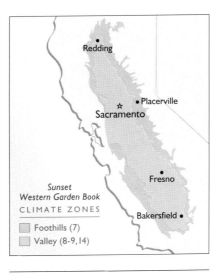

Sunset Western Garden Book CLIMATE ZONES

❑ Foothills (7)
❑ Valley (8-9,14)

get home, place the tree in a stand that holds water, and keep the reservoir full (check daily the first week).

Before moving living or cut trees indoors, wash off the foliage with a hose, or use insecticidal soap to reduce insects. Living trees should be kept indoors two weeks at most. Keep all trees away from heaters, and avoid hot-burning tree lights.

❑ **CLEAN UP.** Remove dead foliage and stems from dormant perennials. Rake leaves from the lawn. Chop refuse into

tiny pieces, using loppers or a shredder. Except for leathery leaves like those on evergreen magnolia, most of it can be composted. To reduce overwintering pests, dispose of leaves and fallen fruit gathered from around fruit trees.

❑ **PROTECT AGAINST FROST.** Killing frosts often hit this month. Watch out for still, starry nights, and be prepared to protect tender plants. Cover citrus trees with perforated plastic or burlap supported by some type of frame that keeps the cover from touching the foliage.

❑ **PRUNE.** As you cut greenery from conifers, holly, laurels, magnolias, and pittosporum, you can do some light pruning as well. Also start pruning dormant fruit trees, roses, and shrubs.

❑ **TEND GIFT PLANTS.** Place plants in a cool spot with bright, indirect light and away from drafts and furnace vents. Don't let them sit in water; cut a hole in the bottom of decorative foil and place pot in a saucer. Feed every two weeks with high-nitrogen fertilizer.

PEST AND WEED CONTROL

❑ **SPRAY.** After leaves have fallen, apply dormant sprays. If you haven't already done so, use fixed copper (in wettable powder form) or lime sulfur to control peach leaf curl. Repeat in January or early February. To smother overwintering insects such as aphids, mites, and scale, apply horticultural oil to roses and deciduous flowering and fruit trees after leaves have fallen.

It has to be December. The mail-order garden catalogs have piled up so high on my desk that the ones on the bottom are starting to compost. With all the holiday chaos, the cold weather outdoors, and downtime for TV football, December is a good time to peruse and file my catalogs.

Garden catalogs make interesting reading, but sometimes they frustrate the gardener in me. (Their pretty pictures promise lush flower borders that could fry in valley heat.) Let's round up all the English-style gardeners from back east and make them garden in the San Joaquin Valley for a summer—then they'd learn the meaning of drought tolerance.

And the rose catalogs! They burst with promise! Let me guess: this year's "world's greatest ever" rose might be called something like 'Easy Free' (it waters and prunes itself, grows happily as a ground cover, hedge, or shade tree, and bears flowers as fragrant as old roses).

I'm sounding a little cynical. In truth, I love garden catalogs and get excited about every one that appears in my mailbox. They always offer something new to try. You just have to be a bit careful when you choose plants for the hot, dry Central Valley and surrounding foothills. And if the hype gets to you, do what I do. Pull out the A. M. Leonard catalog (Box 816, Piqua, OH 45356). It has every tool and garden gadget you'll ever need. Paging through it is like shopping in

CENTRAL VALLEY
Garden Notebook
BY LANCE WALHEIM

an old-time hardware store. Now, that's fun! Or try the good old Gurney's Seed & Nursery Co. catalog (110 Capital St., Yankton, SD 57079). Sorting through all the fruit, vegetable, and flower varieties will make you wonderfully dizzy.

•

Cyclamen are among my favorite holiday plants, although I never leave them indoors for more than a day or two. Instead, I place them on my shady but bright front porch and keep them moist. There they bloom unselfishly until midspring.

THAT'S A GOOD QUESTION

Q: The fruit on my Satsuma mandarin trees got dry and puffy before I could eat them. What happened?

A: Unlike many types of citrus, Satsumas don't hang well on the tree for a long period after reaching maturity. A Washington navel orange will keep getting sweeter on the tree, but a Satsuma will often only get puffy and dry out.

To get the best crop next season, make sure the trees are moist throughout the growing season, be careful not to overfertilize, and start picking a little earlier. In warm areas, many Satsumas will start tasting good in mid-November, even though the rind may be tinged a little green and be fairly tight. You should be able to pick fruit through the holidays. If you're not using enough fruit, try juicing some.

PLANTING

☐ **SHOP FOR BARE-ROOT PLANTS.** Coastal, inland- and low-desert gardeners (climate zones 22–24, 18–21, and 13, respectively) can plant bare-root this month. Look for artichokes, asparagus, cane berries, deciduous shade and fruit trees, grapes, and roses. Plant as soon as possible after purchase.

☐ **FINISH PLANTING BULBS.** It's not too late for coastal, inland, and low-desert gardeners to plant anemones, daffodils, freesias, ranunculus, and other spring-blooming bulbs. Tulips, crocus, and hyacinth that have been prechilled for at least six weeks in the refrigerator can go into the ground, too.

☐ **ADD WINTER VEGETABLES.** Plant replacements for the winter crops you harvest. Choices include beets, broccoli, brussels sprouts, cabbage, carrots, cauliflower, head and leaf lettuces, kale, kohlrabi, peas, radishes, spinach, Swiss chard, and turnips.

☐ **PLANT NATIVES.** Unless soil is soggy, this month is still a good time to plant many California natives. Other drought-resistant plants can be planted now as well. If rains are light, water regularly to get plants established.

☐ **PLANT WINTER COLOR.** Set out blooming plants of calendula, candytuft, cyclamen, Iceland poppy, linaria, nemesia, ornamental kale, pansy, primrose, and viola. In frost-free areas, you can also plant cinerarias.

SOUTHERN CALIFORNIA
CHECKLIST
DECEMBER

Bishop

NEVADA

CALIFORNIA

San Luis Obispo

Tehachapi

Santa Barbara

Lancaster

Los Angeles

Palm Springs

Sunset Western Garden Book CLIMATE ZONES

☐ 1-3 ☐ 11
☐ 13 ☐ 14-24

San Diego

MEXICO

MAINTENANCE

☐ **CARE FOR GIFT PLANTS.** Remove wrapping paper or foil so that water can drain from the bottom of the pot. Indoors, give plants natural light but no direct sun; keep them away from heating vents. Don't overwater poinsettias.

☐ **PRUNE FOR HOLIDAY DECORATIONS.** Cut branches of holly, juniper, nandina, pittosporum, podocarpus, pyracantha, and toyon; save clippings for holiday decorations. Cut to side branches, or to about ¼ inch above buds.

☐ **FERTILIZE.** To promote steady growth, feed fall-planted winter vegetables and annuals regularly.

☐ **CUT BACK RASPBERRIES.** Low-chill raspberries bear fruit over a long period on new wood. Rejuvenate plants this month or next by cutting back to the ground all canes that have fruited.

☐ **CARE FOR CHRISTMAS TREES.** Keep your living tree outdoors until shortly before the holidays. Water regularly so the rootball won't dry out. Indoors, place the tree away from heating vents and fireplaces. Move the tree outside after a week or two. Always put a cut tree in water as soon as you get it home, but first saw off the base of the trunk so the tree can take up water.

PEST AND WEED CONTROL

☐ **PREVENT BEETLE DAMAGE.** Prune eucalyptus, pine, and other trees susceptible to bark beetles now while borers are inactive. Chip prunings or cover firewood tightly with a tarp to prevent beetles from laying eggs in it. (Beetles lay eggs on both dead and live wood.)

☐ **APPLY DORMANT SPRAY.** As soon as leaves fall, spray roses and deciduous flowering and fruit trees with dormant oil to smother overwintering insect pests such as scale, mites, and aphids. For diseases such as brown rot and peach leaf curl, mix lime sulfur or fixed copper into the oil. Spray the branches, crotches, trunk, and ground beneath the tree's drip line.

While researching low-chill fruit trees this summer, I met an extraordinarily generous group—the California Rare Fruit Growers. These gardeners—even more than most—clearly love to share the fruits of their labor.

While the surplus harvest they inevitably sent home with me was always delicious, I relished their well-researched advice even more. This group attracts people who keep records, take notes, compile charts, read manuscripts and texts, and sometimes write them, too. When someone from CRFG talks, it pays to listen.

So, if you're in the market for a pome or stone fruit tree—this is an excellent month to plant one—and you don't know which one is best for your microclimate, get acquainted with someone from CRFG. The group has eight chapters in Southern California. To find the one nearest you, call (714) 526-7198.

•

At Disneyland, a showplace for the art of annual color, red poinsettias and white cyclamen combine to stunning effect in its winter color beds. "You don't need to cover every inch of soil to achieve an ornamental effect with these two plants," says Ken Inouye, Disneyland landscape project manager. In fact, he says, the crisp, ruffled foliage of cyclamen (which he considers the plant's main asset) needs some empty space around it to be properly appreciated.

SOUTHERN CALIFORNIA Garden Notebook
BY SHARON COHOON

If you borrow this idea, make sure you choose acclimatized plants, warns Inouye. Purchase plants displayed outdoors at a nursery, not florist stock.

•

If you want to plant a street tree, or just want to know the name of the pink-flowered one that's blooming now on the next block, check out *Street Trees Recommended for Southern California* (Anaheim Street Tree Seminar, Inc., 1994; $35). If your library doesn't have a copy, call (714) 991-1900 to order.

THAT'S A GOOD QUESTION

Q: I wish I hadn't planted 'Queen Elizabeth' next to 'Dainty Bess' last year. Is it safe to dethrone her?

A: Very likely. Bare-root planting season—now through February—is an excellent time to move a rose, according to Virginia Carlson, founding member of the Orange County Rose Society. Roses that have had a brief reign in one spot, like your 'Queen', are easiest to transplant. Prune the plant back fairly hard before you move it, suggests Carlson. (This will also make it easier to handle.) Once you've dug up the plant with a spading fork, gently brush or wash away as much of the old soil as possible to expose the roots, and prune root tips lightly. Then replant just as you would a new bare-root rose.

CHECKLIST
DECEMBER

PLANT CARE

❑ **CARE FOR GIFT PLANTS.** Christmas gift plants do best with plenty of light, regular water and feeding (especially while they're blooming and setting fruit), and freedom from drafts.

❑ **CARE FOR LIVING CHRISTMAS TREES.** Keep indoor trees away from fireplaces and heater vents. Water regularly; take your tree to a sheltered place outside immediately after Christmas to let it acclimate.

PLANTING, ZONES 12-13

In the intermediate and low deserts, many plants can be set out or started from seed this month.

❑ **ANNUALS, PERENNIALS.** Plant calendula, candytuft, cyclamen, dianthus, Iceland poppy, larkspur, pansy, petunia, primrose, snapdragon, stock, sweet alyssum, and viola. If you live in a frost-free place, set out bedding begonias and cineraria as well.

❑ **BARE-ROOT STOCK.** Berries and roses are usually the first to come in, followed by fruit trees and perennial vegetables such as asparagus, horseradish, and rhubarb. Keep roots moist between nursery and garden, and plant as soon as you get home. If the roots dry, the plant dies.

❑ **BULBS.** Plant daffodils, gladiolus, ranunculus, and prechilled tulips as early as possible this month.

❑ **CROPS.** Sow seeds of peppers and

Sunset Western Garden Book
CLIMATE ZONES
1-3
10-11
12-13

tomatoes in a warm indoor spot now. Give them plenty of light, regular watering, and light fertilizing; transplants will be ready for the garden by late February or early March.

❑ **NATIVES.** Plant, water in well, and mulch. Then watch the weather: if you don't get much winter rain, follow up with regular deep watering to help roots get established.

MAINTENANCE

❑ **CHECK STORED BULBS.** Look over stored summer bulbs (such as those of

begonias and glads), throwing out rotting ones. You can save imperfect dahlia tubers by cutting out bad spots, dusting with sulfur, and storing them away from the others.

❑ **CUT HOLIDAY GREENS.** This is pruning: make each cut just above a side branch, thinning the plant evenly as you work. Also remove dead, diseased, and injured branches; to finish the job, prune for shape.

❑ **MAKE COMPOST.** Compost piles work year-round if they have oxygen, moisture, and food (equal parts green and brown garden waste). Keep adding garden waste to your pile, turn it weekly, and add water when needed.

❑ **MULCH.** It's not too late to put a 3- to 4-inch layer of mulch over perennial, bulb, and shrub beds that might be damaged by alternate cycles of freezing and thawing.

❑ **SPRAY DORMANT PLANTS.** Zones 12–13: Spray roses and deciduous flowering and fruit trees with horticultural oil to smother such overwintering insects as aphids, mites, and scale. You can also control brown rot, peach leaf curl, and shot hole by mixing lime sulfur or fixed copper into the oil. Spray all parts of the tree, including the crotches and furrowed bark.

❑ **WATER.** When the weather is above freezing, water dry spots in the garden—especially plants in containers and under house eaves.

INLAND WESTERN STATES
Garden Notebook
BY JIM McCAUSLAND

Bill Gates, Warren Buffet, and I could probably all agree about one thing: the importance of long-term thinking. For Gates, it has built a computer software empire. For Buffet, it has paid off in investments worth billions of dollars. And it has rewarded me with four beautiful birch bark cherry trees along my driveway.

I've purchased other ornamental cherry trees ('Shirotae', for example) so I could enjoy just three weeks' worth of spring flowers and pretty autumn leaves. But birch bark cherry (*Prunus serrula*) rewards me every time I see the sun shining through the branches, illuminating the peeling translucent red bark so that the trees look as if they are on fire. If you live in *Sunset Western Garden Book* climate zone 1, 2, or 3, you too can enjoy the long-term benefits of growing this tree.

Birch bark cherry is just one of several Himalayan trees that excel in the winter garden. As striking in its own way is that whitest of all birches, *Betula jacquemontii* (zones 3–11), from northern India.

●

It freezes regularly and snows occasionally where I live in Port Orchard, Washington, so ice is a slippery reality. I never use salt on

garden walkways or the driveway, since it can hurt plants. Instead I sprinkle sand for traction. Don't try that, however, on decks: sand will scar the wood.

●

With this month's mail, all but lost among the Christmas cards, garden catalogs start dribbling in. Take time to read a few. Even if you don't order, the catalogs inspire garden planning and get you thinking about the planting season ahead.

THAT'S A GOOD QUESTION

Q: Why is the bark cracking on my new dogwood tree?
A: When they're young, dogwoods and many other trees have thin bark. In winter, as freezing air chills the bark, the low midday sun hits the trunk's south-facing side and warms it. This cold-warm combination causes the bark to split and opens the sapwood up to insects and disease. (In summer, leafy branches shade the tender trunk.) To protect against winter sun damage, wrap the trunks of young trees loosely with fabric or commercial tree wrap. Nurseries stock it, or you can order a 6-inch-wide, 150-foot roll for about $7.50. One good source is A. M. Leonard (800/543-8955).

Greens and fruits capture the spirit of the season. On these eight pages, they combine in elegant new ways to make...

Nine Glorious SWAGS

HOLIDAY DECORATING WITH foliage has an ancient heritage: Druids draped their huts with evergreens to welcome the spirits of winter. Today the mystical associations of greens with spirits are gone, but swags of evergreen boughs remain a tradition, presiding over home and hearth during the holidays.

Garden swags can be as simple as clusters of fir boughs strung together and hung between two points, but the most handsome ones artfully combine several types of fresh foliage with berries, flowers, and fruits. You can drape swags almost anywhere—indoors or out.

The possibilities are endless. Frame a front door with a swag of cedar and fir boughs accented with berries and dried hydrangea blossoms. Or drape a banister or entry hall with a swag of California bay leaves to fill the house with fragrance. For a special holiday fete, suspend a swag gracefully across a fireplace mantel and top it with an elegant bow.

The nine swags shown on these pages illustrate the bounty of plant material Los Altos, California, designer Françoise Kirkman found in gardens on the San Francisco Peninsula.

The swag of manzanita, deer brush, and oak gall combines elements of Western chaparral, while the one that weaves together conifers, lichens, and cones reflects the cool, rainy Northwest. The palm and banksia swag topped with anthuriums (the only swag made of plant material from a florist) nods to the warm-winter climates of Southern

BY LAUREN BONAR SWEZEY

PHOTOGRAPHS BY KEVIN CANDLAND

SOUTHWEST SWAG (FAR LEFT)

Bay leaf

Statice

Red chilies

CALIFORNIA SWAG (LEFT)

Hollyleaf cherry

Pittosporum eugenioides

Cotoneaster lacteus

Crabapples

LIGHT AND LACY SWAG (RIGHT)

Asparagus retrofractus

Cushion bush

Quince

DOOR SWAG made of red cedar, pine, redwood, eucalyptus, pepper berries, and hydrangea is tacked to door frame.

MARK DARLEY

California and Hawaii. Your own backyard may yield a very different array of plant material, giving you the opportunity to create a swag you can call your own.

The swags are simple to put together and, depending on size, take about 2 hours to make.

For the base material, gather clippings from evergreen shrubs and trees with thick, shiny, or textured leaves, or use a variety of conifers (Douglas fir, fir, pine, and redwood hold needles longer than deodar cedar, spruce, or Western hem-

lock). Select foliage with contrasting colors and textures.

Other good choices include boxwood, California bay, camellia, citrus, eucalyptus, holly, hollyleaf cherry (*Prunus ilicifolia*), hollyleaf sweetspire (*Itea ilicifolia*), Japanese aucuba (*A. japonica*), juniper (*Juniperus sabina*), mahonia, manzanita, osmanthus, Pacific wax myrtle, pittosporum, podocarpus, and Western red cedar.

For the fall leaf swag (shown on page 328), Kirkman collected ginkgo, ornamental pear, and red oak leaves in prime

FIREPLACE SWAG includes deer brush, manzanita, and painted oak galls. It's attached to mantel with tape.

fall color. You can also use leaves of other deciduous trees if they have long leaf stems (so they can be securely attached to the swag), such as cherry and liquidambar.

Cut branches with plenty of branchlets attached (always use appropriate pruning practices—never leave stumps or ragged bark—and maintain an attractive plant shape). Collect foliage in a large, sturdy garbage bag. Half a bag packed with California bay branches or similar foliage makes an 8-foot-long swag. Eight 1-foot-long juniper branches make a 6- to 7-foot swag.

Almost any kind of berry, cone, long-lasting fruit, or pod makes a handsome accent. Kirkman used California pepper tree berries and foliage, cones, cotoneaster berries, cushion bush (*Calocephalus brownii*), deer brush (*Lotus scoparius*), dried pomegranates, dried poppy pods, lacecap hydrangea flowers, lichens, oak galls, and tea tree (*Leptospermum*). She purchased crabapples, Japanese persimmons, quince, and red pimiento peppers at the grocery store.

MAKING THE BASIC SWAG

GATHER MATERIALS AND TOOLS

At a craft or floral supply store, buy:

- **natural jute twine** (2 or 3 ply), ribbon or raffia
- a spool of **green paddle wire**
- **water picks** (tubes to hold cut flowers or berries in water)

At a nursery, buy:

- an **antitranspirant** to keep foliage fresh longer

Around the house, gather:

- **pruning shears**
- **scissors**
- **wire cutters**

Wire supports most of the swags pictured on these pages. The swag accented with *Asparagus retrofractus* on page 323 has a grapevine base (birch or weeping willow also work). To save time, you can buy a plain swag made of conifer greens at a nursery or Christmas tree lot and add your own accents.

Swags hung outdoors last longer than swags hung in warm, dry locations. And foliage such as hollyleaf cherry and manzanita just naturally looks fresh for weeks. Other foliage (*Asparagus retrofractus,* California bay) dries out quickly. Spray such swags with an antitranspirant just after constructing them, to prolong foliage freshness and color.

MEASURE THE AREA TO BE DECORATED

The size and shape of the area you're going to decorate determines the best way to put the swag together. Follow these guidelines:

- To surround a door, make the swag in three lengths (one for the top, two for the sides).
- To decorate a banister, make one long swag, or construct one in whatever lengths you are most comfortable working with.
- To festoon a fireplace wall, make one long swag.
- Before you start your swag, separate the foliage and accents into individual piles.

STEP 1 Unroll a length of twine on a flat surface. Make a loop (to hang swag later) on the end and knot it tight. Place the loop on your right side (so you can work from right to left; left-handers may want to work the opposite way, placing the loop to their left), and tie wire on loop. Leave twine and wire spools attached until you're finished.

STEP 2 Gather together three or four 6- to 9-inch-long branchlets of greenery (use one kind of foliage or a mixture of greens). Place the bunch on top of the loop and lay stems along the twine. Hold stems together against the twine with your left hand; use your right hand to bring wire over top of stems. Continue looping wire under and all the way around stem and twine; pull tight.

STEP 3 Make a second bunch of greenery, and position it so it overlaps stems of the first bunch; bind it to twine as described in step 2. Continue adding greenery until the garland is the length you want. To avoid a uniform look, use branchlets of varying sizes. If using fresh flowers, insert stems in water picks and attach with wire along with bunches of greenery (berries and some delicate accent foliage also last longer in water).

ATTACHING FRUIT AND GOURDS

To attach fruit, berries, gourds, and pods, wrap stems with wire and leave long ends. For oak galls and cones, attach eye screw (poke a hole with a nail first), then insert wire through the eye screw. Wrap stemless fruit (such as quince) in a piece of ribbon made of gold netting; tie the top with a long piece of wire.

MIXED GREENS SWAG

Photinia serrulata

Camellia

Variegated osmanthus

Pieris flower buds

Japanese persimmons

STEP 4 To finish the swag, make a knot with wire and then tie the wire and twine together securely; make a loop and knot it. Then add decorations. Tie on berries, fruit, red peppers, and pods with wire (for methods of attaching wire, see upper right). Use larger fruit singly; cluster together bunches of berries, peppers, and pods. Space them at irregular intervals along the swag. Cover the loop with a bow.

FALL LEAF SWAG

Gingko   Ornamental pear   Red oak   Redwood

For a 5-foot swag, collect half a large grocery bag of fresh unblemished leaves. **To preserve the leaves,** buy a 16-ounce bottle of glycerin at a pharmacy. Mix one 16-ounce bottle of glycerin with 2 quarts of warm water in a large bucket or dishpan. Immerse the leaves in the mixture. Cover the container with plastic wrap or a plastic bag; push plastic down on top of leaves to help hold them under liquid. Set the container in an unlighted place for 8 to 12 days. Remove the leaves from the container and rinse them in soapy water. Lay them flat on a newspaper to dry. Once dry, the leaves will remain supple. Red and green leaves turn reddish to dark brown. Yellow leaves stay yellow. **Assemble the swag:** Follow the instructions for making a mixed greens swag, but instead of using branchlets, bunch eight or more preserved leaves and bind stems to the twine. Mix in redwood branches.

UNRAVELING A VINE WREATH

To make a swag from a purchased wreath of birch, grapevine, or willow, soak the wreath in warm, soapy water for a few hours (soak grapevine for three days); remove from water. Unravel and pull the vine pieces apart in clusters of three or so; overlap ends of each cluster, and wire clusters together at 12-inch intervals until you've reached the desired length.

Gather a small bunch of greens with lower leaves stripped off, insert their stems between the vine pieces, and wire them in place. Cover the base lightly so it shows through the foliage. ■

TROPICAL SWAG (LEFT)

Palm

Ti leaves

Leucodendron

Banksia

Lycopodium

Anthurium

CHRISTMAS SWAG (RIGHT)

Douglas fir

Redwood

Lichen

California pepper berries

Eucalyptus pods

Pine cones

Poppy pods

Wanted: Perfect partners for lonely poinsettias

Artichokes, azaleas, and other surprising plant companions

BIG TRUMPETS *of blooming amaryllis are the center of an assortment of plants, including azalea, poinsettia, and trailing rosemary, assembled in a wicker basket. Spray-painted white branches add lacy filler. Designer: Joyce Gauntt.*

I T WOULDN'T be Christmas without a poinsettia. You buy one on impulse at the grocery store or receive a gift plant from a party guest. Then it sits all alone on the coffee table because its gaudy tropical foliage and foil-clad pot seem to clash with everything in sight. Whether it's red, white, or pink, a poinsettia can be the ugly duckling of the holidays.

It doesn't have to be that way this year. We asked two Seattle floral designers to create displays costing no more than $50 each that would turn the poinsettia into the focal point of a holiday room. Our problem-solvers were Joyce Gauntt, floral designer at Swanson's Nursery, and Michael Prihoda, floristry instructor at South Seattle Community College's School of Floristry. As you can see here, their arrangements combine plants with readily available materials (live,

dried, and manufactured) in attractive containers.

Scout your house for large containers that will hold several plants; don't overlook nontraditional choices such as wooden wine boxes, soup tureens, and enamel wash pans. To form a waterproof liner for most containers, use 8- to 10-mil plastic sheeting.

Leave purchased plants in their pots. Before arranging the plants, let them sit

CEDAR SNIPPETS *are wound with lights and ribbon around a planter hanger to make a showy frame for a poinsettia in an Italian terra-cotta pot. Designer: Michael Prihoda.*

overnight in a sink or bucket with enough water to cover the tops of the pots. This ensures that the soil is thoroughly moist and will remain absorbent when you water later.

As you arrange plants in a container, use Spanish or sphagnum moss or excelsior to fill in around the pots and create a uniform surface.

Place the container in bright light—not direct sun—and well away from heat sources. Use a long-necked watering can to give the plants a drink at least twice weekly. Provide enough water to keep soil moist, but not so much that it pools up in the bottom of the container. Clip off leaves and blossoms that fade. ∎

By Steven R. Lorton

DRIED ARTICHOKE BUDS *and fresh-cut salal and eucalyptus (in water-filled glass jars) join a pink poinsettia in a birch bark basket. Designer: Joyce Gauntt.*

DAVID McDONALD

TOUGH AND RELIABLE *garden tools make great gifts. Pictured clockwise from upper right are: trowel by Bulldog of England, Felco shears, soil knife, hand weeder, Wilkinson shears, mud gloves, and Japanese pruning saw.*

Can't-miss garden gifts

Seven hand tools that Sunset garden writers simply can't live without

SOME GARDEN TOOLS are like old friends—they never let me down. I turn to them time after time when I need help digging or pruning. Eventually they lose the glow of youth—their surfaces get a little rougher and they require a bit of care to stay in shape. But they remain tough and reliable.

Every avid gardener has a set of "old friends" in the toolshed. My fellow garden writers at *Sunset*—Sharon Cohoon, Steven R. Lorton, and Jim McCausland—each depend on at least one tool that's always by their side during the gardening season. Any of their favorites, along with a couple of my own, are perfect gifts for a gardening friend or relative.

Trowel by Bulldog of England ($15, Smith & Hawken). This trowel with an ash handle is made of sturdy carbon steel that never bends or breaks. It keeps on giving even though I leave it out in the rain and periodically lose it in planting beds.

Felco 7 pruning shears ($45, A. M. Leonard). The handle rotates as the shears open and close, reducing the chance of blisters and fatigue. "My always-with-me tool, which I use almost daily," says McCausland.

Soil knife ($20, A. M. Leonard and Smith & Hawken). This tool digs, cuts, pierces, and saws with a strong 6- to 6½-inch blade. "The *hori hori* (Japanese soil knife) is an indispensable tool," says Lorton. "It acts as a small trowel and works like a charm for weeding between cracks in paving and removing deep-rooted weeds."

Hand weeder ($12, Smith & Hawken). The thin 4¾-inch-wide blade is very sharp and designed to penetrate the soil easily. "Weeding is the thing you do most in the garden," says McCausland. "And this tool is perfect for uprooting small broad-leafed weeds."

Wilkinson Sword 900 Series pruning shears ($35, Kinsman Company). These professional pruners have the most comfortable grip of any shears I've used. The alloy body is durable; the coated blade reduces friction. A thumb catch at the top of the handle prevents accidental closure.

Mud gloves ($8, Little's Good Garden Gloves). These machine-washable, rubber-coated cotton gloves with double-knit cuff are resistant to thorns. "They're flexible enough to let you feel what you're doing, but the rubber keeps hands dry and fingernails clean," says Cohoon.

Japanese pruning saw ($29, Tashiro's). This folding saw has a hard steel blade that stays sharp for a long time and prunes quickly. "This is a serious pruning tool," says McCausland. "I use it to trim a 40-foot row of arborvitae—with maybe 30 4-inch trunks—in an hour."

MAIL-ORDER SOURCES FOR THESE TOOLS

A. M. Leonard, Inc., Box 816, Piqua, OH 45356; (800) 543-8955.

Kinsman Company, Inc., Box 357, Point Pleasant, PA 18950; (800) 733-4146.

Little's Good Garden Gloves, Box 808, Johnstown, NY 12095; (518) 736-5014.

Smith & Hawken, 2 Arbor Lane, Box 6900, Florence, KY 41022; (800) 776-3336.

Tashiro's Sharp Japanese Tools, Box 3409, Seattle, WA 98114; (206) 621-0199. ∎

By Lauren Bonar Swezey

KENTIA PALM *adds a touch of the tropics. This 7-foot plant thrives in a large pot.*

PAUL HAMMOND

Palms that work indoors

Eight choices that adapt well to life in the house

I F YOU TRACE THE HISTORY OF palms as interior adornments, you'll find they go all the way back to the royal palaces of ancient Egypt. But in the modern West, palms are gaining new popularity as house plants. Never has such a wide variety of palms been so readily available—and affordable. Wholesale growers are producing large quantities of field-grown and greenhouse plants for the retail market.

Palms are easy to grow and care for. They live happily in containers. Most grow relatively slowly, so you don't need to repot frequently. Best of all, since many kinds of palms are native to the heavily shaded floors of rain forests and jungles, they will thrive in the low light of a house.

Palms have two types of leaves, or fronds: on feather palms, the leaflets are arranged in ranks on opposite sides of the central stalk or midrib; on fan palms, the leaflets are arranged at the end of the

stalk like fingers on a hand.

Eight good choices are described here. The prices listed are ballpark retail figures—what you can expect to pay for a plant in a 5-gallon container. Although most will take relatively low light, they'll do best next to a south- or west-facing window or under a skylight.

Bamboo palm (*Chamaedorea seifrizii*), $85. This fast-growing palm produces a clump of bamboolike stems that can reach 8 to 10 feet. Feather fronds reach 18 to 30 inches (the bottommost ones die as the plant grows taller). It is one of the few palms you can control for height—if a single cane gets too tall, cut it off at ground level and allow other canes to emerge. Give it medium to strong light.

Fan palm (*Livistona chinensis*), $100 to $120. This slow-growing palm will reach a height of 15 feet in 40 years and has 3- to 6-foot-long fronds. It's highly resistant to pests such as spider mites. An excellent candidate for an unheated sunporch, it needs plenty of light but will take temperatures down to 22°.

Fishtail palm (*Caryota mitis*), $90 to $110. Until recently, this slow-growing palm was rarely used as an indoor plant. It eventually reaches 20 to 25 feet. Its 6- to 10-foot feather fronds are made up of dozens of wide triangular leaflets with broad, irregular tips resembling fish tails. It needs medium to strong light.

Kentia or paradise palm (*Howea forsterana*), $120 to $150. This feather palm grows slowly to a height of 9 feet. Its 4- to 6-foot fronds arch out and droop down. It tolerates low light but not overwatering.

Lady palm (*Rhapis excelsa*), $140. One of the best palms for low light, this fan palm grows slowly to a height of 5 to 12 feet. It thrusts up straight canes with brown hairy fibers and fronds about

the size of a large human hand. Given bright light, it will grow faster.

Neanthe Bella palm (*Chamaedorea elegans*), $50 to $85. A first cousin to the bamboo palm, with similar feather fronds, this single-stemmed plant grows slowly to a height of 3 to 4 feet. It does well in low light.

Pygmy date palm (*Phoenix roebelenii*), $40 to $75. This slow-growing palm will eventually reach 6 feet in height. Its 4- to 6-foot feather fronds look especially showy when it's planted in a terra-cotta pot. It needs ample light.

Triangle palm (*Neodypsis decaryi*), $75 to $105. This palm is unusual not only for its sturdy triangular leaf bases but also for its strong vertical form. Magnificent 4- to 6-foot gray-green feather fronds jut up and then arch out slightly on plants that eventually reach 18 to 20 feet in height. This palm actually likes to dry out occasionally between waterings. It does well in low light.

CARE AND FEEDING

Plant palms in rich potting soil in sizable containers that provide good drainage. Water plants regularly; place them where air circulation is good.

Feed palms in their active growing period—April through August. Suzette Clause of Indoor Design Plant Service in Palo Alto, California, suggests using a half-strength solution of water-soluble 15-30-15 fertilizer twice each feeding month.

Repot plants about every three years. Turn the pot on its side and gently pull the plant out. Shake the rootball to remove as much of the old soil as possible. Repot the plant with fresh potting mix in a container bigger than the old one, and water it well. ∎

By Steven R. Lorton

A DIVERSE DUO *of plants: Neanthe Bella or parlor palm (left) forms a dense mass of feather fronds; pygmy date palm (right) sends up spiky feather fronds.*

Article Titles Index

General Subject Index

Abutilon megapotamicum, 108
Acer, 75, 295, 296
Achillea, 266
African daisies, 78
African fern pine, 21
Agapanthus, 188
Agastache, 165
All-America selections for 1995, 8
Anemone hybrida, 266, 295
Anisodontea hypomandarum
  'Tara's Pink', 89
Annuals
  heirloom, seed exchange for, 30
  quick bloomers from seed, 78
Apples
  bagging developing fruit, 161
  best new varieties, 68
  'Fuji', 243
  pests of, 215, 297
Aquatic plants in Bainbridge
  Island, WA, 235
Aquilegia, when and how to plant,
  286–288
Arabis fernandi-coburgii
  'Variegata', 157
Araucaria heterophylla, 21
Arbutus unedo, 315
  A. u. 'Oktoberfest', 89
Arctostaphylos uva-ursi, 92, 307
Arizona, climate zones in, 55, 57,
  58, 59, 61
Artemisia, 91
Asparagus, 313
Aster, 265, 295
Asteriscus maritimus, 92

Baby blue eyes, 78
Balloon flower, 188
Ballota psuedodictamnus, 91
Bamboo muhly, 90
Bamboo palm, 332
Baptisia australis, 188
Bare-root planting, 16–19
Basil, 143
Beans
  colorful varieties, 139
  early lima ('Betty'), 143
Beaucarnea recurvata, 21
Bed-and-breakfast inns around the
  West, beautiful gardens at,
  118–124
Bee balm, 144
Bellflower, 188
Berries, planting bare-root, 18–19
Betula, 23
Big-tooth maple, 75
Birch, 23
Birdseed, squirrelproof, 316
Bluebeard, 241
Blue-flowered perennials, 10 top
  choices, 188
Blue star creeper, 304
Bolax gummifera, 307
Boltonia, 87, 266

Bonsai
  display ideas for, 289
  from grapevines, 140
Border penstemon, 87
Bottlebrush tree, culture tips for, 77
Bottle palm, 21
Boulders as garden accents,
  290–291
Bromeliads in Balboa Park (San
  Diego, CA), 144
Buddleia, 77
Buffalo grass, 110
Bulbs. *See also* specific bulbs
  antique types, catalog of, 145
  chilling before planting, 268–269
  planting tips for moisture-
  sensitive types, 275
Butterflies by mail-order, 198
Butterfly bush, 77

Cactus for the holidays, 315
Calamagrostis acutiflora 'Stricta', 90
Calendula, 78
  C. officinalis 'Touch of Red', 225
Callistemon citrinus, 77
Callistemon viminalis 'Little John',
  89
Calylophus hartwegii, 92
Campanula lactiflora, 188
Candytuft, 242
Cannas, 197
Cantaloupe, heirloom type, 109
Cardinal flower, 266
Carex comans, 90
Caryopteris clandonensis, 241
Caryota, 20, 332
Centaurea, 188
Central Valley, gardening infor-
  mation and ideas for
  drought-tolerant garden in
  Exeter, 243
  garden checklists & notebooks.
  See Garden checklists &
  notebooks in the Article Titles
  Index
  public gardens, 76
  seedless grapes, 10
  single roses, 30
Ceratostigma plumbaginoides, 307
Chamaedorea, 332
Charentais melons, 158–159
Cherry trees for small gardens, 10
Chilean jasmine, 171
Chile peppers, 67
Citrus, when to feed, 10
Clarkia amoena, 285
Clematis for arid climates, 141
Cleome hasslerana, 76
Climate maps of the U. S., 77
Climate zones, Western, as
  defined by *Sunset,* 36–61
  in Central Valley, 45, 47, 48, 49
  defining factors for, 37
  in inland Western states, 38, 39,
  54, 55, 56, 57, 58, 59, 60, 61
  maps of
  Central California, 48
  Eastern Washington, Eastern
  Oregon, Idaho, 38
  Los Angeles and inland,
  46–47
  Nevada, Montana, Wyoming,
  Utah, Colorado, 56
  Northern California, 44
  San Diego and environs, 52

Climate zone maps, *cont'd*
  San Francisco Bay Area and
  inland, 50–51
  Southwest deserts: Arizona,
  58
  Southwest deserts: New
  Mexico, 60
  Southwest deserts: Southern
  California, 54
  Western Oregon, 42
  Western Washington, 40
  in Northern California, 44, 45,
  46–47, 49
  in Pacific Northwest, 38–43
  in Southern California, 48,
  50–51, 52, 53, 54, 55
  in Southwest deserts, 54, 55,
  57, 58, 59, 60, 61
Colorado, climate zones in, 56, 57
Columbine, when and how to
  plant, 286–288
Composting, home program for,
  198
Container plants
  arbor with misters for, 221
  hanging baskets in Victoria,
  B. C., 186–187
  New Zealand flax, 313
  ornamental grasses, 157, 172
  rooftop garden in San
  Francisco, 190
  salad greens as, 242
  trees, 20–21, 332
  catproofing, 30, 298
  white-flowered, 314
Coral bells with striking foliage, 97
Corn
  ornamental types, 132–133
  supersweet white, 108
Cornus alba 'Kesselringii', 314
Cortaderia selloana, 111
Corydalis flexuosa 'Blue Panda',
  188
Cotoneaster, 307
Crabapple, new golden variety, 28
Cranesbill, 86
Creeping St. Johnswort, 307
Crocus
  C. chrysanthus, 274
  chilling before planting, 268–269
Crowea exalata, 89
Cut flowers
  sunflowers for, 178–181
  tips for sending by mail, 195

Daffodil, scented ('Curlew'), 244
Daylilies, 72, 171–172
Decollate snails, 74
Decorations for home or garden
  decorative grains, 132–133
  fall bouquets, 294
  gargoyles, 298
  gazing balls, 316
  gourds and squash, 276
  with poinsettias as focal point,
  330
  from recycled garden materials,
  296, 313
  swags for the holidays, 322–329
  white-flowered plants for the
  holidays, 314
Deer-resistant perennials, 130–131
Delphiniums, encouraging growth
  of, 274
Diascia vigilis, 86, 295
Digitalis purpurea, 169, 196

Dimorphotheca, 78
Diseases
  apple canker, 297
  Dutch elm disease, 107, 224
  fireblight, 30
  oleander gall, 171
  pitch canker, 275
  powdery mildew, 142
  rust, 143
  of trees and shrubs, book about,
  168
Dogwood, dark-stemmed, 314
Dorycnium hirsutum, 91
Drought-tolerant plants. *See also*
  Water conservation
  in Exeter, CA, garden, 243
  in front-yard "meadow" (Arroyo
  Grande, CA), 160
  ground covers, 92
  new to *Sunset Western Garden
  Book,* 89, 92
  in Niguel Botanical Preserve, 27
  for Pacific Northwest, 77
  roses, 76
  in Ruth Bancroft Garden, 216
Dwarf periwinkle, 304
Dwarf plumbago, 307

Echinops exaltatus, 266
Elm that resists Dutch elm
  disease, 107
Epimedium rubrum, 307
Erigeron karvinskianus, 194
Eryngium alpinum, 188
Euonymus japonica, 156
Euphorbia amygdaloides
  'Purpurea', 86
Evergreen euonymus, 156
Evergreen pear, treating for
  fireblight, 30

Fall planting ideas from public
  gardens, 256–261
False indigo, 188
Fan palm, 332
Feather reed grass, 90
Ferns, culture tips for, 30
Ficus, 20, 21
Fire safety, landscaping for,
  282–284
Fishtail palm, 20, 332
Flannel bush, 144
Flax, miniature, 108
Flowering locust, 28
Flowering maple, 108
Forget-me-not, 78
Foxgloves, 169, 196
Fremontodendron californicum, 144
Fuchsias, hardy, 99
Fungus gnat, 111

Garden ideas. *See also* Decorations for home or garden
  aquatic plants in Bainbridge
  Island, WA, 235
  at bed-and-breakfast inns
  around the West, 118–124
  boulders as garden accents,
  290–291
  cracked patio "softened" by
  creeping plants in
  Kensington, CA, 98
  fall planting ideas from public
  gardens, 256–261
  fanciful artist's garden in Albany,
  CA, 182–183